'One of the most significant works on India's economic policies, this brilliant prescription for the country's future by two practitioners could not have come at a better time. Dr Kelkar has played a role in many major financial reforms since liberalization. What is most alluring about the book is its approach of tackling difficult economic concepts and making them accessible and engaging for the lay reader. A must-read for everyone!' NANDAN NILEKANI

'It's a fascinating read about the art and science of using economic policy to solve a country's problems. It describes some inefficient policy choices made in India in the past, and how to create an environment for best policies in the government.' N. NARAYANA MURTHY

'Two respected economists, who have worked in government and for government, have produced a remarkable and wonderful book, examining government, governance and state intervention in a charming and reader-friendly way. A book in the service of every citizen.' BIBEK DEBROY

'This marvellous book is a wonderful guide to thinking about public policy. It combines three things that rarely come together: clear analytical thinking on first principles, a good sense of historical judgement and a commitment to the values of freedom and fairness. It is the work of masterly professionals making their thinking accessible to a wider public.' PRATAP BHANU MEHTA

'Kelkar and Shah have written a masterly book, combining in-depth personal experience and sound economic principles. With simple language and vivid examples, they offer many home truths about the why, when, what and how of policy, and even more important, when to do nothing. I hope India listens.' AVINASH DIXIT

'Kelker and Shah give us one of the best examples of simple and straightforward prose writing, of commonsensical policy design, and of synthesizing a century of social science on social change, all rolled into one book. They are Indian economists, living and working there, who have spent most of their careers trying to make the state and the economy work for people. If you live in a liberal democracy anywhere in the world (including the United States) and you want to try to make your government function better, this is one of the top five books you can read.' CHRIS BLATTMAN

'How can India achieve accelerated inclusive growth fuelled by innovative public policy, which preserves the foundations of our liberal democracy as also the integrity of our institutional frameworks? This insightful book by two of our iconic masters in the art and science of public policymaking is an invaluable guide to achieve this objective. An absolute must read for all interested in building new India of our dreams.' RAMESH A. MASHELKAR

'The book is a perfect combination of esprit de geometrie and esprit de finesse; the hard-nosed analytical framework sine qua non for policy formulation and all the soft and "artistic" elements descendant from empiricism. Dr Kelkar and Dr Shah have, through great mastery of the subject, simplified the discourse on policy making, demystified the flaws and foibles in vigour and provided a ready intellectual template that is of immense value to policy framers. In substance, the reach of this book is way beyond the policy establishment and should be required reading for legislators, bureaucrats, politicians, management and strategy experts, governance gurus and all students of policy making.' RAHOOL S. PAI PANANDIKER

'The book is a must read for anyone interested in public policy, as decision maker or student. The volume is a veritable feast of lucid and non-technical enunciation of concepts illustrated with real-life examples.' URJIT PATEL

'This is a remarkable and a very important book, being perhaps the first comprehensive and authoritative study of all aspects of economic policymaking and execution. When and why should a policy be introduced (or abandoned), how and in what manner should it be implemented and so on—questions that every practitioner of public policy ought to ask—are all answered here by two eminent economists with enormous experience in policy formulation and execution. Written in a simple, elegant and a very engaging style, this book is a must read for every student of economics and public administration and also every civil servant in the country.' SUDHAKAR RAO

REVISED AND UPDATED

IN SERVICE
OF THE
REPUBLIC

THE ART AND SCIENCE
OF ECONOMIC POLICY

VIJAY KELKAR
AND
AJAY SHAH

PENGUIN BOOKS
An imprint of Penguin Random House

PENGUIN BOOKS

USA | Canada | UK | Ireland | Australia
New Zealand | India | South Africa | China

Penguin Books is part of the Penguin Random House group of companies
whose addresses can be found at global.penguinrandomhouse.com

Published by Penguin Random House India Pvt. Ltd
4th Floor, Capital Tower 1, MG Road,
Gurugram 122 002, Haryana, India

Penguin
Random House
India

First published in Allen Lane by Penguin Random House India 2019
This edition published in Penguin Books in 2022

Copyright © Vijay Kelkar and Ajay Shah 2019, 2022

ISBN 9780670093328

Typeset in Bembo Std by Manipal Technologies Limited, Manipal
Printed at Gopsons Papers Pvt. Ltd., Noida.

www.penguin.co.in

To our parents,
who set us out on this path.

Contents

Preface   xiii

Part I: Foundations

1. The Purpose of Government   3
2. The Limited Toolkit of Intervention   21
3. A Long History of Failure   26

Part II: Diagnosing the Indian Experience

4. Anatomy of Our Policy Failure   37
5. Why Do Things Go Wrong?   44

Part III: The Science

6. People Respond to Incentives   71
7. Going with the Grain of the Price System   82
8. More Competition, Always   96
9. Trace Out the General Equilibrium Effects   107

10. Go to the Root Cause, Use the Smallest
    Possible Force   112

11. Redistribution Is Fraught with Trouble   121

12. Private Solutions for Market Failure   129

13. Bring Cold Calculations into the Policy Process 139

14. Ask the Right Question   150

15. Taking Decentralization Seriously   158

Part IV: The Art

16. The Problem of Organizational Capacity   173

17. Evolutionary Change for Society, Revolutionary
    Change for Government   181

18. Cross the River by Feeling the Stones   188

19. Adapting from the International Experience?   197

20. Test Match, not IPL   212

21. What Is Hard and What Is Easy   227

22. Confident Policymakers Work in the Open   235

23. Criticism and Conflict Have Great Value   245

24. Coming Out Right, Always, Is Too High a Bar   256

25. A Country Is Not a Company   261

26. Beware the Rule of Officials   269

27. The Digital Pathway to State Capacity   279

28. State Power That Reshapes Society in the
    Digital Age   289

Part V: The Public Policy Process

29. Policymaking Is Siege-Style Assault   303
30. Reforming in a Crisis?   311
31. Choosing from Pillars of Intervention   318
32. Building the Foundational Processes   328
33. The Decision to Spend Public Money   344
34. Walk Before You Can Run   350
35. Building the Knowledge Foundations   369
36. Low State Capacity Changes Policy Design   387
37. Rolling up Your Sleeves to Build State Capacity   401
38. Do No Harm   421

Part VI: Applying These Ideas: Some Examples

39. The Path to Decarbonization   435
40. Building the Perfect GST in a Low-Capacity State   442
41. Health Policy   445
42. Vaccines for Covid-19   459
43. Financial Economic Policy   468

Part VII: Reimagining the Indian Development Project

44. Institution Building, Not Just GDP Growth   485
45. Looking Forward   492

Acknowledgments   501
Notes   507
Index   547

Preface

India has come into middle income, with a $3 trillion economy. We got a great surge of growth from 1991–2011, drawing on a new intellectual framework of policy that was put into place from 1977 onward. For the first time in India's history, in these two remarkable decades, there was a substantial decline in the number and the share of those in poverty.

The period after 2011 has seen a retreat from the optimism of the two remarkable decades. Growth in exports has stalled, private investment has declined, and the number of persons working has grown poorly. Present economic and demographic trends suggest that we will get old before we get rich.

We need to change course, to obtain the sustained economic growth through which we will utilize our workforce and get to the edges of the advanced economies in 30 years. We must do this in order to transform the lives of hundreds of millions of people, and to meet our tryst with destiny. We must do this to avoid the social stress that goes with a large mass of people who are not working. The great question of the age is: *Why did the reforms process from 1977 onwards deliver success in 1991–2011, but falter thereafter?*

In this book, we try to tell a story about why we under-performed, and how to get back on the growth turnpike. Intensification of the 1977–2011 strategies will not suffice: what is required is rethinking the foundations. While we have rapidly created a $3 trillion economy, we have been slow to build the institutional frameworks for a dynamic middle-income emerging economy.

Modernization of the political system and of the economy are taking place at the same time and feeding into each other. Establishing the foundations of liberal democracy—building the republic—is integral to solving the economic malaise. The pursuit of economic growth requires new respect for the principles of debate, dispersion of power, the rule of law and the curtailing of executive discretion. The tradeoffs and compromises inherent in democratic politics determine the policy choices in the real world. Our thinking draws as much on the timeless themes of building the republic as it does on public economics.

Economic policy lies within the subject of political economy, the dark crossroads where economics and politics meet. Both disciplines have a core of scientific thinking: the areas where the analytical foundations and empirical evidence are strong. And then, beyond that, there are a large class of questions where the picture is less clear, where intuition, inspiration and the wisdom of experience must be brought to bear on questions. This is the art of public policy. In this book, we take on the left brain and the right brain aspects.

We care about the ideas and we care about translating them into action. Some parts of the book are more analytical and conceptual, while other parts of the book are more practical and link directly to action.

When the rubber hits the road, there are tangible policy questions in each area, such as oil exploration or inflation targeting. There are many fascinating areas of work in progress, all across the Indian landscape, where there is the 'slow boring of hard boards' of policy reform, with passionate sectoral experts grappling with the state failure that permeates the Indian policy landscape. While we draw on 79 examples from many sectors, this is not a handbook of policy papers. We offer general insights that are valuable across diverse fields.

We live in an age of social media. The degradation of norms of discourse, and the noise in the policy discourse, has harmed the ability of liberal democracies to find politically stable compromises. In this book, we help to recover common ground, to find a shared intellectual framework and vocabulary that a lot of us may be able to agree upon. We have, therefore, stuck to what we hope is relatively non-controversial terrain. This has involved downplaying issues of ethical preferences and income redistribution.

Together, the authors have 65 years in the field, and have been talking about these grand questions for the last 20 years. The genesis of this book lies in Shekhar Shah's invitation to Vijay Kelkar to deliver the C.D. Deshmukh Memorial Lecture at National Council of Applied Economic Research (NCAER) on 27 January 2017. The enthusiastic feedback from that lecture led to the idea that an extended version of this would be an interesting book.

The enthusiastic feedback from the first edition of November 2019 propelled us into writing this revised and expanded edition, the publication of which coincides with the 75th anniversary of India's Independence.

Part I

Foundations

1

The Purpose of Government

Everyone has felt the irritation of having multiple chargers for different devices. There is a chaos of chargers with USB-B, USB-C, Apple Lightning, etc. interfaces, all of which are incompatible with each other. This adds expense, inconvenience, clutter, and electronic waste.

To engineers, 'standards wars' are inefficient. To consumers, a plethora of standards can appear irritating and confusing. A single standard would allow device makers to focus on making devices, while other companies focus on producing universal chargers. To many people, this will result in lower prices, more convenience and less waste. An exasperated person may say *Can't we have a government that standardizes this?*

It seems easy to think about finding a great leader, who will choose the one correct technical standard, and then the government forces everyone to fall into line. While this might be plausible at first blush, when we go deeper into the problem, there are all kinds of difficulties; human society is not amenable to engineering intuition. This, in turn, brings us to the twin questions of what a government *can* do versus what a government *should* do.

Could a government add value by coercing all electronics companies to make only one kind of charger? At first blush, this may seem like an appealing idea. This is the sort of thing a muscular Indian government might come up with—a law that forces all technology companies to only sell consumer products in India that use (say) the USB-C charger. This is something that the European Union is doing.[1]

If we had to have a government choose the one charger to rule them all, let's think about how the standard will be established. Who will choose? How would we be sure that these persons would think in terms of the best interests of society, and possess the requisite intellectual capacity? How do we know that the right decision will be made, despite intense lobbying by all technology companies? What if there are certain devices made in Taiwan, which are extremely capable and cost effective, but use a prohibited charger. Will we ban Indian consumers from using them?

Suppose the USB-C charger is made a standard via government imposition. What if there are small devices, such as wrist watches, where the USB-C charger is too bulky?

How will charger standardization be enforced? Who will watch out for violations? Will we have customs officials keeping an eye on goods shipments to prevent equipment from coming in, which uses any of the forbidden chargers? Will we have the police raid factories looking for violators who produce equipment with the wrong charger? What about individuals who travel abroad and are carrying their own personal equipment, which they promise will not be used in India? What penalties will we impose in all these cases? Will a black market develop for chargers that violate the rule? Will we enforce against it?

Or is all this too difficult, and we turn to taxation and subsidies? Perhaps we can tax equipment which has the wrong charger and subsidize equipment that has the right charger. That will have its own difficulties: who will choose the correct standard, and the correct level of the subsidy? And, we have to ask, will the gains exceed the (large) welfare cost associated with the use of public funds?

Engineers see standards wars as wasteful. But standards wars are the path to technological innovation. If the government forces the USB-C charger upon the world, what will happen to the process of scientific discovery and innovation? Will innovators stop thinking about making a better charger, when the government is backing one standard?

Standardizing chargers for electronic devices is not a particularly important problem! It is a tiny, inconsequential problem. But in this small illustration, we see how government intervention, even in such small problems, rapidly turns into a mess.

We recognize the technical genius of the USB-C standard. In our personal lives, we use this, and encourage others to do similarly. But there is a line between friendly ad-vice and the use of state power. Things become difficult when a state tries to get involved in either developing a technological standard or in using state power in pushing the economy towards one chosen technology. The process of development and adoption of technological standards is best conducted in the private sector. As an example, a firm like Google has a place in pushing the Android ecosystem in favour of certain standards.[2] And, a ceaseless process of innovation must always flourish, where new things go up against the alternatives that have high market share. Standards wars are the sound of a flourishing innovation machine.

What Objectives Should the State Pursue?

As we have seen with a simple problem like USB chargers, it is not easy to choose the problems where we want intervention by the state. The first question in the field of public policy is *What objectives of public policy are appropriate?* Should the government own or operate an airline? Courts? Restaurants? Watch-making factories? Parks? Should a government gift money to poor people? Feed poor people? Run hospitals? Out-patient clinics?

Factories that make medicines? Factories that make medical instruments? Trucks? Tanks? Standardize chargers?

The state is the most powerful actor in society. The state has the capacity to coerce, the capacity to inflict violence upon private persons. Many people get giddy at the prospect of wielding state power, and come up with woolly ideas for state intervention. Each of us has a few pet peeves, and we are quick to propose the use of state power to pursue our own value judgements.

In India, we have a government that runs temples, restaurants, airlines and banks. Some of us may think it is obvious that the government should not run restaurants, but the Tamil Nadu government runs *amma kitchens*, and seems to do this rather well. Meanwhile, others think it is obvious that the government should not run a factory that makes wrist watches, but the public sector company 'Hindustan Machine Tools (HMT) long had a monopoly in making wrist watches in India.

There is a vast array of objectives that a state can potentially pursue through government action. But there is a big gap between dilettantism in public policy and the professional capability of actually making it work. We need the intellectual capacity to envision how a plausible sounding intervention will actually work out. The first milestone in this journey is asking: Should the government be doing this? Can we go beyond gut feeling, to an analytical toolkit through which we can think about the appropriate objectives of government?

Remarkably enough, we can. In the last century, considerable knowledge has been developed on this question, which we summarize ahead.

Freedom Works Well

> *Little else is requisite to carry a state to the highest degree of opulence from the lowest barbarism, but peace, easy taxes, and a tolerable administration of justice; all the rest being brought about by the natural course of things. All governments which thwart this natural course, which force things into another channel, or which endeavour to arrest the progress of society at a particular point, are unnatural, and to support themselves are obliged to be oppressive and tyrannical.*

—Adam Smith, 1776

To understand what the state should do, we should first appreciate what free men and women do when left to themselves. Most of the great achievements of mankind can be traced to the creativity and drive of free persons.

The normal rhythm of the market process is one where firms compete to obtain greater profit. Firms energetically look for actions that will yield higher profit. This drives a ceaseless process of improving the product and reducing the cost of production. This is done by understanding the consumer better and through technological change.

Firms are given no guarantee of profit or survival. The market system demands ceaseless innovation. Every now and then, some firms that fail to cater to the needs of customers go out of business. And, when the profit rates of incumbents become attractive, new firms are created to compete in this business.

Therefore, firms must endlessly run on a treadmill, trying harder to please consumers with better and cheaper products. The productivity gains of a firm (through greater capital investment or through better technology) generate higher wages for workers as their contribution to output goes up.

All these good things result from the self-interest of firms and consumers. This free-market process induces prosperity, creativity, innovation and individual freedom. No central planning or control is required, to get to an endless process of economic growth and prosperity.

There are innumerable elements of the near-miraculous gains in technology and product quality that have arisen in the last 200 years. In 2010, the average refrigerator required an energy consumption that was one-fourth of those sold in 1975, but had 20 per cent more volume and a 40 per cent lower price.[3] Moore's law is the proposition that the number of transistors on a chip doubles every 18 months. Every 18 months, great feats of engineering come about, that generate the next doubling of the number of transistors. All these things come about through the creativity, imagination and hunger of individuals and private firms, not from governments.

The societies where the freedom of individuals is prized are the societies which harness the energy of their people. The most prosperous countries of the world are liberal democracies. Every now and then, there is envy of the growth rates that an authoritarian regime in China has been able to produce, but few would want to live there. *Immigration is the sincerest form of flattery*, and this is where liberal democracies stand out.

We in India are very used to state domination over society. But we ought to remember that the remarkable achievements in history were mostly born of individual initiative.

We tend to assume that the exploration of (say) Antarctica is the work of some government agency. But it was a private person—Vasco da Gama—who found the first sea route from Europe to India. A private person—J.R.D. Tata—first purchased planes and set up an airline in India. These achievements were not planned and run by the Portuguese or British governments; they took place at the initiative of *private* persons.

Similarly, in India, we tend to think that space exploration is the work of Indian Space Research Organization (ISRO), which is a government organization. But the frontiers of space exploration today are increasingly going from government organizations like NASA or ISRO into private hands, such as Blue Origin or SpaceX. The reuse of rockets yields an 80 per cent cost saving, and this frontier is being pushed by private space exploration firms.

Engineers can often visualize simple designs, and are too quick to thrust their schemes upon society. As we have seen with USB chargers, there is a big gap between engineering and public policy. A recurring theme of this book is an appreciation of 'self-organizing systems', of the uncoordinated decisions of individuals left to themselves, that discover order by themselves. The organic development of the economic system, with freedom in the hands of each individual, often works better than instructions from the top.

This does not suggest favouring anarchy, i.e., an absence of government. There is a role for government, in creating conditions for freedom. The main body of this book is about finding the appropriate role for the state, and the mechanisms through which the state becomes useful as opposed to oppressive. The first milestone in that journey is to see the primal role of the individual in society.

At the Heart of the State Is Coercion

> *A state is a human community that (successfully) claims the monopoly of the legitimate use of physical force within a given territory.*

—Max Weber, The Vocation Lectures, 1919

While the state is often seen as benign or benevolent, almost like an uncle or a parent, there is violence at the heart of the state. As Max Weber's definition goes, the state is the community that acquires a monopoly upon violence. States establish conditions where nobody but the state is permitted to engage in violence. States use the threat of violence in order to obtain obedience on taxation and behaviour. The state is not a parent, a philanthropist or a friend.

The individual has a soul but the state is a soulless machine. The state can never be weaned away from violence to which it owes its existence.

—Mahatma Gandhi

All state activities fall into two categories. In the first case, the state can use force to modify behaviour. A law can be enacted that forbids a certain activity (e.g., killing, defamation or sedition) and threatens violators with punishment ranging from monetary penalties to imprisonment to death. In the second case, the state obtains tax revenues and spends this money in certain ways. But obtaining tax revenues is itself done through the threat of violence. The state demands that residents must pay certain taxes, and threatens us with monetary penalties or even prison time if these demands are not complied with.

A failed state is one which fails to achieve a monopoly on violence in its territory—e.g., one in which militias and gangsters also have the capability to inflict violence upon the people. A successful state achieves a monopoly on violence in a given territory, and after that, we face questions about the extent to which it works in the best interests of the people. The big idea of liberal democracy is to limit state violence to a controlled, predictable and just form. In an ideal democracy, we consent to an ethical regime of coercion. But when the checks and balances surrounding the state are imperfect, state violence is deployed in unjust ways.

Every state action comes at the cost of coercing private persons. These restrictions limit individual freedom, which reduces human welfare in and of itself. When we impose a tax of Re 1 upon a person, we take away that person's freedom to spend that Re 1.

Addressing Market Failure Is the Legitimate Ground for Coercion

The important thing for government is not to do things which individuals are doing already, and to do them a little better or a little worse; but to do those things which at present are not done at all.

—John Maynard Keynes

The role for the state is born of a class of problems where freedom does not work so well, where the free market yields poor outcomes. This is the zone of 'market failure', where free men and women, all by themselves, obtain results that disappoint. Where the free market fails to deliver efficient economic outcomes, this is termed 'market failure'. Market failure comes in four kinds: Externalities, Asymmetric information, Market power and Public goods.

Externalities are the situations in which persons impact upon each other in ways that are not intermediated through voluntary agreements between these persons, where people impact upon each other in ways that were not negotiated. Consider a flat owner who takes in a paying guest with a noisy hobby. The flat owner can price in the loss of peace and quiet; therefore, the noise is part of the negotiation and commercial contracting between the flat owner and the paying guest. The neighbours, however, are not part of the negotiation; for them the noise pollution is a 'negative externality'. It is a channel of influence from the paying guest to the neighbour, which was not part of a negotiation.

Pollution comes in many kinds: from the burning of fields, to loudspeakers,[4] to electric lights,[5] to sneezing. All these can induce negative externalities upon other persons without their consent.

There are also *positive* externalities. A homeowner may sublet the ground floor to a paying guest who builds a garden; the garden imposes 'positive externalities' upon the neighbours. A university that triggers off a hotbed of entrepreneurship in its neighbourhood is inducing a positive externality. It imposes beneficial impacts upon nearby households, without their consent. Research and development expenses, that produce new knowledge, impose positive externalities upon society at large.

An urban transportation system imposes large positive externalities upon neighbourhoods that get connected. People choose better people to engage with, when the choice set is enlarged through urban density and swift transportation. Firms are able to obtain lower costs when employees are able to travel over longer distances. Even the non-users of the system, who live in proximity to the system, are beneficiaries of it. The gains to society are much larger than the direct revenues of the urban transport system.

A forest that protects biodiversity and captures carbon induces a positive externality upon the world.

Whether positive or negative, externalities involve gains or harms that are imposed upon bystanders, which do not directly feedback upon decision makers through the normal market process.

When externalities are present, in general, freedom does not give the best outcomes. The producer of a negative externality tends to not care about harms upon third parties and therefore tends to over-produce. Conversely, the producer of a positive externality tends to not care about the gains obtained by third parties and therefore tends to under-produce. When externalities are present, there may be a role for the state to step in, exercise its monopoly of coercive power, and induce better outcomes.

As an example, when one person inflicts personal harm upon another person, this is a negative externality. The state runs the criminal justice system, through which the negative externality of crime is blocked.

Asymmetric information is found when a customer steps into a restaurant. The customer has no reasonable way of knowing whether the kitchen is clean. This fear changes the behaviour of customers and (ultimately) restaurants. Similar issues arise when a customer buys a medicine at a drug store. The customer has no way of knowing if the medicines are adulterated.

A high degree of asymmetric information can create conditions under which voluntary or market-based transactions become infeasible. As an example, these situations are seen with credit or insurance markets, where the market can even cease to exist owing to the inability of private persons to solve the problem of asymmetric information. These 'missing markets' fall under the problem of market failure associated with asymmetric information.

Market power is the lack of competition. Monopolies tend to reduce the output and raise the price. Left to itself, the free-market system delivers poor outcomes in the areas where one side of the market wields disproportionate power. For example, the Italian firm Luxottica controls 80 per cent of the global market for eyeglasses.[6] This gives them the ability to earn supernormal profits.

Finally, *public goods* such as clean air are under-produced by the free market. In technical jargon, public goods are the things that are 'non-rival' and 'non-excludable'. Clean air is 'non-rival', as my breathing clean air does not diminish the amount of clean air available to you. Clean air is 'non-excludable', as it is not possible to exclude a newborn child from breathing in clean air.

An important example of a public good is safety. When the armed forces make us safe from war, this safety is non-rival and non-excludable. The same issue arises with safety within the country, which is produced by the justice system.

By definition, public goods are non-excludable. It is not possible to exclude any person from the benefits. Excludability is essential for firms to obtain a revenue stream. No private firm would produce public goods such as clean air as residents cannot be billed for the services rendered. Hence, we require state action to obtain tax revenues and provide the public good.

The term 'private good' is the opposite of 'public good'. It does not denote 'the things that are privately produced'. For example, telecom services are a private good, whether produced by a government or by a private person.

The free market does not, on its own, solve these four kinds of problems: public goods, externalities, asymmetric information, market power. The interventions by the state should be primarily located around these four problems.

This classification sheds new light upon many things that we do in economic policy. As an example, health care is commonly seen as being the work of the government. But health care is a private good. The services of a doctor or a hospital are rival and excludable. When I am on a hospital bed, you cannot at the same time be on that hospital bed. It is in *public health*—the public goods of health—that there is a clear role for the state. We need to be more careful in understanding market failure in the field of health, and designing optimal policy pathways for what the government should be doing in the field of health.

When faced with a proposed state intervention, our first question should be: What is the market failure that this seeks to address? When market failure is *not* present, we should be skeptical about state intervention. This is a valuable way of drawing the line between central planning and legitimate intervention in the economy.

Market Failure: From Ideas to Action

The idea that freedom works well, apart from the role for the state in four classes of market failure, was evolved by economists over centuries. It always lay at the foundation of debates about state intervention. From the 1980s onwards, it came to be formally deployed into the formal rules that determine the working of governments.

As an example, in the United States, market failure was placed into the formal rules that govern the working of all federal agencies. Executive Order 12866 of 30 September 1993 has this text in Section 1.b.(1):

Each agency shall identify the problem that it intends to address (including, where applicable, the failures of private markets or public institutions that warrant new agency action) as well as assess the significance of that problem.

The Office of Management and Budget (OMB) guidance document, *Economic Analysis of Federal Regulations Under Executive Order 12866*, explicitly uses the term 'market failure'.[7]

Redistribution as the Subsidiary Ground for Coercion

All states engage in redistribution: in raising tax revenues and giving resources to some people at some times. Redistribution contains a fundamental moral challenge: when is it okay for a state to threaten person A with violence, to take money away from person A, and give it to person B? Unlike market failure, there is no technical foundation for redistribution; it relies solely on the political preferences of each person.

As an example of redistribution, all states engage in disaster relief. After a natural disaster, the state expends resources in rescuing people and in post-disaster reconstruction. This is a redistributive activity that most of us might be willing to support.

All states also transfer resources to the poorest persons of the country. This reflects a mixture of altruism and self-interest. Helping poor people is a moral imperative, and in addition, everyone is better off when the poorest are protected from the extremities of poverty and hopelessness.

There is one important calculation in redistribution to address poverty. There are about 0.1 billion poor people in India, so when a government gives them Rs 100/day, this comes at a cost of Rs 3.65 trillion per year. This is a feasible value in union government budgets in India today. The scale of redistribution in India today is vastly larger than this.

As with all government activities, there is a state capacity challenge in translating such objectives (disaster relief or a subsidy program) into action. There is quite a management challenge in identifying the 0.1 billion poorest people, and accurately delivering Rs 100 to them every day. The pressures of electoral politics generate incentives to increase the magnitude of subsidy and the range of people who are paid.

Infrastructure

It is generally assumed that state intervention/production is always legitimate for anything that is 'infrastructure'. Infrastructure is the class of problems which are excludable, plausibly non-rival and natural monopolies.

As an example, consider a highway. It is excludable: It is possible to put a toll booth at the entrance and exclude the people who refuse to pay for it.

It is non-rival under normal traffic conditions: your use of the highway does not diminish my access to the highway. However, once we approach congestion, this stops being true, and your use of the highway imposes negative externalities upon me.

And, most highways are natural monopolies, there is no alternative way to get through from one point to another without using the highway.

These are the three tests that should be applied for something to be infrastructure: it should be a natural monopoly, it should be non-rival and it should be excludable.

Most computer engineering systems are not infrastructure as they are not natural monopolies. Google search is not infrastructure as it is easy to have multiple rival competing search engines. Payment systems are not infrastructure as it is easy to have multiple rival competing payment systems. Credit information systems are not infrastructure as it is easy to have multiple rival credit information companies. Anything that can be done just fine, by having multiple rival private firms that compete, is not infrastructure.

Open source software, that you can download from a website, is a public good, it is not infrastructure. It is fully non-rival (your downloading the code in no way diminishes my access to the code) and it is not a natural monopoly (it is easy to fork a project and start a new one).

There is a great deal of confusion around the terms 'private good', 'public good', and 'infrastructure'.[8] Many mistakes in policy thinking can be solved by being more precise around these terms.

When a problem (e.g. highways) is infrastructure, there are two possible pathways for state intervention: production (the government can build and run the highway) or regulation (a private person can run the highway, but the government regulates the monopoly to prevent it from earning supernormal profits).

Summing Up

The first question in the field of public policy is: What should the state do? A great deal of good policy reform can be obtained by putting an end to certain government activities, and by initiating new areas of work that better fit into the tasks of government.

The state has a monopoly of violence. All activities of the state are grounded in coercion: either directly (when the state demands that private persons behave in certain ways) or indirectly (when the state uses threats of violence to collect tax revenues, and then spends them in certain ways). Coercion of private persons is the unique thing that only the state can do. Coercion is an unpleasant thing and can easily go wrong. Building the republic is about creating ethical control systems that contain and channel state violence for the common good.

The founding intuition of the field of public policy is the notion that freedom works pretty well. Left to themselves, free men and women achieve reasonably good outcomes in most situations.

Freedom works well most of the time, but there are exceptions: the four kinds of 'market failure'. These are: Externalities, public goods, market power and asymmetric information. On its own, the free market often fares poorly at dealing with these situations. This is where the state can add value in society, by intervening in some situations where there is market failure.

Mistakes, failure, unintended consequences happen all the time. Private initiatives fail, government initiatives fail. Things that sound simple—like a government that forces the USB-C charger standard—are much more complicated upon more careful examination.

'Public good', 'private good', and 'infrastructure' are technical terms and are often used incorrectly in the conventional policy discourse. In policy advocacy, the phrases 'public good' and 'infrastructure' are used too often, for policy proposals that do not create public goods or infrastructure.

All states do some amount of redistribution. For example, relief work done by the government after a natural disaster is a case of transferring the money obtained in coercive ways (through taxation) from the populace to the persons affected. Electoral politics creates incentives to do more redistribution.

2

The Limited Toolkit of Intervention

The word 'policy' is often used loosely in India. The Indian government landscape is littered with documents such as a 'National Map Policy'.[1] These documents are written by officials in the executive branch. They lack legislative backing. In a constitutional democracy, only the legislature can authorize the coercion of private persons, through laws. What can government do? There is a limited menu of interventions which can be utilized in order to address market failure.

Coercion That Modifies Behaviour

The state has the monopoly over violence in society. This can be utilized to enact a rule that bans a certain behaviour, backed with the threat of penalties for non-compliance. For example, a law approved by the legislature can define a speed limit for cars, and a punishment that will be meted out upon wrongdoers, through steps initiated by persons in the executive branch.

Officials do not have the power to give arbitrary orders to private people. Officials should not have the power to inflict arbitrary harm upon private persons. In a constitutional democracy, officials only have the authorization to enforce laws, which can at most imply initiating litigation against errant individuals which will then be adjudicated in court. Only judges have the power to write orders that inflict harm upon private persons. It is a departure from constitutional democracy when laws are poorly drafted, thus giving officials expansive power, or when the power to inflict harm upon a private person is in any way available to an official.

Coercion to Pay Taxes

Coercion can be used to force people to pay taxes, thus creating a resource base for expenditure. Every detail of tax policy is coded into the 'Finance Act' that is authorized by the legislature.

The objective of modified behaviour and the objective of raising taxes can be interlinked. The state can tax a certain behaviour in order to deter it, e.g., taxing cigarettes.[2] Subsidies can also be delivered to tax payers in this fashion, e.g., through a favourable tax treatment of purchases of infrastructure bonds.

Using Budgetary Resources to Produce Public Services

The state can use its budgetary resources in order to directly run production of certain services within a government organization, e.g., monetary policy or the police.

Expenditure programs require the authorization of the legislature through the Finance Act.

Using Budgetary Resources to Give Out Subsidies

The state can subsidize certain activities; e.g., if you install rooftop solar equipment, the state can pay part of your capital expenditure. Similarly, education vouchers leave the school choice decision to parents, and state resources flow to the school chosen by parents.

Research and higher education produces externalities, which justifies public resourcing, but this resourcing is generally devoted to high externality areas (e.g., research in all areas, or fields such as philosophy or mathematics) and not the areas with low externalities (professions such as doctors, engineers, lawyers, accountants where education is just a private good).

Subsidies are not necessarily connected to externalities; they can be pure redistribution.

All these kinds of expenditures require the authorization of the legislature in the form of the Finance Act.

In many fields, we see three pillars of intervention: producing (e.g., government running schools), regulating (e.g., government regulating private schools) and financing (e.g., government paying kids to attend private schools). These flow from the limited toolkit of intervention.

Thinking Like a State

Some people are giddy when wielding state power. When the rule of law is weak, officials and politicians achieve the ability to orally demand things from the people who may comply out of fear. In authoritarian environments, there are no limits upon what a state can do. But in a properly functioning state, there is actually a well-defined and limited toolkit of intervention.

Thinking about public policy involves thinking about only four highways—coercive threats that modify behaviour, coercive threats that induce tax payments, public spending to run programs, public spending to pay out subsidies. A disciplined approach, of understanding these four channels and achieving high capability on these four paths, is wise.

None of these four channels are under control of ministers and officials in a constitutional democracy: the legislature must sanction all these pathways. All use of force to demand modified behaviour requires authorization in the form of law, and all taxation or spending requires authorization in the Finance Act.

Summing Up

What can a government do? There is a narrow toolkit of intervention. The state can demand certain behaviour and threaten violence against the private persons who refuse to comply.

The state can demand tax payments from the populace, backed by threats of violence against people who do not comply. The tax rates can vary based on the situation. Private persons overproduce things that impose negative externalities (such as pollution) and under-produce things that impose positive externalities; modifications to tax rates can help improve the outcome.

The state can choose to spend tax revenues in two ways. It can run state organizations such as the police, which produce certain public goods. Or, it can transfer money to private persons. These transfers can be linked to market failure (e.g., using education vouchers to address the externalities in education) or they can be pure redistribution.

Policy thinking must be channelled into only four highways—coercive threats that modify behaviour, coercive threats that induce tax payments, public spending to run programs, public spending to pay out subsidies. These are generally grounded in laws that define the behaviour of government. Taxation and expenditure programs are spelled out in the Finance Act, which constitutes the budget of each year. The Indian government often produces 'policy' documents which do not mean very much.

The power to give orders to private people attracts many people into working in government. Much of that power, in today's India, derives from the extent to which India is not a well-functioning constitutional democracy. When the Indian state matures, private people will have more freedom, and entry into public life will be motivated to a greater extent by the desire to serve the people.

3

A Long History of Failure

During the Cultural Revolution in China, there was a cult of personality surrounding Chairman Mao. In public, everyone claimed that Chairman Mao was their great leader, who had their best interests at heart, and had the right answers to all policy questions. Chairman Mao extolled practical knowledge and denigrated intellectualism.

One day, Chairman Mao organized millions of people to kill all the sparrows in China, on the grounds that sparrows eat grain.

Even if we ignore the ethics of this intervention, we would have to conclude that it was an objective failure. With the sparrows removed from the scene, the insect population surged, and the insects ate the grain instead. Chairman Mao may have had good intentions, and he may have had practical experience of sparrows eating grain, but the intellectual foundation of the intervention was faulty.

Has the Indian-Style Developmental State Worked?

India obtained freedom in 1947 with great expectations of rapidly rising to the ranks of a prosperous liberal democracy.

This did not happen. A few rare countries that were poor in 1945 have graduated to prosperity and the freedoms of a mature liberal democracy, but most did not, and we in India fall in the latter group.

Our founding fathers had the best of intentions, and initiated numerous policy programs, as part of a state-led strategy for growth which is termed 'the developmental state'. However, good intentions do not suffice, and we have poor outcomes in a large number of areas, such as the criminal justice system, the judiciary, the tax system, and financial regulation. Social change has been quite limited; we continue to be hobbled by superstition and prejudice. All across the Indian landscape, the development project has not worked well.

Example 1: Safety of the People

Safety of the people is the most important function of the state. But after 9 p.m., over half of New Delhi feels it is unsafe to go to an ATM, and 90 per cent believes that it is unsafe for an unaccompanied woman to be outside the house. Only 13 per cent of Mumbai believes that an unaccompanied woman is safe outside the house at any time of the day, and for New Delhi this drops to 2 per cent.[1]

Example 2: Carnage on the Roads

In India, we have 130 fatalities per 100,000 vehicles per year. The comparable value for the UK is 6 fatalities per 100,000 vehicles per year.[2] We are 22 times worse.

The appropriate measure that should be used in this comparison is fatalities per kilometre, but this is not measured in India. Each vehicle in India probably travels fewer kilometres per year than is the case in the UK. In this case, road safety in India is *over* 22 times worse than in the UK.

Poor road safety has significant implications upon the health of the people. The Union road transport and highways minister Nitin Gadkari said, 'the main reasons are faulty road engineering, defective DPRs (detailed project reports), bad designing of junctions, inadequate signage and road markings'.[3] In addition, state regulation of drivers, including driving tests and poor enforcement of traffic rules, are a source of low safety.[4]   ••

Example 3: Elementary Education and Health

In India, teacher absenteeism is at 23.6 per cent[5] and the absence rate for medical personnel is 40 per cent.[6] Immunization rates are at about 60 per cent.[7]

The per-student expenditure in government schools rose from Rs 7245 a year in 2008–09 to Rs 19,233 a year in 2016–17 (all values in 2011 rupees). This was an increase of 2.7 times. Learning outcomes in government schools *declined* in this period. In 2010, 50.7 per cent of children in class 5 in government schools could read a class 2 level text, but this declined to 40 per cent in 2016–17.

The government spends over Rs 2000 a month per student on its production of schooling. Private schools have median prices of about Rs 500/month (rural) and Rs 1000/month (urban). Parents face the choice between using a free government school versus paying for a private school.[8] Parents voted with their feet from 2010 to 2016: enrolment in government schools fell by 11.1 million while it rose by 16 million in private schools.[9]

At the end of many decades of very large expenditures in health and education in India, and large-scale intensification of old-style expenditure programs, we are left with dismal outcomes.   ••

Example 4: In Which Year Was the US at the Present Indian Level?

India in 2021 remains a poor country when compared to the frontier of advanced economies in the world. It is useful to look at some measures and ask:[10] *In what year in the past was the United States at the present Indian value?*

With women's labour force participation, the present Indian value of 9.2 per cent (which is similar to Pakistan's level) was found in the US prior to 1890. For per capita GDP expressed at PPP, the present Indian value of $6806 was found in the US in 1896. Six per cent of households in India have a car, a value that was achieved by the US in 1915. These values show a gap of about a hundred years or more between the place where India is today, and the historical developmental journey of today's advanced economies. This raises questions about the Indian development strategy of the last century.   ••

Example 5: The Difficulties after 2011

In 1991, we thought we were at the dawn of a new age of freedom. There was a strong growth episode from 1991 to 2011, but after that there have been significant difficulties.

For the first two decades after 1991, exports growth averaged 11.3 and 21.3 per cent per year. In the decade after 2011, this growth dropped to 2.8 per cent.[11]

Private investment is well measured by the stock of private 'under implementation' projects as seen in the CMIE Capex database. This had average real growth of 19 per cent in the 2001–11 decade and -7.9 per cent in the following decade.

The number of persons working has been broadly stable from 2011, while the number of persons of working age has risen.

••

Example 6: Political Freedom Is Limited

Freedom House classifies India as 'Partly free'.[12] Reporters Without Borders computes the 'World Press Freedom Index', and places India at rank 142 out of 180 countries.[13] The Indian policy strategy is faring poorly on both prosperity and freedom, and there is the possibility that feedback loops have set in between economic and political freedom.

••

The Problems of State Intervention

> *A government can no more suffice on its own to maintain and renew the circulation of sentiments and ideas in a great people than to conduct all its industrial undertakings. As soon as it tries to leave the political sphere to project itself on this new track, it will exercise an insupportable tyranny even without wishing to; for a government knows only how to dictate precise rules; it imposes the sentiments and the ideas that it favors, and it is always hard to distinguish its counsels from its orders.*

—Alexis de Tocqueville

The murder of sparrows in China may appear to be an extreme example. It is not an exception. Across a large number of situations, state intervention works poorly. Once the state achieves a monopoly on violence in a given territory, it is easy for the state to use this power to compel in all kinds of ways. Human history is littered with state power being used in unpleasant ways.

India has a hundred years of a 'developmental state', a strategy where the leadership in society lies with the state, where the state has considerable arbitrary power, individual freedom or initiative is low, and the main focus of the state is upon redistribution. The results of this are visible in the form of mass poverty in India. Vigorous and plentiful state intervention has been tried in India, and it has not delivered an advanced society.

There is a gap between the ideal state and the real world.

'Public economics' is the idealized world of economic analysis, where market failure is identified. This leads to policy analysis, about how state interventions can be undertaken in order to address market failure. These are implemented through organizations, and their design and management lies in the field of 'public administration'. In an ideal world, we would detect market failure using public economics, and then do public administration in order to intervene in society so as to address it.

In the real world, many interventions are ill-advised: they are not motivated by the desire to address market failure. And many interventions fail. The state is supposed to be a machine that converts coercive power into human welfare. But human societies fare poorly on controlling and channelling the monopoly on violence into welfare and justice.

The Law of Unintended Consequences

Unintended consequences inevitably attend purposive social action.

—Robert K. Merton

There is black humour in the phrase 'the law of unintended consequences'.[14] A government intervention that is intended to have a certain outcome will very often end up yielding a very different result. Such failures happen so often that these have been elevated to the level of a humorous 'law'.[15]

A Coercive Agent Is Poorly Placed at Solving Failures of Negotiation

Why does the state fare poorly at addressing market failure? Ordinarily, freedom works well, and we have negotiations and voluntary choice by individuals all across society. The essence of market failure is the channels of influence between two persons which are not governed by negotiations and choice:

- *Market power* : One party in the negotiation has little power and experiences a loss of choice.
- *Asymmetric information*: The process of negotiation works poorly as there is a lack of information.
- *Externalities*: There are channels of influence between two parties that are not negotiated.
- *Public goods*: The individual is not given the opportunity to negotiate and choose.

Market failure is rooted in weaknesses of negotiations and choice. We think we are bringing in the state to address market failure. But the state is a coercive agent, and is ill-placed at addressing a lack of negotiation.

The Impossibility of Paternalistic Policy

Paternalism is the idea that an altruistic government understands the desires of its populace and seeks to do good for them. The assumption is a paternalistic government is like a parent. It knows what a person desires, works in her best interest, and does nice things for the person.

But the only power of a government is coercive power. A government can force people to do certain things, and a government can force people to pay taxes. State paternalism can then only be in favour of some and not all. A government that makes Person A happy by forcing Person B to gift her Rs 1000 is a government that makes Person B unhappy.

We need to change course, from a view of government as a benign paternalistic agent that means well, to a more skeptical view of government. We need the state, in order to address market failure, and we the people must give the state the monopoly of violence, but we have to be skeptical about the things that will be done by the state. The people are the principal and the state is the agent, and the puzzle lies in reshaping the agent to serve the interests of the principal.

Summing Up

There is a long history of failure in the field of public policy. Over and over in history, we see governments that try to do things and fail.

The Indian state constitutes a certain design that came together over the past century. It features domination of the state, a 'developmental state', and low initiative or freedom in the hands of the people. Particularly from 2011 onwards, the results of this strategy have been poor. These failures call for a re-examination of the design of the Indian state.

There is a 'law of unintended consequences', where an initiative often ends up inducing an outcome that was different from what was intended, and indeed was completely unanticipated.

The state is a coercive agent. At the heart of market failure is a failure of coordination, of a lack of negotiation. There is a tension at the core, where problems of coordination are not easily solved through the tool of coercion.

Some people might like to have a paternalistic government. Coercive power gives the state the ability to take from one and give to another, but this will make some people happy at the expense of others. Paternalism by the government is an impossibility.

In a republic, the citizen is the principal and the state is her agent. The citizen consents to the coercive power of the state. But there is a problem of constraining the agent to work in the best interests of the principal.

Part II

Diagnosing the Indian Experience

4

Anatomy of Our Policy Failure

Understanding Indian State Failure

The Indian state is overwhelmed. Day-to-day crisis management tends to dominate, and there is little effort or ability to engage in the long, slow journeys that are required to genuinely solve problems. As the financial economist Harsh Vardhan says, '*we work through panic, package and neglect*'. The Indian state works poorly, experiences panic when faced with a crisis, comes out with an announcement of a policy package that seeks to address the crisis in a short-term way, and retreats back into neglect (alongside triumphalism about the supposedly successful crisis response). Smooth, capable working on an everyday basis has not come about.

The urgent is prioritized at the expense of the important. There is an obsession with practical things to be done today, with an eye to the headlines of the coming week. The internal life of a government organization is mostly about taking an imperfect stab at the crisis of the week, and moving on to new crises next week. The 'field orientation' is extolled, and the ability to engage in strategic thinking has atrophied.

Under these conditions, state failure in India is the norm and not the exception. Whether we look at the statistical system, financial regulation, agriculture, health policy, taxation or spectrum allocation, there are fundamental difficulties in the working of the Indian state.

In each sector, we can speak with sectoral experts, who will describe, with great feeling, the precise nature of the malady that afflicts their sector. It is possible that there are unique twists of intellectual failure and political economy constraints that are hampering every different sector in India. Occam's razor guides us, however, in favouring a more parsimonious explanation: *State failure in India is pervasive because there are features of the Indian state, present in every sector, that are inimical to high performance.* Oddly enough, as these problems are *not* sector specific, they tend to not become the priority of sectoral experts.

This book is about these sector-neutral, cross-cutting features which are present in all sectors, which present a simple explanation of Indian state failure. Most of the chapter titles of this book are sector-neutral, and these chapters contain 79 displayed examples, which are drawn from a wide range of sectors.

This approach holds the possibility of finding high impact pathways to solve these problems. When these cross-cutting constraints upon state capability are addressed, we will reap the fruit of this labour all across the Indian state.

There is a conventional classification scheme, where government failure is decomposed into two parts. First, there is the political economy problem, and governments are hijacked by special interest groups to aim for the wrong objectives. And then, there is the state capacity problem, where government fails to achieve the objective that it seeks to solve.

This organizing structure is inaccurate insofar as in the first stage, it thinks that government is itself pristine, and is only nudged off course by external forces. There is an excessive willingness to give legitimacy to the objectives of the state.

A basic feature of a weak political system is that in many situations, the objectives that a government sets out to achieve are not in the best interests of the citizenry. We cannot assume that governments desire the right things but only have a state-capacity constraint in execution. Low state capacity emerges from the principal-agent problem between citizen and state, and under these conditions, the very objectives of policymakers are often suspect. Supporting policy makers achieve their objectives may often be harmful.

We find it useful to analyse policy failure in four ways.

- *State action where none is required.* In most cases, doing nothing is a good answer. There is no market failure, and there is no need for the state to intervene, the best option is for freedom to prevail. In fact, the 'law of unintended consequences' suggests that well meaning but unnecessary action will worsen the situation.

  Consider the SEBI rules that force exchanges to only work in the Indian daytime. There is no market failure when exchanges stay open for business at any time of the day or night, and there is thus no case for SEBI to coerce exchanges on their trading hours.

  In 2022, the union government proposed a new law that gave sweeping powers to interfere in the working of the fertilizer industry.[1] There is no rationale for this in terms of market failure.

There is no market failure in philanthropy, and there is no case for government interventions, whether the mandatory 2 per cent CSR, or MCA rules that direct how this money should be used, or the FCRA that blocks cross-border grants.

- *There is market failure, but the politics goes wrong.* In some situations, market failure is present, but the search for the right state intervention is hijacked by special interest groups, and the very objectives of policy go astray. An example of this is the problem of ground water in Indian agriculture.

- *There is market failure, and the objectives of policymakers were sound, but the design of the intervention was wrong.* In some situations, the identification of a market failure is correct, but the intellectual clarity was lacking, and hence the wrong interventions were chosen. An example of this is the Delhi government's odd-even initiative, where half the cars were sought to be taken off the roads every day, in order to improve air quality. This was based on a lack of understanding of the sources of the air quality crisis, that afflicts all of North India. The intervention imposed a high cost upon society and delivered low benefits.

- *There is market failure, the correct intervention was attempted, but the implementation failed.* The leadership thought of the right thing, e.g., mosquito control, but was not able to execute it.

This four-part thinking is more useful than the more conventional classification scheme of 'political economy problems' (which fits the second category) versus 'state capacity problems' (which fits the third and fourth categories). It is also more useful than the concepts of 'first generation reforms' (simple stroke of the pen reforms) versus 'second generation reforms' (those that require the construction of state capacity).

The Obstacle Course of Public Policy

The three key steps in policy thinking are:

1. *Are we facing market failure?* If not, there is no role for the state.
2. *Does the proposed intervention address this market failure?* Sometimes, we see proposed solutions which do not address the claimed problem.
3. *Do we have the ability to effectively implement the proposed intervention?* Many times, an idea might be sound but, under present capacity constraints, the implementation of the proposed intervention may be infeasible.

In India, there is a vast unfinished agenda of market failure where not enough work has been done. The justice system should be the first priority of civilization; this requires far reaching work in rethinking laws, police, prisons, public prosecutors and courts. We have major new dimensions of health crises emanating from air quality, road safety, antibiotic resistance and substandard medicines. All these areas require subtle understanding of market failure, and commensurate state interventions. The competition perspective is required all across the working of economic policy, to address the problem of market power.

Numerous elements of state coercion that are present in India lack justification, insofar as there is no market failure that can justify the use of state power.

Why does the state control the time at which a stock exchange opens and closes, or the objects that it trades in? Why does the state seek to imprison a farmer if her produce is not sold at a physical market specified by the state? Why is the state forcing corporations to spend 2 per cent of their profit on good works? When a donor outside India wishes to gift money to an organization in India, why does the Indian state have veto power over whether this gift should take place?

The list of erroneous interventions runs into thousands. India will obtain great progress by identifying and removing these intrusions upon freedom.

Summing Up

When faced with a potential government intervention, it is useful to ask three key questions: Is there market failure? Does the proposed intervention address the identified market failure? Do we have the ability to implement the proposed intervention? A disciplined approach of carefully walking through these three steps will result in improved economic policy thinking. It adds up to a powerful and non-trivial toolkit for thinking about the world.

There are four classes of errors in Indian public policy that call for reform: (a) Situations where freedom works well, where the right thing for the government is to do nothing but the government is doing something; (b) Market failure is present, but the politics pointed state power in the wrong direction; (c) Market failure is present, the politics worked out right, but the wrong intervention was chosen; (d) Market failure is present, the right intervention was chosen, but the implementation was lacking.

A successful political system is one which is able to navigate this minefield. It should hold back from engaging in interventions where there is no market failure. It should be able to channel democratic politics away from the traps of populism or special interest group politics. It should be able to foster expertise in understanding problems and devising the right solutions. And finally, it should have the execution capacity of implementing the right idea.

In a republic, the citizen is the principal and the state is her agent. When democratic checks and balances work poorly, the state becomes a ruler, the citizen becomes a subject, and many objectives that the state chooses to pursue are less than legitimate.

5

Why Do Things Go Wrong?

Public policy failures are born of: (1) The information constraint; (2) The knowledge constraint; (3) The resource constraint; (4) The administrative constraint; and (5) The voter rationality constraint. These five problems interact, and jointly generate government failure, of both kinds: pursuing the wrong objectives and failing on the objectives that have been established.[1]

Element 1: The Information Constraint

Why do things go wrong? Because we are flying blind. India is in poor shape in terms of the range of information available to policymakers, the errors in data, and the delays in data. Policymakers just do not know what is going on.

The criminal justice system in Delhi should evolve based on a quarterly 'Crime Victimization Survey', which measures the outcomes of the criminal justice system based on asking a random sample of persons. This information infrastructure is lacking in India. Under these conditions, episodes like a horrific rape event impinge upon the policy process and dominate perceptions.

In the modern age of electronic and social media, these outliers gain visibility and become clickbait. Practitioners tend to be well informed about outliers, and outliers exert a disproportionate influence upon forming a view of the world. This is a poor way to proceed. Systematic measurement, and the formal analysis of evidence, yields a better understanding of the world and the design of better public policy.

Our ability to undertake rational analysis of interventions, and conduct post-mortems of policy initiatives, is bounded by our availability of information. *What you measure is what you can manage.* We will be able to rationally reform the criminal justice system only when fine-grained data about the criminal justice system can be interrogated. This involves comprehensive measurement of crime, courts, police, prosecutors, and prisons.

A particularly disappointing feature of the Indian statistical environment is that in addition to having limited data, some of our standard public data sources are also flawed. Terms like 'GDP' have institutional legitimacy in the international discourse, but in India we have to be cautious about errors in measurement. Economists in India are doctors without stethoscopes; we suffer the unique agony of trying to do macroeconomics without a well-measured GDP.

Example 7: Education and Air Quality

Statistical system constraints loom large in education and in air quality.

A standard recipe in public policy is to demarcate between inputs, outputs and outcomes. To use education as an example, the inputs are school buildings and teachers. The outputs are students enrolled that go through the motions of being taught. The outcome is the knowledge that students achieve. We have to worry about inputs not yielding outputs (e.g., the teachers do not show up to work) and outputs not yielding outcomes (e.g., the students do not learn much).

Assessing the situation, and undertaking management changes, requires a vast statistical system. Without high-quality fine-grained data, management is impossible. Hard won public resources are being spent in the pious belief that education is important, but the 'bang for the buck' is abysmal.

Similarly, facts are in short supply on air quality. The policy process on air quality involves pursuing a series of questions: *How bad is air pollution in India? What is the root cause? What are the interventions which can make a difference? When interventions were undertaken in the past (e.g., shifting taxis to CNG), did they deliver useful results?*

Making progress on these questions requires fine-grained data on air quality at thousands of locations in India. At present, this data does not exist. *What you measure is what you can manage.* We will only be able to rationally confront the air quality crisis of North India once the requisite statistical system has been constructed.   ••

Information Constraints Hamper Paternalism

A paternalistic government does nice things for each person. For this, it would need to know the preferences of each resident, to know what that person desires. Paternalism is infeasible because no government has such databases.

When redistribution is done, cash transfers are particularly attractive as they leave the choice of consumption goods in the hands of the recipient. No government knows what each individual wants, but the market economy is able to present each individual with a vast array of choices within which each individual obtains a best basket of consumption goods, in exchange for cash. This encourages us to focus redistribution, in India, into cash transfers.

Element 2: The Knowledge Constraint

Why do things go wrong? Because we do not know enough to do the right things.

Designing state intervention into the working of human society is an act of research. Whenever the state intervenes, a high level of knowledge is required about the problems it is seeking to solve, and predictions are required about how a proposed intervention will solve those problems. The understanding of the problem, and the prediction about the impact of the intervention, require research. Every intervention must flow from a theory of change, and our ability to theorize in India is quite limited.

Without deep roots in knowledge, the policy process degenerates into a contest of political and business special interests that harness the coercive power of the state to their own ends. Where we do not have high intellectualism, we get raw power play.

One way in which many countries ensure that state intervention works as applied research is by mandating that state agencies justify their intervention by providing the rationale in the form of an analysis of expected impact of the intervention. For example, some countries require analysis of benefits and costs to be done before any regulation or law is finalized, and usually this analysis is to be periodically reviewed to ensure that it still stands the test of evidence. Inputs into this analysis are given by myriad studies and reports that are available in the public domain or are accessed or created by the agency looking to intervene in the economy.

The kind of research that serves as input for most of policymaking is social science research. Economists, sociologists, psychologists, political scientists, anthropologists, and others apply the methods of their respective discipline and subdisciplines to present a picture of our world in a manner that is able to help us understand the general patterns, persistent trends, and notable exceptions in social phenomena.

In a process of iterative refinement, they help policymakers make sense of their world, and understand whether their perceptions, the petitions from stakeholders, the pressures from interest groups, and other sources of ideas are consistent with what the evidence is telling. In the modern world, the policy process consists of feedback loops from intervention, into the analysis of big data (either administrative data or private data sets), feeding back into refining the intervention.

Research and evidence is essential, not just in formulating policy responses, but also in making the decision to not act. On many problems, it requires sophisticated analysis to conclude that there is no substantial market failure, or that all the feasible tools for intervention are likely to work poorly.

We in India have a dire shortage of knowledge resources to serve as inputs into the policymaking process. As argued in the chapter on the statistical system, the basic information systems in India are weak.

We produce far less research than we need to. The bulk of state-supported research tends to be oriented towards science and engineering. However, the knowledge that is required to feed into public policy comes primarily from the social sciences and the humanities. The atrophying of intellectual capabilities in the social sciences and the humanities has adverse implications for the possibility of a sound policy process.

Most committees and commissions that we have been associated with have been hard-pressed to find the data and research required to make recommendations based on sound evidence. In the absence of sound evidence, it is difficult to take sound decisions. The process of policymaking is always about decision-making under uncertainty, but in the absence of proper data sources and sound research, the uncertainty increases considerably.

As an example of the importance of thorough policy work, demonetization was proposed as an answer to the problems of black money, tax compliance and digital payments. There was a lack of knowledge about the empirical facts, the claimed market failure and the efficient interventions on each of these three fronts.

Analysing social systems is hard in the best of times. In the public policy context, however, there is an additional problem: The Lucas critique.[2] When we look at the data, it may show certain patterns. But when the policy changes, people will re-optimize, so those patterns will change. Many patterns in the data are not exploitable by policymakers. The hardest research projects are those that seek to illuminate policy thinking.

Element 3: The Resource Constraint

Why do things go wrong? Because every rupee of public expenditure is more expensive than we think.

We generally think of a rupee of public expenditure like we think of a rupee of our personal expenditure. However, raising one rupee of tax revenue from the economy is not a simple matter. People respond to incentives, and hence people change their behaviour when faced with a tax. Through this, every tax policy design induces distortions upon the working of the economy.

Taxation imposes a cost upon society owing to these distortions. The total cost of public expenditure is not just the Re 1 that is directly spent, but also the distortions or lost GDP associated with raising Re 1 of tax revenues.

These issues lead up to a powerful concept in public finance: the *marginal cost of public funds* (MCPF). The MCPF tells us the cost to society of Re 1 of public spending. This is typically much larger than Re 1.

> *Every tax ought to be so contrived as both to take out and to keep out of the pockets of the people as little as possible, over and above what it brings into the public treasury of the state.*

> —Adam Smith, *The wealth of nations*, 1776.

In India, the sources of inefficiency from the existing tax system are as follows:

1. Income tax distorts the work-leisure trade-off and the savings–consumption trade-off.
2. Commodity taxation distorts production and consumption, particularly when there are cascading taxes (i.e., the

multiple application of taxes at the links in a production chain).

3. We in India have a menagerie of 'bad taxes' including taxation of inter-state commerce, cesses, transaction taxes such as stamp duties or the securities transaction tax, customs duties, and taxation of the financial activities of non-residents. From 1991 to 2004, we thought the tax system was being reformed to get rid of these, but from 2004 onward, things have become steadily worse, starting with the education cess and the securities transaction tax. All these are termed 'bad taxes' in the field of public finance. When money is raised in these ways, the MCPF is large.

4. India relies heavily on the corporate tax, and has double taxation of the corporate form. In the last decade, corporate income tax and the dividend distribution tax added up to 35 per cent of total tax collection. The double taxation induces firms to organize themselves as partnerships and proprietorships. Production and corporate structures are placed outside India in order to avoid Indian company taxation. These behavioural distortions drive up the MCPF.

5. There is the compliance cost by taxpayers and tax collectors, which is a pure dead-weight loss. Raids and litigation by tax collectors intrudes upon the mind space and imposes costs upon private persons. Costs are imposed upon society by illegality and criminality owing to corruption in the tax system. When some firms get away with tax evasion, this changes the incentives of ethical firms to invest, which imposes enormous costs upon society as the most ethical firms are often the highest productivity firms. As India has one of the highest tax compliance costs in the world, we

would be likely to have a high value for the marginal cost of public funds.

6.   When we do not have a simple single-rate tax system, this has adverse consequences for GDP. E.g., if there was only one customs duty (e.g., 5 per cent), this is much better than having different rates, as small differences in tariffs can induce highly divergent effective rates of protection based on the extent of value added. Similarly, 80 per cent of the countries which introduced the GST after 1995 have opted for a single rate GST. In India, various pressure groups lobby for higher or lower taxes on one industry or another, and this distorts the resource allocation of the economy. This drives up the MCPF.

7.   At the margin, public spending is actually financed out of deficits which constitute deferred taxation, intermediated through the processes of public debt management. Hence, in thinking about the MCPF, we must think about deficits and their financing also. Additional costs to society appear here, as we in India do financial repression (some financial firms are forced to buy government bonds), and have many mistakes in how public debt management is organized.

8.   Under a broad class of situations, the distortion associated with a tax is proportional to the square of the tax rate.[3] In India, many tax rates are quite high, such as the peak rate of income tax and the peak rate of GST. Some sectors such as telecom suffer from extreme taxation. These extreme tax rates tend to increase the cost imposed upon society associated with a rupee of expenditure.

All these factors induce high inefficiencies upon the economy when the government chooses to spend Re 1. There is remarkably little work on measuring the MCPF in India. We believe that the value for India may be about 2.5 to 3.5. As a thumb rule, it is useful to reckon that the cost to society for every rupee of public spending is around Rs 3.

The notion of MCPF brings a whole new perspective upon revenues and expenses of government. It encourages us to be very frugal in spending. We should only spend Re 1 when we are sure that the gains to society exceed Rs 3.

Example 8: Bailing Out Banks

The marginal cost of public funds puts a whole new perspective on using taxpayer money to bail out failed banks. Micro-prudential regulation is supposed to avoid a large-scale banking crisis. Micro-prudential regulation in India failed, and we got a banking crisis. Does this mean that between Rs 5 trillion to Re 10 trillion of public resources should be used to recapitalize banks? We should visualize that these are costs for the economy of between Re 15 trillion to Rs 30 trillion, using the multiplication factor of 3×.

These are astonishingly large numbers. For a comparison, each Rs 1 trillion of public expenditure buys 10,000 kilometres of four-lane highways. Perhaps the right sequencing is for India to have a small banking system, and first learn how to do micro-prudential regulation of banks.   ••

In the Long Run, This Problem May Subside

The institutional failures in tax policy and debt management, which are giving the large Indian value for the marginal cost of public funds, will take a while to resolve. In the long run, we may expect that India will achieve fundamental reforms of tax policy, tax administration and public debt management. Once these changes are achieved, the marginal cost of public funds will go down. In the best advanced economies, the numerical value for the MCPF is from 1.5 to 2.

Until those changes are implemented, however, the rule of 3× is a major constraint upon public policy thinking in India.

Element 4: The Administrative Constraint

Why do things go wrong? Because it is difficult to build effective management structures in government.

We in India know a lot about the management of large private firms. This makes it easy to think that such knowledge can be brought into government contexts. However, a country is not a company.

Government organizations are bigger than anything seen in the private sector. Indian Railways employs 1.3 million people, while TCS has 0.4 million.

In all large organizations, there are principal–agent problems. The employees care about their own interests, and not the objective of the organization. Management is about establishing procedures for overcoming this conflict of interest.

Public administration, the management of government organizations, is harder than management in the private sector, for three reasons. The government wields coercive power (to compel private persons) or the power to spend public money (that is, in turn, obtained by coercing private persons to pay taxes. This is not found in private firms. Private firms keep score using profits or share prices. There is no comparable dashboard in government. Private firms have competitors, and face the threat of going out of business, while the government is a monopoly that will never go out of business.

Government organizations thus contain the hardest management problem. How do we obtain good behaviour from employees that wield coercive power, while lacking good measures of performance, and having no threat of organizational extinction?

Three cross-cutting problems that are found in all organizations are human resource management, the financial process and the government contracting process. In the Indian state, so far, these processes have not been properly established. This hobbles the working of all parts of the Indian state.

Large organizations require well-structured process manuals, and internal audit mechanisms to ensure that the process manuals are being complied with. In the Indian state, there are process manuals governing homeostatic functions— e.g., how pencils are purchased—but organizations generally lack formal processes for the substantive content of their work.

The decision process in sound organizations is organized around a policy document (generally in English) that is refined across multiple meetings (which generally take place in English). Such capabilities are the exception in the Indian state where generally we have oral discussions (in a non-English language) which result in a decision, that is written into the government file and associated legal instruments (often in English).

In every organization, there are front-line producers and then there is an enormous overhead of monitoring, measurement, management and strategy. A low 'teeth-to-tail ratio' is required for the organization to work well. Too often, in India, we have organizations which are all teeth and no tail. In the Mumbai police, the bulk of resourcing goes into hiring front-line policemen, and there is little time or prioritization for the 'overheads' of information, planning, management. This induces poor management and thus poor performance. Similar problems are found in hospitals, courts, etc., where the typical government organization is all teeth and no tail; there is negligible management capacity.

More generally, in the Indian policy discourse, we tend to glorify the field perspective, and downplay policy thinking. We tend to denigrate the knowledge obtained from the analysis of data, from meetings in air-conditioned offices. This generates poor functioning of organizations. A great beat constable does not make a good head of police.

Finally, there is a connection between administrative capacity in the country and the administrative capacity in the state. An example of this problem is seen in the GST, which calls for substantial record-keeping capabilities in all firms. When most firms by number are in the informal sector, this hampers the possibilities for building capability in the government.

These factors have induced a severe administrative constraint that hampers performance in the Indian state. The best designed policy pathways yield poor outcomes because we lack the institutionalized capabilities to build capable organizations.

Politics without Romance

When the State trespasses beyond what is legitimately within its province, it just hands over the management from those who are interested in frugal and efficient management to bureaucracy which is untrained and uninterested except in its own survival.

—C. Rajagopalachari[4]

Why do things go wrong? Because we have a rosy-eyed view of the state.

Many decades ago, we used to think of the state as a pristine, benevolent actor who would work for the best interests of the people. Now we should think about the *incentives* of politicians and officials, who pursue their own personal objectives. Many mistakes which were made in India, in the early years after 1947, would not have been made if such an unsentimental approach were applied to all policy questions.

We in India have a lot of experience with the working of the state, and are often cynical about the motives of politicians and officials. If employees in the government were benign, we would not have large numbers of undertrials in jail for periods that exceed the sentence that they would have received if they were pronounced guilty.

This intuition was formalized in the field of 'Public Choice Theory', which used economic analysis to think about the objectives of politicians and officials.[5]

Public choice helps us see the difference between the people and the state. The country is a collection of people living in a given territory, and the state is the self-interested community which has achieved the monopoly of violence in this territory. The two are quite distinct, and phrases like 'we' (for the superset of state and people) or 'India' (for the Indian state) need to be eschewed.

The Yearning for Heroes

> *Andrea: Unhappy is the land that breeds no hero.*
> *Galileo: No, Andrea: Unhappy is the land that needs a hero.*

—From *Life of Galileo* by Bertolt Brecht, 1939

No matter how famous or well reputed a person is, when she is hired as an official in a government agency, there is a gap between her personal interests and the public interest. Public choice theory encourages us to engage in 'politics without romance'. We will not build the republic by finding benevolent people. What we need are the frameworks where various kinds of self-interest are in conflict in the public arena, through well-specified rules of the game. The objective of reform is not to hire saints, but to achieve a state which yields good outcomes when each actor is self-interested.

Public choice theory has an important implication for institutional design. There was a time when we would try to hire a competent and benevolent person to head an institution, and then leave all the decisions to her. Public choice theory has helped us see that we should stop searching for heroes and that we should not concentrate power in any one person. The capability of an institution lies not in personnel choices but in the arrangement of information, incentives and power. A sound institution is characterized by checks and balances, that create forces of accountability, that push the leadership of an organization to serve the people of India and not pursue their own self-interest.

The authors of the Constitution of India thought that the Speaker of the Lok Sabha was a gentleman, who would always be ethical and fair when performing his functions such as determining whether a given piece of legislation is a money bill.[6] For a contrast, the authors of the United States Constitution, envisioned a President like Donald Trump. They wrote a document which is not a statement of hope about what a good president can do. Rather, it is a document that is focused on limiting the damage that a bad president can do.

Example 9: The Fruit of the Poisonous Tree

Consider the problem of policemen tapping phones. We cannot assume that policemen or their masters are benign people who mean well. We need tight restrictions upon the state apparatus for surveillance.

Suppose a policeman engages in illegal surveillance, illegal entry, or torture, which *successfully* identifies a criminal. Should we condone the violation of laws governing due process, on the grounds that this illegal activity yielded a good result?

Under the 'fruit of the poisonous tree' doctrine in the US, all illegally gathered evidence is inadmissible in court, and policemen who violate laws governing surveillance are personally subject to punishment. Whether illegal surveillance found the criminal or not, the fruits of this poisonous tree cannot be used in court.

This is the only way to create incentives for policemen to live within the rules. If policemen were benign, we would not need laws governing surveillance, or we could have overlooked the occasional blemish where a well-intentioned policeman was so caught up in the pursuit of a criminal that due process was violated. Public choice theory teaches us that enforcement personnel are not benign. Strong limitations are required on their behaviour.

The lack of this doctrine in India—the implicit belief that policemen are benign persons who mean well—is a major source of arbitrary power and thus the abuse of power by enforcement agencies in India.   ●●

Who Will Mind the Minder?

Without the toolkit of public choice theory, we tend to think that the solution to one failed bureaucracy is to set up another. We are willing to believe that the Lok Pal will be better than the Central Bureau of Investigation (CBI). We are willing to think that a new independent agency which reviews official statistics will be better than the Central Statistics Office (CSO).

Public choice theory encourages us to think that all officials and all politicians are cut from the same cloth. We have to construct systems of checks and balances, that will work through rational incentives of all parties, and without assumptions that any one person is a saint.

The Limits of Public Choice Theory

Public choice theory views every official and every politician as purely self-interested. In reality, every individual in public life has a mixture of personal and altruistic elements. We should see public choice theory as a cautious approach: we should design institutions assuming self-interested actors, and we will do better to the extent that some saints are recruited.

A more substantive critique of public choice theory is that substantial state capacity has generally required the construction of a professional ethos, of harnessing the inherent human desire for each person in the policy process to give an account of one's work to peers and to earn the respect of peers.

At first blush, the misbehaviour of policemen will be checked by requiring that they wear body cams which record videos and audios of their every move. But going beyond that, the next level of state capacity can only come about when policemen think that they work for the common good. Being good should be important to each policeman, over and beyond the check and balance that is brought about by wearing body cams.

Our view is that India is at an early stage in the journey to state capacity. At our levels of capability, a simple-minded use of public choice theory is particularly useful. In future decades, as capabilities develop, we would shift gears in favour of the importance of professional ethos.

Element 5: The Voter Rationality Constraint

Democracy is the system where wicked people lie to stupid people.

Why do things go wrong? Because the people lack incentives to know about public policy. The romantic notion of democracy involves listening to the people, but the people generally do not know much about policy.

In 2014, when Russia invaded Crimea, the *Washington Post* ran a poll asking whether the US should intervene militarily in Ukraine. One in six could find Ukraine on a map, but there were plenty of strong views on military intervention. In 2015, Public Policy Polling ran a poll asking whether the US should bomb Agrabah. Agrabah is a fictional city from a Disney movie. A full 43 per cent of Republicans and 55 per cent of Democrats had a clear opinion on this question.[7]

Incentives of Voters

There is a simple economics problem about individuals and policy: the average person does not have the incentive to invest in learning about policy problems. Individuals are very interested in the knowledge that matters to them directly—e.g., a person learns about motorcycles before buying one. But the learning that is done prior to voting is limited. Individuals will not take the trouble to understand GST or PDMA. This is because people respond to incentives: The improvement to the life of an average person, from devoting 10 hours to learning GST, is roughly zero. Hence, individuals will not learn about policy questions.

Consider a range of economic issues. Why nations become wealthy, the benefits or drawbacks of markets and international trade, the role of financial markets, the effects of regulation, the origins of inequality, the benefits of soft borders and immigration. Generally, there is a large disconnect between professional economists and folk beliefs on these questions. Until Donald Trump educated the world about walls on national borders, most people in India may have supported an impermeable wall on the India–Bangladesh border.[8] If the average person would devote time and effort to study these issues, insights will surely arise, but the problem lies in the fact that there is no incentive to obtain this knowledge.

This is not a new idea; it has been known since *The Republic* by Plato, which was composed in 380 BC. Direct democracy does not work well.[9] Taking policy questions to individuals, through referendums, does not work well, as individuals lack the incentive to invest in knowledge about public policy choices.

There is a lot of unhappiness that the voters in the UK or Italy chose the wrong option in the referendums of 2016. But we should not be surprised when referendums fail to give good outcomes. The Constitution of India may not have won a referendum either in 1950 or today. Similarly, demonetization was shown to be reasonably popular in opinion polls in early 2017.

> *The fact of having the majority on one's side does not in any way prove that one must be right. Indeed, humanity has always advanced through the initiative and efforts of individuals and minorities, whereas the majority, by its very nature, is slow, conservative, submissive to superior force and to established privileges.*
>
> —Enrico Malatesta

Direct democracy also suffers from majoritarianism, the idea that policy should be made based on the views of 51 per cent of the population. We must question the extent to which 'the voice of the people' is the oracle that must be followed. There is much more to liberal democracy than winning elections.

The Limits of Voting Systems

The great economist Kenneth Arrow proved an 'impossibility theorem', which shows that voting systems are not able to consistently aggregate the preferences of voters.[10] Specifically, Arrow defined three sensible criteria that a reasonable voting system ought to simultaneously satisfy, and proved that no voting system could achieve all the three at the same time. This emphasizes how voting and elections are less useful than meets the eye, in finding the right pathways for policy.

Popular Policy Ideas

Judging a policy initiative by its popularity among the masses is unwise. Pursuing the policies that have wide support among the people often leads to outcomes which are against the best interests of the people.

As an example, NAFTA created enormous prosperity in the US, but it is generally unpopular in opinion polls. In India, opinion polls have often revealed hostility to eminently sound policies, e.g., on subsidy reform. We should not judge (say) GST by its popularity—the full general equilibrium effects will not be understood by the average voter.

Indeed, it is the institutional function of capable economic policymakers to be unpopular. A Minister of Finance has to make ends meet, and this involves angering many powerful people who want to spend more. When special interests lobby in favour of harnessing the state to suit their own objectives, it is the institutional function of the Minister of Finance to incur their wrath.

In Britain in 1624, King James had a Treasurer named Lionel Cranfield, who made powerful enemies by opposing an expensive war. When Cranfield was locked in the Tower of London in chains, King James said *All Treasurers, if they do good service to their masters, must be generally hated.*

A good Minister of Finance will generally leave office with less political capital than where she started, and vice versa. In terms of the incentives of public life, a successful Minister of Finance should earn respect for the rest of her life, after demitting office. When a sitting Minister of Finance has confidence, that high performance will generate that exalted status in the deep future, she will become more comfortable making decisions which make powerful people unhappy.

Representative Democracy

The strategy that, instead, works better is *representative democracy*. We as individuals elect persons to represent our *interests*. We expect municipal councillors, MLAs and MPs to invest time in understanding policy questions, on our behalf. Legislators are expected to have *shared values* with voters, and obtain intricate knowledge of public policy in pursuing the best interests of their constituents.

This is not easy: there is a principal–agent problem where the individual (the principal) faces difficulties in ensuring that the elected politician (the agent) works in her best interests. Making this work is difficult, but it is more feasible than asking voters to understand policy choices.

Transformative change in many countries has not come from a bottom-up phenomenon of insights appearing in the populace. The countries that have achieved transformative change were greatly influenced by a capable intellectual elite. Whether we think of the founding fathers of the Indian freedom movement, or the founders of the United States, the ideas of the elite mattered greatly, and these ideas were generally unlike the cosmology of the masses.[11]

Incentives, Not Technology

Democracy is supposed to be the rule of the people, by the people, for the people. It is easy to carry this too far, by asking the people about policy decisions. We could just put things to vote. Some technologists think that the complicated structures of representative democracy were invented because, before modern computer technology, it was impossible to listen to each individual. This leads to design proposals where every person votes, using the Internet, on various policy questions.

The large-scale use of referendums is, for the first time, technologically feasible. Direct democracy is, for the first time, feasible. The problem runs deeper. It is not incentive-compatible.

Our only way forward is to make representative democracy work. This is not to say that representative democracy always works well. But our way forward as a republic lies in learning how to make representative democracy work, and not in taking policy questions to the people.

Summing Up

In an ideal world, the state is a benevolent actor, which establishes the right priorities, and is able to marshal the resources to achieve good outcomes. This is not the world that we live in. Public policy in India is characterized by a great deal of failure. We tend to establish the wrong objectives, and then we tend to fail on achieving these objectives.

What are the sources of state failure in India?

1. The *resource constraint*. Each rupee of state expenditure in India is likely to come at a cost of Rs 3 for society.
2. The *information constraint*. Policymakers mostly lack high-quality data about the society in which they seek to operate.

3. The *knowledge constraint*. Public policy is a research process, and we in India lack the foundations of knowledge for operating this research process.
4. The *administrative constraint*. We fare poorly at resolving the principal–agent problem between the individual and the state. We must approach politics without romance. Politicians and officials pursue their self-interest.
5. The *voter rationality constraint*. Individuals lack the incentive to think about policy problems, and organize themselves to influence the policy process.

Many reform proposals suffer from a clear-eyed view of the present and a rosy-eyed view of one reform proposal. By internalizing the deeper sources of state failure, we will become more realistic about our pet ideas in policy.

Part III

The Science

6

People Respond to Incentives

Humans Optimize

In 1902 in Hanoi, under French rule, there was a rat problem. A bounty was set—1 cent per rat—which could be claimed by submitting a rat's tail to the municipal office. But for each individual who caught a rat, it was optimal to amputate the tail of a rat, and set the rat free, so as to bolster the rat population and make it easier to catch rats in the future. In addition, in the outskirts of Hanoi, farms came up, dedicated to breeding rats. In 1906, there was an outbreak of bubonic plague that killed over 250 people.[1]

Sometimes we think that people are stupid, or that people are hide bound in following traditional behaviour patterns. Economists have found, in field after field, that people are not wood, they are not stones. People think intelligently about their own self-interest and change their behaviour in response to changed incentives.

This is also the reason why simple laws have not been found in economics. The difference between economics and astronomy is that when Jupiter goes around the sun, he is not a sentient being pursuing some objective.

This has far-reaching implications for policy thinking. It is dangerous to look at the world, come up with a design of an intervention, and hope that it will have a narrow impact as expected.

Some Chinese universities mandated a fitness requirement measured through steps as counted on the mobile phone. A business sprang up, of firms who would shake a phone and artificially drive up the number of steps recorded on it.[2]

Human beings look at policies and rethink their optimizations. When kerosene is cheaper than petrol, we should expect that people will adulterate petrol using kerosene.

In the 16th century, Dutch authorities levied taxes on individuals based on the width of their houses. This has led to narrow houses. The narrowest houses in Amsterdam are 80 centimetres wide.[3]

The response to changed incentives is often small in the short run, but in time, big changes come about. Far reaching changes in behaviour are feasible, over the medium term, when the price system gives out the correct incentives.

India has long had difficulties in vaccine production, which were rooted in fixed-price arrangements. When more remunerative production arrangements were made, vaccine production in India has bloomed, and India is now an important exporter of vaccines.[4]

Politicians and Officials Also Respond to Incentives

People respond to incentives.
Politicians and officials are people.
Therefore, politicians and officials respond to incentives.

Many times, we criticize the working of a government organization, and get worked up about the mindset of the staff. The economist Percy Mistry has always emphasized that in public policy discussions, we are not allowed to ask for a change in the mindset.

Politicians and officials are not benevolent; they are self-interested actors. What appears to be an entrenched mindset, or an entrenched organizational culture, is always endogenous to incentives. A government organization that is riven with corruption is not one which was unlucky to get a lot of corrupt people. It is one where the rules of the game facilitate corruption.

Conversely, when the rules of the game are changed, this will generate changes in the most entrenched mindset, in the most established organizational culture.

The task of public policy research is to identify the formal rules which have incentive implications for the behaviour of officials and politicians. When the rules change, the culture will change.

Politicians and officials respond to incentives: this has a big and optimistic implication. Changes in the rules of the game will generate behavioural changes on politicians and officials also.

The behaviour of politicians and officials is malleable. The puzzle of policy design is that of finding the checks and balances, and the rules of the game, through which politicians and officials will generate good outcomes for society when they pursue their own self-interest.

Example 10: Monetary Policy Committee

People respond to incentives.
Monetary policy committee members are people.
Therefore, monetary policy committee members respond to incentives.

In previous years, monetary policy decisions in India were dominated by the RBI Governor. When the Ministry of Finance wanted certain things done in monetary policy, they would engage with the governor and a negotiation would take place, outside the public eye. In any such situation, the negotiation may not yield the best outcome.

The solution to this lies in handing over the monetary policy decision to a committee that is called the Monetary Policy Committee (MPC). This is analogous to going from one judge to a bench of judges. Each MPC member is asked to vote and to release a rationale for the vote in public. When individual MPC members make poor decisions, they suffer reputational damage, and thus there are incentives for each MPC member to do better in their decision-making. This arrangement harnesses the incentives of individual MPC members to get them to make better decisions, and avoids the problem of centralized power with one person.

The present design of the Indian MPC still gives too much power to the RBI Governor. The MPC has three RBI staffers, three external people, and the RBI Governor has the casting vote. This implies that even if all of the external members have a contrary view, the RBI Governor still controls the outcome. In this sense, the reform has not yet induced adequate dispersion of power, e.g., as is the case with a bench of judges where no one person dominates. ••

Deploy Incentives with Care

Caution in Setting Up High-Powered Incentives

Economists are proud of having understood how people respond to incentives. The simple-minded application of this idea into management and public policy, however, leads to many difficulties.

It is easy to propose very high monetary pay-offs in return for a simple measure of performance. In the 1860s, the US Congress paid railroad builders per kilometre of rail. This gave incentives to builders to take the longest route between two points.[5]

When such 'high-powered incentives' are set up, the agent single-mindedly focuses on achieving that measure, and sacrifices everything else. When a financial trader is paid millions of dollars of bonuses in return for high trading profit, the trader tends to take very high risks. Such risk-taking is probably not what the employer had in mind.

In the confines of simplistic micro-economic models, incentives work out nicely. In the real world, there are many objectives, and it is seldom possible to capture all aspects of performance into an incentive formula. Under these conditions, the simplistic use of high-powered incentives gives poor outcomes. In most management contexts, low-powered incentives work better.

This proves to be particularly important when transplanting ideas from advanced economies into India. In an advanced economy, there are many elements of checks and balances emanating from the legal and institutional environment. Those are often lacking in India. A high-powered incentive that works well in that environment often results in difficulties in India, because the remaining checks and balances are lacking.

Caution in Setting Up Incentives around Statistical Measures

When a measure becomes a target, it ceases to be a good measure.

—Goodhart's law, 1975

Suppose we think that a certain examination is a good measure of the knowledge of students. If we give teachers bonuses for the exam scores of their students, there is the danger that teachers will then narrowly 'teach to the test'. They will make sure the students do well on the examination. The apparent test scores will go up.

But the examination was never the end; it was the means. The examination was intended to be an instrument for measuring certain deeper knowledge. High-powered incentives that push teachers to deliver exam scores will succeed in obtaining higher test scores, but those test scores will be less informative in portraying what they were supposed to measure.

Or, consider hospital beds. All over the world, the number of hospital beds is used as a measure of capacity of the health care system. There are thumb rules which are supposed to shape the number of ICU beds, ventilators, etc. that are present per unit bed, and then counting the beds makes sense. But once politicians and officials are praised for increasing the number of hospital beds, there is a temptation to cut corners on the full implementation of a hospital bed. As an example, in India, hospital beds tend to be rolled out without the commensurate ratios for the number of ICU beds, ventilators, etc.[6]

Example 11: Goodhart's Law in Innovation Policy

At the starting point in India, there were researchers like S. Ramanujan, C. V. Raman, C. R. Rao, S. N. Bose and J. C. Bose: they had very high intrinsic motivation and produced deep and original research. Despite the barriers of colonial rule and extreme limitations in resourcing, India produced remarkable scientists who mattered on a global scale.

Later, universities brought high-powered incentives into the management of researchers. Universities demanded publication-orientation from researchers. This was done by counting publications in general, and particularly valuing publications in 'high prestige journals'.

Once researchers were given career gains in return for publications, there was a strong incentive to increase the number of publications, even if this reduced the quality of research. In the extreme, 'predatory journals' have sprung up, which exchange money for publications.

Similarly, many researchers choose projects which are likely to get into high prestige journals, and have de-emphasized their own judgement about what is likely to be a fruitful line of inquiry.

Human networks are built to get into high prestige journals, e.g., by befriending editors and referees, or finding co-authors who are well networked. Many research projects are constructed with Indian co-authors playing subsidiary roles, while co-authors abroad exert creative control.

Universities sought to spur research by creating high-powered incentives, such as jobs and promotions, in favour of publication in high prestige journals. We now have more publications including those in high-prestige journals, but along the way we have paid a price in curiosity, creativity and innovation. We are pushing less important research into more prestigious journals.

This problem is present the world over. Vast increases of resourcing into research have been accompanied by poor bang for the buck.[7] As the statistician Andrew Gelman says,

> This is not at all to single out this particular article, its authors, or the editors of the journal that published the

paper. They're all doing their best. It's just that they're enmeshed in a process that produces working papers, published articles, press releases, and news reports, not necessarily scientific discovery.[8] These distortions are particularly harmful in the social sciences and humanities, where scholars who are pursuing high prestige journals outside India are likely to lose their engagement with the most important questions as seen in India. ●●

People's Responses to Incentives Can Be Wonky

Typically, we think that humans have unique preferences, that are hard for an outsider to understand, and each human pursues her own self-interest. This is a very fertile line of thought which has given immense insights into the world around us.

The first thing that we learn in economics is to respect the preferences of others. When we see someone else doing something that appears incomprehensibly wrong, there is generally a good logic in favour of those decisions, based on the preferences and budget constraints of that person. Liberalism—the respect for the values, beliefs and decisions of others—is integral to economics as it is to no other branch of human knowledge.

But at the same time, there are disconcerting gaps in the paradigm. The first chink in the armour is the cost of acquiring and processing information. It is too easy to slip into the world of the model, where humans are perfect in obtaining and processing information. In practice, obtaining and processing information is costly. Humans are rational in choosing where to expend such effort.

As an example, humans think carefully before buying a microwave oven, because the gains from wisely choosing a microwave oven are large compared with the effort expended in understanding them. But humans do not bother to vote, or expend minimal effort in choosing how to vote, as there is a low link between effort spent in understanding alternative political parties and the self-interest of the voter. After 1945, voters in Europe at first carefully avoided authoritarians, but as the years went by, the memories faded. In a rational world, voters would read history books and not forget.

Consider the choice of soap. We do not live in a world where a consumer assembles all information and solves out once for the optimal choice of soap, and then stays fixed with this choice as long as tastes and prices are stable. Consumers start out somewhere, and gradually learn their way to an optimum. The key element of this process is the fact that buying soap is done frequently. Each person tends to converge upon a subjective choice of soap. This comes from an iterative process of experimentation, experience and slow learning. On the scale of a life, changes in preferences, technology and budget constraints happen to everyone, and the choice of soap shifts gradually.

This process of groping for the optimum does not come about for purchases that are made only rarely, such as a home loan. Therefore, these markets tend to work poorly.

Consider the process of an entrepreneur doing an IPO. The IPO is an important event in the life of the entrepreneur. She has not done it before, it is important to her, and she is keen to get it done successfully. There is no problem of rational inattention or under-investment in information and information processing. However, there is no possibility of a learning process, as almost nobody does more than one IPO in a life. This hampers the working of the market.

The second chink in the armour lies in thinking across long time horizons. The field of behavioural economics has emphasized that humans seem to exhibit a very low regard for events deep in the future. There is a certain kind of short-termism that is wired into us; we tend to make decisions based on outcomes nearby in time.

These concerns about human decision-making have becoming increasingly prominent; they have gone from novel criticism of the mainstream, with the 'bounded rationality' of Herbert Simon of the 1950s, to becoming the mainstream, with the economics Nobel prize of 2002.[9]

These problems are particularly important in health and pensions. Humans have little understanding of the incremental contribution of a medical professional. We tend to be swayed by the bedside manner, and fail to understand malpractice. We fail to think correctly about how health-related decisions play out over many decades. Similarly, it is difficult for humans to make savings and investment decisions starting in the twenties that will yield income in old age, from the age of 70 to the age of 100. The optimal stance of policy is not obtained if we think of human beings as perfectly effective at understanding information and making sound decisions.

Summing Up

People respond to incentives. Human behaviour is not fixed; it changes when the incentives change. When policy changes, human behaviour changes.

The behaviour of politicians and officials is also not fixed; it changes when the incentives change. There is nothing innately Indian about malfunctioning civil servants, politicians, mindset, or low state capacity.

However, changing incentives should not be done in a simplistic way. When high-powered incentives are introduced, there is the danger of individuals pursuing those incentives to the exclusion of everything else. This can often result in unintended consequences.

When incentives are established based on a certain statistical measure, there is a greater risk that this measure will be tampered with.

While human beings mostly do well in understanding incentives and doing the best for themselves, the new field of 'behavioural economics' has documented many kinds of mistakes that human beings make in understanding information, risk and time.

7

Going with the Grain of the Price System

The great economist Paul Samuelson narrated a fable about agriculture that is quite revealing. Suppose there is a bumper harvest and the price crashes.

If farmers make decisions based on last years' price, then this will give reduced sowing and reduced expenditures on agricultural inputs. Now, the harvest will be reduced and prices will go up.

In the next season, if farmers make decisions based on last years' price, then this will give increased sowing, and then the cycle goes on and on.

This 'cobweb model', a story of prices and incentives and behaviour, is an example of the intimate connection between prices and public policy problems.

The price system is the vast mechanism through which the uncoordinated decisions of millions of people come together to make prices, and prices turn around and reshape the production and consumption behaviour of millions of people.

The price system is the opposite of central planning. Central planning is the control of technology, products, processes, the resource allocation, in the hands of the government (it could be at any level of government, not just the union government). The opposite of this is decentralized decisions by free persons, the organic evolution of the self-organizing system, of information processing and decision-making in the price system.

Economics has a great deal of understanding of the price system, and this offers five valuable rules in the field of public policy:

1. Supply and demand make the price.
2. Demand curves slope downward and supply curves slope upward.
3. There is a law of one price.
4. The policymaker should have no opinion on the price, and no tools to directly control it.
5. The most efficient resource allocation arises from the price system.

Supply and Demand Make the Price

If there is a lot of demand, and not enough supply, prices will go up. If there is a lot of supply, and not enough demand, prices will go down.

The price will move till the market is cleared, i.e., the supply and the demand are equal. As an example, consider the price of salt. The per capita consumption of salt is essentially fixed; there are no substitutes and there is no possibility for most people to consume less. When a small shortage of salt comes about, a very large price adjustment is required to get some people to buy less salt, and thus remove the gap between supply and demand.

The consumption of (say) salt or wheat is price-insensitive, therefore, there will be large price fluctuations. The consumption of (say) avocados is highly price-sensitive, so there will be small price fluctuations.

Indira Gandhi claimed that inflation in the 1970s was caused by hoarders and speculators. It was actually just a simple matter of supply and demand. Excoriating, coercing, or imprisoning the hoarders and speculators changes nothing in terms of creating new supply. The economic theory of the persons hostile to the price system is wrong.

Policymakers have regularly tried to ban futures trading when the price of a commodity goes up. This is based on the mistaken notion that futures trading causes the price to go up. The price is made by supply and demand and not by trading. Our extensive experience in India with bans on trading show that these do not work in influencing the price; they only damage the working of the market.

A gap between supply and demand is the problem that is solved by the price system. Prices move in order to remove imbalances between supply and demand. The movement in price solves this problem by inducing changes in both supply and demand. Every time a government interferes in the movement of a price, it hampers this adjustment process.

The most important price of the country is the exchange rate. Every day, the exchange rate should change, to catch up with changes in macroeconomic conditions. Changes in the exchange rate impact upon capital flows and international trade. When a government interferes with the movement of the exchange rate, this hampers macroeconomic adjustment: the underlying problem that was driving the change in the price persists.

Demand Curves Slope Downward and Supply Curves Slope Upward

When the price goes up, less is demanded ('demand curves slope downward'). When the price goes up, more is supplied ('supply curves slope upward'). People are rational and change their behaviour. At a higher price, there is more supply and less demand. If prices of vaccines are higher, more vaccines will be produced and fewer vaccines will be demanded.

Example 12: Minimum Support Price (MSP)

If a government announces a high minimum support price (MSP), farmers will see the prospect of higher profits per kilogram of output. They respond to this high price by spending more on inputs. These inputs include sown area, electricity to pump water, fertilizer, insecticides, etc.

Hence, after MSPs are raised, we get a supply response. There is a surge of production. Now, there are exactly two possibilities. Either the government will succeed in running a purchase operation all across the country, to buy this enhanced production at the promised MSP, and put it away in warehouses. Alternatively, the government lacks the administrative ability to buy the product, and this glut will reach the market, where supply and demand make the price, and result in a crash in prices.[1]

This yields a teachable example of unintended consequences in public policy. The government raises MSPs because it thinks this will make farming more remunerative, but this yields a crash in prices and farmer profitability.   ●●

Example 13: Rent Control

Some policymakers became unhappy at high rents, and imposed rent controls. The coercive power of the state was used to force rents to a low level. But supply curves slope upwards: when the price is driven down, the supply of housing available on rent declines. Shortages of housing will inevitably develop when rent control is imposed.

The policymaker who sets out to make rented housing cheaper for the middle class makes rented housing unavailable for the middle class. ••

There Is a Law of One Price

The same object cannot command two different prices. If this is the case, there will be *arbitrage*. If gold is cheap in Mumbai and expensive in Delhi, people will buy gold in Mumbai and sell it in Delhi. This arbitrage tends to make the price difference go away. Similarly, if gold is cheap in Dubai and expensive in Mumbai, people will buy gold in Dubai and sell it in Mumbai.

Many governments have experimented with 'dual exchange rate regimes' where the government forces one exchange rate for importers and another for exporters. These schemes never work.

Policymakers of a socialist vintage are hostile to the word *arbitrage*. However, arbitrage is the basic human instinct of removing the difference between two different prices for the same thing, and earning a profit while doing this.

The Policymaker Does Not Control the Price

Every now and then, policymakers see a market price that they do not like. Perhaps the price of wheat is too low in the eyes of a policymaker, perhaps the price of wheat is too high in the eyes of a policymaker, perhaps the price of stents is too high in the eyes of a policymaker. The coercive power of the state is sometimes deployed into a price control. These never work.

A price of wheat that is too low in the eyes of the producer is a bonanza in the eyes of the consumer of wheat, and vice versa. For every exporter who gains when the rupee depreciates, there is an importer who gains when it appreciates. Once policymakers get into having an opinion on prices, they have to adjudicate conflicts between different groups of people who see prices from the buyers perspective versus the sellers perspective. There is only one objective way to think about price: the correct price is the one made by supply and demand, untrammelled by political influences.

> *The market is not an invention of capitalism. It has existed for centuries. It is an invention of civilization.*

> —Michael Gorbachev

Policymakers need to learn to respect the prices that come out of the large numbers of free people buying and selling. Sometimes, prices go wrong because of market failure. As an example, a monopoly tends to drive up the price and earn supernormal profits. If so, the solution lies in addressing the root cause—the market failure. Controls on prices are illegitimate and do not work.

Policymakers of a socialist vintage feel they should have a large number of levers of control through which prices can be controlled. Modern thinking in public economics guides us into focusing on the appropriate role for policy: Addressing market failure. The state should not be here to control prices based on rival political influences; the state is here to address market failure.

The term 'price system' is sometimes misunderstood. A sector works through the price system when and only when all buyers and sellers come together in a market to make the price, and the price reshapes their production and purchase decisions, and all these actions take place in a state of freedom. The mere existence of prices at stores in the erstwhile USSR, or in the purchase of electricity in India today, does not mean that the price system is in operation. The price system is only in operation when there is no state coercion upon the actors, who work through the market, who make the price through their supply and demand decisions, and have their behaviour in turn reshaped by prices.

In India, we started out with a government which controlled the price of steel and cement, and many other things. By and large, mainstream economics knowledge in India has reached a point where there is no interest in price control for cement and steel. But should you bring up the exchange rate, policymakers switch back to craving for state power in setting the exchange rate, or as it is more euphemistically stated these days, in 'controlling the volatility of the rupee'.[2]

Breaking Out of the Cobweb Model

Samuelson's story, at the start of the chapter, gives us an insight into the problem of boom and bust in Indian agriculture. The price of onions surges under shortages; this attracts sowing; the price of onions crashes in a glut; this discourages sowing; and so on.

How do we break out of the cobweb model? *Storage* (also called 'hoarding') is the technique through which goods are transported from a time point where they are cheap to a time point where they are expensive. *Futures trading* looks into the future, and produces a forecasted price at the harvest date which can be used for sowing decisions or storage decisions.[3] *Free trade* (within India[4] and across the border[5]) generates arbitrage, where cheap goods are taken away and additional supply brought in when prices are high.

We suffer from the cycle of boom and bust in Indian agriculture because the state has disrupted all these four forces of stabilization—warehousing, futures trading, domestic trade and international trade.[6] The state makes things worse by having tools like MSP and applying these tools in the wrong way. Better intuition into the working of the price system would go a long way in shifting the stance of policy.

When private persons fail to achieve the right decisions on sowing and storage, this has larger consequences. Food supply crises and inflation crises impose negative externalities upon the larger populace. If anything, addressing this market failure calls for subsidizing the stabilizing responses of warehousing, futures trading, domestic trade and international trade.

The Most Efficient Resource Allocation Arises from the Price System

In every economy, there is a configuration of labour and capital through which production and consumption is organized. As an example, consumers of electricity choose whether they should use LED bulbs or air conditioners, which shapes their demand, and the production side of electricity comprises myriad decisions about how to organize generation, transmission and distribution. The configuration of the economy is termed 'the resource allocation': this is the description of how labour and capital are organized in the economy.

When the price system is in operation, there is a two-way street: the decisions of all buyers and sellers come together into the market, to make the price, and the price reshapes the behaviour of all buyers and sellers. When the price is high, sellers respond by producing more and buyers respond by purchasing less. Technical change is continuously driven by rational buyers and sellers responding to the outlook for prices. The resource allocation is thus continuously reshaped by the price system. Prices are an information system: buyers and sellers only see prices and respond to them, and grand movements in the resource allocation of society come about through everyone's self-interest.[7]

A remarkable feature of the price system lies in its efficiency. The price system discovers the most efficient resource allocation. Detailed decisions, about techniques and methods of production, at millions of locations and persons all across the country, are best made through the price system. If a central planner tries to instruct people on (say) using LED bulbs, or if a muscular Indian state will try to supplant the Indian retail industry by purchasing LED bulbs and selling these in India, this will always result in an inferior resource allocation.

A central insight of modern public economics lies in the value of keeping the state out of central planning, i.e., of any say in the technology, products or processes of the economy. The private sector will find the most optimal answers, and ceaselessly modify them in response to prices, when the price system is allowed to function. Whether it is the payments system, bill payments, e-commerce, or credit information: there is no role for the government in technical design, technical standards, business process design or industrial organization.

As an example, if decarbonization of the economy is required, the right role for the state is in taxing the CO_2 pollution, which directly addresses the negative externality. Once this is done, the price system will discover the most optimal resource allocation that achieves the required decarbonization. Direct government control of energy production or consumption technologies will always yield a higher cost of decarbonization.[8]

Reshaping Resource Allocation Takes Time

When the pandemic started, there was a surge in demand for masks. The price of masks skyrocketed.

This price rise was the sound of the price system in action.

The price system was sending messages to every firm that there are profit opportunities in making masks. Myriad firms, all over the world, worked feverishly to increase the production of masks. There could not be a bigger and faster mobilization of productive resources (i.e., capital and labour) for producing masks, when compared with what happened in early 2020 based on the two- to ten-fold increase in the price of masks. Private people moved mountains, overcoming supply chain dislocations, innovatively repurposing equipment and raw materials that had not been intended to make masks, so as to ramp up mask production. Firms who had never made masks before, such as Fab India, got into this business.

All this creativity and innovation only required one input: high prices.

Practical people think that this is price gouging, or that it is unfair that the price of a mask is so high. Upon reflection, we should see that this is the sound of the price system doing its work. In a few weeks and months, global production of masks surged and mask prices crashed. To know economics is to be patient with the short-term response (huge changes in the price) as this is the best pathway to the long-run answer (changes in demand and supply).

The price system achieves the most optimal adjustment, and state power can only degrade the outcome when compared with this. Every interference by policymakers, in the market for masks, only harms the adjustments of the price system. A country becomes great when the political system creates the conditions of economic freedom for the price system to work its magic.

Prices, Fast and Slow

Some people get unhappy when prices move rapidly. A big change in the price, over a short time period, i.e., high volatility of the price, raises concern in their minds. But the one thing worse than a price that adjusts rapidly is a price that does not.

Suppose an imbalance between supply and demand builds up. Would we rather have the imbalance closed quickly or slowly? A better functioning economy is one in which a shortage *rapidly* generates a higher price. This yields reduced demand, and incentives to increase supply. In time, increased supply will kick in and help bring down the price.

If the government blocks the movement of the price, the responses of supply and demand will not come about. If the government forces the price to adjust slowly, the responses of supply and demand will come about slowly. These are inferior outcomes when compared with a rapid movement in the price.

Consider the rupee. Suppose there is a big change in economic conditions and a large rupee depreciation is called for. Suppose RBI decides to reduce the volatility only. As an example, suppose a movement from Rs 70 per dollar to Rs 80 per dollar is required, for the big change in economic conditions, and suppose RBI decides to 'reduce volatility' and spread out this change over 10 months.

What would the consequence be? For every person, it is now efficient to sell domestic assets, take the money out of the country, and bring it back after this process is complete. A person would sell Rs 70 billion of domestic assets, convert them to $1 billion held abroad, wait out the 10 months, and bring them back as Rs 80 billion, which is a cool profit of Rs 10 billion in 10 months. The authorities may try to impose capital controls which interfere with such movement of money across the border, but India is now too internationalized, and there are too many avenues through which these steps can be executed.

This is a teachable moment in unintended consequences: the policymaker thought she was reducing volatility of the rupee, but kicked off an asset-price collapse in the domestic economy. And, the general principle here is, the best functioning economy is one in which changes in supply and demand *rapidly* result in a change in the price.[9]

In the field of medicine, an *iatrogenic illness* is an illness that you contract at a hospital. You go to hospital trying to get cured, and instead you contract an illness. Larry Summers has introduced the phrase *iatrogenic volatility*, of policymakers who make mistakes when trying to stabilize markets and in fact end up destabilizing them.[10]

Summing Up

Supply and demand make the price.

When prices go up, demand goes down. When prices go up, supply goes up. The price system sends messages to everyone, through prices, which reshape their behaviour in these ways.

Free men and women will buy things where they are cheap and sell them where they are expensive, and thus arbitrage away pricing discrepancies.

The price system reallocates resources and delivers the required economic adjustment: at first, there are large adjustments in prices and small adjustments in the resource allocation. Changing the resource allocation is time consuming. Gradually, the structure of production and consumption change, and the early overshooting of prices is reversed. A good political system is one which has the patience to allow the price system to do its magic.

When there are large changes in a price in a short time, this can be disconcerting and impose problems upon some people. But if the government forces the price to change slowly, this makes things worse. Prices are the mechanism through which the market economy adjusts to shocks; by hindering price movement we postpone adjustment.

In India, the legislature, the executive and the judiciary have all repeatedly undertaken actions which go against the grain of the price system. These actions are doomed to failure. When the policymaker tries to control the price, this is harmful, and the greatest harm is done when the policymakers try control both the price and the quantity.

The policymaker should have no opinion on prices and not try to control prices. Policymakers must strengthen their intuition into the working of the price system, and go with the grain. The field of public policy is about identifying and addressing market failure, not controlling prices.

Under conditions of economic freedom, the price system is in operation. The price system induces the most efficient resource allocation. Central planning—government control of technology, products or processes—always yields a less efficient resource allocation compared with this.

8

More Competition, Always

One of the four categories of market failure is market power, i.e., uncompetitive market conditions. The market economy yields good outcomes for society when, and only when, there are high levels of competition. Competition pushes firms to cut costs, to innovate, and to deliver the best bargains for customers. When competitive pressure is lacking, firms degrade into inefficiency but obtain supernormal profits. This works badly for the economy. Every lever of public policy should be applied to address this market failure, to reduce entry barriers and increase competition.

Every Firm Wants Peace of Mind

When competition is achieved, the market economy pushes firms to ceaselessly work hard. Every CEO is looking for a way out of the grind. Every firm is looking for a way to obtain some edge, that others cannot compete with, after which wealth and peace of mind can be obtained.

As an example, IT entrepreneurs are very focused on creating 'network effects' through which a firm like Facebook or Amazon is able to set up a position on the market that is unassailable, and then earn supernormal profits and peace of mind. The phrase 'network effects' is freely used by technologists but it should make us uncomfortable. Market power is market failure, whether this is done by old style cartels or new age technologists.[1]

Creative Destruction and the Death of Firms

Every firm constantly tries to adapt to the changing world of what consumers want and what technology makes possible. Every firm peers into the future, and speculates about the kinds of products and production processes that will prove to be profitable. Some firms will always make mistakes in this speculation and go out of business. Their departure frees up labour and capital that can go to more productive firms.

When a firm goes out of business, we feel a certain sorrow about its departure. But a key idea of economics is that birth and death of firms is healthy and desirable. The great economist Joseph Schumpeter termed this process 'creative destruction'.

In India, we have traditionally felt that all firm failure is a bad thing. As Montek Ahluwalia says, the very phrase 'sick company' suggests the need for a hospital to nurse it back to health. We need to shift gears, and marvel at the process of creative destruction. There is a great circle of life, and both firm creation and firm destruction are required for a sound ecosystem of firms.

For this to work properly, we require a well functioning bankruptcy process. In this, the key distinction is between firms with valuable organizational capital and those without.[2]

Some firms possess value in their organizational capital. They are sound as a going concern; they just need to be refinanced through a new financing package where the erstwhile owners and creditors take a loss. As an example, European telecom companies overbid in spectrum auctions. Many companies were not able to service their debt. But they were sound organizations, and the bankruptcy process found value in these organizations. The bankruptcy process imposed a 100 per cent loss upon shareholders, a large loss upon creditors, and recreated a new all-equity ownership structure which preserved organizational capital. Customers of these telecom companies experienced no interruption of service when the old firms were put through the bankruptcy process and were recreated under a very different balance sheet.

Sometimes, the very organizational capital of a firm is faulty and it needs to be dissolved. Such a firm goes into the bankruptcy process and is liquidated. This improves the profitability of competitors and frees up labour and capital that can go into better performing firms. The critical call that the bankruptcy process has to make is whether there is organizational capital that justifies firm survival or not.

There are two pathways to the resolution mechanism. For most firms, the right answer when faced with default is to hand over control of the firm to a 'committee of creditors' who decide how best to extract value for themselves. When a financial firm has a large number of individual creditors (e.g., a bank or an insurance company), this committee would prove cumbersome, and a more state-led bureaucratic solution is preferred, this is called the 'Resolution Corporation'.

In Indian economic history, Financial Sector Legislative Reforms Commission (FSLRC, 2011–2015, led by B. N.

Srikrishna) came at these questions first, at a time when neither the bankruptcy code nor the resolution corporation existed. It designed the resolution corporation, and anticipated the coming Bankruptcy Legislative Reforms Committee (2015–2016, led by T. K. Viswanathan), which designed the main bankruptcy code. The 'FRDI Bill' is essentially the sub-component from the draft Indian Financial Code, which creates the Resolution Corporation, and it has not yet been enacted.

Zombie Firms

The Japanese experience in recent decades has inspired the phrase 'zombie firms'. These firms are the walking dead, the firms that ought to have died, but have been artificially kept alive through state or bank support. The lingering presence of these firms increases the cost of inputs for healthy firms and reduces the profitability of healthy firms. When a policy framework encourages the lingering survival of failed firms, this harms healthy firms in that sector. Japan experienced remarkable problems through the combination of zombie banks who did evergreening for zombie firms. Their story of macroeconomic difficulties is an important warning in favour of sound banking regulation, blocking evergreening, and encouraging exit by banks and non-banks.

By this logic, the presence of one large zombie airline harms the viability of all private airlines. When Air India was privatized, and the flow of public money into Air India was halted, all private airlines benefited; it became an environment of fair competition.

In the Indian context, zombie firms are particularly harmful given the weak discipline of the budget process. When a government faces a soft budget constraint, there is a greater temptation to support zombie firms to walk the earth for a few years more. This is one reason why public sector companies are a problem for the economy: there is a greater risk of them becoming zombie firms backed by the exchequer. This is bad for public finance and bad for the economy.

Another pathway through which a kind of zombie firm comes about is when some firms violate laws or evade taxes. In India, we see many markets where low productivity firms coexist with high productivity firms. The competitive market process should force the exit of low productivity firms. This does not happen when the low productivity firms violate laws, e.g., a low productivity firm may emit pollution, while the high productivity firm incurs the higher costs associated with the pollution control required in the law. In similar fashion, a low productivity firm may survive, in competition against a high productivity firm, by evading taxes.[3]

When enforcement capabilities, of laws or of taxes, are improved, low productivity firms will exit. Production will shift from low productivity firms to high productivity firms. This reallocation will yield GDP growth, in and of itself.

In some areas, we have seen the meteoric rise of certain firms that are allied with the prevailing ruling party. For some time, such politically connected firms fare well, through harmful means such as obtaining support from regulators. When the sweetheart arrangements break down, such firms tend to collapse, as their skill lies in political manoeuvering and not in achieving high productivity. When institutional quality improves in India, the time period for which such firms will have a happy ride will come down.[4]

Economic Dynamism Requires Closure

Creative destruction is the ceaseless process where people try out ideas, build a business, and when they find that it does not work, they close it down. Many innovations are attempted, out of which some turn out to work well. When an incumbent firm develops a high profit margin, others jump in and compete this excessive profit away.

Creative destruction requires closure in the form of firm exit. There are three kinds of frictions in firm exit. Some firms are artificially kept alive as zombie firms. Other firms face a messy exit owing to the infirmities of the bankruptcy process.[5] Finally, there is the case when the agencies come in. When business failure turns into investigations, there is no closure.

The willingness of entrepreneurs to start a business requires an economic environment of limited liability, where the entrepreneur will be able to give up, put the firm into the bankruptcy process, and walk out of it with nothing more than a bruised ego, reputational damage, and valuable experience. A society that pillories entrepreneurs, and turns business failure into protracted disputes or entanglement in agencies, is one which will have less entrepreneurship.

Business Cycle Fluctuations and Firm Failure

Bankruptcy at the level of firms or individuals is intertwined with the macroeconomics of business cycles. In good times, many firms do well, whether capable or not.

Downturns are an *agni pariksha* (trial by fire), which certain firms do not survive. This has its own cleansing impact. Similar issues prevail about firm creation also: the firms that get started in bad times seem to be a bit more capable.

Conversely, there is a link between institutional mechanisms for exit and recovery from a downturn. Consider a future date when the bankruptcy process works well. Under such conditions, when a business cycle downturn commences, weak firms will go into the bankruptcy process *and get rapidly processed*, their swift exit will improve profit margins of the survivors, and the resource reallocation will generate GDP growth. The faster that this process can play out, the shorter the downturn will be.[6]

Credit stress in financial and non-financial firms in India was visible from 2012 onwards. About a quarter of the firms were under substantial stress. In a world with a well-functioning bankruptcy code, and a well-functioning FSLRC resolution corporation, these firms would have been processed by the resolution frameworks in about two to four years. By 2016, the slate would have been wiped clean, and the economy would have been poised for recovery.

A sound bankruptcy process thus gives less severe business cycle downturns. This aspect is distinct, and over and above, the traditional macroeconomic policy thinking on stabilizing business cycles.[7]

Living in Creative Destruction

Many of us live in the cossetted formal sector, where our salaries and pensions are assured to us. We are used to very high levels of income and organizational stability. There is a vast India out there where things are more dynamic.

As an example, India saw the rise and fall of a million-man industry in the form of STD/PCO booths.[8] At first, a traveller in India was stuck for want of long-distance calling; then came a period where the STD/PCO booth industry took off after long-distance calling ('STD') rates collapsed; and then they vanished when mobile roaming became affordable. The market economy quietly mobilized the capital and labour for this new industry, and the market economy quietly presided over its dissolution. This was creative destruction at its best.

Similarly, each visit to a mall in India shows a new set of establishments that are hawking their wares. There is a constant pace of entry and exit. This shows that small firms in India are living the economists' ideal world of a high rate of entry and exit. There is nothing special about the Indian environment which makes this infeasible.

The Government as a Source of Market Power

The job of the state is to address market failure, and in this case, to combat market power. However, all too often, we have had state actions in India that have created or fostered market power.

As an example, the powers of banking regulation have been utilized to block competition against incumbent banks (e.g., by preventing foreign banks from operating in India, and by preventing the entry of new Indian private banks) and competition against banking (e.g., by preventing adjacent industries from competing against banks for their business). In Indian banking, market power has been induced by RBI.

Similarly, the market for agricultural products has been organized around monopoly power for Agricultural Produce Market Committee (APMC). The state has promised to punish farmers if they sell to anyone other than the APMC. In Indian agriculture, market power has been induced by the APMC Acts.

Market power results in bad outcomes, regardless of whether the actor in question is public or private. We should be as zealous about dismantling state-induced barriers to competition as we are when attacking market power created by private persons.

Policy questions in many areas have a remarkable impact upon competition. As an example, when port reforms were done by bringing in multiple competing operators at the JNPT, this was an inspired leap of combining greater competition with private production of infrastructure services. For a contrast, when the same vendor controls the old and new Mumbai airports, this is a lost opportunity in terms of improved competition.

The Dark Side of Competition

In many industries, when there are high levels of competition, there is a 'race to the bottom' on the bad behaviour, on the market failure. Some kinds of market failure can be flipped around to obtain the list of bad behaviour that private firms can engage in: impose negative externalities, be stingy on imposing positive externalities, and abuse situations with asymmetric information.

In banking, under conditions of high competition, the way to earn supernormal rates of return is to take on high levels of risk. Ordinarily, this should be blocked by a financial regulator.

In insurance or in health care, under conditions of high competition, firms can go down the path of customer abuse. Ordinarily, this should be blocked by law and regulation.

These things are supposed to be controlled through the regulatory apparatus of the country. But when regulation works poorly, higher intensity of competition induces a higher extent of bad behaviour. In a country like India, where law and regulation work poorly, these concerns are more important.

Summing Up

The desire for vigorous creative destruction animates our interest in competition policy. All across the economy, we require a progressive outlook supporting entry and competition. Political economy generally favours the incumbent, and leads us towards stagnation where one industry after another are locked up by a few powerful incumbents.

At present, Indian public policy does not give pride of place to competition policy. Far from always promoting competition, many state actions at present *hamper* competition. Market power is market failure, whether it is in the hands of a new age technologist or an old-style mining tycoon.

Policymakers must constantly use the power of the state to prise open closed systems, to create conditions of extreme competition, and to see the bright side of firm failure. The prolonged survival of a weak firm, based on artificial life support, induces negative externalities upon healthy firms. The exit of these 'zombie firms' is a positive for the economy. It is likely that business cycle downturns will be shorter, once the bankruptcy process is in place, for non-financial firms and for financial firms.

The Indian economy features the co-existence of high productivity firms that abide by laws with low productivity firms that violate laws. When law enforcement improves, and weak firms exit, GDP growth will be obtained through reallocation of labour and capital.

Creative destruction is not alien to India: for small firms, it is the everyday reality. It is only with the large firms, and the areas connected with government, where competitive dynamics is poor.

When state institutions that address market failure are weak, conditions of intense competition can create a 'race to the boom' where competitive pressure results in successful firms engaging in bad practices.

9

Trace Out the General Equilibrium Effects

A deep insight of economics is general equilibrium: the interaction on an economy-wide scale of all economic agents. Every small shift in one firm or one industry imposes adjustments all over the economy.

As an example, suppose the world price of memory chips goes up. This will drive up the cost of computers in India. This will, in turn, kick off myriad adjustments. The supply function of software will shift (as software companies are users of computers); the price of software will go up slightly. Costs in user industries such as finance will go up slightly and depending on elasticities of demand, these will show up as changed prices. In the labour market, persons who have skills in using computer hardware more efficiently will be paid a bigger premium compared with people who get things done while wasting resources. This will feed through into demand for books, conferences and the other purchases of highly skilled computer scientists.

We can go on enumerating a very long list of effects. The key intuition of general equilibrium is that prices change all across the economy in response to one such stimulus. The changes may be small, but they are real.

By this reasoning, the effects of a given policy change may not show up in a concentrated fashion. But if small changes are spread over a large number of economic agents all over the economy, they may add up to a substantial impact (whether benign or malign) even if they are not sharply visible at any one place.

A good thumb rule about general equilibrium effects is that there will be no feel-good newspaper story, no photographs on social media. There will be no sharp impact, no human-interest angle. There will be small changes spread all across the economy, which can add up to substantial impacts.

By default, we are wired to look more narrowly. For reasons of functional specialization, the lines of turf, and the limitations of our minds, it is easier to look at one firm or one sector at a time. This is 'partial equilibrium' thinking. But every policy thinker must maintain a general equilibrium perspective in the back of her head.

When we think about tax policy, it is important to narrowly look at the incremental effects of every move. But it is even more important to see these moves in a general equilibrium context.

A great deal of the debate about GST is made up of practical squabbles about this commodity or that location. But the best insights into GST are obtained by thinking at the level of the full economy, about how incentives of all private persons will change, how the resource allocation will be reshaped, and how production and prices will change on an economy scale.

Similar issues are faced in international economic integration. Opening up to the world is always a problem for one narrow sector or constituency, which is placed under competition from overseas. Policymakers tend to often reflexively protect the Indian persons who face new challenges emanating from overseas.

But the great insight of trade theory is grounded in general equilibrium effects. International engagement shifts labour and capital from certain industries to other industries, and in the aggregate, we become better off. This is why, to economists, 'protectionism' is a bad word. But seeing this requires a general equilibrium perspective.

Example 14: Agriculture

In the field of agriculture, we have a large number of distortions: restrictions on input prices, output prices, transportation, international trade, etc. Taken one at a time, each of these restrictions appears difficult to remove.

But the key is to apply general equilibrium reasoning, and envision the world where *all* of them are removed. In that world, India will use a different set of inputs, produce a different set of outputs, which will have a different set of prices, and India will be major part of global agricultural trade. We will grow a lot less of wheat and rice (which are capital intensive) and do more fruits and vegetables (which are labour intensive). The overall outcome will be very good for India, but we would not see that if we think of one distortion at a time.[1]   ••

Example 15: Universal Basic Income

Suppose there is a GDP of Rs 100, and we think that Rs 4 should be used to pay out a 'universal basic income' (UBI) to everyone. Perhaps this fiscal space can be obtained by eliminating existing subsidy programs and raising the tax rate.

The UBI will, however, play out in general equilibrium. People who get paid a UBI will be less keen to work: the supply curve of labour will be modified and the labour market will clear at some new price. Higher taxes will also result in reduced work, reduced saving and reduced investment. The marginal cost of public funds will kick in: the cost to society of raising (say) 3 per cent of GDP to spend on the UBI will be much higher than just 3 per cent of GDP.

It is not easy to see the overall outcome that would be obtained. It is, however, a useful caution: we should at least intuitively try to visualize how the UBI will play out in general equilibrium.[2] The result will diverge from the simple notions about UBI.   ••

Short Term versus Long Term

There is a relationship between the short run versus the long run, and partial equilibrium versus general equilibrium. In the short run, we see the first effects of a policy change, which are smaller in their scope. But with the passage of time, all parts of the system adjust, and we achieve the full general equilibrium effects. Conversely, to think about the long run requires general equilibrium thinking. These themes are visible in thinking about trade liberalization, the GST reform, Direct Tax Code, customs reforms, etc.: In each of these, there is a short run effect, which is often fairly painful for a narrow section of society, but with a lag, the full general equilibrium effects kick in, which give overall gains to society.

There was a time when customs duty collections were as large as 3 percent of GDP, and it was easy to argue that trade liberalization would present considerable fiscal difficulties. Indian policymakers were particularly clear-headed in going forward with duty reductions, which apparently gave reduced tax revenues. The key idea was that deepening ties with the world would improve GDP and thus feed back into other tax revenues. This insight was borne out by the outcomes. While customs duties vanished in importance, the other taxes grew well, based on the buoyant GDP growth that was assisted by trade liberalization.

Summing Up

We normally see a few firms or an industry at a time. But actually, all parts of the economy are connected together in 'general equilibrium'. Every change in one firm or one market induces ripples in every other market. The full general equilibrium effects play out slowly.

In areas like tax policy, globalization, agriculture, or universal basic income, general equilibrium thinking has a lot to offer in understanding the policy issues.

10

Go to the Root Cause, Use the Smallest Possible Force

Road safety in India is over 22 times worse than in the UK. Every hour, a large number of people face a health crisis owing to a road accident on the highways. Would we solve the problem by building additional hospital capacity along highways?

Treat the Disease, Not the Symptom

If a person has malaria, we do not attack the fever. The same idea holds with market failure. Market failure generates visible consequences. Practical people are often attracted to use the power of the state to reverse those visible consequences. But we should understand the anatomy of the market failure, and address it at the root cause.

The right way to address the road safety problem is to go to the root cause, to the public goods of highway management. The lowest cost interventions are found there, by building better highways and managing highways better.

Example 16: Antibiotic Resistance

Consider the problem of antibiotic resistance. There is market failure here: When person X misuses antibiotics, and helps create antimicrobial resistance (AMR), she imposes an *externality* upon others. Actions by person X have an adverse impact upon an innocent bystander Y, an impact which is not intermediated through market transactions. This increases health care costs for person Y, who is no longer able to get a swift and rapid solution for simple illnesses.

How could the state change things? One way is to go to the *consequence*. We could possibly pay a subsidy to person Y, to compensate for the increased cost of health care suffered by her. Alternatively, we could address the root cause, which is the abuse of antibiotics.   ••

Occam's Razor of Public Policy

> रहिमन देख बड़ेन को, लघु न दीजिये डारि।
> जहाँ काम आवै सुई, कहा करै तलवारि॥

> *Don't use a sword when a needle will suffice.*

—Baba Rahim

In science, there is a concept named 'Occam's razor'. When two alternative explanations are equally effective at explaining the facts, we should favour the simpler explanation. In similar fashion, we should employ an 'Occam's razor of public policy':

> *When two alternative tools yield the same outcome, we should prefer the one which uses the least coercion.*

There is wisdom in this approach as the use of force is always problematic. Government intervention interferes with personal freedom. Government interventions are always imperfect and have unintended consequences. If we can get something done using less coercion, that is always better.

Going up to the root cause generally yields a reduced use of the coercive power of the state. The two objectives—reduced use of coercive power and solving a problem at the root cause—are related.

Consider market failure associated with asymmetric information. The root cause of the market failure is certain gaps in information. Hence, addressing this market failure at the root cause requires interventions in the structure of information.[1]

These are issues where economics has much to contribute. Practical people see a problem in society, and often come up with a simplistic attack which directly hits the *manifestation* of the problem. But we have to be careful in distinguishing between the symptom and the disease: we should not respond to bad road safety with more hospitals. Good economic analysis will often show us the upstream cause, and it is better to address the upstream cause rather than the manifestation.[2]

What interventions are more intrusive? In some situations, it is easy to compare two alternative interventions and identify the one which is more intrusive or more coercive. Imprisonment is more intrusive than a fine (civil penalties are always less intrusive than criminal penalties). Imprisonment is less intrusive than chopping off a hand. Any state intervention which involves forcibly touching a human being against their will is more intrusive than one which does not.

Mass surveillance is more intrusive than narrow targeted surveillance. Snooping on people without their knowledge is more intrusive than sending a letter demanding information. An income tax department that does not raid a private person is less intrusive than one that does. A pre-dawn raid is more intrusive than a daytime raid. Spending tax money and offering to vaccinate people, at their choice, is less intrusive than using state power to prohibit vaccination.

Government spending is based on taxation, and taxation is based on violence, so expenditure proposals are more intrusive than meets the eye.

But in many situations, these comparisons are less clear. Policy thinkers need to evolve a moral philosophy and quantitative toolkit that guides this thinking.

Example 17: Subsidies

Too often in the Indian policy discourse, policymakers first reach for subsidies as the instrument of choice to address the consequences of market failure. Proponents of subsidies tend to inadequately consider the marginal cost of public funds, of the welfare cost and the violence that has to be inflicted upon society for the government to obtain tax revenues. In addition, when we carefully look at subsidies, often times the root cause analysis leads to the need to address a market failure, in which case that is always preferred.

The government may think it should pay a subsidy to people who are suffering from respiratory ailments in north India. It would be better to go to the root cause, and achieve clean air.

Policymakers have responded to the difficulties of digital payments by giving subsidies to digital payment transactions. It would have been better to go to the root cause and solve the policy mistakes of the field of payments.

Practical people see a problem in society, and are readily able to visualize a subsidy that counters the problem. Economic reasoning helps us understand the root cause of the market failure, and use less force by focusing the intervention upon the source of the market failure.   ••

Example 18: The Problems of Infrastructure Financing

Infrastructure financing requires equity financing until the infrastructure asset is generating cash flows, as there is considerable political and contracting risk in the early phase. After the asset starts working, and generating cash flows, there is a role for long-term debt. This requires a bond market. In India, we have errors at the foundations of financial economic policy, and the bond market does not work. This problem needs to be solved at the root cause.

Policymakers have responded to the difficulties of bond market financing for infrastructure projects by giving subsidies to infrastructure bonds. It would have been better to make the bond market work.

Policymakers have tried to create specialized infrastructure financing companies, in the public sector, given the failures of the foundations of finance: these included ILFS (1987), IDFC (1997), IIFCL (2006) and now NIIF (2016). It would have been better to go to the root cause and make the bond market work.[3]   ••

Example 19: Addressing Domestic Distortions through Trade Barriers

Domestic market imperfections can hamper domestic firms when faced with international competition. This leads to demands for protectionism. But tariffs induce their own distortions. Bhagwati and Ramaswami offered a key insight into this.[4] They showed that it was better to go to the root cause: to address the domestic distortion. This old idea, from 1963, needs to be resurrected every year, when a different set of players comes up with a new demand for protectionism. It is better to solve the 'disabilities' faced by firms operating in the Indian environment, rather than setup a 'Production Linked Incentive' (PLI) scheme.   **••**

Example 20: Know Your Customer

The global community embarked on a movement of 'Countering the Financing of Terror' (CFT). There was an attempt to establish a mass surveillance system in finance. As part of the global community, the Indian policy process chose particularly cumbersome pathways to 'know your customer' (KYC) requirements in finance.[5]

This worked out poorly. In terms of constitutional morality, all mass surveillance is disproportionate. The surveillance of formal financial transactions has not proved to be important in anti-terrorism.[6] The mass surveillance system on finance imposes costs upon legitimate users of finance, while there are ample avenues for terrorists to get their work done through untraceable transactions that utilize cash and gold. Alongside this, the Indian-style KYC imposed high costs of compliance when doing legitimate financial transactions, particularly for poor people.

The Indian policy community chose to combat this problem by establishing a biometric identity system. This has not worked out satisfactorily. On one hand, every mass surveillance system constitutes an excessive intrusion into the lives of the people. Alongside this, poor people continue to find it difficult to comply with onerous KYC requirements even under the biometric identity system.

It would have been more effective to undertake root cause analysis, and to address the foundations, by questioning the mass surveillance system, and questioning the cumbersome KYC requirements.   ••

Criminal Sanction

Criminal sanctions are highly intrusive upon the individual. Under conditions of low state capacity, criminal penalties put supreme power in the hands of enforcement agencies. Harsh punishments go with wrongful raids, arrests, prosecutions and even convictions. They set the stage for abuse of power, corruption, and a collapse in state capacity.

They are generally not required in economic law. In economics, all that a person stands to gain from violating laws is unlawful profit. A penalty that is larger than the unlawful profit, on expectation, suffices to take away the incentive to violate a law. The standard textbook problem in public economics involves a parking violation where a person dodging a fee of Rs 10 is caught with a probability of 0.25. Setting the fine to Rs 40 suffices in generating compliance. There is no need to ratchet up the level of interpersonal violence in society, with threats of incarceration, in order to obtain compliance with parking charges.

We look back at the 1970s as a peak of the license-permit raj, with an intrusive and powerful state apparatus. However, we now have more criminal offences in economic law when compared with the 1970s. We were supposed to have transitioned from FERA to FEMA in 1999. Violations of capital controls were supposed to have become a civil offence with FEMA, in contrast with the draconian FERA. However, in recent years, criminal sanctions have crept back into FEMA.

Forcing companies to spend 2 per cent of their profit on 'corporate social responsibility' is a use of the coercive power of the state that is not connected with market failure. Companies are rational economic actors, and if there is a problem with non-compliance, monetary penalties would suffice. When the law threatens to put individuals in jail for violating the rule, this is an excessive use of force.[7]

We now have hundreds of criminal offences littering economic law. This is one of the channels through which populist politics—which play off the supposed hostility between 'the people' and 'the elite'—hampers economic performance.[8]

Summing Up

We should solve the disease and not the symptoms. We should solve dengue epidemics by controlling mosquitoes and not by building hospitals; we should solve respiratory ailments by improving air quality and not by building hospitals; we should solve accident-related health problems by improving road safety and not by building hospitals. This calls for root cause analysis of market failure.

In the class of solutions that are available for addressing a given situation with market failure, we should favour the one which intrudes upon the lives of private persons as little as possible.

These two ideas are related. The lowest cost interventions are often found by understanding the market failure and addressing it at the root cause.

Intruding into the home of a person, viewing private conversations of individuals, interfering in personal life, incarcerating a person, touching a human body, these are the most intrusive things that the state can do. These high intrusions should be used with great restraint by policymakers. In economic law, there is rarely a case for criminal sanctions: once ill-gotten gains will be taken away from wrongdoers on expectation, the incentive for wrong behaviour goes away.

11

Redistribution Is Fraught with Trouble

Difficulties with Paternalism

Discussions about poverty often involve person X getting unhappy that poor people do not buy (say) music lessons. This may reflect poverty. It may also reflect preferences (poor people may not value music lessons much). There is an ever-present danger of paternalism, of policy thinkers who feel they know how poor people should lead their lives.

Poor people have their own tastes and their own budget constraints. We should respect what they are doing. Poor people have minds and preferences and pursue their own objectives. All over India, millions of poor people are *choosing* to walk away from a free public school and pay for the services of a private school. We should respect what they are doing and try to find out the reasons for this choice.

When we organize public policy around the problem of market failure, there is the possibility of rational discussion around the identification of problems and the identification of interventions. We can debate whether market failure is indeed present, we can debate whether the proposed intervention is the lowest cost intervention, and we can debate whether the costs to society are outweighed by the benefits. Where paternalism begins, however, we are down to value judgements. When one person wants to use state coercion to give shoes to poor people, and another wants to use state coercion to give shirts to poor people, there is no rational way to settle the disagreement.

Public choice theory encourages us to be skeptical when a politician or an official engages in paternalism. In addition to the lack of empathy (i.e. the policymaker is unable to step into the shoes of a poor person, and see the world from her eyes), state actors act in their own interests.

Poverty Will Not Be Solved by Redistribution

Most of us feel an urge to help the poorest. When this impulse translates into private philanthropy, it constitutes pure altruism: there is no state coercion in the picture. There is also value in creating state programs which deliver money to the poorest persons in society.

At the same time, we should recognize that no country got out of poverty through redistribution. All countries which managed to escape from mass deprivation did so through sustained GDP growth that played out over many decades. As the economist Lant Pritchett emphasizes, 99 per cent of the cross-sectional variation across countries, of the poverty rate, is explained by one number: the median income. Everything else that poverty scholars take interest in—redistribution, poverty programs, welfare programs, income distribution, etc.—accounts for the last 1 per cent.[1]

We should never lose sight of this prioritization of growth-oriented policies.

In the main, government action should be about identifying and addressing one market failure at a time. This creates conditions for growth that is led by the accumulation of resources in private firms and productivity growth in these firms. Growth is the most powerful, and only effective, anti-poverty weapon.

The main machinery of public economics consists of understanding market failure and addressing it. Poverty or inequality do not constitute market failure. Certain people in every society have a low income compared to others, and this can happen in a perfect economy without any market failure present. Establishing a state which competently addresses market failure, and does little else, is the most important building block for poverty alleviation through sustained GDP growth.

Alongside the main body of a sound state, which is focused on market failure, there is the role for redistribution in the form of disaster relief and one lean anti-poverty program.

Distortions in the Market Economy

Sometimes, policymakers intervene in the working of a market in order to help poor people. As an example, the government may use state power to coerce fertilizer companies to sell fertilizer at a low price.

While this may indeed make fertilizer cheaper for some intended beneficiaries, it also distorts the resource allocation of the economy. The overall cost-benefit analysis is generally not favourable. We are better off letting the price system work, and addressing the problem of poverty through a poverty program. When looking at a given industry, such as the fertilizer industry, the only consideration should be to identify and address market failure if this exists. The best resource allocation for the fertilizer industry is that which is obtained through the price system; every state-induced modification of what the price system would do is a productivity-reducing distortion.

We should let the price system do its job of effectively allocating resources, of obtaining high GDP growth. The market economy would grow the pie, the government would tax a slice of the pie, and use this money for redistribution.

Subsidy payments distort the behaviour of recipients. Poor people should be striving to obtain skills and jobs. When welfare payments are reliably obtained, this would induce some to subsist on the subsidy and not strive to climb out of poverty. This 'moral hazard' is not a problem when the subsidy design is perhaps Rs 100 per day that is paid out to 0.1 billion people, but it does become an issue when subsidies become bigger, as is the case all over India today.

So far, we have taken a somewhat static view: that the interventions which try to address poverty hamper the *level* of GDP. The problems are more severe when the poverty objective clashes with GDP *growth*. Many interventions of the government are done with the intention of reducing poverty, but they end up causing damage to growth and increasing the decades spent with mass poverty.

Fiscal Risk

In an ideal world, subsidies would be paid to the poorest 0.1 billion people in India, and all others would be too proud to ask for subsidies from the government. Liberal democracies, however, tend to succumb to a competitive process of pressure groups mobilizing to demand larger subsidies for themselves.

Politicians see a ready opportunity to obtain votes by paying out cash. This tends to induce an excessive focus on subsidy programs, and a loss of prioritization in addressing market failure. In India, we have a state capacity crisis in the core activities of the state. Many politicians are despondent about the extent to which expenditures in addressing market failure might impact upon voters, and are inclined towards subsidy programs.

Fixing the police and the courts is hard; pandering to special interest groups is easy.

There is an ever-present danger of expanding the list of beneficiaries, well beyond the poorest 0.1 billion people, and in expanding the subsidy to well beyond Rs 100 a day. When subsidy payments are sent out to a large number of people, there is a greater danger of imprudent fiscal policy.

The marginal cost of public funds (MCPF)—the cost incurred by society for each rupee of public expenditure— is about Rs 3 in India. In mature market economies, the institutional arrangements for taxation and debt management are in good shape, which yields a lower marginal cost of public funds, which makes subsidy programs more attractive. A redistributive state is a luxury that is better afforded by countries with good institutions.

Loss of Focus Weakens Accountability

A key flaw of Indian public policy in previous decades, a deeply held element of the Indian-style developmental state, was to view all government actions as anti-poverty programs. The assignment principle teaches us that one tool of policy should be devoted to one objective. The policy analysis of (say) fertilizers should be about solving market failure (if any) in the market for fertilizers. Poverty or redistribution should not be a consideration when making fertilizer policy. Once multiple objectives are mixed into government programs, it is harder to create accountability for sound policy formulation or execution.

We note in passing that when the Indian state got going paying subsidies *per kilogram* of fertilizer consumed, the magnitude of the subsidy obtained is proportional to the amount of land owned. A program that was built under the excuse of addressing poverty ended up delivering more money to rich farmers. This is a recurrent theme in the political economy of redistribution.

Example 21: Workfare Programs

In the late 1980s, there were good experiences in Maharashtra with employment guarantee schemes.[2]

The key insight of a successful workfare program is that the only people who will show up, to earn Rs 100/day in doing manual labour, are those who are facing extreme economic stress. It was felt that the mainstream labour market would not be distorted when the state paid out a below-market wage in a workfare program.

Policy thinkers were attracted by three key features of workfare programs. They are *self-targeting*: Only the poorest would utilize them. They are *self-adjusting*: When there are remunerative activities, e.g., associated with an agricultural cycle, there would be an automatic reduction in workfare. Finally, they are *self-liquidating*: Once incomes in a certain region go up, through economic growth, nobody would want to do manual labour at Rs 100/day. Over the years, these programs would tend to fade away on their own.

These assumptions hinged on the idea that the wage in a workfare program is lower than the wage seen in the labour market. In practice, the way the National Rural Employment Guarantee Scheme (NREGS) was implemented in India, the wage paid was higher than that seen in the labour market. There has been great economic growth in India after NREGS was born, but there has been no decline in the number of persons participating in NREGS. As a consequence, many of the beneficial features, originally envisaged of NREGS, were not obtained.

This gap, between workfare programs in theory versus NREGS in practice, is a reminder of how the best thought-out redistributive programs often go wrong. Successful redistribution makes great demands upon the capabilities of the policy process. ••

Summing Up

It is hard for the state to be paternalistic as it does not know enough about individuals. Each person is different, and only the individual can choose what is best for herself. When the government tries to be paternalistic, value judgements are made by policymakers which are not amenable to rational discourse.

Poverty is not a market failure. Inequality is not a market failure. No country solved poverty through redistribution. The first priority of policymakers should be to establish a vibrant market economy, through which the size of the pie grows strongly. After this, taxation can be used to obtain budgetary resources which are then redistributed. The price system holds the key to allocating resources efficiently, and setting the stage for high GDP growth.

Distortions of the market economy, induced in the pursuit of redistribution, hinder GDP growth. Subsidies distort behaviour of recipients, and hinder GDP growth. That is tantamount to killing the golden goose.

The marginal cost of public funds in India is high. The cost imposed upon the economy for Re 1 of public expenditure is about Rs 3. This implies that subsidy programs induce a large adverse impact upon GDP.

It is easy to build state capacity for paying out subsidies such as NREGS; it is hard to build state capacity for public goods such as the police. Competing political parties tend to enlarge subsidy expenditures as a way to win elections, and avoid the hard work of actually being a state. The establishment of large subsidy programs, and the sense of entitlement that tends to arise around them, creates fiscal risk.

Fighting poverty should be the clear objective of one or two anti-poverty programs. The objective of the remainder of government should be to address market failure, without bringing distributional considerations into the picture.

12

Private Solutions for Market Failure

Consider the pollination services of bees. The beekeeper gets honey, but the presence of the bees imposes a positive externality upon other farmers, who get free pollination services. The standard economic analysis teaches us that the free market will get this wrong. The beekeeper spends money on beekeeping till the point where *her* gains from bees are matched against her expenses from bees. She does not value the positive externality that her bees impose upon her neighbours. There will be an under-production of pollination services.

The first cut of public economics lies in understanding that when there are externalities, there is market failure. We may want to indulge in some intricate intervention into society in trying to address this. The great economist Ronald Coase brought fresh insight into this field, with what is called the 'transaction costs perspective'.[1]

Let us look at the problem of bees and externalities in a different way. It is possible for the farmer to pay a beekeeper who will place beehives at the centre of the farm. While some of the bee activities will still spill over beyond the farm, there is a strong connection between the work of the bees and the pollination services received by the customer. This creates a viable business model where some people specialize in owning and transporting beehives to locations chosen by customers.

In Maharashtra, there are professional beekeepers now charging farmers anywhere from Rs 1,000 to Rs 3,000 for renting out boxes for a month.[2] This presence of a private market for pollination services shows that this contractual solution is a feasible one. Through these private contracts, we have solved the externality problem, without a requirement for state intervention.

There is a general idea here. Detailed bureaucratic solutions can be brought into addressing externality problems. But there are also other ways out of the problem: Private persons can enter into contracts, which internalize the externality.

When we set up a detailed bureaucratic state intervention, there are considerable difficulties in obtaining the full knowledge of prices and technology within the government, through which optimal decisions can be made. Public choice theory teaches us that state actors pursue their own self-interest, and not the interests of the people. In contrast, when private persons negotiate with each other, the full knowledge of prices and technology is brought into play by well-incentivized actors, in order to find the right solution.

The canonical example of this field concerns a steel mill and a fishery. The pollution emitted by the steel mill imposes a negative externality upon the fishery.

If the same person owned the fishing company and the steel mill, the emission of pollution would be optimal. The single owner would weigh profit from fishing, profit from steel-making, and the cost of pollution control. We cannot predict what the correct answer would be, but the unified owner would understand the trade-offs and choose the optimal path, without requiring government coercion on emission of pollution. This is the simplest case.

In this simplest case, the knowledge of technology and prices that the single owner has would yield an optimal answer, that would generally be better than a government agency that worked on pollution control.

Let us now move to the case where the fishery is distinct from the steel mill, but property rights are clear. The structure of rights must be so configured that the fishery and the steel mill are forced to negotiate a voluntary arrangement. The two sides will explore all contractual possibilities and come out with a contract that works the best for both of them. We cannot predict what the outcome will be. Either the fishery will pay the steel mill to emit reduced pollution, or the steel mill will pay the fishery and emit a certain amount of pollution. The key point is that when property rights are clear, both sides are brought to the table to negotiate, and the result is superior to any bureaucratic intervention.

Before Ronald Coase, economists viewed negative externalities as a story with a perpetrator and a victim. It is easy to slip into the assumption that the fishermen are the ones who have to be protected. However, the Coasean analysis yields an important result. Whether the fishermen have property rights, which limit the steel mill's ability to pollute, or the steel mill has property rights, which limit the other side's ability to fish, is not important. As long as property rights are clear, both sides will be brought to the table to negotiate. Coase showed us that both parties have a shared interest in finding the right solution, and minimizing total harm. The answer lies in their negotiation, and when this is feasible, we do not require state coercion.

Example 22: Windmills That Emit Noise

Consider a windmill company which places noise-making wind turbines near a residential community. The command-and-control approach is to view the noise as a negative externality. We would build a government mechanism which caps the noise that windmills can make. We would set up a bureaucratic procedure to identify violations and punish them.

The Coasean approach consists of bringing the residents and the company into a negotiation. The company should pay something to the residents in return for the discomfort. If the residents are intransigent, the windmill company will just go somewhere else, and the residents will get no noise and no money. The negotiation will result in an agreement that the company will pay each individual a certain sum of money per year. Such a private negotiation is the best of all worlds.

In this approach, many private adaptations will simultaneously take place. As an example, people can weigh the choice of spending money on double-wall glass windows that will diminish the noise. In other words, the recipient can also invest in pollution control. These are optimal responses, from the viewpoint of society at large, which would not easily be obtained through a bureaucratic solution.   ••

Example 23: Trading in Emission Permits

A great success story of the Coasean approach is the trading in pollution permits. Under this system, scientists define a cap for the amount of a pollutant such as sulphur dioxide that can be emitted by society at large. The government establishes a rule: firms that wish to emit must buy permits. The magnitude of permits sold is set to the cap that is set by the scientists. The government enforces the rule, inflicting punishments upon firms that emit pollution beyond the permits that have been purchased by them.

A market for these permits comes about. Each firm looks at the cost of the permit on the market versus the cost of pollution control, and optimally chooses what to do. At some firms, pollution reduction is easy: these firms prefer to reduce pollution. At other firms, pollution reduction is hard: these firms prefer to buy emission permits.

This results in the ideal outcome for society, where pollution control is done at the plants where the cost of reducing emissions is the lowest. For a contrast, it would be very difficult for a pollution control bureaucracy to understand which factories should reduce emissions.   ••

The Role of the State in Coasean Solutions

The Coasean approach requires the state to play a role in clearly defining property rights. In the steel mill example, the state needs to establish the powers of the steel mill in controlling fishing or the powers of the fishery in controlling pollution. Or a neutral one between these two paths is taken; in both cases, the outcome works out to be optimal from the viewpoint of society. The key point is that property rights should be clear enough that imposing an externality upon a person calls for a negotiation.

The Peruvian economist Hernando de Soto, and his downstream literature, has rightly drawn attention to the importance of property rights in land. This has motivated a big effort worldwide to improve clarity of legal rights for various uses of land. Land is the biggest asset class in most economies and is an important factor of production. The full Coasean vision, however, sees property rights as much more than land. For example, the person on the land should have property rights over the noise in their airspace, so as to bring the windmill company to the negotiating table. The field of property rights needs to embrace the larger problem, and not confine itself to land.

Public policy also plays another role in the Coasean approach, through the judicial infrastructure of contract enforcement. In many practical situations, the traditional UK concepts of tort law give rights to persons harmed, which are conducive to a Coasean negotiation. Greater effort is required in India, to lay the foundations of tort law, and to build the courts through which these disputes can be efficaciously adjudicated.

Once property rights are defined and private persons can search for contracts, good outcomes are obtained without requiring a heavy-handed command-and-control intervention. By this logic, policymakers should put a high priority upon the reforms that clarify property rights, and the reforms that improve the working of the judiciary.

There are many problems where a large number of individuals is involved, and it is difficult to bring all persons together into a negotiation. It is in those problems that the first cut of public economics holds true. Under these circumstances, there is a role for the state to engage in the more conventional machinery of public policy, ranging from taxes/subsidies to regulation to production.

Traditional Community Solutions to the Tragedy of the Commons

The standard idea in economics about common pool resources is the 'tragedy of the commons'.[3] We cannot easily control access, and then a scarce resource tends to be depleted by excessive usage. The classic example is the fish stock in the sea. It is hard to control fishing boats, so the fishing tends to be overdone, giving a fish population collapse. Each person has an incentive to over-use the commons, which induces a negative externality upon all other users of the commons.

All non-excludable goods are not depleted by excessive usage. As an example, consider a large number of people tuning in to a radio channel. The number of people who tune in does not diminish the radio signal available. This discussion is limited to common pool resources which are depleted by excessive usage.

We could combat this market failure in three ways: state control, privatization, or a Coasean solutions involving private contracts. Each of these solutions has problems:

- State control requires setting up a complex bureaucracy that will monitor, allocate and enforce. In many situations, the magnitude of the resources being allocated (e.g., pasture land associated with a village) does not justify the expenditure on the state solution.
- Privatization is infeasible in some problems (e.g., the open sea). Cutting pasture land into small plots can yield an inferior solution as the grass may grow in different places at different times of the year.

- A Coasean solution does not easily come about, as it is difficult to get a large number of people (e.g., all fishermen) to come together and negotiate.

The political scientist Elinor Ostrom discovered that many practical institutional arrangements, established by traditional communities over very long periods of time, achieve good results. Some of the examples that she has studied have been practiced for hundreds of years or even for a thousand years. Her examples include communal tenure of high-mountain meadows and forests in Switzerland and Japan, the 'huerta' irrigation systems in Spain and the 'zanjera' irrigation system in Philippines.

Much research is required in India, on traditional arrangements that have been brushed aside in the first flush of modernization, to look more deeply about how well they perform. For instance, the moratorium on eating fish during Shravan is commonly understood to tie in with the spawning season. But we have not studied the roots of such arrangements from the lens of solving common goods problems.[4]

In previous years, we in India were much more optimistic about state-led solutions. Some of that early optimism about the state has subsided. We should have greater respect for self-organizing systems that do not require state capacity. As an example, the Forest Rights Act tried to give a better place to forest dwellers. But the Act retains a substantial role for the state and emphasizes allocating rights to individuals than to communities. There may be a better pathway to a good outcome, based on researching traditional community arrangements among forest dwellers in India, in the light of Ostrom's insights.

This is another surprising dimension to modern public economics. Intuitively, we should see these organically grown institutions as being akin to the system of markets. These institutions emerge and evolve on their own, aggregate a large amount of information, and result in an efficient allocation.

Pushing Regulation Down to Private Firms

Consider the problem of regulating taxis. One possibility lies in setting up a bureaucratic machinery that engages with each taxi driver. Another pathway lies in contracting out this regulation to private taxi companies. Aggregation business models, such as AirBnB, have an incentive to utilize customer feedback and supervisory staff to improve the quality of their customer experience.[5]

The strength of this approach lies in reduced intrusion into the lives of people based on threats of state violence. A taxi driver *chooses* to become part of an Uber or Meru system. If the system works badly, they can walk away. In contrast, nobody has the choice of escaping state coercion.

This approach has been particularly successful with 'financial market infrastructure institutions' (FMII) such as stock exchanges. Exchanges work as the front line of regulation, and engage in detail with hundreds of financial firms performing a large number of transactions. This reduces the demand for state capacity at the regulator. The problem that flows from this approach is the tension between the profit motive of an exchange and this regulatory function.

Summing Up

The first cut of public economics asks us to find market failure and address it. Sophisticated public economics whittles down the role for the state when compared with this first cut.

When property rights and contract enforcement work well, private persons will negotiate their way to many good solutions. And even in the extreme, where large numbers of people are involved, some traditional community solutions achieve optimality. When feasible, these pathways are superior to the traditional toolkit of state intervention, as they involve less coercion.

The conventional Indian discourse slips into moralizing, into a populist approach that favours the interests of the fishermen over the steel mill. This does not yield the optimal answer. We are all in this together, and negotiations are better than supporting the supposedly wronged person.

This pathway involves establishing property rights (e.g., when a windmill makes noise near a house, the homeowners should have the power to force a negotiation), judicial capacity (to adjudicate disputes), and modern business model innovation (e.g., regulation by AirBnB).

13

Bring cold calculations into the policy process

State power was used in India to force large companies to gift money (in ways that are tightly controlled by the government). This superficially seems like a good thing, as some poor people get more gifts. But what about the costs to society? Forced donations by companies are no different from a higher tax rate, in that the rate of return on equity goes down. Fewer investment projects make the grade, and the overall investment and growth of the economy goes down.

We should not just see the benefits (for some special interest groups) from state intervention. Every use of state power imposes costs upon society as well. We should look at the full picture, of the costs and the benefits.

Tallying Up the Costs and Benefits

The public policy process involves a stylized set of questions:

1. What is the problem that we are out to solve? Are we sure that there is, indeed, market failure?
2. What are the alternative interventions that could be used? What is the least intrusive intervention that gets the job done?
3. How would we implement the proposed intervention? What are the state capacity constraints that we would face? How would we build state capacity for our desired intervention? Are we certain that under our real-world implementation constraints, the proposed intervention will indeed address the malady under examination?
4. Do the benefits outweigh the costs?

Proponents of many policies are convinced they are correct. Cost-benefit analysis is the discipline of trying to tally the numbers. The first element of costs is the direct costs borne by government. The second element of cost is the intrusion upon private persons that is caused by the policy proposal. Against this, we have the claimed benefits.

In God we trust, all others must bring data. *Did we choose the least intrusive alternative? Are we sure that the benefits to society outweigh the costs?* Such a formal process helps diminish many of the flaws of human decision processes.

Formal calculations of cost are, of course, important in economic policy. They are also useful in other areas of public policy. In October 2002, the US Congress authorized the then President George Bush to use military force against Iraq if this was felt appropriate by him. In December 2002, the economist William D. Nordhaus made a calculation of the economic consequences of the war in Iraq.[1] These calculations showed a sombre outlook.

The war began in March 2003, and ran till December 2011. With the benefit of hindsight, we know that the Nordhaus calculation of December 2002 was largely sound while the reasoning of the US national security establishment was not. This shows the opportunity for improved decision-making through careful calculations, going beyond economic policy.

Accounting for the Interests of Persons Not in the Room

Human decision-making tends to think about the impacts upon the persons who have been in face-to-face conversations with policymakers. This creates a bias in favour of special interest groups that are able to mobilize for lobbying. A sound cost benefit analysis tries to quantify the overall costs and benefits to society, and not just the narrow zone of the people who are lobbying the government.

Every regulator tends to intensively engage with its regulated persons. TRAI tends to talk to telecom service providers (TSPs), RBI tends to talk to banks. Over time, the regulator tends to adopt the worldview of regulated persons, and think of their interests. This can go beyond ordinary human nature to a more malign notion of 'regulatory capture'. Explicit calculations help ensure that the interests of the larger populace are brought to the table.

Consider the disaster resilience of a bridge in the Himalayas. In the event of an earthquake, there is a direct cost to the PPP contractor who owns the bridge, if the earthquake destroys the bridge. However, if the bridge were to be destroyed, it would also impose significant harm (a negative externality, a market failure) upon persons who live on both sides of the bridge.

A sound cost benefit analysis for improving the disaster risk resilience of the bridge would take into account the full costs and full benefits to society and not just the interests of the PPP contractor.

Long-Term Thinking

By default, human decision-making tends to focus on the short term. A sound cost–benefit analysis would look deeper into the future, and thus green light policy initiatives which impose costs in the short run but result in valuable improvements in the long run.

Consider a state intervention to provide or to subsidize nutrition for the young. If this is properly implemented, this yields costs in the short run and generates good results for society for decades thereafter. Most sensible things in tax policy involve sacrificing tax revenues in the short run, but higher GDP growth is kicked off, which (in turn) generates higher tax revenues as a consequence.

Combating Sunk Costs

As humans, too often, we tend to look back and are shaped by costs that have been paid in the past. Sunk cost fallacies are found in government also: once a lot of time and effort has been put into building a scheme or an institution, policymakers are tempted to continue in the same direction. Intensification of effort comes easily to a bureaucracy, fundamental reform does not. It is hard to sign a peace agreement once a lot of lives have been lost: stopping the flow of death seems to do injustice to the stock of death.

Systematic cost–benefit analysis is useful insofar as it combats the intuitive human failure of the sunk cost fallacy. Formal calculations for cost benefit analysis help us to look forward, and thus reduce the extent to which we are deluded by the sunk cost fallacy.

Ex-Post Review

Every legal instrument should state its objective at the outset. After three years have elapsed, an empirical examination of whether these objectives were met should be mandatory. In some situations, there is a role for 'sunset clauses' where laws are automatically repealed after a certain time period elapses.

As an example, land reform in Maharashtra, through the Bombay Tenancy and Agricultural Lands Act, 1948, was considered a revolutionary step forward in its time. We can debate about whether it was optimal in its time, but there is little doubt that it is out of touch with the questions that we face today. Under this act, even farmer-to-farmer leasing of land is prohibited. A systematic mechanism of ex-post review would bubble up such laws into periodic review.

Too often in India, interventions are put into place without explicitly stating the problem that is sought to be solved. A first objective is articulated, but the moment it is clear that this did not work out, the goal post is shifted. It is a healthy discipline to require the release of a documentation packet, associated with each intervention, where the problem that is sought to be solved is clearly stated. This will support ex-post evaluation of whether the intervention did indeed help solve the problem that it set out to solve. This formal documentation will take away the possibility of shifting goal posts.

This will help reveal mistakes that need to be reversed. Clarity about objectives, and the calculations associated with cost-benefit analysis, will help the CAG work on policy initiatives in a more effective way. The staff in an intervention, who expect such review, will be more accountable and hence do better work.

Ex-post review is highly relevant in the main track of public policy: using state coercive power to change the behaviour of private persons in ways that address market failure. However, at the same time, we have to be careful when we think of crisis-management actions.

Hindsight is 20-20 vision. It is important to respect the view of the world as seen contemporaneously by the crisis manager. Many actions are taken, at the peak of a crisis, to stave off bad outcomes. Ex-post, these may appear to be a waste. We should put ourselves in the shoes of the decision-maker, when doing ex-post analysis, and respect the fact that many of the actions that appear irrelevant in hindsight were actually expenditures on risk management.

The relevant comparison is not the overall expenditures in the path taken, but a comparison against the counterfactual, the path not taken, of either doing nothing or undertaking other decisions.

Example 24: A Success Story: Solving the UTI Crisis in 2002

Consider the actions taken by Yashwant Sinha's Ministry of Finance in response to the UTI crisis. The government paid a fiscal cost by paying out money to UTI unit-holders. The government purchased certain securities from the problematic UTI schemes, and placed these into a new organization named 'SUUTI'. Ex-post, we know that when these securities were sold, the government made a tidy profit. This seems like a successful intervention from a simple financial point of view.

Suppose this had not worked out this way. Suppose Nifty had moved in a different way, and the government had suffered a loss when selling off the SUUTI holdings. Would we then excoriate the decision makers of the time, on the grounds that their intervention in the UTI crisis was (ex-post) a mistake? This would be an unfair assessment.

It is important to think from the perspective of the policymaker in 2002. A disruptive mess at UTI would have triggered off panic selling by large numbers of small investors. This is the counterfactual of doing nothing, which was on the minds of policymakers in 2002. Even if the SUUTI holdings were, later on, sold at a loss, the important thing that was averted in the UTI crisis management was a panic among individual investors.   ••

How Precise Can This Be?

We have no illusions about the scientific precision that can be achieved in this analysis.[2] These kinds of calculations are notoriously vulnerable to changes in assumptions. However, there are two reasons why such analysis is valuable. First, the very act of conducting the analysis forces the decision makers to improve their understanding of the problems that they seek to solve.

An integral part of a sound cost-benefit analysis is asking the question: Is there another and superior way through which we could got the job done? Could we achieve the desired objective with a lower use of state coercion? When calculations are absent, the policy process tends to degenerate into a contest of rival political influences. Systematic cost–benefit analysis encourages an exploration of alternative policy pathways, and generally yields better thinking.

Second, with all its imprecision, cost–benefit analysis is able to block some egregiously wrong initiatives. The formal step of cost benefit analysis, in our opinion, will block perhaps one fifth of the blunders of policymakers in India.

The Zone of Applicability of Cost–Benefit Analysis

The economic theory of market failure is well established. Interfering in the price system, when not narrowly addressing market failure, will always fail a cost-benefit analysis. This is the power and usefulness of theoretical public economics.

Cost-benefit analysis is a valuable tool when the state intervenes in society, either through tax-and-spend or through making rules that coerce private persons. This is the zone where there is value in seeing the full picture, and tallying the costs and benefits. The costs and benefits under examination are the costs and benefits *to society*. The honest work process consists of working out the numbers for multiple rival pathways to intervention, and then discovering which of them has the best benefits and low cost.

A great deal of work in the policy process is internal reorganization of government. Cost–benefit analysis is less useful here. For an analogy, a corporation works very carefully when testing a new product that it shows customers, but it moves more with deductive logic when internally reorganizing itself.

An Institutionalized Application of Mind

Cost-benefit analysis is thus about creating an institutionalized application of mind. It is a way of ensuring that the right questions are asked, and alternatives evaluated, before a decision is made. This helps avoid impressionistic and casual approaches to policy formulation, and reduces the extent to which sectarian considerations dominate.

For the gains to be obtained, the key decision makers must do the cost–benefit analysis themselves. Sometimes, there is the temptation to arrive at a decision in an intuitive way, and then hand out the task of writing up an attractive cost–benefit analysis to English-speaking assistants. It is better to apply cost-benefit analysis to a group of plausible alternative interventions, and let the calculations reveal which is the best intervention.

The release of documents with cost-benefit analysis improves the policy process as independent persons will critique the assumptions and the calculations, often bringing fresh insight into the question.

In the demonetization episode, such practices would have been quite useful. It would have helped to clearly state the objective up front. It would have helped, to undertake calculations about the costs being imposed upon society. It would have helped, to ask whether there were less intrusive interventions through which the same objectives could be achieved.

Policy thinkers have emphasized the importance of formal cost-benefit analysis and ex-post review for a long time. As with other aspects of deep thinking in the policy process, there is lip service and low adherence. In the hurried real world policy process, there is an extreme emphasis on fire-fighting and *rapidly* pushing initiatives out the front door. We *plan in haste, and repent in leisure.*

A member of the board of directors of RBI once remarked in a meeting, *'If we do such thorough work, we will only be doing research, and not regulating'.* The rest of the room replied in unison, *'Precisely'.* Wielding the coercive power of the state should not be done lightly. It should be backed by complete and thorough thinking.

Public choice theory shows us that officials of an agency will not adopt these practices by themselves. It is not in their interests to reduce their arbitrary power. Agencies are the agent of the Parliament. Parliamentary law must encode requirements for cost-benefit analysis and ex-post review of laws and regulations.[3] From the 1980s onward, under the influence of 'new public management', laws of mature market economies have built in these provisions: cost-benefit analysis, ex-post review, notice and comment, etc. Such codification in Parliamentary law, of sound processes that accompany the delegation of coercive power to agents of the legislature, is the frontier of building state capacity in India.

Summing Up

Going beyond the qualitative recognition of market failure, it is important to quantify the benefit that would be obtained for society by addressing it.

If the cost-benefit analysis shows that the costs imposed upon society, by the best solution, outweigh the prospective benefits, then the cure is worse than the disease.

The formal process of cost-benefit analysis helps avoid emotion, respects the interests of persons who have not mobilized to campaign or lobby for their own interests, helps bring long-term considerations into the picture, and combats the sunk cost fallacy.

Every new policy initiative should be launched with a clear statement of the problem that it seeks to solve, the demonstration that there is market failure, and the cost benefit analysis that was used to discover the best intervention. After a few years, it is useful to engage in ex-post review, and change course if the original objectives were not met. Cost–benefit analysis is not a science and there is a significant imprecision in all such estimates.

We always see things more clearly in hindsight. The idea of ex-post review is not to pillory the people who looked at the information at a certain point in time, e.g., in a moment of crisis, and made a decision. It is to establish feedback loops through which a process of iterative refinement sets in.

Cost–benefit analysis is required for government *intervention* into society. It is not essential when doing internal reorganization of government organizations.

The laws that give power to government agencies to intervene in society must codify the processes of cost-benefit analysis and ex-post review. Through this, it induces an institutionalized application of mind, and improves the quality of work.

14

Ask the Right Question

There is a vision of black money, perhaps drawn from Hindi movies, where there are suitcases of cash that are stored. Such a problem statement leads to a certain style of attack on black money, such as demonetization.

But black money is a flow and not a stock. It is paid and received every day as part of business activities that evade taxes, bribe government employees, etc. Once we pose the problem of black money as a flow, the solutions that may be attempted change considerably. We may like to remove executive discretion, improve tax policy and tax administration, remove capital controls, etc. in the attempt to address black money as a flow.[1]

When we are 'seized with a problem', we are often seized with the political manifestation of a problem. The problem that seizes you is sometimes not the problem that is worth solving.

This may appear trite, but it is actually often difficult to pose the right question. The *problem* is an elephant, and we are all blind men coming at it from various directions. There is every possibility of the policy process getting hijacked into side lanes.

In the 1970s, Indian policymakers used to compare Indian textile production against that of South Korea, and claim that India was doing better because there was lower import content. While Indian textile production did, indeed, have a lower import content, Korea ran far ahead in value added and exports. It would have made much more sense to focus on value added in textiles, or export of textiles.

In similar fashion, the objective of 'Make in India' can go wrong if this morphs into an attempt to reduce import content, in which case it will become much like the old policy strategy of 'import substitution' (IS).

Common Sense on Taxes

In the field of tax policy, the objective is often stated in terms of a desired high value of the tax/GDP ratio. This is the wrong way to think about the problem.

Collecting taxes induces distortions upon the economy, and harms GDP. We should be asking how the tax system can yield a desired *level* of tax revenue, while GDP is as high as possible. When tax reforms reduce distortions and yield higher GDP growth, we should be delighted, even if the tax/GDP ratio were to come down. Faced with a choice of a GDP of Rs 100 and a tax/GDP ratio of 20 per cent, versus a GDP of Rs 200 and a tax/GDP ratio of 15 per cent, we should prefer the latter. A single-minded focus upon the tax/GDP ratio is inappropriate; we must see the larger picture.

On a similar note, the emphasis on revenue neutrality in the GST, in the short run, was a mistake. Government is an important buyer of goods and services, and a low single-rate GST would yield cost savings for all levels of government.

There are strong inter-linkages between GST and direct tax collections. The VAT chain induces legibility for the state, and this legibility induces higher direct tax revenues also. A successful GST reform will yield higher direct tax collections also. Looking for revenue neutrality between the new GST and the old indirect taxes is an incomplete vision.

Looking for *budget neutrality* in the induction of GST, instead of *revenue neutrality*, would have been better.

In addition, fundamental tax reforms always involve giving up revenues in the short term and making it up on higher GDP growth. Consider the reduction of Indian protectionism: there was an immediate loss of customs tax revenues, but more global integration resulted in higher GDP growth, which fed back into income tax and VAT. GST should similarly be seen as a structural GDP-enhancing reform. We should have been comfortable running up larger budget deficits in the short run. An insistence on achieving revenue neutrality in the short run was a mistake.

Not All Deficits Are Bad

Every now and then, we get unhappy when there is a large bilateral trade deficit between country i and country j. As an example, Donald Trump has expressed concern about the bilateral US–China trade deficit. It is easy to slip into nationalism and nativism through the lens of the bilateral trade deficit.[2]

However, international trade should always been seen in its entirety. The US imports cheap manufacturing from China, uses this to produce high end services, and exports these to affluent countries. What must be judged is the overall trade balance of a country, and never a bilateral trade balance.[3]

> *Our trade deficit ballooned to $817 billion. Think of that. We lost $817 billion a year, over the last number of years. In trade! In other words, if we didn't trade, we'd save a helluva lot of money.*
>
> —Donald Trump

Some people view a large current account deficit as a failure to export. However, the macroeconomic identity teaches us that the current account deficit is the gap between investment and savings. When the investment of a country is larger than the savings of a country, this shows up as a current account deficit. If the financial system is allocating resources well, investment results in GDP growth, and it is better to import capital. A reduced pace of investment is worse than a large current account deficit—where we are importing capital for the purpose of investment.

The legitimate concern about the import of capital lies in ensuring that there is a high degree of diversification. Capital should be coming into the country from a heterogeneous class of players, through many different financial channels, into many different kinds of domestic assets. This diversification will generate sustainable financing of the current account deficit. Once this is achieved, there is no difficulty associated with investment that is larger than savings.

On a similar note, for many people, large fiscal deficits are always a bad thing. The analysis of the fiscal deficit must, however, be placed in two contexts.

Macro policy is working well when the fiscal deficit is highly dynamic and managed in a responsible way. In most years, there should be a small primary surplus, i.e., in most years we should be paying down debt and the debt/GDP ratio should be declining. This establishes fiscal soundness. Once this is in place, a sharp enlargement of the deficit occasionally, when the economy is faring badly, is perfectly healthy and legitimate.

This is predicated on the underlying fiscal soundness. The government should be highly solvent. In India, we should aspire for a credit rating that is better than the edges of speculative grade. This involves putting an end to conscription of savings through financial repression, running a small primary surplus in most years, sound fiscal and macro data, etc.

Once fiscal soundness is achieved, the ability to rarely run a large fiscal deficit, e.g., as was done by the UK in 2008/2009, is the triumph of a fiscal policy that stabilizes. We should not reflexively think that all big fiscal deficits are bad. It is *chronic* deficits that are a bad thing; in most years, we should have a (correctly measured) primary surplus and the (correctly measured) debt/GDP ratio should decline.

One Tool, One Objective

A valuable element of the economics toolkit is 'the assignment principle', which comes from the great economist Jan Tinbergen. Each tool of policy can cater to one objective. We have to assign an objective to each instrument. After that has been done, that instrument has been 'used up'. It cannot then pursue multiple objectives. This is a simple and powerful idea. It helps cut through numerous conundrums in the field of public policy, where failure is inevitable when n instruments are being used to chase m objectives, but $m > n$.

The most famous example of the assignment principle lies in monetary policy. There was a time when we thought that RBI would pursue multiple objectives. Now we understand that the most that RBI can do for us is deliver low and stable inflation. Hence, the RBI Act was amended in 2016 to enshrine CPI inflation of 4 per cent as the objective of RBI. Once this has been done, it is no longer possible for RBI to pursue auxiliary objectives such as the level of the rupee, export promotion, SME financing, promotion of cashless transactions, etc.

On a similar note, there is a certain degree of mission creep and confusion about NREGS. Is this an anti-poverty program, or is it about creating rural infrastructure? Going by the assignment principle, it is best to think about NREGS as a pure poverty program, and not burden it with additional objectives.

The assignment principle links to some of the thinking in the 1950s about the role of the Ministry of Finance versus the Planning Commission. The idea at the time was the Ministry of Finance would think on a one-year budget horizon, wielding the instrument of the budget, while the Planning Commission would think about deeper issues in public policy formulation wielding an array of different instruments. Now that the Planning Commission has been disbanded, we will need to build a medium-term budget system that incorporates both points of view. There is a need to clearly define the role and function of NITI Aayog in this new environment, so as to fill these gaps in the mainstream policy apparatus.

The assignment principle shows a founding defect in the IMF.[4] At the core of the IMF is a 'quota regime'. This is a single instrument which aims to pursue three goals. Quotas determine the contribution of countries to the IMF. Quotas determine the access by members to the IMF's resources. Finally, quotas determine voting power within the IMF. By placing three problems—contribution, access, voting—within one instrument, we have created a problem. An arrangement of quotas which appears sound with respect to any one objective will appear wrong on the others.

Why do organizations find themselves in situations with more objectives than instruments? Jan Tinbergen's assignment principle has been around since the 1960s; surely everyone knows it by now.

Public choice theory predicts that public organizations will *favour* multiple objectives as this gives reduced accountability. Clarity of purpose is efficient for the principal and not the agent. It is our job, as policy thinkers, to hold the metaphoric feet of every agency to the fire, and hold it accountable for a narrow set of goals associated with a narrow set of powers. This requires drafting modern laws that clearly articulate objectives and establish commensurate accountability mechanisms.

Formal Process Helps

In the informal ways of policymaking, the risk of failing to pose the right question is greater. In the conventional informal ways, many things are talked about orally, a vague picture is assembled of a problem, and actions are proposed, yielding a three-page note.

The formal discipline of policymaking generates improvements by forcing a due process. We are forced to write down: What is the problem that we are trying to solve?

Are we able to demonstrate that there is market failure? Do we have an instrument through which the identified problem can be addressed? Has this instrument already been used up to pursue other objectives?

Formal documentation is required, before every move in public policy, which conducts such analysis. Without such formal statements, we run the risk of degenerating into shifting goal posts: An objective is stated, it fails to work out, the authorities then claim that the true objective was a different one.

Summing Up

The first stumbling block in the policy process is posing the right question. When a policymaker wants large resources in order to run subsidy programs, the right objective to pursue is *tax revenue* and not *the tax/GDP ratio*, and the path to this lies in low tax rates that foster high GDP growth. The field of economic policy is littered with analytical fallacies that have set off entire policy communities in the wrong direction.

Jan Tinbergen's 'assignment principle' teaches us that one policy instrument can only be used for one objective. Monetary policy has only one instrument—the short-term interest rate—and can hence deliver only one objective, e.g., the targeted inflation rate. A great deal of policy confusion in India stems from placing multiple objectives upon policy initiatives.

Public choice theory predicts that officials will favour multiple objectives so as to avoid accountability. A publicly stated and clear objective, on each policy initiative, improves the policy process.

15

Taking Decentralization Seriously

The Constitution of India is imbued with federalism: it envisions India as a union of States. It cut up all the work of government into three lists. The Union government would deal with List 1 questions, the States would deal with List 2 questions, and the two sides would amicably figure out how to deal with the concurrent list.

India is a vast and diverse country. The most salient problems vary from one place to another, and the most effective solution varies from one place to another. The constitutional scheme is a wise one. What constitutes a good solution for education policy in Kerala (where schools are closing down as the number of children is declining) is likely to differ strongly from the corresponding solution in Uttar Pradesh.

When schools are financed through the union government's scheme *Sarva Shiksha Abhiyaan*, however, there is considerable standardization all across the country. Such centralization of policy design, at the union government, has come about in numerous areas. In many respects, we have deviated from the constitutional scheme, and gone too far in centralizing power in New Delhi.

In the US, the phrase 'laboratories of democracy' has come to be used about states. This emphasizes the role of democratic processes in multiple states coming up with different policy strategies, out of which knowledge and experience is improved for the entire country. If there was only one powerful central government, these gains from experimentation would be lost. In each field, 'regional role models' should emerge, e.g., perhaps southern states might look up to the solutions adopted in Karnataka on urban water supply.

We wince every time the word 'central government' is used in the popular discourse as this is suggestive of central planning and an exaggerated conception of the role of New Delhi. The phrase 'union government' is an accurate description of the constitutional scheme, and a more modest phrase.[1]

The Problems of Intra-India Disparity

India is a continental economy, and there is very high heterogeneity within the country. There is heterogeneity about conventional economic measures such as income and capabilities. There is also heterogeneity of political and social preferences, where the South and the West is making more progress on social issues such as the agency of women.

Some facts illustrate the extent of heterogeneity:

- We identify the five poorest 'homogeneous regions' (HRs) as seen in the CMIE CPHS household survey, in the last pre-pandemic months of September–October–November–December 2019. They are districts in UP,

Odisha, Madhya Pradesh and Bihar. The average value of the median income, across these five HRs, is Rs 11,027 per month. The five richest HRs are districts in Maharashtra, Haryana, Chandigarh and Delhi. This average of median income is Rs 47,201 per month.[2]

Thus, the richest places are 4.3× richer than the poorest places.

- We turn to the probability that a person has a mobile phone. This reflects a combination of household income and intra-household resource allocation. We identify the five HRs where the fraction of females owning a mobile phone is the lowest. The value here is 4.7 per cent. That is, of all females in the population, 4.7 per cent have a mobile phone. (The comparable value for males was 36.5 per cent, i.e., 7.71 times higher than the value for females). We identify the five HRs where females have the most mobile phones. The mean value here is 84.2 per cent. That is, 84.2 per cent of females have phones. The male value is slightly higher at 85.41 per cent.[3]

Thus, the best places are 17.8 times ahead of the worst places.

In this evidence, the best places are 17.8 times or 4.3 times ahead of the worst places.

Similarly, consider self-reported health as seen in household survey data. Research with this data shows enormous geographical variation in the raw self-reported ill-health rate, the predicted ill-health rate of a fixed typical household, and the extent to which the rich are healthier than the poor.[4] This heterogeneity emphasizes the need in health policy to look deep, within each small group of 10 million people in India, in a process of identifying, diagnosing and solving public goods problems.

We may have had a mental model at one time that once economic development takes root in India, intra-India heterogeneity will subside. So far, there is little evidence of this convergence taking place.[5] There are other elements of the international experience, such as the poverty traps in the US or Italy, which have persisted for hundreds of years despite attempts by policymakers to change things. While we may desire convergence, and while some economic theory predicts convergence, we should not assume that it is afoot.

The heterogeneity of economic and social development, across the regions of India, generates heterogeneity in the public policy pathways desired by different groups of people. A policy position that is well liked in Uttar Pradesh may not be liked in Kerala, and vice versa. This creates conflict in a centralized public policy process.

These problems are addressed in a federal structure at three levels. The first involves reducing the extent to which decisions are taken at the union government. While monetary policy and defence need to be done at the union government, drinking water and elementary schools need not. The preferences of Kerala's population, on the role and status of women, will diverge from those in Uttar Pradesh, and this should play out into policy thinking in Kerala. Kerala may create rules requiring that half of all policemen should be women before this is done in Uttar Pradesh.

The optimal design of processes *within* government also varies with locale. As an example, the cost of engaging a schoolteacher in Kerala should diverge from that in Bihar. The Mumbai municipality should have a different organization design when compared with the Kolkata municipality. By imposing uniformity in the working of government, we inevitably reduce the quality of working of government.

The second involves creating structures that favour migration. When wages are higher in Kerala, or when women have greater freedom in Kerala, this creates an incentive for people to migrate from Uttar Pradesh to Kerala. Alongside this, free movement within the country of capital and enterprise helps exploit the 'equalizing differences' feature of the market economy. If labour is cheap in Uttar Pradesh, firms may like to reduce costs by investing in UP. This process is limited by the extent to which basic public goods in UP are of acceptable quality and the extent to which goods and services move freely through the country.

The third involves fiscal transfers through which the per capita resources available to the state government in poor states are higher than the per capita taxation that is done in those states. This creates the opportunity for local politicians to undertake actions that make progress on policy problems within a larger budget set than would be feasible if local tax revenues were the only resource base.

Rethinking State and Local Government

The 'subsidiarity principle' asserts that a function should be placed at the lowest level of government where it can possibly be performed. Mosquito control programs can potentially be run by the union government, a state government, or the municipality. By the subsidiarity principle, these should lie at the municipality as this is the lowest possible level.

Why does this make sense? At the local level, there is the best local knowledge in prioritizing problems and devising solutions. There is greater accountability when voters are closest to the local government.

Implicit in the subsidiarity principle is a great value for local knowledge. Social systems are not physical systems. In physics, Newton's Laws work everywhere, but social systems have complex inter-relationships that vary strongly with culture, institutions and history. An expert on urban transport policy in London is not an expert on urban transport policy in Pune. An expert on urban transport policy in Pune is not an expert on urban transport policy in Patna.

Each place has its own rhythm, and we require deep local knowledge in every corner of the world in order to understand problems and solve them. In his book *Seeing Like a State*, the great political scientist, James C. Scott, used the word 'metis' to convey deep experiential local knowledge.[6] Each of us has to study our backyard, build knowledge about it, and solve problems in it.

This approach has far-reaching consequences.

It implies that on List 2 and List 3 questions, cities and states have to develop their own capabilities for policy planning and execution. Each state will have to cultivate its own ecosystem of intellectuals, research organizations, staff that supports legislators, debates about legislation, and policy capabilities in the bureaucracy.

Health policy in Madhya Pradesh is as complex as health policy in Germany, considering that the two regions have a similar population. This suggests that the health policy capabilities in Madhya Pradesh—data sets, researchers, research organizations, government—need to match the richness of what is found in Germany. Bombay, with 20 million people, needs a policy intellectual ecosystem that is comparable with that seen in Australia, with 26 million.

The great research institutions of the country need offices in many states, and needs to get deeply involved in public finance and policy at the level of multiple states and cities. International interlocuters and funders, who find it convenient to only engage with ministries and organizations in New Delhi, need to engage with the complexity of sub-national India. As an example, the bulk of Indian public health lies in a variety of ministries in the states, and not in the union Ministry of Health.

While the Constitutional scheme gives considerable latitude to the union government on List 3 questions, the norms need to shift to an environment where these subjects involve little work by the union government.

In the field of mineral resources, there has been a long history of tension between the union government and state government. An attractive solution is for the union government to completely vacate this space and leave it to state governments.

Smaller States, Cities as States

Uttar Pradesh is a vast and heterogeneous state. It may make sense for it to be divided into multiple smaller states, each of which would then find solutions that are the most appropriate for local conditions. Jairam Ramesh has emphasized that such actions can be taken by the Parliament acting alone.[7] The map of about 100 'homogeneous regions' from CMIE offers fresh insight into a practical arrangement of sub-national units of government in India.

If the biggest cities become states, as has been done in China, this would help urban governance. This may be particularly appropriate as, in the future, the identity of many individuals will be tied closer to a home city than to a home state. Participation in local politics will become more natural if it is organized around a city rather than a state.

In the modern economy, cities are the engine of growth. Sustained growth in India is critically linked to achieving sound urban governance. If cities are empowered with their own tax base (by becoming states), there would be incentive compatibility in governance. City governments would issue bonds, improve local public goods, which would foster greater consumption in the city, which would feed back to the tax revenues of the city through the GST, and these tax revenues would be used for debt servicing.[8]

Decentralization within States

The subsidiarity principle is the essential foundation for cities that have local political arrangements for local public goods. When we see the city governance of New York or London or Sydney, we see a large array of functions being placed at the city level, which are found in India at the union or state governments.

The slogan of policy thinkers in this field is the need to place 'funds, functions and functionaries' at the local level. While a great deal of progress has been made in Indian tax policy, one piece which has yet to fall into place is a foundation of tax revenues for cities. The logical place for this is to carve out a component of the GST associated with a place. The GST is based on a consumption principle. It is collected at the point of consumption. It is easy to count the GST associated with consumption in (say) Aurangabad. It would make sense to transfer a fraction of this GST revenue—attributable to consumption in Aurangabad—to the city government of Aurangabad.

State-level politicians, who preach the cause of greater autonomy from the union government, need to consistently carry this through and devolve full powers to the city governments within their states.

The Role of Migration

In prehistory, when there was no sustained population growth, states competed to obtain more *people* including through coercive methods of forced resettlement. The prosperity of the society is determined by the number and capabilities of each people, and so is the tax revenue obtained by the state. Land area does not help: the number of people is what counts. Now that the world is coming back to stationary or declining population growth, we come back to the simple idea: states compete for people and not land.

Bad governance matters not because it controls some territory, but because it influences the lives of some people. The opposing force is exit of the people. The people vote with their feet, and shift from badly governed places to better places.

The population of Western Europe has swelled in recent years with the flight of people from Afghanistan, Syria, Libya, Ukraine, and Russia. Proponents of the 'China model' need to ponder why so many well-to-do young people from China tend to see their future elsewhere. The places that attract migrants tend to have individual rights, rule of law, competitive markets, independent news sources, safety from expropriation, and freedoms of thought and speech. The countries that fare poorly on these issues tend to lose people, which adversely impacts on aggregate GDP and thus the tax revenues that those states can obtain. There is a Darwinian process in which resources move to the territory of the best states.

A similar process is underway within India. The people are moving from misgoverned places to better places, thus fuelling economic prosperity and tax revenues in the good places. Conversely, state failure in the bad places is rewarded with fewer people to mis-govern and reduced tax revenues.

To the extent that city/state governments obtain tax revenues that are linked to the city/state GDP, this creates increased incentives for local politicians to make progress that attracts migrants. Redistricting will also, in the long run, award political power to the places that receive migrants. The better places in India need to rise above nativism, and create a more migrant-friendly society based on the requirements of migrants from within India and from abroad, in order to harness this phenomenon.

The Limits of Decentralization

Greater decentralization is criticized on the grounds that there is low capability in many state and city governments. This does not mean that centralization of power at the union government—which has been tried for 75 years—is the answer. Low capability at sub-national governments is partly a consequence of our historical journey.

In an age where the Planning Commission and the union government dominated decisions about (say) education in

Maharashtra, this inevitably gave an atrophying of policy capabilities in Maharashtra. When policy thinking was centralized at the union government, we got more field orientation at state and city governments. When the political/ bureaucratic system at states and cities is asked to play policy functions, at first, there will be a gap in capabilities. As decentralization progresses, policy capabilities will need to emerge in state or city level organizations, which may presently appear to have a mere field orientation.

While shifting power to states and to cities is desirable, political system reforms is required in establishing deep decentralization and commensurate checks and balances. The powers of the union government on the concurrent list need to be modified. The chief minister of the typical Indian state faces little by way of checks and balances: winning one assembly election yields extreme power. The five pillars of checks and balances—data, intellectuals, media, legislature, judiciary—all work poorly upon state governments.

Once these political system reforms are implemented, the pressure of accountability to local voters can be stronger in states and cities, than is the case with the union government. A voter sees a street lamp that does not work and is able to translate this into an opinion about the performance of the city government. In contrast, the policy actions of the union government are largely out of sight and out of mind.

While decentralization is a sound approach, there are two areas which we should be careful about.

The first issue is about problems that require coordination *between* states. As an example, the transportation system requires design at the level of the country, about how highways and gas pipelines and ports will be placed. The Union government can play a leadership role for this planning.

The second issue is about the possibility of severe capacity constraints in a state or a city. There is the possibility of a geographical region falling into a vicious cycle, where talented people leave, which gives a shortage of skills in the public policy process, which exacerbates elite flight. We need to keep a watch out for these vicious cycles and have a set of strategies to address them.

Summing Up

India is a continent, with very high heterogeneity. There is no one answer to policy questions, on most problems. The fact that many union territories—run by the union government—work better than many states should not lead us to question decentralization. Decentralization of government helps produce local answers to local problems. The 'subsidiarity principle' asserts that a function of government is best performed by the lowest possible level of government where it can be performed.

The Constitution of India is imbued with federalism. The evolution of the republic shows an inappropriate extent of centralization, of schemes that are designed by the union government and rolled out everywhere. The phrase 'union government' is preferable to 'central government' as the latter suggests greater control. Similarly, there is an inappropriate level of control of cities and villages by the capital of the state government. The appropriate role of the union government lies in coordination problems (e.g., the design of infrastructure networks that cut across states) and in addressing poverty traps where the conventional feedback loops of liberal democracy have broken down.

In a truly federal structure, state and local governments will have to design their own schemes. This requires capacity building in public policy at states and cities all over India.

States compete for people, not land. This has created pressures within India, where the people are relocating to better places, which fuels economic growth and tax revenues in the good places at the expense of the others.

For decentralization to work, the political system at the level of the state and the city requires reform, in order to achieve adequate checks and balances and dispersion of power.

Part IV

The Art

16

The Problem of
Organizational Capacity

When we think of government, we tend to personalize it into one prime minister or one official. When we think of the private sector, we tend to personalize it into one private person. However, in the modern world, most of what is happening is within *organizations*. It is the behaviour and capabilities of *organizations* that shapes outcomes. To desire a sophisticated society is to desire one which contains capable private and state *organizations*.

Whether in government or in the private sector, large organizations hold the possibility of assembling vast quantities of labour and capital and translating it into remarkable output. One person with a gun can be a field operative. To pull off a military campaign requires coordinated behaviour by hundreds of thousands of people, based on complex policy ideas in strategy, operations and tactics, and harnessing trillions of dollars of equipment.

The Question in Organization Design

Building organizations is difficult owing to the principal– agent problem: The fact that the objectives of the individual inside the organization diverge from the objectives of the organization. In a private sector setting, the individual inside the organization behaves in ways that are not aligned with the best interests of the principal, the shareholder. In a government setting, the individual inside the organization behaves in ways that are not consistent with the best interests of the principal, the citizen.

There is a caricature of corruption, where suitcases of cash are paid and a particular action by an official or politician is obtained. While this is indeed corruption, it is just a variant of the core problem: of officials or politicians pursuing their own self-interest and not doing the things that serve the objectives of the organization.

While low knowledge and training do hobble people in all organizations, the wrong actions of individuals in organizations are primarily a problem of incentives. This is the essence of public choice theory: The idea that individuals in government organizations are self-interested and not benevolent.

A successful organization is one that delivers on the objectives of the organization. The path to this lies in *organization design*, the orchestrated dance through which the individuals within the organization act. To do public policy is to be able to design public organizations well, and to envision how alternative methods of organization design would induce different outcomes.

Elements of Organization Design

The design of an organization consists of seven elements:

Objectives An organization must have an objective. In the private sector, the objectives of an organization are relatively clear: to generate a flow of dividends for the shareholders. In government, the objectives of the organization are generally not clear. The first task of organization is to establish the objectives of each government organization clearly. People can only be held to task when their task is clearly identified.

Leadership An organization needs a leadership. The job of the leadership is to develop a situational awareness every day and undertake actions which pursue the objectives of the organization.

Formal design An organization must have an organization diagram and a set of process manuals. These documents are vital components of the organization design, where clarity is established on who does what and how things will be done. Processes must be actually obeyed in practice.

Who is in charge of a given task? The hallmark of an advanced economy is that there is clarity on the positions and organizations where each decision is taken. The hallmark of underdevelopment is that it is never clear who is in charge of a given decision. Diplomats representing foreign governments, living in India, are constantly being asked who is actually running the show on a given subject.

Checks on coercive power Government organizations wield coercive power. A set of checks and balances must be in place, to prevent the arbitrary use of coercive power. This is called 'the rule of law'. Key elements of this involve

citizens knowing the law, the law being made in ways that
has democratic legitimacy, the presence of formal processes
controlling how coercive power is wielded, with harm being
imposed on private persons only through hearings/appeals in
front of judges.

The board The management of every organization is self-
satisfied and convinced about their virtue. The board holds
the management accountable and keeps them honest. The
composition, powers and process of the board (which is
termed 'the governance structure') is a key element of the
organization design.

Feedback loops Organization design requires feedback
loops, through which success and failure impact upon the
organization, in a short-term sense (personnel being rewarded
for doing well), and a long-term sense (organization design
that is changed in response to failure).

It is a time-consuming process: to design an organization, write
process manuals, encode them into software systems, have a
formal job description for every position in the organization,
to train every employee in understanding their task and the
enterprise IT systems through which the tasks are performed,
and to establish the systems for audit and measurement that
oversee the overall process.[1] Under the best of circumstances,
it takes years to build organizational capacity.

While the phrase 'organization design' suggests a designer,
most organization design in the real world emerges from
feedback loops and incremental improvements. Organizations
only learn by doing something over and over, and the feedback

loops generate slight improvements every year. Modest-sized feedback loops add up to major gains over a few decades, but this has really come about in only a handful of poor countries that became advanced economies in about 50 years. In most poor countries, the feedback loops are largely absent, and state capacity does not improve over time.

The word 'capital stock' tends to be associated with factories and highways. The most important capital stock of a society is in human and organizational capabilities. Conventional accounting does not see the intangible capital, of the years spent undertaking expenditures on organization building, that add up to a capable organization.

Organizational Capability Cannot Be Switched Off and On at Will

The private sector always desires profit, but organizational capacity in the private sector also does not come about easily. It takes many years to build a large organization that is good at doing something. As a consequence, capabilities in *private* organizations cannot be switched off and on at will. When there is a ban, capabilities are dissipated, and it takes years to rebuild them. Once private persons know that a ban can possibly take place, their willingness to commit resources for organization building are diminished.

Example 25: Banning and unbanning Foreign Investment in Indian Corporate Bonds

To some economists, foreign investment in Indian corporate bonds sounds like a frictionless activity, where large-scale capital flows will instantly arise in response to attractive risk/ reward situations.

In reality, these capital flows arise out of *organizations*. Large teams are required, in financial firms, which understand the Indian corporate bond investment landscape, which find the 10,000 key decision makers in global finance, carry knowledge about the investment opportunities in India to these customers, earn their trust, overcome practical frictions, and get started on a gradual process of trust building and investment.

These teams have to establish databases, process manuals, and knowledge about Indian corporate bonds. They have to achieve trust in the eyes of the ultimate investors, and build relationship-capital in engaging with one investor at a time. The fundamental problem in international capital flows is the incomplete information that foreign investors have about developing countries. The teams that work in financial intermediaries are the carriers of information to investors, that help produce better decisions by investors.

When an Indian policymaker bans foreign investment into Indian corporate bonds, these teams in financial firms are disbanded. No financial firm will carry on the stream of expenditures for this team, that works on foreign investment into Indian corporate bonds, once the Indian government bans foreign investment into Indian corporate bonds. The team will be disbanded, the knowledge will be dissipated, the relationship-specific capital with investors will be lost.

When, at a future date, an Indian policymaker chooses to reverse the ban, there will be a slow process of recreating that organizational capital. This recreation will be slow because building organizational capabilities is always hard, and also because decision makers in private firms will be wary of putting capital to work in building these capabilities, given that the Indian state has proved to be untrustworthy in the past.

This example has played out repeatedly in recent decades, because RBI established a 'quantitative limit' for the total investment by all foreign investors, put together, in the Indian corporate bond market. When this limit (e.g., $50 billion) is reached, all new investment stops, and the teams that work in financial intermediaries in this field are disbanded. The disruption of these teams leads to a decline in foreign participation in Indian corporate bonds.[2]

There is a feedback loop here. When policymakers are mistrustful of financial markets, there are more bans, and these bans interfere with the construction of organizational capability in the private sector, which leads to greater malfunctioning in the financial sector. Dirigisme breeds dirigisme. The puzzle for every society is to flip to the opposite virtuous cycle.   ••

Summing Up

State actions are taken by organizations, not individuals. To get to a successful state, we require good organization design.

Officials and politicians pursue their own interests and not the interests of the people. Organization design is about public choice theory, it is about this principal–agent problem, it is about creating the conditions where these individuals are pushed off course, from their own interests, to cater to the interests of the people.

The design of an organization comprises a written down document with (a) Objectives, (b) Leadership, (c) Formal design, (d) Clarity about who is in charge of a given task, (e) Checks on coercive power, (f) The board which exerts governance, (g) Feedback loops. Every time we look at a government organization, we should understand it in these seven dimensions.

Organizations are not designed, they evolve under the pressure of feedback loops. At its best, when the feedback loops work well, it takes many years to achieve a high-quality organization. Most Indian government organizations lack feedback loops and are not getting better over time.

In the private sector as well, organizational capability cannot be achieved quickly. When policymakers ban something, that capability is lost, and a mere unbanning does not bring back the capability.

17

Evolutionary Change for Society, Revolutionary Change for Government

The Pursuit of Life, Liberty and Happiness without Interference

We must create an environment in which the public has stability. Stability means many things. Stability means the confidence of planning a life, of starting a family, knowing that there will be no upheaval in society for a lifetime, which means a horizon of 80 years for a 20-year-old adult. Stability means the certainty that one will not face violence for the next 80 years. Stability means the ability to create savings without fearing expropriation by the state or by a private person. Stability means being able to embark on a business plan knowing that no disruption in the political or economic environment will arise.

These are primordial values in their own right. We must value such stability and endeavour to achieve it. This requires a respect for each individual in society. In public policy, we should not undertake actions that will disrupt the lives of the people on a large scale.

It is all too easy, in the world of public policy, to slip into the mode of directing people on how to lead their lives. But the pursuit of happiness by each person is best achieved when the state creates conditions of stability and vanishes into the background.

> *The ideal non-violent state will be an ordered anarchy.*
>
> —Mahatma Gandhi

At its best, the state should not impinge on the consciousness of individuals. People should have the ability to pursue their own values, with complete concentration, for decades on end, without intrusion from the government. One may wish to be a painter, another may wish to be a trader, for each of them there should be the opportunity to be absorbed in the desired zone for decades, without noticing the existence or actions of the state. When the state impinges on the minds of individuals, this is an intrusion.

Social Engineering Is Inappropriate

This pursuit of non-intrusiveness, stability and order has one powerful implication: We should favour small impacts upon the lives of the people over large ones. Social engineering, even if for ostensibly noble goals, should not be attempted. Every political system has Jacobin elements, which are attracted to transformative projects, that need to be kept in check.

Even if we were comfortable with interfering in the lives of others, large-scale schemes of social engineering have a long track record of failure. Social systems are very complex and outcomes are generally greatly different from those that the planners may have desired. Social engineers have, all too often, ended up inducing a capricious set of upheavals in the lives of the people. There is value in a precautionary principle here: we should be very concerned about initiating a move that will cause harm. For these reasons, even if social engineering were desirable, it is infeasible.

We see social engineering as infeasible and inadvisable, we prefer gradualism. When a government tries to redesign society, to create a new man, this is overreach.

> *If economists could manage to get themselves thought of as humble, competent people on a level with dentists, that would be splendid.*

> —John Maynard Keynes

The demonetization episode was a large shock upon the economy. Even if a cost-benefit analysis showed that the benefits outweighed the costs, the fact that it was a large disruption should have been a consideration in the decision.

China's one-child policy illustrates many themes of this book. It was inappropriate for a government to embark on it, because it constituted social engineering. It was also inappropriate as it involved a high degree of intrusion into the personal space of individuals. In the event, the one-child policy has induced serious problems for China. It illustrates how social engineering often goes wrong: we know too little in order to safely meddle into human society in most areas other than market failures.

Example 26: The Pitfalls of Social Engineering: Organic Farming in Sri Lanka

On 27 April 2021, the Sri Lankan cabinet banned the import of over 600 items, including chemical fertilizers. In his speech at the UN Food System summit, in late July, President Gotabaya Rajapaksa cited chronic health problems and ecological destruction as the reason for the ban. There was an element of nativism in play; advisors of the government such as Dr Anuruddha Padeniya made claims that in ancient times, Lankans lived to 140 years.[1] Many civil servants who opposed the proposal were sacked. Some observers painted a future with a rapid transition to organic farming, improved health and high value exports. However, this sudden use of the coercive power of the state (to interfere in cross-border transactions on fertilizers, to do industrial policy) was disruptive for the economy.

In July 2021, food prices rose by three to five times. There were protests by farmers and a black market for chemical fertilizers. The government raided 'hoarders' of fertilizers, pesticides and food. The Rajapaksa government announced that subsidies of up to Rs 12,500 per hectare, for up to two hectares of land, would be given to farmers.

In August 2021, $188 million was allocated to import organic fertilizers from China. Upon delivery, these shipments proved to be of substandard quality. Food prices shot up in September 2021. Mr Rajapaksa declared a state of emergency. By late 2021, the government reversed the policy initiative. ●●

Turning from social engineering to hard engineering, modern thinking on 'megaprojects' warns us that the worst projects are the ones that get built, and that mega projects are consistently over budget and over time.[2]

Gigantism is not a useful strategy.[3]

This Is Not a Defence of the Status Quo

Liberal democracies have achieved far-reaching change through small changes over long time periods. We applaud these changes. We favour a world where society evolves in far-reaching ways.

The values and imagination of the *people* should drive the changes of the world, rather than the values and objectives of a few central planners. Respect for each individual takes us to this notion of self-determination, which views the evolution of society as the outcome of millions of thoughts and actions by the people, rather than by a small group of rulers.

Communicate Till It Hurts

This pursuit of non-intrusiveness, stability and order has a second implication: a bias in favour of communication. We in the world of policy should always copiously talk about what is being done. We should prepare people for what is coming. We should never give out bad surprises. All new policy decisions should be discussed in the public domain, and once a decision is taken, the effective date should be many months or years away. This reduces the extent to which the policy decision induces instability.

Too often, we see a big policy change that was planned in secrecy, and then there is an uproar, and then we get a policy reversal. It would have been much better to have done the developmental work in the public eye. Sometimes, the early feedback would have been so negative the decision may never have been taken. In general, people react better when they are adequately sensitized.

Revolutionary Change for Government

When it comes to society, we should respect every person going about her daily life in a stable way based on her own search for happiness. Policymakers should not be the source of upheavals, of crises, of disruption.

A very different approach is required when it comes to redesigning *government systems*. As policymakers, we should be quite willing to ask civil servants to do new things. There is no need to respect the stability of the life of a civil servant. There is a need to constantly redesign organizations, rearrange turf, design better operating procedures, etc., to push public bodies to higher levels of performance.

As a thumb rule, each doubling of GDP (in real terms) calls for a fairly far-reaching change in the organization structure of government. It calls for a substantial rethinking of the boundaries and functions of departments and agencies, and of government processes. In India, most of the organization design seen today dates back to the time when India had one-tenth of the present GDP. Greater energy is called for, in organization design in government.

We should prioritize the good night's sleep of the populace but not of civil servants.[4] We should pursue revolutionary change for government structures, but evolutionary change for the people.

It is when the state interacts with private persons—either by coercing them or by setting up an expenditure program—that we should be cautious in our movement, and undertake cost–benefit analysis at every step of the way. When reorganizing management structures and organization designs in government, there is little role for formal cost–benefit analysis.

Summing Up

A good society is one in which individuals plan and live on their own terms, in a state of confidence over long time horizons. The purpose of public policy is to create the enabling conditions for such a life. As an example, the right way to structure monetary policy is a formal inflation targeting system, as it rules out inflation surprises, and makes personal financial planning possible over multi-decade horizons.

The best framework of public policy is one in which the state impinges upon the lives of individuals as little as possible. This is not a defence of the status quo. Society can and should evolve, gradually, through the thoughts and actions of the people. The state should not engage in social engineering, i.e., it should take no leadership role in the evolution of society.

Non-intrusiveness, stability and order is fostered by better communication. The government must say what it will do and then do what it just said. There should be no surprises.

Within the structures of government, however, it is permissible to undertake large scale reorganizations. We do not need to bring stability to the life of a civil servant.

18

Cross the River by Feeling the Stones

The phrase, from Deng Hsiao Ping, has gone deep into the world of public policy. What exactly does it mean to cross the river by feeling the stones? There are three elements to translating this idea into tangible policy strategies.

Element 1: No Silver Bullets

There is sometimes a temptation in thinking that what is required is one big bang and then the problem is solved. This is never the case. No problem is susceptible to a big one-time policy effort.

In every successful policy effort, there will be a large number of decisions, and iterative refinement based on empirical experience. We have to plan for sustained work over many long years rather than one big bang reform. This calls for capacity building process of a stable team within government, the organizational structure within which that team will work, and a supporting intelligentsia outside government. If any of these three elements are neglected, then an initiative is likely to falter after the big bang.

As an example, the reforms of the Indian financial markets consisted of analytical work through the 1980s, and the establishment of a non-statutory SEBI in 1988. This work leaped into high priority after the Harshad Mehta scandal of 1991/1992. This involved the establishment of institutional infrastructure with the closure of the Controller for Capital Issues, establishing the Capital Markets division at the Ministry of Finance, enacting the SEBI Act, setting up NSE, and the emergence of data-sets and an academic community in the field. This combination—a strong team within government, organizational structures in government, and a supporting intelligentsia outside government—was able to work on a sustained basis from 1992 onward. This gave fundamental progress over the 1992–2001 period.[1]

Similarly, the 'R group' reforms in the petroleum sector took place through a stable team over a six-year period.

Policy proposals such as demonetization have a certain silver bullet appeal. We are encouraged to take one bold decision, and after that the problem of black money will be solved. Similarly, it is claimed that the HR problems of government will be solved by bringing in 500 lateral recruits. Real world public policy success is generally found in more wonkish territory.[2]

Consider the field of financial inclusion. Poor people are excluded from the formal financial system for a variety of reasons, shaped primarily by the difficulties of financial regulation and weaknesses in competition. When the established firms are handsomely profitable while only serving the top quartile of India, there is no reason to take the effort to reach out into the middle class and the poor. Alongside this are the problems of the uniquely onerous KYC rules which have arisen in India.

Some people have been enamoured by the silver bullet of computer technology. It was felt that UIDAI and UPI, and other such computer systems, will solve the problem of finance for the poor. While computer technology is useful, the problems primarily lie in the infirmities of financial regulation and have resisted the silver bullet.

Element 2: Participatory and Therefore Slow Process

Policymaking that is done by a few people in government, under conditions of secrecy, is inadvisable as it lacks democratic legitimacy. It also yields poor results. No small team knows the answers. Wider participation, from experts and from practitioners, improves policy work. In addition, the process of participation seeds the private sector with a sense of what is coming, so they can develop business strategies ahead of time.

The sound process of drafting legal instruments consists of the following:

1. Clearly identifying a problem that needs to be solved.
2. Demonstrating that there is market failure.
3. Using a systematic process (cost–benefit analysis) to identify the lowest cost intervention that would address the problem.
4. Drafting a legal instrument that expresses the chosen best intervention.
5. Releasing these draft documents for public discussion.
6. Responding to all substantive points that are made through the public comment, including modifying the

legal instrument in response to some comments which proved to be correct.

7. A senior level discussion about the entire documentation packet, and the consequential modifications to the legal instrument.

8. Releasing the final legal instrument with a future date on which it becomes effective.

9. Conducting an ex-post review, three years later.

This process for drafting law induces the institutionalized application of mind, through which legal instruments are slowly drafted, one by one, that genuinely solve problems, and earn the respect and trust of the private sector.[3]

At present, one state agency in India—the Insolvency and Bankruptcy Board of India (IBBI)—uses such a procedure. Nowhere else is it used. In the absence of such a thorough process, policymaking is tantamount to crossing the river based on ideology or political compulsions. When law is drafted without such a careful and slow process, the private sector sees the government as a source of regulatory risk.

The sound process described above is encoded into the draft Indian Financial Code as the process prescribed through which financial regulators must write regulations. This is similar to the methods applied in mature democracies, where Parliamentary law requires agencies to work in this fashion. As an example, in the US, the Federal 'Administrative Procedures Act' (APA), 1946, prescribes such a machinery that must be used by all federal agencies.

Element 3: Small Moves Coupled with Feedback Loops

Experimentation is valuable. Too often in India, interventions are unveiled without the requisite level of knowledge about social systems. That knowledge can be slowly constructed through a systematic process of experimentation.

As an example, suppose SEBI believes that there are problems in the world of high-frequency trading, and suppose there is an intent of unveiling an intervention into the world of high frequency trading. SEBI could choose a set of 20 randomly chosen medium-sized firms, and the intervention could be rolled out for a period of one year for these 20 firms. This would permit a comparison between these 'treated' stocks and a set of similar 'control' stocks where no intervention was made, to assess the extent to which the intervention was useful. Once this is known, the intervention can either be scaled up or rolled back, based on empirical evidence about what works. This is analogous to the 'beta testing' that private firms do, where new products are tested out before they are rolled out more widely.

In the US, the securities regulator, the Securities and Exchange Commission, regularly undertakes policy experimentation in this fashion.[4] As an example of the difficulties in India, consider the problem of cash settled versus physically settled derivatives. Single-stock derivatives were cash settled from their launch in 2001 onward, and this system had worked well. In 2017, SEBI decided to force these to be shifted from cash settlement to physical settlement. This is a major action, which has a substantial impact upon the life of market participants. The decision was taken without identifying market failure, measurement, or experimentation. There was no ex-post review, so we do not know the magnitude of the adverse impact of this decision upon market quality.

The approach to experimentation is one valuable feature of the Chinese experience. The word 'ShiDian' is used in China for 'Policy Experimentation' or 'Policy Piloting'. This refers to political–administrative procedures that discover and test novel instruments and thereby propel policy innovation or institutional adaptation. The Chinese have engaged in spatially, sectorally and temporally limited policy trials so as to reduce the risk and cost of major reforms.

Abhijit Banerjee, Esther Duflo and others have emphasized the importance of 'randomized control trials' in learning about economics. We see this as being a valuable part of the economic policy toolkit, in the process of iterative refinement at the level of doing economic policy.

The corollary to favouring small moves, coupled with feedback loops, is the need to not let big problems build up. Once a big problem has built up, it is much harder to resolve, as small moves no longer defuse the crisis. This idea features in many situations.

A floating exchange rate delivers a small adjustment to the economy every day. In contrast, a managed exchange rate runs the risk of a big mistake building up, after which small moves are no longer feasible. Under sound banking regulation, the equity capital shortfall of the banking system would never cross 1 per cent of GDP, but when banking regulation is weak, large shortfalls of the equity capital in the banking system have repeatedly built up. It is better to have a system of individual insolvency, with a 'fresh start' program, instead of building up a large mass of bankrupt individuals, after which there is a greater risk of a loan waiver backed by state coercion.

Example 27: Bans on plastic Plastic Packaging Materials

There is a global problem with the use of plastic in packaging. This plastic is creating litter in the natural environment, particularly in places where the handling of solid waste is weak. Plastics are not bio-degradable and the residue will linger for 500 years.

As a consequence, in 2018, single-use plastics were banned in Mumbai.[5] This is a big disruption for the packaged foods industry, which has come to value the impermeability of plastic as a tool for avoiding bacterial and insect infestations in food.

It would perhaps have made sense for the government to start by experimenting with these bans in small towns, and simultaneously establish a data gathering and research process to measure the impacts. Perhaps the scaling up could be from a few towns to a district to a group of districts. At each step, evidence is required before making the next move. The packaging industry would also have time to develop and scale up plastic-free alternatives. ••

Policy Reversibility

> *Do things that you can undo.*
>
> —James C. Scott

In the US, 1 in 25 of the persons who were sentenced to death were, in fact, innocent.[6] The prosecution claimed, and the judiciary agreed, that these persons were guilty of heinous crimes, beyond all reasonable doubt. And yet, in fact, 1 in 25 of the persons killed by the state were innocent. Under conditions of low state capacity, this error rate is likely to be higher. Death cannot be undone. We in India should be even more hesitant about the death penalty as compared with thinkers in the US.

Where is greater reversibility found? The presence of measurement systems helps. If an action will yield an impact that will be well measured, then there is a better chance of seeing a mistake and reversing it. In contrast, when measurement systems are absent, policymaking is fraught with greater risk.

The distinction between 'first generation reforms' (stroke of the pen reforms) versus 'second generation reforms' (those that involve establishing complex government organizations) is useful here. It may be possible to reverse first generation reforms, when it is understood that there was a mistake. It is harder to close down a bureaucracy once it has been created. Second generation reforms are more irreversible.

Irreversibility is thus inherent to some things (e.g., death of a person), is greater when measurement is lacking, and is greater when the action involves establishing an implementation structure in government. These are the areas where greater caution is required in state intervention.

Summing Up

There are no silver bullets. The reforms that matter are complex multi-year journeys that require a large policy community. Most simple, quick and easy solutions are wrong.

Participatory policymaking works better than small groups working in secret. They tap into the full knowledge, that only lies in the people and not in a small ruling class. The job of the leadership is to facilitate the process through which the knowledge out there is discovered.

The ideal mechanism is to have measurement systems, and make small moves. Based on the feedback from the measurement, the small moves can be refined and modified as part of a larger strategy.

Do things that you can undo.

Beware of the things that you cannot undo. When the measurement is weak, mistakes will not be caught, and there is a need for greater caution. Stroke of the pen reforms are easier to reverse, but when a government organization has been setup, it is hard to undo, and there is a need for greater caution.

Many a mistake will not be undone, so there is wisdom in intervening less.

19

Adapting from the International Experience?

The harms associated with state access to information about individuals are well understood through the experiences of history, particularly in the authoritarian governments of the 20th century that were able to create significant information systems. The prime problem in state surveillance is the need to restrict government access to information about individuals. This problem has been largely solved in the advanced democracies. In the UK and in Europe, over the centuries, state surveillance has been tied down into rule of law procedures with highly limited ability for officials to snoop on individuals.

In recent years, there is fresh concern about the abuse of information about individuals by firms such as Facebook. European policymakers have pushed to the frontiers of the field with the 'General Data Protection Regulation' (GDPR) in the EU.

A simple reading of the contemporary literature on privacy in mature democracies is, then, misleading. Such a reader would see the bulk of the contemporary policy discourse as being the debates around GDPR and its enforcement. A reader of this literature would think that Facebook is a major problem in the field of privacy. Policy recommendations in India may flow from this study of the international experience: that we have to block information access about Indians by Facebook using a legal instrument on the lines of GDPR. This position would be treated warmly by persons in India who are hostile to foreign companies.

Such transplantation of the international experience would, however, be incorrect. Access to personal information by the state is far more dangerous for individuals as compared with access to this information by private firms.

The Indian state possesses unchecked surveillance powers over its territory. It would view firms like Facebook as useful enablers of the surveillance system. It may seek to use its considerable powers over such firms in ways that enhance surveillance. The behaviour of the Indian state, vis-a-vis such firms, is likely to diverge from what is seen in mature democracies where state surveillance is placed under limited and rule of law mechanisms.

A law like GDPR makes assumptions about UK or EU state capacity. To favour creating a new privacy regulator that will coerce private firms on the question of privacy, without the checks and balances prevalent in the EU, would work out poorly in India.[1] In the Indian discourse, we have rapidly run ahead to proposing criminal sanctions, in the hands of the proposed 'Data Protection Authority'.

The interesting policy question on privacy in India is not about how to transplant UK common law or the EU's GDPR into India. The prime question in the Indian privacy debate is about reining in intrusions into the privacy of individuals by the Indian state. This requires understanding the existing surveillance system and bringing it up to the qualities of state surveillance seen in healthy democracies.[2] Alongside this, we need to ask: *What is a modest and minimal scale of coercion of private firms, to increase the privacy of individuals, which are feasible under Indian levels of state capacity, which deliver the bulk of the gains?*

There is a tremendous prestige associated with the successful institutions of the first world. However, we should not be the sorcerer's apprentice, we should not engage in what the economist Lant Pritchett calls 'isomorphic mimicry', we should not mechanically copy the international experience.

It is always interesting to review international experience. But the core thinking about public policy in India must always be first principles reasoning that is deeply grounded in the Indian institutional context.

The policy thinker needs to envision how component X will work, in the context of all the other elements of the Indian landscape that are left intact. The policy analysis should envision how many policy alternatives will work—when placed in the Indian landscape—and then propose the possibilities that will work out best.

The Problem with Simple Transplantation

> *Every bad policy has been adopted in at least one good country.*
>
> —Ashok Desai

When faced with a policy question—e.g., the working of agricultural markets—one easy path is to do a literature survey of what advanced economies are doing. As an example, the policy thinker may study the working of agricultural markets in the US, the UK, Australia and Canada. Or, the people more oriented towards development economics might look at the country experiences in Brazil or Mexico or Thailand. Some combination of the institutional apparatus seen in these countries is then proposed as a policy reform for India.

In this age of Google searches, many policy notes in India are written in this fashion. A problem is proposed, the experience of a few mature market economies and emerging markets is reviewed, a few countries are identified where the outcomes are good, and some remix of the solutions adopted in those countries is proposed. This is particularly taking place with young law students and people who have studied outside India.

This is a faulty way to do policy thinking.

Go Beyond Description to Understand Why Things Work

Practitioner knowledge from other countries is generally of a descriptive nature. A UK insolvency practitioner can describe how the UK insolvency process works. But the problem in policy analysis is that of going below the 'thin description' to understand *why* something works. What are the incentives that hold the pieces together? What is the combination of norms, laws and enforcement that produce good behaviour?

For these reasons, practitioner knowledge has limited value in policy thinking. As Lant Pritchett says, a first-world policy practitioner is a bit like a New York taxi driver. The New York taxi driver knows how to perform rides and get paid, but has no conception of *why* the taxi system of New York works. Policy institutions in advanced economies have been refined for hundreds of years, and most people in close proximity to those institutions lack an awareness of *why* things work.

Invisible Infrastructure

When we look at one narrow piece of a policy puzzle, e.g., in the health system in France, we fail to see the *'invisible infrastructure'* upon which it depends. A large number of elements of state policy interact with the visible decisions of health policy to add up to the successful French health system. A frontline worker in the French health system does her job reasonably well because there is invisible infrastructure of the civil servants HR process through which she will face sanctions for not doing her job well. A visitor to France who focuses on studying the health system may admire many design elements of the French health system. But these are often not transferable into a different context, where the invisible infrastructure is lacking. Visitors tend to see elements of health system design in France, and not notice this invisible infrastructure.

As an example, we in India look at the US Securities and Exchange Commission (SEC) and think of it as roughly analogous to SEBI. We often fail to see the capability of the US *judicial* system, through which 'Administrative Law Judges' (ALJs) hear cases brought by the US SEC. Hearings at the SEC are conducted by *judges*, not by SEC employees, and the separation of powers at the US SEC is protected. This is made possible by the invisible infrastructure of a well-functioning legal system. We in India have an inferior arrangement, where the SEBI Act does not enshrine the separation of powers.

SEBI employees who also perform legislative and executive functions, and lack judicial independence, are performing the judicial function.[3] The lack of this invisible infrastructure— separation of powers and judicial independence—results in lower capability at SEBI when compared with the US SEC.

Similarly, securities law is only one small part of commercial law, and many schemes that break laws go beyond violations of securities law. We tend to not see the key role played by the law enforcement apparatus of the State of New York, and the US Department of Justice 'Southern District of New York (SDNY)' office. The SEC is one piece of a complex policy apparatus. When we look at the SEC alone, we tend to not understand the remainder of this apparatus and the role played by it.

In the US, ordinary courts work well; lying in court is dangerous; lawyers, investigators, prosecutors and judges have high capabilities. All this is the invisible infrastructure that shapes the working of the US SEC, which is lacking in India.

When we read policy papers and blog articles which engage in contemporary policy debate in advanced countries, they tend to focus on the frontiers of *their* policy environments. The US has the Food and Drugs Administration that broadly works well, and standing on that foundation there are fervent debates about a contemporary problem such as (say) medical implants. If we transplant that worldview into India, we tend to over-emphasize the problems of medical implants and under-emphasize the foundations, the invisible infrastructure of a well-functioning agency like the US FDA.

Many small countries are more unitary, but India is a continental economy and the Constitution is imbued with federalism. This federal architecture of the Indian state has important implications for most policy questions, and this limits the extent to which experiences from more unitary countries are transplantable into India.

Envisioning Policy Choices in the Indian Context

Every individual state intervention takes place in a context. That context is shaped by the organization of the economy and the existing structure of state interventions. There is path dependence; the history of the country and of past actions of policymakers shapes where we are and how we see things. A policy pathway that is successful in (say) Australia may not work in India as it is being placed in a very different setting. Envisioning how a given policy initiative will work in India requires deep knowledge of the local context. We need to visualize all the moving parts and think about how one proposed piece will fit into the larger context. This requires knowledge of history, institutions and politics.

As an example, infrastructure development is done by private persons in many parts of the world. But in India, private infrastructure development ran afoul of an array of problems that are unique to the Indian context.

As an example, we see many countries where regulators investigate violations of their law, and then initiate prosecution in ordinary courts. If that were brought into the Indian context, it may work poorly, as courts in India have many difficulties.

The international experience is a valuable source of knowledge about higher design principles. Concepts such as freedom, the public discourse, human rights, the rule of law, dispersion of power, negotiation, scientific inquiry, etc. are all drawn from enlightenment values. These are universal principles. It is when we come down to practical problems (e.g., how to organize the agricultural spot market) that the portability of ideas across countries breaks down.

Example 28: A Success Story: Tax Information Network

In 2002, we proposed the 'Tax information network' (TIN). This was envisaged as an IT system which stored facts about the income tax deducted at source, by the employer, and supported reconciliation with the claims by the employee about income tax already paid by her. The key insight for the TIN was related to the thought process of VAT credits, but it was relatively new when applied into the income tax context. TIN was envisaged as a system that would be run by NSDL, the information utility.

When these ideas were exposed to many international experts, their first response was negative. They felt this was a complex system, and an unproven idea in the international discourse. They also alluded to the ways in which the problem does not arise in mature market economies: If an individual falsely claims taxes deducted at source, there is a small probability of getting caught and very large penalties. Mature market economies did not have the problem that we were trying to solve.

The TIN was implemented and it was a great success. This example shows a sound approach to doing public policy in India: understand local conditions, and engage in first principles problem solving. The solutions adopted here will often diverge from those seen elsewhere.   ••

The Way Forward

We require a creative stage where possible solutions are proposed. The international experience is a useful source of early-stage candidates for this funnel. As an example, when we discover that in Brazil, public sector banks have been channelled exclusively into financial inclusion work, we should think *How interesting, could that possibly be useful in India?* We should also design from the ground up, exploring policy pathways that are unique to India. We should prioritize the points of pain in the Indian setting, which will often diverge from the problems being debated and solved elsewhere in the world.

All these candidates should go into a process of envisioning that is deeply grounded in the Indian context. In this analysis, we will often discover that a policy initiative that succeeded elsewhere is likely to fail in India, and vice versa.

The simple description of international experience, drawn from websites or from practical experience, is not useful for policy analysis in India. Sound policy analysis in India requires authenticity. It calls for deep experiential local knowledge ('metis'). The most valuable people in the Indian policy story are those who have authentic knowledge of India, and are able to imagine and envision how policy choices will play out in the Indian setting.

This calls for intellectual capacity in the Indian policy process. It is useful to think of three levels of intellectual capacity.

At Level 1, we come up with nutcase proposals, unmoored in logic or analysis.

At Level 2, we use Google and unthinkingly copy what other countries are doing. At this stage, we will avoid mistakes like the Chinese Great Firewall, which controls Internet access of the populace, and is abhorrent in all healthy democracies. It would have helped to know that no country has ever taken 86 per cent of its currency notes out of circulation in one fell swoop. It would have helped to know that no mature democracy bans crypto-currency investment or trading. However, at this stage, we will make many mistakes, that come from inappropriate transplantation of policy designs.

At Level 3, we have acquired metis, we are authentically grounded in our backyard, and engage in creative problem-solving from first principles. We would be fully knowledgeable about how the rest of the world works, we would creatively imagine new solutions on our own, we would be authentically grounded in the Indian reality in envisioning how various policy alternatives would work. We would be fully able to debate with policy thinkers elsewhere in the world, and present Indian solutions as optimal pathways under Indian conditions, while carefully warning other countries that they have to think for themselves. We would be confident about our work, but recognizing the importance of metis, we would not think that our success stories are the blueprint for other countries. The puzzle before the Indian policy community lies in nurturing the intellectual capacity for Level 3 work.

Free Riding on State Capacity Outside India

There are, however, some situations where international economic integration brings the possibility of simple free riding on state capacity that exists in mature democracies.

Example 29: Regulation of Food and Drugs

In the field of food safety, regulation in India is weak. Market failure in the form of asymmetric information is present when buying boxes for food storage and transportation. The consumer cannot know the extent to which the box is made of harmful substances.

Lacking such regulatory capacity, the typical plastic box for food storage and transportation, that is sold in India, may contain harmful substances. One easy solution *for a consumer* is to buy such plastic boxes from places where food safety regulation is strong. As an example, perhaps Tupperware plastic boxes sold in India benefit from US FDA regulation of food safety. When this is done, the Indian consumer is free riding on the US regulatory system.

In the field of medicines also, the same market failure (asymmetric information) is present. When we buy medicines in India, there is a risk that these are ineffective or counterfeit, owing to weak regulation of drug safety.[4]

As with Tupperware plastic food storage boxes, one could think of Indian consumers buying medicines which benefit from the oversight of mature democracies and thus free ride on their regulatory capacity.

In general, a bottle of aspirin purchased in a developed country is superior to a bottle of aspirin purchased in India. But this possibility for consumers of purchasing imported drugs is hampered by the Drug Price Control Order (DPCO), which forces very low prices for drugs in India.

In the field of drugs and food, the US and EU authorities run active inspection programs through which certain factories in India obtain the rights to produce drugs which can be exported to the EU or the US. Consumers and policymakers in India can sometimes free ride on this work.

Perhaps, a chyawanprash sold in India may be more trusted by consumers when it has a 'USDA Organic' label. Perhaps, an Indian drug safety regulator can say that the privilege of selling drugs in India is limited to factories that have earned the permission to export drugs to mature democracies. Perhaps there can be a way for manufacturers to say that a certain packet of biscuits is authorized by the US FDA for sale in the US: this would improve the respect of consumers in India for the level of food safety that has been attained.

This approach also breaks down in the field of drugs owing to the Drug Price Control Order: drugs that are manufactured to FDA standards are unprofitable when sold at DPCO prices. This is a special case of the general proposition in economics, that all price control is harmful.   ••

Example 30: A Success Story: Securities Listed Overseas

In the field of finance, there is an interesting dichotomy between firms listed purely in India versus firms that are also listed in the US.

Disclosure laws in the US are better in certain important respects. A firm with an American Depository Receipt ('ADR') listing in the US, like ICICI Bank, releases information owing to US disclosure rules, which is not ordinarily available to Indian shareholders of banks.

Similarly, owners of ADRs on Satyam got damages from Price Waterhouse in the US, while the Indian owners of Satyam shares did not.

With better disclosures and greater liabilities, Indian firms that have ADR listings may behave better with their shareholders. When this happens, Indian shareholders are free riding on the US regulatory environment.   ••

Example 31: Success Story: US FCC design of Spectrum Allocation

In the field of telecom, regulation is required to deal with one market failure, an externality. This is the possibility that one device may pollute the airwaves and hamper the working of another device. Regulation is required to share the scarce natural resource—the electromagnetic spectrum—and to ensure that each device works within certain rules of the game for emission of radiation. This requires a daunting level of state capacity where every device that is sold on the market needs to be tested in a government approved laboratory to ensure that it plays fair within the rules. It is difficult to set up this state capacity.[5]

There are other countries where this state capacity is present. As an example, the US was traditionally a large market for such devices, and the US FCC does such testing. As the US market is an important one for any global devices vendor, these vendors generally obtain a US FCC approval. It is, then, possible for a regulator to free ride on this testing process. For example, an Indian regulator can require US FCC approval for devices that are to be sold in India.

This free riding works if and only if the policy framework for spectrum utilization in India is the same as that in the US. For example, this means that India should allocate spectrum for unrestricted use in a way that is similar to the Industrial, Scientific and Medical ('ISM') bands used in the US.   ••

Example 32: Data Protection

Indian residents have low protection against data surveillance by the Indian government. Mature democracies feature much stronger protections against state access to data. In Europe, memories of Nazi and Communist rule have given strong protections against the government.

Indian residents can free ride on the hard-won liberties of other countries, by choosing where to place their data and computers. Perhaps Indian state power should be used to have data localization requirements for health data of Indian individuals, where health care organizations operating in India are forced to store this data in a GDPR country.   ••

Summing Up

Many policy notes in India are written by reviewing what is done in a few other countries, and patching together some plausible sounding policy proposal for India. This approach works poorly. Enlightenment values port across the world, the bumper stickers of FREEDOM or CHECKS AND BALANCES port across the world, but tangible policy designs do not.

We must go from a 'thin description' of what is done elsewhere in the world to a 'thick description', an incentives-based understanding of why officials and private persons behave as they do in advanced countries.[6]

A great deal of what happens in advanced economies relies on an 'invisible infrastructure' of state apparatus and check-and-balance that is not immediately within view when focusing on a narrow problem of policy. The US SEC does certain things right because the United States Constitution establishes certain protections, but when we focus on how the US SEC works, these foundations tend to be overlooked. A lack of awareness of invisible infrastructure is a greater concern for narrow domain experts.

To do public policy in the Indian context requires envisioning how a proposed design of an intervention or a government organization will work *in the Indian setting*, with a deep understanding of the surrounding conditions. We only change one piece of policy at a time, while everything else stays unchanged. We have to find the best given the constraints of the environment.

Ground-up design of solutions, from first principles, for the Indian environment will often look different from those seen elsewhere.

The institutions of the first world carry enormous prestige. The sum total of these institutional designs adds up to modernity and prosperity. Alternatively, each developing country has one area in which they did things well. However, when one element at a time is sought to be transplanted into India, we run the risk of being the sorcerer's apprentice (who uses the spell without knowing why it works) and engaging in isomorphic mimicry (copying the form without copying the function).

Public policy thinking in India requires 'metis': deep experiential local knowledge. Level 1 thinking is coming up with nutty proposals. Level 2 thinking is copying from websites. Level 3 thinking is grounded in metis, in first principles thinking, in authenticity.

There are some situations where it is possible for policy thinking in India to free ride on state capacity outside India. When this can be done, this is welcome, as it reduces the scope of work in building state capacity in India.

20

Test Match, not IPL

Let's start with a classic example: trade barriers on a certain product are eliminated. This yields immediate gains for the economy at large, as the price of that product comes down, though this gain may be imperceptible to most people as the magnitude of purchases of this particular product, by any one person, is small.

The existing producers of the product suffer from a decline in profitability and greater pressure to increase productivity. The pain is focused upon these persons.

Over time, some of these existing producers go out of business, thus freeing up capital and labour. The reallocation of this capital and labour into more productive uses gradually yields gains for the economy at large.

Entrepreneurs would see new business opportunities, including possible export markets, for business plans that involve buying this cheaper product. Gradually, these new businesses arise, and give gains for the economy at large. It takes time for the full 'general equilibrium' gains to play out. Public policy work is a test match, not an IPL.

Delays in Building State Capacity

When the Insolvency and Bankruptcy Code (IBC) was enacted in 2016, this had no immediate impact on the ground, as the state and private institutions that were required to implement the law did not exist.

A multi-year process began, which included building the National Company Law Tribunal (NCLT) and the Insolvency and Bankruptcy Board of India (IBBI). On the private side, individuals started specializing in the field of bankruptcy, and the slow development of 'information utilities' and 'insolvency professional agencies' began.

It takes years for these changes to play out, for adequate capabilities to develop on all these fronts. For this reason, the gains for the economy, from enacting the IBC in 2016, are obtained at a later date.

The bulk of the gains from the bankruptcy reform come from *modified behaviour* of private persons, taking place in the shadow of the law. The threat of the law is expected to induce modified behaviour on the part of borrowers and lenders. This also takes time. At first, the threat of the law has to change. In time, this will induce changes in culture, in the ways in which contracting and negotiation take place. The full impact unfolds over time.

Lags of Policy Impact

The most important reforms impose pain that is concentrated upon a few people, and gains that are diffused over the entire country. The pain comes early and the gains come with a lag. The political puzzle of reforms lies in managing these two tensions.

The art of politics lies in understanding the map of interests and pulling off such reforms. This involves understanding who will lose in the short run, negotiating with them and influencing their view of the world, modifying the reform in non-fundamental ways so as to reduce the pain upon these persons, and sometimes compensating them through other instruments. It involves harnessing the support of the gainers from the reform.

Policymaking on the Election Clock

The clock that counts the years to the next elections weighs heavily upon this thinking. The art of politics lies in thinking through these time horizons, launching a portfolio of reforms in year 1 and 2, which induce pain (attenuated by specific transfers to affected parties) in year 2 and 3, and yield overall gains by year 4 and 5.

This requires extreme capability in the team that wins power. The incoming team cannot just land up in power, take control of the levers of power, and wield power in in tactical or expedient ways based on political compulsions and ideology. They need to have a portfolio of policy proposals, backed by teams of experts, with fully articulated planning of actions, anticipated impacts, design of the measurement system to monitor the process on an ongoing basis, identification of the persons negatively impacted, and possibly the design of compensatory transfers to defuse the unhappiness.

There is a crucial role for the communication strategy that is put into play from the date the cabinet is formed. In this age of Twitter, 'communication strategy' consists of catchy slogans, catchy slogans, choice abuse, managing the headlines, and 'controlling the narrative'. The true role of communication, however, lies in improving coordination on an economy scale. The political and technocratic leadership must have a shared strategy and shared messaging, through which the full picture is consistently and strongly communicated. This would help align expectations and ensure that private persons change their strategies in ways that are coherent with the strategy of reforms.

If there is no strategy in reforms, or if it is not properly communicated to the private sector, then businesses and financial investors will make mistakes in the formulation of their strategies, which will result in reduced economic performance. This will increase the time lag between the policy change and its full beneficial impact.

Example 33: A Success Story: Cutting the Peak Customs Rate by 5 Percentage Points Every Year

In 2000, the Vajpayee government chose a path: the peak customs rate would drop by 5 percentage points every year. Everyone in the administration understood the strategy and consistently communicated it.

At first, there was an uproar from incumbent firms, and the government had to deal with their anger in year 1. From year 2 onward, firms understood that the peak rate was going to be down by an additional 20 percentage points by year 5. This set off India's firms on paths of fundamental productivity growth, and improved the choice of investment projects. Every step of the way, as customs duties were cut, tradeables in India became cheaper, and this kicked off an export boom.

This combination of communication and staggered introduction of the reform induced synchronization between the government and the private sector. This was critical for the economic boom which started in 2003.   ••

Before the First Year

In the world of business, there is a balance between building a great product and selling it on the market. An extreme emphasis on a sales and advertising team can yield a brief surge of customer interest, but this does not translate into sustained success if the product is not of high quality and the machinery of production and distribution is not in place. In other words, a firm needs not just sales and advertising: it also needs research, design and operations management. It needs a great product and the capability to produce and distribute the product, on top of which the sales and advertising offensive is essential.

There is an analogy with the world of politics. Running an election campaign is analogous to the sales and advertising problem. To win power, this is essential. But if this is all that is done, sustained voter satisfaction will be elusive. Political parties need to prepare to govern, alongside campaigning to get elected. Once the election results are in, every day lost in establishing the team and kicking off a portfolio of reforms is a costly delay. We are doing too little transition planning in Indian politics.

When out of power, political parties should have a shadow cabinet. There should be a sustained process of engagement with research organizations, data sets and intellectuals, in order to cogitate about what is going wrong. The emphasis in an opposition party should be not just on criticizing what the ruling party has done, but on developing a set of plans for what would be done when in power.

The incumbent ruling party equally faces this problem. At year 5, a successful ruling team is jaded, and an unsuccessful ruling team is demoralized. Yet, it needs to think through the possibility of re-election, and find the energy for transition planning.

This preparatory work would be particularly valuable when it is fed into the manifesto of the political party and, when coalition governments are formed, the negotiation for a common minimum program. The paragraphs in such documents matter disproportionately, but receive inadequate attention ahead of time.

Long range thinking, and capacity building, is required in each political party, to develop the capability to succeed in the event of winning elections. When such developmental work is not done, ahead of time, we translate remarkable election outcomes into failures on policy.

Playing the Long Game

A cult of *jald baazi* is taking root in India. This is the notion that a problem can be understood in a few days, and solved in a few weeks. Powerful policymakers tend to whip up a frenzy of getting things done quickly. Every expert in India has gone through the surreal experience of being ignored for years, and then asked to deliver a reform document overnight.

You rush a miracle man, you get a rotten miracle.

—*The Princess Bride*, 1987

This is a harmful approach. In some rare situations, a team is available in India, which is fully imbued with a problem, has the right understanding, has the right human networks in the country, has learned how to work with each other, and can move at high speed in executing a reform. Even under these conditions, drafting laws and building state capacity takes a long time.

In most situations, there is a starvation of intellectual capacity in the country. We lack data, knowledge, experts, and the teams that know how to work with each other. There is thus a slow process of understanding problems, designing solutions, going up from individuals to teams with esprit de corps, and implementing reforms.

The cult of speed yields failure in both cases. Even when the best teams are assembled, if the work which requires two years is compressed into a few months, this will be done badly. With weak teams, the pressure of solving a problem in a few months surely yields failure.

There is a pipeline in the policy reform process: data to research to policy proposals to consensus to government decisions to policy implementation. It is not possible to short circuit this process. Some fields are at a weaker stage, where the basics of data and research is not in place. In these fields, the only horizons over which meaningful policy reform can be achieved is a long time horizon.

The cult of speed is ultimately derived from management failure in government. We are faring poorly on establishing institutions which contain harmonious teams that impound information and expertise, we are unable to make long-term plans, and stay focused on them. We suffer from a strong pace of personnel changes, which prevent the development of knowledge and rapport within policy teams. We suffer from three-page notes of individual reform measures, typically written by interested parties, which lack strategic thinking. We fluctuate from one topic to another, based on the crises that engulf us each day. When a government flits from one issue to the next based on the news cycle, there is no strategy.

> *Fast is slow, and slow is fast.*
>
> —Charles Sherr[1]

We should be skeptical about silver bullets, about solutions that are hawked in three-page notes.[2] We should be slow and cautious. We should set a high bar on the minimum level of knowledge and evidence required before embarking upon even a modest intervention into the lives of private people. We should embark on the long journeys to establish checks and balances, to build state capacity.

Example 34: The Bankruptcy Reform

The Parliament enacted the Insolvency and Bankruptcy Code (IBC) in May 2016. There was a great rush in quickly getting the Insolvency and Bankruptcy Board of India up and running, and in declaring the IBC open for business. Many corners were cut in getting to a quick launch.

By early 2019, many difficulties in the working of the IBC were visible. The big cases have proved stubbornly hard to process. Consider an alternative history. Would it have made sense to lay the groundwork from May 2016 to May 2018, and only then declare the IBC open for business? We suspect that things would have looked better by early 2019, if that slow path had been taken. ••

Example 35: The Rhine Was Not Cleaned in a Day

In 1986, a blast at the Sandoz chemical plant in Basel, Switzerland, leaked tonnes of toxic chemicals in the Rhine, Europe's longest river. The 1,233 km long trans-boundary river, passes through Switzerland, Liechtenstein, Austria, Germany, France and Holland. This presented complex multi-nation problems of policy coordination, in order to clean the river.

In 1987, the Rhine Action Plan was drawn up, with a simple and bold target: *by the year 2000, there would be salmon in the Rhine again.* The implementation plan employed a variety of measures and instruments to clean the river: from expanding and equipping biological sewage treatment plants, to working with non-profits like Greenpeace to monitor emissions levels, and industrial regulation and enforcement. While the original plan had a bold target of an outcome in 13 years, in reality, it took 30 years and 45 billion Euros, and the fish were back.

After this, the Rhine Action Plan was reformulated as the more ambitious goal, over a 10-year horizon, that the riverine ecosystem would become a thriving environment for all creatures.[3]

••

Building a Bridge vs Building Institutions

Policymakers in India now understand how to build a bridge. They know that building a bridge is expensive, that it requires professionals to build, that there will be a project plan, that many steps have to be undertaken, and these take time, and only then can a bridge be inaugurated.

The same approach is required with state capacity! When a new government organization is required: (a) It will be expensive; (b) It requires professionals to build it; (c) There must be a formal project plan in order to build the organization and its capabilities; and (d) Implementing this project plan will take time. Only when the project is completed, can a new organization be declared open for business.

We have repeatedly seen new organizations being launched in the Indian state in a casual and informal way. The present ways—of hiring a few people and declaring a government agency open for business within a very short time horizon—are downright harmful. Right at the outset, the organization is crushed with demands that it is ill prepared for. The fledgling organization is under-funded and under-resourced in every possible way. It gets into a fire-fighting mindset, makes mistakes, and generally never recovers from the early failures.

We in India have learned how infrastructure projects require time and money. We need to carry this professional approach into building state capacity in government organizations.[4]

The equity market reform started at the G. S. Patel committee report in 1984. A humble researcher in this team, R. H. Patil, was central to the establishment of NSE. SEBI was begun as a non-statutory organization in 1988. The pieces of the equity market fell into place by 2001. There was an exciting journey of ideas and action, with the establishment of SEBI, NSE and NSDL, which ran from 1984 to 2001. This gave fundamental progress on the equity market.

We may have thought that once completed, this would stand in place. In the event, there was a dissipation of the institutional memory. The experiences of the 1980s and

1990s, which shaped decisions of the 1990s, were forgotten. The community that understood and led this policy work was disbanded. In numerous aspects, there has been a retreat in the capabilities of the financial markets in the recent decade. As an example, the first settlement failure in the history of NSE, and the first settlement failure in the Indian equity market after a gap of 19 years, took place in 2019.[5]

Similarly, the pension reforms began with Project OASIS, led by Surendra Dave, in 1998. This led up to the decision in December 2002 to implement the New Pension System for new recruits into the government. PFRDA was setup, and the law enshrining PFRDA was only enacted in 2013. However, there was a dissipation of the institutional memory. The experiences of the 1990s, and the logic of the NPS, were forgotten in many important ways. The community that understood and led this policy work was dissipated. On 23 February 2022, the Rajasthan chief minister announced a reversal of this reform for Rajasthan civil servants.

These experiences underline the importance of building stable teams which are able to engage with the reforms process over long time horizons. Each area of work is a complex problem with many moving parts. As policy projects unfold over long time horizons, we require teams and policy continuity over long time horizons. When there is high instability for the thinkers and doers in government and outside it, and when institutional memory is lost, we lose ground.

Building the Republic Takes Time

It took hundreds of years to build the US, the UK and the other mature liberal democracies of the world. As an example, the US Constitution was written in 1776, but the 'fruit of the poisonous tree' doctrine—which is absolutely fundamental to limiting the power of investigative agencies—only came together in the early 20th century, i.e., 154 years after the founding of the country. It was only in the 1970s that US lawmakers shut off domestic operations by the CIA, and brought electronic surveillance by investigative agencies under the rule of law.

Similarly, it took 70 years from 1947 for India to decriminalize gay sex. Assuming there is progress towards freedom and the rule of law in the future, it will prove to take over 70 years to get to basic elements of civil liberties including de-criminalization of defamation, removal of sedition from the IPC, and placing electronic surveillance of the populace under a rule of law framework. These are long and slow journeys.

We should not look for the newspaper headlines, the quick wins, the buzz on social media. We should instead dig into the long and slow process of genuinely building the republic.

The Slow and Gradual Approach Reduces Uncertainty

A well-functioning liberal democracy gives an environment of stability to private persons. Whether we think about building a business, or entering into an infrastructure contract with a 50-year horizon, or planning at age 20 for old age income from age 70 to 100, or planning to have a child: these transformative decisions by private persons are greatly shaped by the uncertainty of the environment.

Many people dream of a muscular government, that is able to solve problems overnight. These notions are particularly prevalent among persons with intellectual foundations outside the humanities or the social sciences. However, if the law or the working of the executive can change overnight, then it can change again the day after. *A government that can give you anything that you want is one that can take away everything that you have.* All private persons are thrown into a zone of supreme uncertainty when placed in such an environment.

We recall a discussion of securities law in the UAE many years ago, where a senior government functionary said *Just bring the perfect securities law to me, and I will enact it overnight.* But if a law can be enacted overnight, then it can also be changed overnight, and then there is low legal certainty. Private persons will not commit resources to building a securities business under such conditions.

The Constitution of India is hard to change, even over long time horizons. We are at the early stages of hoping that the core of the Constitution, the 'basic structure' cannot ever be changed. This immutability of the foundations of the republic is what generates certainty, in the minds of private persons, about the world that they will inhabit in coming decades.

A slow and participative process gives confidence to private persons in two ways. First, private persons are protected from abrupt change: there will be ample time in which an observer will see policy proposals move towards the finish line, time in which business plans can be adjusted. Second, private persons placed in such an environment are citizens and not subjects. They have confidence that there will be a debate about the policy questions, and they will have a seat on the table when the decisions are made.

We should have tremendous intellectual capacity, we should work hard, and the result should be a slow and participatory policy process that incrementally addresses market failure. The slow pace of a sound policy process is *a feature and not a bug.*

Summing Up

When a policy reform takes place, the full gains are obtained through the reallocation of resources in the economy. The policy reform requires private persons to fully internalize the new environment, and re-optimize for it. Many policy reforms require the construction of institutional capacity within government and in the economy. These adjustments takes time. For this reason, the pain is front-loaded and the gains come with a lag. Policymakers need to understand who will lose in short run, negotiate with them, and find compromises with them.

After elections take place, and the leadership faces a five-year horizon, it is useful to think of year 1 as the time to launch complex initiatives, which will mature through years 2,3,4 and show positive impacts by year 5. This imposes demands on the team formed after the elections. It needs to choose the major projects, staff them, and communicate this to the economy so as to reshape expectations. This requires considerable work within political parties before winning the election.

Such thinking over long time horizons diverges from the cult of speed that is often found in Indian public policy, where there is fascination for silver bullets, where three-page notes are written over a weekend and implemented over the week. Such actions tend to be superficial and achieve little.

There is a pipeline of the policy process, from measurement all the way to policy execution. The institutional memory of each field is contained in a community of intellectuals and policy practitioners. The pipeline and the community need to be nurtured, in order to play the long battles of policy reform.

We in India now know that a bridge across a river is a project that has to go through certain steps. It takes time, money and professional capacity in order to build a bridge. We have to see policy reforms in a similar way. There is no short cut from the date on which it is decided that a bridge shall be built, to the date on which the bridge is inaugurated.

Building the republic takes time. It will take many decades of hard work by the policy community for India to rise to the ranks of the advanced nations of the world. Policy reform is slow, hard work and not amenable to quick wins on social media.

The fact that the policy process is slow and participatory serves to increase confidence. Under these conditions, private persons will enhance their investment in building bridges, firms or children.

21

What Is Hard and What Is Easy

When we think of a given government intervention, we need to judge how hard it would be, for successful implementation. Suppose the Indian state is evaluating a universal HPV immunization program for children. While we know that this is hard, it is in the zone of feasible policy pathways. But suppose the Indian state is evaluating a program where officials will interview unemployed individuals and decide which of them should get welfare payments every month. This seems beyond the reach of the implementation capacity of the Indian state.

What are the general principles through which we can engage in such reasoning?

Four Dimensions of Complexity

Lant Pritchett and Michael Woolcock first posed this question and offered elements of the answer.[1] They predict that implementation is hard when there is more discretion and when there are a larger number of transactions. We enlarge on their work.

Number of transactions. It is easier to achieve state capacity on a problem where there are a smaller number of transactions. A vast sprawling machinery involves greater agency problems; it is difficult to be sure that every element of the administrative machine is working correctly.

Discretion. It is easier to achieve state capacity when there is low discretion. An immunization program is a good example, where there is a population-scale outreach, but the work that has to be done by each civil servant is fixed and there is no discretion.

Stakes. It is harder to achieve state capacity when there is more at stake for private persons. Problems like the criminal justice system, the judiciary, the tax system and financial regulation are the hardest puzzles. Here, the decisions of state agents have enormous consequences for individuals, and private persons will devote considerable effort in trying to influence the outcome.

Secrecy. The bulk of the working of the Ministry of Rural Development takes place in the open. Policy documents and data-sets come out into the public domain. This makes the feedback loops of analysis and criticism more effective. In contrast, the secrecy that surrounds a ministry such as Defence can serve as a cloak for poor performance.

Example 36: Monetary Policy Is Easy, Financial Regulation Is Hard

By this reasoning, monetary policy is a relatively easy problem:

- *Low discretion.* Once inflation targeting is embedded in the law, there is a clear accountability mechanism. Individuals who make the decision have relatively limited discretion. Individuals who make flagrantly wrong decisions will be exposed in public and will suffer lifetime reputational damage.

- *Low number of transactions*. There is no citizen-facing part to monetary policy. It is only four to six decisions a year.
- *Low stakes*. Raising or lowering the policy rate has important consequences for the economy as a whole, but it is of extreme importance, at a personal level, to nobody. Not much is at stake as far as private persons are concerned; there will be relatively little tangible lobbying or pressure in trying to influence the outcome. It is interesting to see that when the monetary policy transmission is weak, the stakes are even lower, as small changes in the policy rate have a negligible impact upon the economy. It is easier to establish central bank independence under conditions of a weak monetary policy transmission.
- *Low secrecy*. A sound central bank has essentially zero secrecy, so there is the full potency of public domain analysis and criticism, thus giving strong feedback loops from failure to improvement.

Hence, monetary policy is a relatively easy puzzle in state capacity building. A small elite is required, which writes the rules of the game, that gets the country up to a modern central banking law. A small elite is required, which mans the monetary policy committee. Central banks can be fairly small, lean organizations. The complexity of solving principal-agent problems in a large organization can be avoided.

In contrast, financial regulation is a difficult problem. A lot of behaviour lies in the shades of grey; there is *discretion* for the investigator and the prosecutor in classifying a certain activity as a violation or not.

There are a large *number of transactions*: there are thousands of financial firms and there is a requirement for perhaps 1000 investigators and prosecutors in India. ·

The *stakes are sky high*. How regulations are drafted and enforced makes a difference of trillions of rupees in terms of the payoffs to private persons. Billionaires have a great incentive to reshape the working of financial regulation in their favour, and they will use every trick in the book in trying to impact on the policy process.

There is *a good deal of secrecy*. Supervision, investigations, enforcement and the quasi-judicial process of financial regulators is cloaked in a good deal of secrecy.

Hence, financial regulation is a difficult problem in constructing state capacity.[2]   ••

Example 37: Judicial Reforms

In the working of courts and tribunals, there are two distinct elements which can be seen as pillars of intervention. There is the highly discretion-intensive problem of the thinking of the judge. Alongside this, there is the low-discretion and transaction-intensive problem of running the operational processes of the court. This is also termed 'the registry' of the court.

It is possible to bring modern business process reengineering into the working of the operational procedures. This approach is likely to give substantial gains in the operational efficiency of courts, while leaving the independence of the judiciary intact.[3]

This is a useful vertical split, between high discretion and low discretion parts of the working of a court. Using modern IT systems, the low discretion part can be rapidly transformed. ••

Solutions That Change from One Dimension of Complexity to Another

Many government offices in India find it difficult to achieve clean toilets. Cleaning the toilets is a transaction-intensive problem, which calls for considerable state capacity in being able to recruit and manage a cleaning crew.

This is a well-defined service function, which does not involve the use of coercive power upon the people, and hence it can be contracted out. Our first impulse might thus be: *Why not replace tenured janitors who do not clean the toilets by a private contractor who will not give tenure to her employees?* This appears to offer gains in one dimension: We are replacing a transaction intensive function (janitors cleaning) by a small number of transactions (procuring and monitoring the private contractor).

In the process, however, we do run up to larger stakes. A tenured janitor gains about Rs 150,000 a year (her wage) from doing no work. In contrast, a private contractor that undertakes cleaning services for an entire building may be paid Rs 1.5 crore (Rs 15 million) a year. The private contractor now stands to gain a bigger amount by doing no work. The stakes are higher. It now requires a large amount of state capacity, albeit in a different dimension, to ensure the contract goes to the right person, using a fair process, and is adequately monitored.

When public–private partnership was first proposed as a way to improve upon low-quality infrastructure built by government departments, this was hailed as a big step forward. With the benefit of hindsight, we see that PPP contracting is hard, as the stakes are high.

The Four Hardest Problems

The criminal justice system, the judiciary, the tax system and financial regulation suffer from the problem of high discretion, high number of transactions, very high stakes and varying amounts of secrecy. How the frontline policeman behaves can make a difference of life and death for a person. This gives extreme discretionary power to the policeman. We need to keep our eyes on the four hardest problems in state capacity: the criminal justice system, the judiciary, the tax system and financial regulation.

Learn to Walk before You Run

Once we see that high stakes harm the construction of state capacity, a natural tool for sequencing is to initially start at low stakes.

If the fine for driving through a red light is Rs 10,000 then there will be pervasive corruption. Jobs in the highway police will be sought after; large bribes will be paid to obtain these jobs. There will be an institutional collapse of the highway police. It is better to first start with a fine of Rs 100, and build state capacity. Once a country has learned how to run a highway police at a fine of Rs 100, we can think of going up to larger fines.

A low tax rate induces low stakes. High tax rates are a high load upon the state, as the personal incentives of tax administrators (to take bribes) become highly divergent from the objectives of the institutions that they represent.

Public anger about the failures of the criminal justice system in India has often given a sharp escalation of punishments. This leads to higher stakes, and thus *reduces* the capability of the criminal justice system.

When we are at the early stages of learning how to be a state, it is wise to start out at low stakes (e.g., low tax rates, low punishments). Once capabilities are fully established, there can be a mature debate about whether the right policy pathways involve higher stakes (e.g., higher tax rates, higher punishments).[4]

Summing Up

When we face a problem in public policy, it is important to assess how difficult it will be, to build the requisite state capacity. Four factors shape this:

1. *Transaction-intensity*: If something involves a large number of transactions, by a large number of front-line civil servants, then it is harder.
2. *Discretion*: If something involves more discretion in the hands of the civil servant, then it is harder.
3. *Stakes*: If there are high stakes, it is harder.
4. *Secrecy*: When there is greater secrecy, it is harder.

Monetary policy is easy while financial regulation is hard because the latter involves a larger number of transactions, a greater use of discretion, high stakes and greater secrecy.

Complexity in this four-dimensional space is not immutable. We can often undertake actions that reduce the complexity, in some of these dimensions, or trade-off complexity in one dimension for another dimension.

The four hardest problems are: the criminal justice system, the judiciary, the tax system and financial regulation. They suffer from high transactions, high discretion, high stakes and high secrecy.

If a government organization is asked to suddenly achieve capability on a difficult problem, it will collapse in an organizational rout. A natural way to sequence the construction of state capacity is to first start with an easier problem, to achieve success, and then escalate the complexity. At an early stage in the republic, it will help to reduce discretion, reduce secrecy and most importantly, reduce the stakes. At first, agencies should be given low powers to investigate and the punishments that can be awarded should be low. This will create better conditions for achieving state capacity.

22

Confident Policymakers Work in the Open

In public policy, we don't just dine with friends, we must also sup with fiends.

—Ashok Desai

There is a long tradition of secrecy in public policy in India. Too often, in India, a reform is pushed through as a sudden *fait accompli* upon the losers. As the complexity of the economy has grown, and as Indian democracy has matured, it is increasingly unwise to maintain this level of secrecy.

Secrecy Harms Planning and Execution

Exposing early drafts to the persons who have a lot at stake may often yield improvements in the work. Particularly when we have low state capacity, the most well-meaning reform is often marred by technical mistakes in the execution. A more open policy process catches more errors and it improves the resulting work.

As an example, most draft laws in India are faulty owing to gaps in capabilities for drafting law in government organizations and in their supporting law firms. A thorough and genuine process of consultation will find mistakes.

One of the reasons why the demonetization decision suffered from difficulties of policy design and implementation was the secrecy in which it was surrounded. The areas of Indian public policy which are shrouded in secrecy (military, intelligence, trading in the RBI treasury) may have the biggest flaws.

The full gains from a reform require a great deal of advance planning and preparation by myriad private persons. This developmental work takes place if there is ample advance warning. The same reform will deliver better results if the overall economy has been primed for the idea adequately.

Losers from a Reform Require Fair Warning

Every reform hurts certain firms and certain persons. With more advance warning, they can plan their life better. This would reduce the costs for the economy as a whole.

As an example, consider the simplest reform: trade liberalization. Certain Indian factories, in areas where India does not have a comparative advantage, have to close down when the trade liberalization is done. We as a country have two choices: To present them with a surprise big bang trade liberalization, or to talk about it every step of the way and give ample warning. By giving ample warning, for many years, firms that expect to lose out will cut back on investments in physical capital and organizational capital into the businesses that are not going to survive trade liberalization. This reduces the destruction of capital that always accompanies trade liberalization.

The Policy Process Is One of Negotiation

There is a valuable political economy perspective upon this question, where we see all reforms as a process of negotiation. Healthy democracies are those where various interest groups are able to sit together, engage in good faith discourse, and emerge with reasonable compromises. The essential foundation for the democratic process of negotiation is trust: a certain presumption of good faith.

We as a society need to experience decades upon decades of decent behaviour with each other, in order to learn how to trust each other, to negotiate in good faith. This will yield a political system in which we are able to rise above partisan hatred and enter into bargains that make everyone better off.

The trust building that is required for this is hampered with policy measures are hatched in secret and suddenly unveiled upon the populace. The persons who get hurt feel that they were not treated fairly. This adversely affects the trust capital of the country, and holds back our emergence as a mature political system.

Give People Time to Change Behaviour

Let us go back to the example of trade liberalization. So far, we emphasized the presence of persons who lose from the reform, and sheer fairness requires that they need to be able to plan for this ahead of time.

But the full impact upon the economy works through a series of adaptations. Some of the affected firms may choose to wind down their business or sell it. Others will choose to push up their productivity. Some firms that *use* the goods that have lower tariffs will now see new opportunities to make things for the local or overseas market, as a consequence of lower prices. This may, in turn, kick off technological changes.

The full impact of a policy measure plays out in reshaping the work of the private sector. It is better for this work to commence as early as possible. For this reason, an open and consultative process works better.

If private persons have ample warning, their adaptations commence at an earlier date. Through this, the lags of the policy process are reduced. The gains for the economy are obtained in a shorter period.

It is easy to deride 'paralysis through analysis'. For many people who are not instinctively comfortable with intellectual discourse, the slow process of public debates and government committees seems like a waste of time. Reaching out to critics is tactically costly as this increases the say that critics have in stalling or subverting a reform. The authoritarian impulse, to favour action over talk, is fashionable.

However, the best policy work gets done in the open. The participatory policy process, grounded in intellectual debate, generates better policy decisions. It helps avoid a policy process that is pure power play. The work is better rooted in the landscape of people and institutions. The mistakes are more likely to be taken out. The negotiations and compromises create support and legitimacy. Policy implementation works out better.

Example 38: A Success Story: Petroleum Reforms, the 'R Group'

An example of this is the 'R Group' which worked on petroleum policy reform starting in 1995. This brought together all parties into the thinking, worked in the open, negotiated short term versus long term elements of the reform, and laid the foundations of an important and successful reform.

A group of young leaders from public sector oil companies—all below age 30—was formed, to prepare a road map to international competitiveness. The idea was that these individuals had a long-term stake in the success of the reform, and would be less invested in the present ways. This was termed the 'below 30' group'.

The 'R group' was set up under the chairmanship of the Secretary, Petroleum and Natural Gas (Vijay Kelkar). The members were the leaders of public sector and private sector firms, and independent experts.

Multiple conferences took place with the leaders of trade unions on the benefits from the liberalization program chosen by the 'below 30' group.

The reforms began by replacing administered prices by international oil prices, for all upstream companies including Oil and Natural Gas Corporation (ONGC). This was coupled with competition in new exploration. ONGC simultaneously got better revenues and greater competition. ONGC also got the freedom to operate in the world, just like any large oil company would.

The next step was open competition in the downstream industry, along with replacing the cost plus pricing regime by international parity pricing. This was introduced sequentially.

It began with industrial inputs such as naphtha and fuel oil, and then for transportation fuels such as petrol and diesel, and last for the household fuels, kerosene and LPG.

Finally, the price of natural gas was linked to international fuel oil prices, instead of a cost-plus pricing regime.

This entire story took place over a six-year period. It led to increased investments in upstream, midstream and downstream sectors, productivity gains and higher accretion of domestic oil and gas reserves.

There was no political friction in this process, as the reforms were extensively discussed, there were no unpleasant shocks either to consumers or producers, and the gains for consumers and for trade unions outweighed the pain. The entry of private firms was done through carefully designed auction procedures, so as to avoid accusations of corruption. ●●

Example 39: A Success Story: Inflation Targeting

Inflation targeting was talked about by some intellectuals in the early 2000s, as a response to the difficulties that RBI was then facing with monetary policy. This public debate at an intellectual level led to the first recommendation in a government committee report by Percy Mistry's 'Mumbai as an international financial centre' (MIFC) report in 2007. This was followed by a similar recommendation in Raghuram Rajan's report in 2009. This was followed by a draft law for inflation targeting by Justice Srikrishna's 'Financial Sector Legislative Reforms Commission'.

There was a great deal of debate in newspaper columns, blog articles, research papers and conference panels. This was followed by an RBI committee, headed by Urjit Patel, which also recommended that inflation targeting be adopted. The implementation was done in two steps: the 'Monetary Policy Framework Agreement' that was signed between the Finance Secretary, Rajiv Mehrishi, and the RBI Governor, Raghuram Rajan, on 20 February 2015, and then the amendment to the RBI Act in February 2016.

It is fitting that alongside the introduction of a 4 per cent CPI target into the RBI Act, simultaneously, the text in the preamble to the RBI Act which established the RBI in 1934 as 'a temporary measure' was deleted.

This was a long and slow journey for the emergence of RBI as a valuable organization in the Indian institutional landscape: from a temporary measure in 1934 to the first intellectual clarity in the early 2000s to the modified RBI Act in 2016. Policymakers developed a strategy and gradually executed it, in a completely open process, to the point where, at the end, it was an inevitable non-event.

A look back into history shows how the path of first doing the Monetary Policy Framework Agreement was inspired from a previous milestone in RBI history. On 26 March, 1997, the RBI and the Ministry of Finance signed an agreement through which the issuance of ad-hoc treasury bills, which were effectively a mechanism for deficit financing through money creation, was brought to an end.[1] This historic milestone was achieved through an agreement that was signed by the Finance Secretary, Montek Ahluwalia, and the RBI Governor, C. Rangarajan. This new arrangement was later formalized into the FRBM Act of 2003. But at first, progress was made through this agreement.

The Ways and Means Agreement of 1997, signed between Montek Ahluwalia and C. Rangarajan, was the direct inspiration for the idea of 2013, of making progress on defining the role of RBI through the Monetary Policy Framework Agreement, signed by Rajiv Mehrishi and Raghuram Rajan. History does not repeat itself, but it sometimes rhymes, not least because the next generation draws analogies from the experiences of its elders. The development of policy capabilities requires knowledge transmission and continuity in the policy community, running across decades, in order to ferry knowledge from the decision-making of 1997 into the decision-making of 2013.   ••

From Date of Announcement to Date Effective

From these points of view, it is particularly important to ensure there is a substantial lag between the date of a policy announcement and the date on which it becomes effective.

One of the most harmful things that is taking place in the Indian state is announcements that show up on a website in the evening, without any previous notice, and are effective tomorrow morning. These impose huge costs upon private persons, and drive up the ex-ante fear of policy risk in the minds of the firms.

Professional Capabilities in Public Policy

There is a pattern in the Indian story, where weak policy teams tend to operate in a more secretive way. There seems to be a lack of confidence in being able to win arguments in the public domain. The weakest ideas are hatched in secrecy and suddenly sprung upon the economy.

This is related to the problems of knowledge partnerships and the comfort with intellectual discourse. The best policy teams in India are well-connected into intellectual capabilities, are comfortable with criticism, and are able to debate with their critics as part of the public discourse. Weak policy teams are more likely to be disconnected from intellectual capabilities, work in secrecy, react in a hostile way to criticism, and deliver poor results in policymaking.

When a policy team is comfortable with articulating and debating a reform in public, and listens to other points of view in order to engage in a process of iterative refinement, this sends a signal to private persons that there is genuine capability in the policy process. This improves the legitimacy of the policy process and increases optimism that good work will be done.

Summing Up

वादे वादे जायते तवबोध।

Good debate to good debate, knowledge grows.

—Ancient Sanskrit proverb

Secrecy harms policy planning and execution.

In a liberal democracy, the relationship between the policymaker and the individual is not the relationship between a ruler and a subject. The policy process is a process of negotiation. The losers from a reform require fair warning. When there is ample warning, the adaptations of the private sector kick in early, and the gains for the economy are obtained in a shorter time.

Confident policymakers work in the open. Working in the open signals capability.

The most harmful events are those where a policy announcement shows up on a website in the evening, without any prior warning, and is effective the following morning. The best episodes are those with an open consultative process, where the legal instrument showing up on the website is a non-event, and there is ample lead time between the date of announcement and the date effective.

23

Criticism and Conflict Have Great Value

निन्दकाचे घर असावे शेजारी ।

Your critic should live right next door.

—Sant Tukaram

As policymakers, we tend to develop a point of view. We should, however, be humble. We are not omniscient, and we are frequently wrong. It is wise to listen to our critics as they are likely to often be right.

In our self-image of India, we used to see ourselves as a healthy liberal democracy. There are, however, many disturbing features which have crept in gradually. As an example, we may think that India has a free press, but India is now ranked 142th out of 180 countries on press freedom, by Reporters Without Borders. There is much less criticism of the establishment than is required for a policymaker to find the right decisions.

Good for Fairness, Good for Self-Interest

A healthy democracy is one in which diverse points of view are able to engage in civil discussions, engage in give-and-take, and search for common ground. Critics see the world from diverse points of view. All these points of view are legitimate elements of the democratic process of negotiation and compromise.

In this point of view, acceptance of criticism is integral to norms of good behaviour in liberal democracy, and is a noble thing.

Respecting and valuing criticism is not just about fair play. As the aphorism by Sant Tukaram at the start of the chapter says, it is also about the self-interest of the policymaker. As our information and wisdom is always limited, it is useful to have people in our midst, who will identify mistakes in our reasoning.

Neuroscientists have described a phenomenon called 'the power paradox': persons who possess power appear to become more impulsive, less risk-aware, and less adept at seeing things from other people's point of view.[1] This makes mistakes more likely. Encouraging and respecting criticism is the key path to avoiding hubris.

Another dimension of the gains from nurturing criticism is related to the idea of crossing the river by feeling the stones, using feedback loops. The best way to make progress is to take small steps, and to listen to the statistical evidence. A distributed system of criticism can tap into a larger knowledge base, and create valuable feedback through which mid-course corrections can be achieved.

The peculiar twist in India is that in many areas, the statistical system is weak. We are down to gathering anecdotal evidence by talking to people.

Critics of public policy strategies are a valuable part of society, and essential for the process of crossing the river by feeling the stones. The critic is not a bad human being; the critic is not an enemy; she is someone who has given you free advice that helps strengthen your work. Each critic is valuable insofar as she represents information from a different subset of the system under examination.

> *We must love them both, those whose opinions we share and those whose opinions we reject, for both have labored in the search for truth, and both have helped us in finding it.*

—St Thomas Aquinas

We need not agree with our critics, but our critics can help us see the flaws in our thinking and make improvements. We should not attack critics, and we should not encourage sycophants. We should foster an intellectual landscape featuring honest analysis and discussion. When person X praises the policymaker and person Y criticizes the policymaker, it is more useful for the policymaker to meet person Y and understand the logic of the criticism. This conversation may result in course corrections.

In an environment where critics are attacked and harmed, these feedback loops will be harmed. The government will then encourage sycophants, who will always praise the government. Mid-course corrections will not take place. Criticism is the essential support system. When this support system is lacking, the government will stumble from one mistake to the next. This is why authoritarian regimes, that failed to nurture the atmosphere of honesty and debate, have repeatedly failed in the human experience of thousands of years.

Conflict in the Public Domain Is the Healthy State

Authoritarian regimes look well organized and powerful, like the clean formations in a military parade. There is a great leader, and everyone is deferential to the positions of the great leader and the inner circle of power. Once a position is taken, everyone falls in line, in public, with a great deal of flattery. The great leader is incapable of making mistakes and must always be praised. There are disagreements and conflicts, of course, but they take place outside the public gaze, and tend to degenerate into pure power play.

> *No government can be long secure without a formidable opposition.*
>
> —Benjamin Disraeli

> *The absence of a true opposition has led to the rapid deterioration of democracy into a kind of totalitarianism.*
>
> —C. Rajagopalachari[2]

In contrast, democracies *look* messy. They are riven with debate, dissension, and a tug of war. Power is dispersed across many individuals and many elements of the government. Neutral and intellectual voices weigh in on the conflicts that are played out in the public domain. This policy process is a world of ideas and rational thinking, and not merely an exercise in power play. The continuous debate in an environment of dispersed power is the *reason* why democracies work well. The continuous process of criticism and debate finds and solves mistakes.

In the best of times, most people are greatly influenced by voices around them. On most subjects, we do not have deep expertise, and tend to go with the mainstream. A vibrant intellectual culture acts as a gatekeeper and protects mainstream thinking.

If novel proposals are not vigorously contested, there is the danger of oddball ideas taking root. This problem is particularly seen in authoritarian countries. When the establishment takes a certain position, and there is a great deal of sycophantic applause, the climate of opinion shifts.

When we think about criticizing the government, it is important to see that government is not a monolithic creature. Government is made up of many individuals and agencies, all of which have different points of view. Criticism of the stated position of an agency generally strengthens the hand of the reformers within the agency.

An environment where all criticism is attacked or proscribed is a recipe for policy paralysis. The really important initiatives will never achieve traction without an extensive reshaping of the larger discourse, in which criticism of the status quo is of central importance.

In an ideal world, the government is like a nice NGO. Everyone is imbued with a shared sense of what is good for the people, and all cooperate in harmoniously building a utopia. Conflicts melt away because everyone appeals to the common good. This is an idealized world of agitprop documentaries.

Public choice theory encourages us to see that everyone involved in government works for herself, and all policy making is marred by conflicts. Conflict is the normal, healthy state. Differences between persons and agencies are normal and healthy, and should be played out in the public domain. Differences arise out of conflicting interests, differences in information sets, and legitimate differences in how information is analysed.

> *If we are all in agreement on the decision, then I propose we postpone further discussion of this matter until our next meeting to give ourselves time to develop disagreement and perhaps gain some understanding of what the decision is all about.*

—Alfred P. Sloan

The protagonists of a conflict criticize each other. The media creates rancour by playing up conflict. We should disagree in polite language, maintain good personal relationships, and work through formal procedures for resolving conflicts. But we should be comfortable with conflict as the normal state. In fact, it is only in an authoritarian regime that conflict is squelched, as persons are too fearful to speak up. *If two people agree on everything, only one is doing the thinking.*

The Under-Supply of Criticism

We must recognize that in every society, there is market failure in the form of an under-supply of criticism. Criticizing the government imposes costs upon the critic. The gains from criticism are diffused; the entire society benefits from the criticism. The self-interest of the critic leads her to ignore the gains for society at large, and thus to under-supply criticism.[3]

In July 2018, Xu Zhangrun, a law professor at Tsinghua University in Beijing wrote a tough review of the hardline policies of Xi Jinping, the revival of Communist orthodoxy and the adulatory propaganda surrounding Mr Jinping and the regime. Prof. Zhangrun's essay has text such as *People nationwide, including the entire bureaucratic elite, feel once more lost in uncertainty about the direction of the country and about their own personal security, and the rising anxiety has spread into a degree of panic throughout society.* Such writing by intellectuals is the essence of building a civilized society, and imposes positive externalities upon the Chinese populace.

However, Prof. Zhangrun is alone in facing the attacks from the regime. He has been suspended, barred from teaching, investigated, barred from leaving the country, arrested, sacked.[4] The externalities do not accrue to Mr. Zhangrun, while the costs do. A few academics are courageous and speak up like this, but most would prefer silence.

This is similar to the standard economics argument about individual incentive leading to an underinvestment in higher education, as the decisionmaker does not value the spillovers, the positive externalities for society at large.

A crank is a piece of simple technology that creates revolutions.

—E. F. Schumacher

When an Andrei Sakharov goes up against a regime, the critic instantly earns respect. When an individual goes up against a billionaire, the details are more intricate, billionaires are able to resort to tactics that governments cannot employ, and there is less moral clarity. There will thus be an even greater under-supply of criticism of billionaires.

In a village economy, everyone knows each other, and economic relationships are efficiently organized under conditions of high information. In a modern market economy, however, many key relationships take place under substantial asymmetric information. In an environment where information is suppressed, there is greater fear about what lies beneath. This hampers trust and arms-length relationships.

As an example, in 2012, the research firm Veritas Investment Research Corporation wrote a research report about a firm. Two years later, the authors of the report were taken into custody by the Gurgaon police. This event changed the behaviour of all writers about firms. In addition, all lenders and investors became more concerned about the possibility that there is bad news about firms in India that is not being honestly revealed into the public domain.

Voting Turns Conflict into Better Decisions

Consider a formal or informal meeting where multiple persons, with diverse interests, come into a room to make a decision. How can the conflict be channelled most effectively, so that the knowledge and the interests of all persons in the room are well-represented and a good compromise is obtained?

When multiple viewpoints come to the table, they are normally intermediated by informal systems of power.

The persons in the room are all in a repeated game, and there is a give and take across many different elements of these relationships. It is all too easy for this process to collapse into an autocratic arrangement, where all power is placed with one or two people. Our cultural mores in India tend to give disproportionate power to the oldest or richest person in the room.

The give and take which occurs in these informal meetings is part of a larger game between these individuals. A person may sacrifice the interests of a certain constituency in one particular meeting in return for payoffs in unrelated settings. Each person who gets a seat on the table has the opportunity to non-transparently make certain trade-offs. In the limit, persons in the room sacrifice the interests of constituents or the public interest in return for personal gains.

How can conflicts be channelled into better decisions? Formal voting systems are a great tool for improving the quality of the discourse. It is useful to think of three stages of a meeting. Stage I is a approximate statement of position, by various persons, and a free format debate. Stage II consists of defining sharp propositions. Stage III consists of voting on them. What prevents persons in the room from arranging side payments in exchange for votes? Public disclosure of each vote, with a rationale statement, helps ensure personal accountability of each person for the position taken.

In India, two formal voting systems are in place: benches of judges in the judiciary, and the Monetary Policy Committee (MPC).

In the MPC, the Stage II is clear. Every meeting of the MPC has a narrow range of discrete choices that can be taken. In this case, the propositions that require voting upon are well understood. An MPC meeting then involves only Stage I and Stage III.

The Indian MPC has three votes for RBI staff and three votes for outsiders. When there is a tie, the RBI Governor has a casting vote. This suffers from the problem that the two RBI staffers are likely to be deferential towards the third vote, the RBI Governor. Thus, in effect, the Governor controls the outcome of the MPC. A better design would have one vote for the RBI Governor and four votes for independents. In that design, in order to have her way, the RBI Governor would need to persuade at least two out of the four independents. This seems like a healthy reduction in the power of the Governor.

Decision-making through a vote, with genuine dispersion of power, qualitatively improves meetings. When one or two persons dominate a room, others tend to be listless and uninterested. The knowledge and interests of all persons are not vigorously brought into the room. When a certain set of persons have a vote, each of them is fully energized to participate in the discussion, knowing that she has equal power and that her vote counts. This improves the very *discussion* that precedes the vote.

When a meeting will end in a vote, everyone in the room thinks better and participates more. This idea can be used in a wide variety of meetings in order to improve the dispersion of power and the brainpower that is brought to bear on a question.

Formal voting systems, backed by transparency, provide a powerful mechanism for aggregating knowledge and resolving political conflicts. Particularly in an early-stage liberal democracy, where the art of give and take in political negotiation is only weakly understood, formal voting systems can often mark a big step forward from the autocratic ways.

Summing Up

We should recognize the scarcity and value of criticism, and create an environment where we disagree without being disagreeable. Every critic is engaged in altruism, and harming her own self-interest, by speaking truth to power. There is market failure, in the form of an under-supply of criticism owing to positive externalities.

It is in the self-interest of the policymaker to engage with critics, so as to improve by discovering areas of weakness in the policy work. When the policymaker is short of time, meeting the critic is more useful than meeting a supporter.

Conflict and negotiation are the healthy normal state of a liberal democracy. Liberal democracy is the endless search for a middle road.

Informal meetings run the risk of collapsing into the power of one or two people. Formal voting systems are a good tool for improving the arrangement of power in the room.

24

Coming Out Right, Always,
Is Too High a Bar

Policymakers in India often like to cultivate an image of being all-knowing. They only occasionally champion an idea, and when they do, they claim that they come out right every time. Mistakes are never admitted.

Adverse Impact upon the Policy Process

When omniscience is claimed, this exerts a chilling effect upon the policy process. Real-world policymaking is difficult: there are few sure wins. A large fraction of policy initiatives fail to achieve the desired outcome. What is normal in the field of public policy is 'complex systems failure'—where there are many moving parts and they came together in an unexpected way. Failure will happen, and when failure occurs, there is no simple concept of identifying the decisive mistake and the key person who made that mistake.

When the outcome is a failure, this can puncture the claim of omniscience. The policymaker who lays claim to omniscience is, inevitably, extremely risk averse. The phrase 'policy adventurism' is a lethal one in the Indian discourse, which can kill off a proposal. The fear of failure feeds into a bias for inaction, or 'bold' policy reforms which are just social media campaigns.

There is another possibility. Under the claim of omniscience, there are policymakers who believe their own propaganda, and get afflicted by hubris. The claim of omniscience leads you to a fork on the road, where one path leads into hubristic mistakes and the other path leads into policy paralysis.

We must necessarily peer into the unknown when we choose between multiple solutions to a visible problem. In most cases, it is not entirely clear which solution is superior. To avoid policy paralysis, we have to be willing to make mistakes. To solve public policy problems, and build the Republic, requires taking actions that involve risk. A policymaker who is not making mistakes is not trying hard enough.

This was a problem in the past, and this will be a greater issue in the future. In the past, Indian policy reform consisted of low-risk projects like dismantling industrial licensing and dismantling barriers to globalization. The analytical clarity on those issues was strong and there was relatively little that could go wrong. But as these first order ideas are used up, future policy work will not be as unambiguous.

Sources of This Stance

Why has this combination of claimed omniscience and risk aversion come about?

The incentives of officials tend to be asymmetric: success is not particularly important, but failure can be career threatening. Given these asymmetric incentives, it is efficient for an official to avoid risk.

The mass media sensationalizes success or failure. It puts frail humans on a pedestal, and attributes god-like powers upon them. Policymakers enjoy the glow of media coverage that comes from claiming omniscience and engaging in propaganda, but this very pleasure creates fear of failure.

Policymakers know that the world is a complex place. In our experience, ministers closely quiz their staff, examining the extent to which the team understands the situation, and the extent to which the team will be able to execute on the proposed reform. When the team has greater knowledge, the minister becomes more willing to take the plunge. Conversely, when the team has low knowledge, the minister is more risk averse.

How to Make Progress

Success in policymaking requires creating an environment that is more supportive of failure. We need to put aside the machismo, honestly communicate our limited knowledge, and approach every policy initiative as a process of hypothesis testing. We start on a journey, and improve things based on criticism and empirical evidence. Conversely, when we insist that no mistakes are made, the process of learning stops.

How credit is allocated shapes the risk taking. In authoritarian regimes, all achievements belong to the leader, which makes it difficult to ever admit that a mistake was made. When credit is given more accurately, to the cast of thousands that work on any one policy initiative, it is easier for the leadership to accept that things have not worked out well and introduce course corrections. The best management culture is one in which we *get credit for not taking credit*. This helps create a healthy environment of trying things, accepting that some did not work, and abandoning or fixing the troubled ones.

If the policymaker claims she knows how to cross the river, there is the danger of mistakes or inaction. If, on the other hand, the policymaker only claims to know how to feel the stones, and approaches the larger community with a sense of humility, this gives an environment that is more conducive to taking risks, learning from mistakes, and refining policy strategies based on evidence.

Experimentation is the controlled process of making mistakes, that induces learning. Wherever humanly possible, new policy initiatives should first be rolled out on a small experimental basis. This will create experience based on which we can make more rational moves in the future. And, if something does not work too well, we can back away from it without having suffered too high a cost.

It takes two hands to clap; an open and participatory process requires a commensurately capable policy community. Such capabilities are often lacking. The early stages of the policy pipeline (data, research, policy proposals) are often weak, and it is hard to find 20 experts in the country on a question at hand. The capability of the policy community is itself a resource, that needs to be nurtured. An approach of acknowledging the uncertainties, and discussing and drawing lessons from failure, in an open and participatory policy process, induces improvements in the capability of the policy community over time.[1]

At its best, a positive feedback loop emerges between a participatory policy process and the capabilities of the policy community. A sound policy process is one which is based on formulating hypotheses, undertaking experiments and learning from the outcomes. This process makes demands on the policy community, and in the process strengthens the capabilities of the policy community which obtains learning-by-doing. As these capabilities become stronger, the confidence of the leadership improves and there is a greater willingness to take risk. At its best, this can yield a spiral of expanding capability.

Summing Up

Officials of the Indian government tend to be averse to changing things. This is rooted in the bureaucratic incentives that penalize failure. In order to make faster progress, we need to create an institutional culture that is more accepting of failure.

Part of the problem lies in the official line, which does not recognize or discuss failure. But most public policy work is characterized by failure, and we would all be better off by discussing this in a comfortable and realistic way.

When a policymaker lays claim to omniscience, it is difficult to admit that a mistake was made. It is better to honestly speak about the uncertainties that are being faced, and embark on policymaking as a process of discovery.

Risk aversion by the leadership is often a rational response to the low capabilities of the team and of the domestic policy community. An open and participatory policy process, of hypothesis testing and experimentation, helps set off a positive feedback loop where capabilities are created, which enables greater risks to be taken.

25

A Country Is Not a Company

Robert McNamara came out of the Second World War and joined the Ford Motor Company in 1946. He was extremely successful in this, rising to lead the company in 1960 (at the age of 44). He was the pioneer of modern management practices, and the company thrived on his watch.

The President of the United States, John F. Kennedy read about Robert McNamara in an article in *Time* magazine on 2 December 1960. The brothers John F. Kennedy and Robert F. Kennedy interviewed McNamara for the position of the US Secretary of Defence on 8 December 1960. McNamara demurred, saying that he did not know anything about government, and Kennedy replied, 'I don't know how to be president either'. A week later, he became the US Secretary of Defence. But his time as US Secretary of Defence, 1961–1968, worked out rather poorly. Why did the starring CEO of the age stumble when he became the equivalent of the union government minister of defence?

Before 1991, most firms in India were managed poorly. We now have a large number of extremely well-run firms in

India. The key persons in these firms are legitimately proud of their ability to run large complex organizations. Alongside this, we see the shambolic Indian state, which is unable to get basics right. Can management skills and techniques carry over from the Indian private sector into government? Unfortunately, the skill and rhythm that is required in the public policy landscape is different from what works in for-profit firms.

Government Lacks Feedback Loops

All big private firms are listed for trading on the stock market and see a stock price. The vast machinery of speculation in financial markets produces a real-time measure of the performance of the firm. Internally, private firms see operational management information system (MIS) statements that are updated daily. Revenue and profit are simple tools to distil the working of the firm down into a numerical yardstick.

Are there comparable measures which can be used in public policy? Is GDP growth a good measure of how the government is faring? Later in this book, we show concerns about chasing the yardstick of GDP growth. In any case, in India, we are at the early stages of learning how to measure GDP.

Is the performance of Nifty a good measure of how the government is faring? The movements of the stock market index express *surprises* in the outlook for corporate profitability; this is only weakly related to the achievements of the leadership.

Is the rupee dollar exchange rate a good measure of how the government is faring? The fluctuations of the exchange rate have nearly no link with how the country is faring. Depreciation is often beneficial for the economy. When a leadership starts viewing the exchange rate as a measure of its performance, this is generally harmful.

There is thus no information system that generates feedback loops for government, in the way that accounting data and stock market data generates feedback loops in private firms.

Government Agencies Are Monopolies

The customers of private firms generally have choices about who they buy from. State agencies are generally monopolies. The only place that you can get a driver's license is a government office; the customer has no choice. The policy thinker, Manish Sabharwal, once said that RBI's bond exchange, the Negotiated Dealing System (NDS), 'has hostages, not customers'. Nobody chooses to be a member of the NDS, they are forced to use it. This diminishes organizational performance.

The leadership of a private firm fears financial nonperformance, which will ultimately lead to the loss of jobs and empire. Persistent weak performance can induce a sale of the firm to a new shareholder, who can impose painful changes upon the firm. Private firms face the threat of a bankruptcy process where the firm can be shut down or fundamentally reorganized.

None of these possibilities influence employees in the government. There are rare events where a government agency is closed down. Politicians fear losing elections. Officials have no fear.

The RBI was created in 1934. Consider the thousand-odd large private firms which also existed in 1934. By 2019, most of these firms had gone under, in the face of competitive pressure.

The survivors (e.g., Tata Steel) were unrecognizably different, in 2019, compared with their organizational capabilities of 1934. But the RBI of 1934 has survived into 2019 without facing any competitive pressure, while having small changes in its organizational capabilities.

With private firms, we see something remarkable in the organizational culture of a Tata Steel or an IBM, firms that have managed to stay relevant over very long time periods. In government, in contrast, the oldest agencies are likely to have the most outdated internal arrangements.

Government's Coercive Power Is Qualitatively Different

In a private firm, the levers controlled by the management cover products, production processes and the internal organization of the firm. In government, there is similar decision-making power about the internal organization of government. But the surpassing feature of government is the monopoliztic power to coerce.

The state has a monopoly on violence. It is able to coerce private persons, either to pay taxes or to change behaviour. This yields a fundamental arrogance about state organizations, that private organizations do not suffer from. The puzzle of public policy lies in reining in employees who have the power to coerce, to prohibit, to raid and to imprison.

Government Has Greater Complexity

A big firm in India has 25,000 employees. Compared with this, state structures are vast. Indian Railways has 1.3 million employees. Even if the efficient staffing at Indian Railways is half this size, it is a vast and complex organization when compared with what we see in the private sector.

The public policy process plays out not just through employees but through everyone, as coercive steps by the state induce changed behaviour by the people, which feeds back into the working of the state, and so on. This further increases the complexity of decision-making. Policy decisions have to take into account the internal behaviour of large complex government organizations, and then the responses of the general public, which in India's case is above a billion people. This is a scale of complexity which is just not found in private firms.

Government Has to Prize Rules over Deals

In a private firm, there is ample room for discretion. The idea is to make many tactical decisions—'a hustle here and a hustle there'—that add up to profit.

As an organization becomes larger and more complex, there is greater use of formal rules. In a 10-man firm, every decision is tactical. By the time we get to a 1000-man firm, there will be an HR policy that will shape and constrain HR actions. If a firm has three franchisees, each of the three contracts can be negotiated separately. But if a firm has a thousand franchisees, there will be a policy framework that determines a few standardized contracts that are applied in all settings.

In government, this evolution towards rules is carried forward to an extreme extent. Given the unique features of government, it is pragmatic to work through policy frameworks and not tactical actions. We establish sound general frameworks, and work within them for a long time. We avoid transaction-specific decisions, even when we see a particular situation where the general policy is yielding the wrong answer.

In addition, Article 14 of the Constitution of India requires the Indian state to treat identically placed persons identically. There is no such constraint upon private firms. Private firms can make deals, but states need rules.

Governments Must Disperse Power

The management of a private firm is often quite autocratic, partly because its internal staff is all that it controls. In contrast, public policy requires dispersion of power. The job description for a role in public policy is a package of policy knowledge, team building and nuanced negotiating ability. These are often elusive for persons with a background of leadership in autocratic firms.

Successful governments feature a slow process of debate, negotiation and compromise. The leadership in the world of public policy requires the traits of listening, respecting and negotiating middle roads. This is a very different organizational culture when compared with what is found in most private firms.

It is interesting to see that the organizational DNA in the largest and most complex firms veers towards the strategies of government. The largest and most complex firms have reduced power of the CEO, dispersed decision-making structures, and a greater emphasis on rules rather than discretion. The challenge of public administration lies in carrying this organizational evolution, from small firms to the biggest firms, further up a hundred-fold.

Governments Operate on Longer Horizons

Many in the world of business have come to revere the Alpine-style assault, where a firm builds something very big in almost no time. Instagram got to 10 million users in a year and was bought for $1 billion in two years. A world-straddling company like Google was only founded in 1998. Successful management teams are often imbued with the idea of saving time.

The rhythm of public policy is quite different: to do good things requires a long slow ascent. Big sudden phenomena in the world of policy are generally harmful and/or failures.

Summing Up

We in India revere success and wealth, and there is a lot of respect for business folk. We tend to assume (say) that sound HR practices in TCS will work well in government. But we should be cautious when thinking about transferring expertise into the world of public policy.

Companies have feedback loops where the daily MIS shows how things are faring, where quarterly financial statements are put out, and the stock price is updated in real time. When mistakes are made, they kick off corrections. Governments have no comparable feedback loops.

Most firms operate in competitive marketplaces. When mistakes are made, they lose customers. Governments have hostages, not customers, and there is no choice.

Firms wield no coercive power. They have to be nice to customers all the time. Governments wield coercive power. The danger of functionaries that mistreat individuals is ever-present. Process design for government organizations involves establishing check-and-balance against this threat.

Big firms are small compared with government organizations.

A lot of decisions in private firms can be tactical. Governments become the most effective when they establish rules rather than discretion and eschew day-to-day tactical responses. Governments are bound by equal treatment (Article 14 of the Constitution) while private firms have no such constraint.

The management of a private firm is often quite autocratic. Successful governments, in contrast, do not have a CEO. Success comes from a long process of debate, negotiation and compromise.

Firms tend to work on short time horizons. The best governments work on long time horizons.

For all these reasons, the expertise on the working of private firms does not carry over into public policy, and vice versa. A country is not a company.[1]

26

Beware the Rule of Officials

Separation of powers is the standard doctrine worldwide, through which we check against the problem of a powerful state. The state is broken up into three branches, which are set in conflict with each other: the legislative, the executive and the judicial branches. This reduces the concentration of power and better protects the individual. Separation of power is enshrined in the Constitution of India and it is part of the basic structure of the Constitution.[1] If separation of powers is built out correctly, it would limit the power of the executive branch.

There are many aspects of the Indian state, however, where the separation of powers doctrine is violated. Consider the judicial wing associated with regulatory actions.

Securities regulators in other countries fuse the legislative and executive functions. They write regulations and they conduct investigations. But the cases brought by the securities regulator are heard in an ordinary court.

In India, given the delays in judicial enforcement, we placed a judicial function at SEBI also. With this, the separation of powers doctrine is absent at a regulator like SEBI. SEBI has become a very powerful organization, by the fusing of legislative, executive and judicial functions, and having a monopoly on enforcing securities law. In the memorable phrase of the policy thinker M. Sahoo, regulators in India are 'mini-states'.[2] This concentration of power may have been expedient in the short term, but it has hampered the emergence of state capacity.

From the Colonial State to the Administrative State

While British India established some legislative and judicial structures, the Indian state was a colonial one, where power was concentrated with a small number of white officials. While there were some elements of rule *by* law, it was not rule *of* law. It was not a democracy in the sense of dispersion of power, e.g., across the three branches of government. These problems did not end after independence: Many design features of the Government of India Act, 1935, influenced the drafting of the Constitution of India and thus shape our world today.

The term 'administrative state' refers to the rule of officials, without the checks and balances of a democracy. The colonial roots of the Indian state created an organizational culture of an administrative state. These were underlined through the slant towards socialism that came after independence. Under socialism also, liberal democratic forces are kept under check, the rule of law is underplayed, and arbitrary power is amassed by officials and politicians.

From the late 1980s onward, India has tended further toward the rule by officials who have fine grained control over the decisions of private persons, with functions that veer into legislative and judicial roles. This generates state coercion of private persons that is excessive, unpredictable and unjust.

The constitutional vision involves laws that are drafted by elected members of the legislature. In modern India, while politicians do green light laws at a high level, when it comes to any level of detail, bills are generally drafted by officials and their research assistants. The role of the legislature in the drafting of laws has wilted away. Once the anti-defection law fell into place, no one member of the legislature has any influence by voting on a law.

The emergence of the administrative state is a major flaw of the modern Indian state. India is supposed to be a constitutional democracy, but in many respects, power is not dispersed and officials possess arbitrary power. We are in an unhealthy world of bad rules and high discretion.

There is much concern about the administrative state in the Western literature. Those researchers cannot imagine the level of arbitrary power than an Indian official commands. These include the power to give oral or written orders to one firm without judicial review, to destroy a business without judicial review, to incarcerate a person without trial under the regime of 'jail is the norm and bail is the exception' and impose harm through lawless surveillance and investigation.

For many educated people in India, there is class affinity with officials (and not with politicians). This has tended to blind the Indian intelligentsia to the emergence of, and the adverse consequences of, the administrative state. The maturation of Indian democracy requires rising above this predilection.

The main machinery of this book involves reforming the administrative state in an incremental way. We treat the presence of a regulator like FSSAI as given, and think about narrowing its powers to address market failure, establishing checks and balances upon its functioning, and becoming stingy in bestowing coercive power upon a low capability agency. We think about getting back to one-MP-one-vote, away from the anti-defection law. We envision a greater role of better-functioning parliamentary committees that will bring back a greater role for the legislature in the drafting of laws.

We now turn to a first principles examination of the administrative state.

The Traditional Case for Strong Contract Enforcement

Let us start at the objective of contract enforcement by courts. This is generally seen as being the foundation of business. When contracts are not honoured, it hampers contracting by governments and firms. It holds back decision-making, risk management and investment planning. Through this, an efficient and independent judiciary is an essential foundation of the market economy.

Under conditions of weak contract enforcement, people would limit their contracting to friends and family.

'Repeated games' would spring up, within which there is good behaviour, but this can only be with a narrow class of counterparties. There would be an efficiency loss, because markets would become less competitive. A new player would not be able to dislodge friends and family from my contracts.

When contract enforcement is weak, firms would specialize less, there would be greater internal production and reduced use of contracting. This would adversely impact upon transactions and thus productivity.

While these effects are present, they are not particularly large. In this first cut of the analysis, the adverse impact of poor contract enforcement is relatively limited. The role of the judiciary, however, runs much deeper: it impacts upon the possibilities for addressing market failure without requiring an administrative state.

Private Solutions for Market Failure

Consider a situation where property rights are clear: you own a garden. There can be a contract between you and me that governs my use of the garden. But suppose I use your garden when you are away, without your permission. This creates a 'tort'. In the common law, this can be the source of private litigation.[3]

Many situations of market failure fit under this rubric. The aggrieved person is able to go to court and ask to be compensated for harm. If person A faces the credible threat that person B can win damages, this will constrain her behaviour.

In these situations, addressing market failure only requires the common law of torts, and courts that enforce this law. There is no requirement of a government bureaucracy that does regulation.

This pathway addresses a significant part of the market failure associated with negative externalities and asymmetric information. This pathway requires judicial capacity and property rights.

What about the problem where the persons adversely affected are many? A factory may emit pollution which may harm many individuals, none of whom have adequate incentive to undertake the expenditure of litigation. This collective action problem is solved using 'class action litigation' through which a group of people organize themselves to demand damages. This pathway requires judicial capacity, property rights and class action lawsuits.[4]

This vision of enforcement relies on the aggrieved person taking recourse to courts. It involves *private enforcement* of law. As an example, if a person or a group of persons were adversely affected by securities fraud, *they* would gather evidence and sue.

In this book, we have emphasized the power of private negotiation, as envisioned by Ronald Coase, for arriving at private solutions to many externality problems. These private solutions can flourish when, and only when, the courts are swift and competent. Otherwise, these contracts are not enforceable and the Coasean approach to addressing certain market failure is infeasible.

From this perspective, a great deal of market failure can be addressed through contracts, torts, class action lawsuits and private enforcement.[5] Looking back into Indian history, this pathway was ruled out when, after independence, there were difficulties in judiciary, and policymakers preferred to concentrate greater power in the executive branch and its agents (the regulators).

Example 40: SEBI's Monopoly on Enforcing Securities Law

Consider the establishment of SEBI, in 1988–1992. In the early drafting of the SEBI Act, it was felt that if private persons could sue, on the grounds of violation of securities law, there was a greater risk of harassment. Therefore, the SEBI Act, unlike the US Securities Act, prohibits private persons from suing for violations of securities law. Only SEBI has the right to initiate such actions. Victims of securities law violations do not have this right.

Alongside this, India lacks a class action lawsuit mechanism, so there is no mechanism for (say) the shareholders of Satyam to sue. The design that was adopted in building SEBI was that *only* SEBI can initiate enforcement actions against a person.

These are the building blocks of the administrative state. Now, persons who have experienced harm are supplicants before SEBI, requesting SEBI to enforce securities law. Now the difficulties of public management impact upon the enforcement process. There is also a perverse effect: As private persons lack the ability to use securities law, there is a bias in favour of using criminal law. ••

Example 41: The People versus the State in the Bankruptcy Process

In the concept of bankruptcy, if any person is aggrieved because of non-performance by a firm, that person can initiate the bankruptcy process.

When it comes to defaults by financial service providers, however, in India, only the state can initiate the bankruptcy process. A private person may be aggrieved but is powerless.[6] ••

The Policy Possibilities for a Country with High Judicial Capacity

India today is at a polar extreme, away from mature common law jurisdictions, with the domination of the administrative state. We are weak on clarity of law, contract enforcement, torts, class action lawsuits and private enforcement. Organizations like SEBI are increasingly stepping into the shoes of the erstwhile central planning system.

In the late 1980s and 1990s, the leadership at the Ministry of Finance and at SEBI was engaged in building SEBI in a practical way. They treated courts as flawed and looked for ways to make progress. While such strategies are useful in the short run, at a deeper level, they have limitations. When power is concentrated at organizations like SEBI, these organizations will find it difficult to achieve state capacity. The detailed interference by the administrative state in the economy saps economic vitality. There is a need to rethink this construction of the administrative state, in order to set India on a path of sustained economic growth into becoming a mature market economy.

The detailed licence-permit raj, and the fear of investigation agencies, are arguably at a peak in India today. How do we restore freedom? The agenda of liberalization and economic freedom requires going back to the foundations of common law: to a world of contracts, torts, negotiation, private enforcement and class action lawsuits. This is what is required to scale back the administrative state.

The traditional conception of economists on contract enforcement has been that courts are required to enforce contracts. When the courts fail in this, the implications are relatively modest: there is reduced specialization and there are repeated games. Our perspective, however, runs deeper. When the courts fail, we get the rule of officials.

After independence, we fared poorly on development of the judiciary. The coping mechanisms adopted by policymakers, in response to the failure of the judiciary, have their own harmful consequences. We need to address these failures at the root cause, through fundamental change in the judicial branch. We need to push back on the new central planning system, this administrative state, and graduate to a world of much greater reliance on the judiciary, a world of contracts, torts, class action lawsuits, and private enforcement.

Summing Up

The 'administrative state' is the rule of bureaucrats. This is a state where the officials manning the executive creep into controlling legislative and judicial functions. In the administrative state, politics—the process of negotiation between interest groups—has a limited role. The Indian approach to central planning of the economy, where officials have considerable control over the life of private persons, is uncomfortably close to the administrative state.

Economists have emphasized the role of the judiciary in contract enforcement, which enables the market economy. While contract enforcement is important, the more important role for judicial capacity lies in private solutions to market failure.

Coasean solutions involve private persons entering into complex contracts, which then require commensurate contract enforcement. Many negative externalities can be solved through tort law, as long as litigation is efficacious. Many classic problems of asymmetric information, where we do consumer protection, can be addressed through torts. When many people are adversely affected in a problem like pollution from a factory, the collective action problem can be solved through class action suits. When private people are able to sue, and state agencies do not have a monopoly on enforcing laws, this reduces the reliance on state agencies for enforcing laws.

The agenda of economic freedom in India is ultimately about scaling back the administrative state. This journey runs through great improvements in the courts.

27

The Digital Pathway to State Capacity

In 1947, the UK had 100 per cent female literacy while India was at 6 per cent. The intellectual community looked at the global cross-section of GDP and felt that education was a big differentiator between poor and rich countries. One path to education lies in industrialized, state-driven schooling. Enormous resources were put into such schooling by policymakers all over the world, and in India.

About 75 years later, when we look back, there are countries like South Korea, which graduated into prosperity and liberal democracy, but there are numerous countries with similar schooling outcomes which did not. If Nehru had been told of an India with about 75 per cent female literacy, he would expect the bulk of the development journey is completed. We cannot help look back at the lukewarm payoffs to the enormous increase in schooling, and wonder *where has all the education gone?*[1] Within each country, more educated people are richer than less educated people, but *across* countries, the expansion of schooling does not correlate with economic growth. Perhaps the state-led expansion of the school system

279

failed to generate much learning. Perhaps schooling is the consequence of a successful economy and not the cause.

> *We see the computer age everywhere but in the productivity statistics.*

—Robert Solow, 1987[2]

In 1990, the UK had a lot of computers in government while India did not. Optimists looked at the global cross-section of computers in government and felt that this was an important differentiator between poor and rich countries. Enormous financial and coercive resources were put into high technology by policymakers all over the world, and in India. As with schooling, technology became the fashionable solution. There were hopes of 'leapfrogging', of poor countries directly transiting into a silicon nirvana, avoiding the stage of legacy paper-based systems seen in many advanced countries.

Many millions of CPUs have been put into the computerization of the Indian state, and in the computerization of the lives of private persons in sync with the demands of the state. More has been done, by way of going down this route, than the dreams of the technology enthusiasts of 1990. In India today, there are more CPUs per unit population, and more CPUs in government per unit population, when compared with the UK of 1990. The computer age seems to be everywhere, but state capability remains elusive. The period with the biggest surge of computers in government in India, after 2011, lines up nicely with the period of reduced growth.

There are also dark undertones. Is the state using information, created and amassed through the computer revolution, to control the people? It was always hard to become a republic: it is always hard for the principal (the people) to control the agent (the state). Has the computer revolution tipped the balance of power in favour of the state? How should we think about the promise and peril of the computer revolution?

Computers for the People versus Computers for the State

In the private sector, individuals and firms have adopted a great deal of computer technology. In the popular discourse, there is dizzy optimism about the benefits. Economists are cautious about the magnitude of the gains. Robert Solow's warning reminds us that casual empiricism about the productivity gains from the computer revolution is not borne out by careful calculations.

Many firms that purchase IT fail to obtain productivity gains. But in the private sector, the arrangement of incentives is reasonably sound, and in numerous situations, IT has worked very well. In India, IT had a decisive impact in exporting of software services. In addition, when processes were digitized worldwide, it became possible to produce services in India which were previously non-tradeable.[3] Both these phenomena—software services production, and the export of services over telecom lines—have worked very well for India. Millions of people are deriving their livelihood from them. For the large firms, IT is now India's biggest industry.[4]

In this chapter, we think about the possibilities for transforming state capability by exploiting the computer revolution. The optimistic reading of IT in the private sector does not carry over to the state sector, for three reasons. IT scored a major impact in the Indian private sector in exports, but the state does not export. When individuals and private firms make decisions about IT adoption, they are reasonably well incentivized, but the accountability and incentives of the state are largely faulty. Finally, the state exercises coercive power, while private people do not.

Technological Change within a Government Organization versus Policy Reform

In most services organizations, it is possible to obtain productivity gains through 'business process engineering' ('BPR'). This involves redesign of processes at a relatively fundamental level.[5] IT systems make possible a rearrangement of information, incentives and power. The improved systems will often impose large-scale changes in the organization. Some people will lose power and others will gain it.[6] Conceiving and implementing such change requires the passion of a correctly motivated leadership.

As an example, the 'Tax Information Network' (2002), which was implemented for tracking tax deducted at source in income tax, was not a mere encoding of existing practices in a computer system. It represented a new idea on how IT could be used to perform a cross-check which fundamentally eliminated TDS fraud. This constituted rethinking the business process, not just encoding existing processes in an IT system.

In contrast, the mere computerization of traditional processes—'lift and shift' projects—tends to preserve the erstwhile arrangement of information, incentives and power, and yields limited gains. This helps us understand the Solow productivity puzzle: many organizations that use IT fail to achieve the requisite organizational transformation.

Most elements of the Indian state have low levels of state capability through the present configuration of information, incentives and power. The leadership of government organizations is generally not well motivated. There is little accountability, there is little aspiration for improved performance. *Policy reform*—and not just automation of erstwhile processes—is what is required.

Policy reform is hard, but buying IT is fashionable. Buying IT does not have to go with policy reform, with rethinking the organization. Under these conditions, a lot of IT is brought in at a superficial level, to computerize conventional processes, with low gains.[7]

And so we see a policy landscape where technology projects abound. There are rent-seeking opportunities in the additional expenditure. The leadership gets to claim that progress is being made, and the press believes that more computer systems are synonymous with progress. Incumbents in the organization know that for the few years that it takes to build and implement the system, the status quo is protected. To paraphrase P. Sainath, everybody loves a new IT system.

It is better to focus on the policy reform. In this reform process, IT can be a valuable element, but it is only an element, and it should not occupy centre stage.

Example 42: A Success Story: Computer Technology in the New Pension System

In the late 1990s, the Indian pension system consisted of a defined benefit pension system that was mandatory for government employees, and the EPFO, which was mandatory for large private firms. Both these systems had fundamental policy problems.

The incremental, plumbing approach to computer technology would have been to automate the working of these systems while preserving the policy framework and associated political economy map of interests.

That is not what was done with the New Pension System (NPS). The NPS represented a fundamental policy reform: an individual account (as opposed to socialized payments to pensioners), defined contribution (as opposed to defined benefits), portable pension account (as opposed to non-portable civil servants pension promises) with private fund management (as opposed to no funds in the pay-as-you-go system).[8]

The NPS could not have been implemented without modern computer technology. The design work for the NPS, in the late 1990s, was futuristic, in envisioning pervasive data connectivity all across India and mobile phones in the hands of each worker. The NPS is often seen as a high technology system. It is a fundamental policy reform, in which the IT is used as a tool.   ••

State Capacity in the Digital Age

In this book, we have emphasized four dimensions that shape the extent to which a problem in public policy is a difficult one (transactions, discretion, stakes, opacity). The computer revolution reshapes this landscape: many difficult problems become easier once IT systems are in play.[9]

Public systems that have to do a large number of transactions are easier in implementation using modern technology. When millions of transactions have to be done, it is difficult to track these using paper-based system, but IT systems fare better.

Sometimes, a high-transaction problem can be converted into a low-transaction problem, by having a government organization release an application programming interface ('API') and a competitive private industry takes care of the last mile. As an example, railway reservation only requires API access to be released by Indian Railways, and after that all travel agents would sell train tickets.

Some high-discretion problems can be turned into low-discretion problems by using computer technology.[10]

Once again, the problem of railway reservations is the canonical example. Control of the information system—of which seats are taken and which are not—was in the hands of the frontline railway employee, and that control was taken away using a computer-based reservation system.

Another good example of removal of discretion is the process of obtaining approval for the name of a new company. In the physical system, the local office of the Registrar of Companies was a source of delays and petty corruption, while in the new MCA-21 system, there is a more rules-based based approval for a name.

This gives us a nuanced toolkit to think about the role of IT in improving the policy landscape in India: it helps in addressing problems with high transactions and some problems with high discretion. It does not obviate the larger complexities of public policy.

The Difficulties of Digital Transformation within a Government Organization

Let us set policy reform aside; let us focus on the electronification of conventional processes. In these projects also, there are many difficulties in getting to useful systems; the landscape is littered with failed projects.[11]

Large-scale transaction processing systems are hard to design as there are many possibilities for what the data and consequential actions have to be. While things are better within a city or a state, at the level of the union government, in a population of 1.4 billion, there are 1400 people who are one-in-a-million outliers. In a transaction processing system that does a billion transactions a year, there are 1000 situations that are rather unusual.

In a human-based system, intelligence and decision-making power at the front-line human leads to relatively sensible, common sensical, and just responses to peculiar situations. In a computer system, considerable capability is required in building a system that caters to all these cases. When state capability is low, the IT system is likely to be weak, and there will be numerous situations where the IT system—accompanied by disempowered frontline employees—will result in nonsensical or unjust outcomes.

In the last decade, there has been an upsurge of engineers becoming civil servants, and there is much enthusiasm to wield the hammer of building a computer system. This has led to many siloed applications built by one official at a time. The data within these applications is locked within the siloed system. Data movement tends to involve manual intervention, incompatible file structures, and delays. Information flows through computer files induces multiple different versions of the data, and thereby, a loss of trust in the data. Siloed systems are sized for the requirements of a small unit of government, and cannot serve information requirements of other users, even if API access is made possible. We need a better strategic sense about how IT in government should be done, as opposed to the proliferation of sub-scale siloed systems.

A classification scheme helps us think about digital transformation projects. At the most basic level, transactions should happen through the system, and not in a spreadsheet or paper register. At this point, basic efficiencies of transaction processing are obtained. Once this is done, discretion is reduced, and it should become possible to obtain better performance from front-line employees. The next stage consists of statistical analysis of the data being captured in the system to introduce better intelligence into the IT system. Finally, the highest level of sophistication is where research induces improved situational awareness, better strategic thinking, and better policy formulation. IT in government needs to walk up this ladder of quality.

When state capability is low, there is significant project implementation risk. In India, we have seen a good deal of project failure in state IT projects.[12] To paraphrase an old adage, to err is human, but to really foul up things requires a computer.

Summing Up

The digital revolution has done a lot for the Indian private sector. We tend to assume that big gains will similarly and naturally flow when digital transformation is done in government organizations. This picture is much more clouded.

In most areas in India, what is required is policy reform, and not mere computerization of the existing procedures. IT projects are fashionable, and we are too quick to settle.

Two out of the four dimensions of what is hard in public policy—high-transaction problems and high-discretion problems—can obtain significant gains through the use of computer technology.

But there is many a slip between cup and lip; simplistic automation projects have higher risk and lower impact than meets the eye. When state capacity is low, it is hard to build and fully utilize IT.

28

State Power That Reshapes Society in the Digital Age

There are two distinct strands of thought in the field of technology and policy. So far, we have talked about the use of computer technology *within* a government organization, in problems such as railway reservation, MCA21, income tax or GST.

We now turn to the distinct strand of thinking, of using state power to control society in this digital age. The central planning instincts of the 1950s have got a fresh lease of life, with the use of state power to force certain technology choices upon private persons. State power is being used to force the use of technology upon society in ways that makes the lives of private people more visible to the state. Greater control of society, reduced levels of freedom for the people, are being made possible through the use of computer technology by the state.

Premature State Legibility

The phrase 'state legibility' comes from James C. Scott[1] and refers to the ways in which the state is able to see the people. A key insight of political science is that enhanced state legibility often has unintended consequences. The state is a community of persons who pursue their own self-interest. When the state knows more about the people, this can be used in ways that are harmful to the people.

There are two paths through which state legibility rises. The growing use of computers in society has created a data trail that the state can see. As Indian democracy is at a fledgling stage, there are no checks against officials surveilling or viewing the digital life of an individual or a firm. Officials have achieved an unprecedented level of invasion into the lives of the people through their ability to force individuals to supply passwords to electronic devices and systems.

Alongside this, the coercive power of the state has been used to force greater use of electronics so that more data is available to harvest. The state has instrumented its territory, with tools like UIDAI, video cameras,[2] black boxes placed inside telecom companies, and mass surveillance in finance. Traditional pathways to privacy have been closed, to force the people to interact inside the zone of mass surveillance ('the panopticon'), e.g., blocking cash transactions above a certain size.

Enhanced state legibility, absent checks and balances, increases the power of the state. This is an additional reason why many new IT projects in government suit the self-interest of persons in the state.

Every time the state obtains more information about the people, there is the need for commensurate checks and balances. In the journey to political modernization of a country, there is a race between state legibility and political maturity. Some countries suffer from '*premature state legibility*'.[3]

The motive force for these problems is not only new elements of state legibility. In many situations, the greater use of information technology in the country, and by the state, has changed the legal effects of *existing* laws.

Consider the laws about electronic surveillance. The Indian state used to have considerable power to snoop on individuals, going back to British times. These laws did not amount to much, as the Indian state did not have the capability of listening in upon too many calls. Things changed, however, with the rise of modern computer technology, with the increased shift of person-to-person communications into electronic form. For the first time, the Indian state now has the ability to obtain and analyse a large volume of electronic communications. The old laws are now the foundation of certain kinds of mass surveillance.

Example 43: Restrictions on Storage of Goods

As an example, consider the Essential Commodities Act (ECA) which forces limits on storage of many agricultural products. When warehouses were owned largely by individuals, the ECA did not matter too much. Every now and then, a local policeman would use the ECA to raid a local businessman, but for the rest, the impact upon the economy was limited.

This changed with the rise of large corporations in warehousing. These corporations have computer systems that capture all information and have a higher compliance culture. They have more at stake and cannot violate a law. Here, for the first time, the ECA has come to be a binding constraint. New life has been infused into an old piece of the repressive apparatus through the emergence of a more legible private sector.   ●●

The growing technological sophistication of the economy thus infuses new life into old elements of the repressive apparatus, and we go from irrelevant dirigisme to oppressive dirigisme.[4]

India aspires for Swedish levels of cashless operation of the economy without Swedish levels of democracy. Under the best of circumstances, it is difficult for a poor country to emerge as a vibrant democracy. Premature state legibility has made this task harder in India.

Premature State Control

Modern computer technology helps generate greater control of the populace in the hands of the state. One part of this control flows directly from greater state legibility. In addition, many projects of state control are more feasible in the digital age.

Example 44: State Control of Covid-19 Vaccination

Health policymakers should have worried about improving supply, augmenting demand by poor people, and creating conditions for the price system to deliver results on vaccines. There were health policy failures when, instead of going with the grain of the price system, a centralized program was built, where the union government controlled every vaccination transaction in India.

The state was not able to carry out enough vaccinations through its state-controlled system, the simplistic and rigid rules of state-led vaccination were suboptimal for many people, and state power was used to block all private efforts that might have augmented vaccination. At two points in time—the deaths in the second wave and the Omicron outbreak—there was much regret about the inadequacies of vaccination.

This allure of premature state control was enabled by IT systems (Cowin and UIDAI).   ••

When liberal democracy works well, this increased power goes along with commensurate checks and balances, and there is hope that the increased control of the people is used in benign ways. When political system maturation is the bottleneck, increased control of the people leads to more problematic outcomes.

Pitfalls

A great deal of traditional knowledge about the difficulties of state intervention, about the limitations of high modernism, carry forward into the computer revolution.

The old wisdom asserts that *the state should not produce private goods*; this is best done by a competitive private industry. This raises questions about many attempts by the Indian state to build public sector organizations that produce private goods, e.g., the Public Credit Registry.[5]

The old wisdom asserts that *the state should not engage in protectionism*, in using the coercive power of the state to interfere in cross-border transactions between consenting adults. Data localization is an example of such protectionism.[6] Similarly, in the field of payments, state power has been used to block foreign companies from operating in India.

The old wisdom asserts that *genuine policy work is hard, and a variety of escape valves will be desired which avoid actually getting the job done.* A good example was the development of Aarogya

Setu, the contact-tracing app, which became the silver bullet solution. In fact, the bulk of contact tracing is a complex, labour-intensive process, which requires institution building, and this was largely not done. Similarly, it was easier to build UIDAI rather than actually solve the Indian mistakes of KYC.[7] By using the coercive power and the deep pockets of the state, it is easy for policymakers to build organizations that achieve revenues, transactions, and empires, by supplanting private businesses.

The old wisdom asserts that *central control is harmful*. In a situation like UPI, the Indian state controlled whether and when WhatsApp was able to become a participant of the retail payments system. In the situation of Covid-19, there was an unprecedented development in India's history, where the state interposed itself into the doctor -patient relationship, and controlled who could get vaccinated, using the Cowin software.

The old wisdom asserts that *central planning induces stagnation*, that the government should not be involved in the details of products, processes or production. As an example, in the field of payments, UPI is a state-backed monopoly where the government controls the details of products and processes. The market economy is an innovation machine, as firms ceaselessly come up with new ideas in response to the needs of consumers and the envelope of technological possibilities. Government-controlled systems, in contrast, are unresponsive to users, and respond to ulterior considerations.

Central planning systems do constitute a state-led mobilization of economic resources and technology and they do yield non-zero results. There have been millions of moments of user delight owing to UPI or Air India. However, state-controlled systems tend to have low productivity (owing to public management), they tend to be monolithic systems that lack in nuance (while the diversity of India requires many different solutions for diverse use cases), and they tend to stagnate (in contrast with the private economy, which ceaselessly innovates on technology and business models).

In his famous essay *The Cathedral and the Bazaar*, the computer engineer Eric Raymond shows the gains of decentralized 'bazaar' development of technology, in the open source community, as opposed to the 'cathedrals' where products are built by cloistered groups within large companies.[8] The lessons of this apply even more when the cathedral is a state-backed technology, and when the bazaar is made up of multiple competing firms.

Our objective should be that the people fare well in innovating, in developing and utilizing new technology. For this, the free-market innovation machine, the self-organizing system, works better than state-controlled technology choices.

Example 45: State-Led Technology Standards versus the Internet

One of the biggest success stories of technological development of the last 50 years is the Internet. What was the role of the state in this story?

Public funding went into the research that led to the Internet. This reflects the presence of a market failure, the positive externalities where everyone gains from this research, the under-investment in R&D that tends to happen when private people make the resource allocation decision.

There was no state coercion to encourage or force the use of Internet standards. In many countries, state power tried to work against the rise of the Internet. There was rivalry between two standards in computer networking. A global club of governments developed and pushed a standard called X.25. An inchoate collection of academics and hobbyists developed an alternative standard called TCP/IP. The self-organizing system won, despite being backed by no state. The organic evolution of TCP/IP gave us the Internet, and X.25 died out.[9]   ••

Market Failure in the New Age

What are the implications, for the new world of the computer revolution, of the standard thinking about market failure as a justification for state intervention, and the constraints of state capacity? Each element of the family of market failure induces clear thinking in the light of the computer revolution:

Negative externalities There are new kinds of *negative externalities*, such as cyber crime. The justice system needs to commensurately chase a larger set of crimes, and old crimes engineered using new tools. These problems are exacerbated when it comes to state systems: a breach of a government sector database is generally more harmful than a breach in a private firm, and it is harder for the managers in government to achieve adequate security.

Positive externalities There is a new dimension to the *positive externalities* of knowledge. The transmission of knowledge has become easier. Therefore, the positive externalities from the production of knowledge go up.

Asymmetric information The root cause analysis of situations with *asymmetric information* takes us to problems of the information set. Computer technology can often be used to rearrange the information set and thus eliminate the asymmetric information.[10] New mechanisms of regulation by firms such as Airbnb, assisted by ratings of customers, can reduce the extent of market failure and the case for regulation.[11]

Public goods In the world of public goods, there are some new ideas for useful *public goods* like the Global Positioning System (GPS) that is run by the US Department of Defence as a global public good. For a public good like the maps made by the Survey of India, the computer revolution suggests a new boundary between private and public: The government should make the maps database and release it, while the private sector should make the maps.[12]

Market power There is a fresh wave of concern, in the world of firms organized through modern computer technology, about *market power*. Two-sided markets such as taxi companies have strong network effects, and there is the threat of predatory pricing that is used to establish a monopoly. Competition policy needs to respond to this new situation.[13] This is an area of active debate and policy experimentation the world over. India can gradually draw on this emerging body of knowledge, and apply it both to global firms operating in India, that have market power, and to Indian firms or systems that have market power.

The main path of policy thinking lies in market failure. In the five aspects described here, the digital age calls for modifying the traditional thinking. Each of these is an area that requires building a body of knowledge and expertise in India.

Summing Up

In the 1950s, there was a great outburst of high modernism, the Nehruvian idea that science and technology—and the experts that carry these—are benevolent, the idea that scientists and thinkers should design a new India. A great deal of these presumptions remain alive and well in the Indian landscape. At many points in the last 20 years, digital transformation has been viewed as the decisive solution to policy problems.

Millions of CPUs were introduced into the Indian development project. Why did the results disappoint? Perhaps the causal claims were incorrect, perhaps the essence of the growth process lies elsewhere.

We can also envision pathways for negative effects. When state legibility went up, this made private people more uncomfortable, and this had an adverse impact upon private investment. Genuine policy work could have been de-emphasized, when officials pursued the silver bullet of an IT system. The resurgence of central planning and protectionism are harming the competitive dynamics of the market economy.

We have to be conscious about harms. Information in the hands of the state, and control of the people in the hands of the state, leads to harm unless matched by commensurate improvements in the checks and balances of democracy. The traditional concepts of market failure reveal themselves in new ways, owing to the computer revolution, and require commensurate modifications of policy frameworks to address market failure in the emerging world.

The computer revolution is a powerful force reshaping the modern world. At many locations in the Indian economy and society, there are gains from applications of high technology. Both authors of this book have undergraduate degrees in engineering. In our practical work, we are at the frontiers of the digital age. We build and release open-source software. We are excited about the possibilities that modern technology offers, both in private hands, and for more efficient implementation in the state.

We are skeptical about high modernism, the willingness to give engineers the power to design society using state coercion. The self-organizing system, of myriad private initiatives and decentralized decisions, holds the best prospect for technology adoption and innovation in the country. State control or state leadership retards technology adoption and innovation.

On the grand scale of history, all the success stories of countries that emerged into high levels of freedom and prosperity did so without the computer revolution. In the UK, the rule of law and the high-quality working of courts was achieved without computers. High levels of state capability came about without computers; the British conquered India without email.

We worry about escapism in public policy, the idea that there are tech-heavy pathways to become an advanced economy without solving the difficult problems of freedom, check-and-balance and institution building. The foundations of Indian progress, in this digital age, continue to lie in political science and economics. Our task in public policy to watch over the use of state power, to protect freedom of individuals, and to channel the state into the narrow task of addressing market failure. Premature state legibility and premature state control have made these things harder.

Part V

The Public Policy Process

29

Policymaking Is Siege-Style Assault

In mountaineering, the climbers choose from two strategies. In the siege-style assault, a large team establishes a base camp, which sets up the second camp and establishes the logistics for resupplying it, and so on. In the case of Mount Everest, there is a base camp at 5,400 metres, Camp 1 at 6,100 metres, Camp 2 at 6,400 metres, Camp 3 at 6,800 metres and Camp 4 at 8000 metres. Finally, from here, a few climbers try to get up to the top, which is an altitude of 8,848 metres. The siege-style assault is slow, expensive and reliable.

In an Alpine-style assault, on the other hand, there is none of this preparation. One or two people try to walk up at the fastest possible pace. When the Alpine-style assault works, the result is always remarkable. But it requires superhuman capabilities, and the probability of failure is high.

We think that the public policy process requires a siege-style assault. Every now and then, there are situations where an Alpine-style assault yields some dramatic gains, but in time, these gains tend to be impermanent.

Example 46: The UK Policy Process on In-Vitro Fertilization

The world's first test tube baby, Louise Brown, was born in the UK on 25 July 1978. There was a great deal of hostility to the concept of a test tube baby, at the time.

In 1982, the UK government established a committee headed by the moral philosopher Mary Warnock, to think about the associated public policy problems. The Warnock Report was delivered in 1984 and led up to the 'Human Fertilization and Embryology Act' of 1990. This Act created the 'Human Fertilization and Embryology Authority' (HFEA) to adjudicate and license all work on human embryos, whether for IVF or for scientific study.[1]

How would this work out in the Indian policy process? We can see a few potential pitfalls:

- Right in 1978, when there was public criticism, there is a likelihood of a simple ban coming about. There is a bias, in India, for muscular responses to current newspaper stories. Letting the field unfold under *laissez faire* for four years is an unlikely event in the Indian policy process. As the securities expert Ashish Chauhan pleads 'First you have to have a market, and only then you can regulate it'.

- If a committee had to be created, it would have been hard to find a moral philosopher to head it, as the humanities have atrophied in Indian universities.

- The translation of the report into the Act would have been done badly.

- The translation of the law into state capacity at HFEA would have been done badly.

The Assisted Reproductive Technology (Regulation) Bill (ART Bill) and the Surrogacy (Regulation) Bill were passed by the Indian Parliament in December 2021, 12 years after the Indian Council of Medical Research first published a draft bill on this issue. The processes surrounding these laws show weaknesses, and no moral philosopher was involved.   ●●

The Policy Pipeline

Stage 1 of the policy pipeline is the establishment of the statistical system. Facts need to be systematically captured. Without facts, the entire downstream process breaks down. Our only hope for truth to matter is for truth to be recorded and widely disseminated.

In the modern world, few actors in the economy have an incentive to do a good job of measurement. As an example, academic economists are quite comfortable doing research with faulty data, because the academic economists who will review their work do not ask questions about data quality.

Stage 2 of the policy pipeline is descriptive and causal research. This requires a research community which will study the data, establish broad facts and regularities, and explore causal connections.

This work should be primarily grounded in the Indian locale. Academic researchers are too often swayed by the curiosity of journal editors and referees in a different continent. This hampers the choice of questions to pursue and the quality of research design through which those questions are sought to be answered.[2]

Stage 3 of the policy pipeline is the creative phase of inventing and proposing new policy solutions. A large menu of choices needs to be at hand, for possible policy pathways. The republic is always short-changed when 'there is no alternative' (TINA) to one mainstream idea.

At present in India, there is no community which systematically looks for fully articulated solutions. Academic journals do not publish policy proposals, hence academic researchers are not keen to invent policy proposals.

Stage 4 of the policy pipeline is the public debate where rival solutions compete with each other. This requires a vigorous process of debate and discussion, in writing and in seminars. A broad consensus needs to come about on what will work, within the analytical community.

In the Indian context, this is often assisted by the expert committee process. The purpose of the expert committee process is to sift through an array of possible policy pathways that are in the fray at the end of Stage 3, and filter down to a few which make sense. The best expert committee reports help mainstream novel ideas in policy reform, and pull together the state of the art into a report. As the late Isher Ahluwalia said, nothing gets done by writing it in a government committee report, but nothing ever got done without it being repeatedly written into multiple government committee reports.

Stage 5 of the policy pipeline is the internal government process of decision-making. This is where ministers and senior bureaucrats take stock of the range of possible policy pathways and make decisions. This is the zone of political economy, and the creative trade-offs that make progress possible.

Stage 6 of the policy pipeline is the translation of the decisions into legal instruments. Most policy decisions must be implemented through law that is enacted by the legislature, or subordinate legislation in the form of rules or regulations. High technical quality, and subtle detail, of this drafting process is of great importance.

In India, all too often, the drafting of law is done by persons who have a superficial understanding of the prior stages of the policy pipeline, which leads to poor drafting of law. While the Standing Committee process can be an important check where draft laws are examined and improved by the legislature, this often works imperfectly, and needs institutional redesign so as to improve the operational capabilities of the members.

Finally, *Stage* 7 of the policy pipeline is the construction of state capacity, in the form of administrative structures, an organization design, that enforce the law.

Looking back into our history, the successful reforms in India were those that fared well on all seven elements of the policy pipeline. This, in turn, required capacity building in all the stages. It is only when there were human capabilities on all seven steps of the pipeline, and enough time had been given for working through these steps, that we got a sound reform.

The first four stages of the pipeline are the process through which we arrive at a shared sense of the truth. In the best of times, this 'epistemic infrastructure of truth' was weak in India. Things have become more difficult in the world of social media, a world where false news reaches people more than the truth.[3] In his important book, *The constitution of knowledge*, the policy thinker Jonathan Rauch poses these questions in the US in the age of Trump.

A harder task awaits us in India: of establishing the community, the institutions and the norms that create a shared truth when starting from a weak intellectual tradition, at a time when many of the traditional institutions have been disrupted.[4] A harder task awaits us in India, in that these capabilities in the policy community are required in all cities and all states, and not just the union government.

An Alternative Depiction of the Policy Process

The economist Satya Poddar has a different conception of the policy process, which is also illuminating. He thinks in terms of a four-part story:

1. Defining the future state, or the preferred policy outcome
2. Preparing a blueprint for the design and specification of the future state
3. Defining the transition path from the current to the future state
4. Building political consensus or garnering public support for the change

These elements are intertwined and are rarely sequential phases in the implementation process. Yet, they serve as a useful framework for project management.

The four parts require different skill sets. For example, we need visionaries and saints for the first element, who can rise above the morass of information, scientific knowledge and cacophony of self-interests. Preparation of the blueprint is science, engineering and public administration. A poorly designed transition path is often the main cause of policy failures, and thinking through a sound transition is more art than science. Consensus building is predominantly an art.

Assessing the State of Maturity of the Reforms Process in a Field

For people who take interest in a field in India—e.g., agricultural reform—it is useful to score the state of maturity at each of the seven stages, every year. At each link in the chain, we should ask: What is the state of knowledge, literature and community? Can we identify 10 highly capable persons (of all ideological persuasions) in each stage of the pipeline? A field is in poor shape on stages 1, 2 and 3 if we are not able to envision ten wise persons who can usefully be members of an important expert committee (at Stage 4).

This classification system can be used to systematically identify the weak links in the chain in a field of interest and strengthen those.

Capacity Building for the Indian Policy Process

> *The best time to plant a tree was 20 years ago. The second-best time is now.*

—Chinese proverb

Capacity building for Indian policy reform requires fostering capabilities in all seven stages. Successful reforms tend to take place when there is maturity in all the seven areas. Activities that do not fit in the pipeline have limited usefulness. Alpine-style assaults are a high-risk strategy; they will often fail or be reversed.

The pipeline flows from left to right, and therefore there are prerequisites. The early stages have to be complete for the late stages to fare well. A systematic strategy of identifying the gaps—e.g., 'in field X, there is a particularly important weakness at stage 3'—can lead to constructive strategies to address these gaps.

The seven elements help us think about areas that are ripe for reform versus those that are not. The first four stages of the pipeline are of particular interest. When these early stages are strong, there is a possibility of making significant progress in actually doing reforms. The leadership which finds itself in such a situation should thank the people who put in the requisite investments, in previous years, to build the early stages.

When these early stages are weak, there is little opportunity to achieve significant reforms. It is quite inexpensive, to nurture these stages of the pipeline, and create reform opportunities for the future. But when a leadership is short-sighted and skimps on this nurturing, this has harmful effects in ways that are not visible at the time.

Summing Up

Progress in policy involves a pipeline that runs from data to research to multiple policy proposals to public debate about rival proposals to decisions to legal instruments to implementation. If we use the letter '|' to denote a pipe then the policy pipeline is data | research | proposals | debate | decisions | legal instruments | implementation. This is a slow, siege-style assault.

For a given field (e.g., property rights), it is useful to formally assess the state of capability in each stage of the policy pipeline. Each stage requires mature knowledge and a strong community. This will help guide the most valuable next actions that need to be undertaken to obtain reform in a field.

30

Reforming in a Crisis?

It's a mistake to believe that the change that has not yet come will never come. On 9/11 the world changed; on 10/26 the PATRIOT Act was passed. The Patriot Act was not written in 46 days. It was simply the instrument that was ready when the moment arrived.

—Persuasive Language for Language Security: Making the case for software safety by Mike Walker, 24 May 2018

The US politician, Rahm Emanuel, famously commented that 'a crisis is a terrible thing to waste'. In a crisis, the 'Overton window'—the range of possibilities that are realistically under debate in the policy process—is enlarged, and there is a larger zone of possibility in Stage 5 of the policy pipeline. Policymakers should be alert to these opportunities. More generally, there is a lot to be said for a policy process where a community chips away at stages 1 through 4 of the pipeline, and waits for the right moment when Stage 5 will use the ideas and Stage 6 and 7 will use the human capabilities.

> *When (the) crisis occurs, the actions that are taken depend on the ideas that are lying around. That, I believe, is our basic function: to develop alternatives to existing policies, to keep them alive and available until the politically impossible becomes politically inevitable.*
>
> —Milton Friedman

The relationship between crises and reforms is, however, highly exaggerated. There are three contrary points of view that have to be kept in mind.

The Early Stages of the Policy Pipeline Have to Be in Place

The possibilities in a crisis are the product of previous work that has been done in the early stages of the pipeline, and the human capabilities for stages 5, 6 and 7 that have been built ahead of time. The apparently high marginal product of crisis is partly grounded in misattribution; a lot of the credit has to go to the investments by the policy community of previous years. When we see the correlation between crisis and reforms, we are exaggerating the role of the runner who carries the baton across the finish line.

Investments in the early stages of the policy pipeline, and in human capacity, have to be in place. Otherwise, a crisis will be wasted. As an example, the 'Nirbhaya rape case' in Delhi in 2012 created a political moment for reform of the criminal justice system. However, as the early stages of the pipeline had not been constructed ahead of time, and human capabilities for stages 5, 6 and 7 were weak, the response that was obtained in that terrible moment was weak.

Chaos Is a Ladder

The second concern that has to be kept in mind is that when the range of possibilities is enlarged, this includes some very harmful ideas. We should not think that the leadership is always benign and intelligent. Crises are dangerous moments when placed in a fragile liberal democracy like India. In a crisis, it is easier to influence events than it is to understand them.[1]

A theme that has been repeated many times in history is the reduction of freedom in the aftermath of a crisis. When the populace is in fear, when criticizing tough new measures would be seen as unpatriotic, it is easier to justify greater powers in the hands of the state, and weakened checks and balances.

Authoritarian rulers chafe against the check-and-balance of a free press, the legislature, the courts and independent statistics. Democratic politics is about the hard work of negotiation, and when it works, heads of state routinely experience defeat. Authoritarian leaders find this a frustrating process; in fact, they are often inexperienced in the culture of democratic law-making. They lack the temperament of sharing power, and are uncomfortable with the traditions of criticism and compromise.

Crises offer aspiring authoritarians an escape from constitutional shackles. When security threats arise, it is easy to label all critics as anti-national. When national security is at risk, the press, the courts and opposition parties are more deferential. We have numerous examples of crises that gave damaging outcomes. Hitler exploited the Reichstag fire in 1933. In Peru, an insurgency and economic crisis gave Alberto Fujimori the opportunity to dissolve the Constitution in 1992. Recep

Erdogan imprisoned thousands of opponents and intellectuals after a failed coup attempt in 2016. Indira Gandhi used the economic and political crisis of 1976 to declare Emergency.

A litmus test about the conduct of policy in a crisis is the extent to which the proposed actions are located at the causes of the crisis. When this is not the case, policy actors have possibly harnessed the chaos to push an unrelated policy agenda, to pull off a 'bait and switch'. As an example, the 1991 reforms were located squarely at the locus of the macroeconomic crisis, and there was a complete link between a diagnosis of the crisis and the policy actions that followed. For a counterexample, in 2020, some people favoured the farm bills as a way of exploiting the Covid-19 crisis. This was less tenable as there was no connection between the farm bills and the pandemic.

> *The confusion, anxiety, and the profound sense of bewilderment about market forces are inevitable when breadwinners must worry whether income will be enough next week to feed the family... You cannot think straight in the midst of hyperinflation. The society becomes unglued.*

> —Jeffrey Sachs

Let us shift gears away from a fundamental threat to the republic, in a crisis. When there is low state capacity, the day-to-day firefighting in a crisis can yield poor results. For example, India repeatedly had inflation crises in the past decades, and each inflation crisis triggered a fresh batch of harmful command-and-control measures. The reform which actually mattered—inflation targeting through the Monetary Policy Framework Agreement of 20 February 2015—was not triggered off by an immediate inflation crisis.

RBI produced 74 regulations in the first 50 days after the demonetization of 2016, an average of 1.5 per day. These crisis-management actions were not RBI's finest hour. The 2013 currency crisis had sustained policy activism over a period of months, with many adverse effects upon the economy.[2]

The Indian Ministry of Health produced 1324 press releases from March 2020 to May 2021, an average of three per day.[3] But the pandemic induced no gains in terms of deeper health policy reforms. The pandemic was instead harnessed as an opportunity to build new mechanisms of control, where the Indian state interposed itself into controlling every doctor–patient relationship across the country in vaccination.

Given weak institutions in India, we should dread a crisis.

Incremental Progress versus Reforms in a Crisis

The third concern is that focusing on opportunities for reform in a crisis tends to understate the value and possibilities from incremental reform. A lot more is possible from the slow process of improving things every day, than is commonly given credit for. The UK got to liberal democracy without a French Revolution. We should not be entranced by dramatic wins; we should have the endurance to engage in 'the slow boring of hard boards' over long decades.

In India, it is often argued that deeper reform will only come about in a crisis. A flip side of this belief is a demoralized view that under normal circumstances, policy reforms are infeasible. We see the policy process as a process of building knowledge and conducting hypothesis tests every day, and we dread a crisis.

Example 47: A Success Story: The Reforms of 1991

The reforms of 1991 are linked, in the minds of many, to the balance of payments crisis and consequential IMF conditionality. A closer examination of that period, however, shows the policy pipeline that was established through the 1980s that made this possible.

The decades in which India grew at 3.5 per cent, while East Asia did much better, had made an enormous impression upon the policy community. The intellectual foundations of the 1991 reforms were laid by Jagdish Bhagwati, Padma Desai, T.N. Srinivasan, Arun Shourie, Manmohan Singh, Anne Krueger, Ashok Desai, Montek Ahluwalia, and the other pioneers of market-oriented policy thinking in India.

The government committee process had established key pillars for reform, including the Dagli committee on controls and subsidies (1979),[4] the P.C. Alexander Committee on Import-Export Policies and Procedures (1977), the Abid Hussain Committee on trade policy (1984), and the G. S. Patel committee on stock market reform (1984).

By the late 1980s, there was a community of key persons in a dozen ministries, who were envisioning a market-oriented India. There was an entire community that was ready to play a leadership role in economic reforms. Indeed, it was the ideas of *this* community which were written into the IMF conditionalities of 1991.

If these elements of the policy pipeline had not been in place, ahead of time, the crisis of 1991—on its own—would not have induced the positive changes that it did. For a contrast, Pakistan had 22 loans from the IMF from 1958 to 2020,[5] but lacked the policy community and the early stages of the policy pipeline, through which these moments of crises could be turned into accomplishments for policymakers.   ●●

Summing Up

There is a widespread belief that crises are an ideal opportunity for reforms. However, crises are difficult times. If the pipeline is not mature, ahead of time, in the heat of the crisis it is not possible to overcome the gaps in knowledge and human capacity. When crises enlarge the range of possibilities, this includes some harmful ideas. Checks and balances are less effective in a crisis. Things can more easily go wrong. Institutions that are weak in normal times are unable to deal with the day-to-day events of a crisis. We should dread a crisis.

31

Choosing from Pillars of Intervention

In many fields, it useful to think of state activities as falling under discrete categories, of 'pillars of intervention'. A government can *produce* education services by running schools. It can *regulate* the working of private schools. It can *finance* private persons buying the services of private schools. These are three pillars of intervention—producing, regulating, financing.

In the world of business, a common phrase is 'make versus buy': a firm can produce a certain good/service internally, or it can buy it from an external producer. The phrases 'make' and 'buy' here map to the pillars of intervention 'produce' and 'finance'.

In this chapter we ask: Under what conditions is a given pillar of intervention appropriate?

Mapping from Market Failure to the Pillars

When there is *market power*, *asymmetric information* and *negative externalities*, this can justify regulation, i.e., the use of the coercive power of the state to force private persons to behave differently.

Private persons under-produce the good which imposes *positive externalities* upon others. This can justify financing: the government encourages the private person through a subsidy, which recognizes the larger gains to society and reshapes incentives.

Private persons will not pay for *public goods* as they are non-excludable. This can be addressed through government financing to a private producer or through government production.

These relationships can also be read backwards, about the pillars that should *not* be used when faced with a certain class of market failure. If financing is being done, it should go with public goods or positive externalities. If financing is being used in any other class of market failure, something is probably amiss. Similarly, production should only happen with public goods. Production or financing are generally not useful when faced with market power, asymmetric information or negative externalities.

The Indian state often produces in the absence of market failure, i.e., when mere purchase would suffice. The fact that the government builds bridges does not justify producing the engineering services of building bridges or producing steel. There may be market failure in the need for a bridge (as it is a public good), but there is none in the market for engineering services or in the market for steel.

Conflicts Introduced by Public Sector Production

When a government is both umpire and player, this induces difficulties. The people in charge of production by the state have a bias in favour of capturing all the resources available for financing. They try to ensure weak regulation for themselves, and would like to place regulatory barriers upon private producers. In the Indian experience, there are many examples where the mixing of regulatory and production functions within one organization has worked poorly.

Example 48: *Government Production of Telecom Services at DOT*

In the old structure of the Department of Telecommunications there was a fusion between monopolistic public sector production and regulatory functions. It is difficult for a state monopoly to regulate itself, which gave poor services. The telecom reforms of the late 1990s separated out regulation into the Telecom Regulatory Authority of India (TRAI), ended the public sector monopoly, and created multiple private providers.   ••

Example 49: *Government Production of Financial Services at RBI*

This mixture of a public sector monopoly with regulatory functions is also found in many aspects of the RBI. Critical bond market infrastructure is owned by RBI which is also the regulator of the bond market. In the field of payments switching, there is a monopoly (NPCI) which is owned by a group of banks, where RBI has significant control. The recent proposal to build a 'Public Credit Registry' raises the possibility of an additional monopoly producer controlled by RBI, while RBI also performs connected regulatory functions.[1] In all these cases, the strategy of mixing public sector production with regulation works poorly, and we would obtain improved outcomes through multiple competing private producers coupled with RBI regulation.   ••

Example 50: Banking

There are two pillars of intervention in banking in India. On one hand, the state *regulates* banking. In addition, the Indian state *produces* banking services through the ownership of banks.

While there may be a case for privatization of banks, at a practical level, the state is a producer of banking services and will be in this business for some years. The public administration problem can then be phrased as two distinct questions. First, how should state capacity be achieved in the regulation of banking? Second, how should state capacity be achieved in the production of banking? Regulatory capability requires setting up a sound banking regulator and commensurate capabilities in a department of government. Owning banks requires setting up organizational capacity for the governance of public sector banks.

There are conflicts between these two lines of thought. Regulation by the state may be indulgent towards its own entities. The persons tasked with production may request a non-level playing field: regulatory restrictions upon private banks but indulgence towards public sector banks. This calls for strong separation between the two pillars.   ••

Example 51: Education

In the field of school education, there are three pillars: Funding, Regulating, Producing:

- There is market failure in the field of education—positive externalities—where the person who obtains education does not take heed of the gains for society that come about as a consequence. This leads to under-investment in education by each individual. Governments fund education in response to this market failure. This calls for the public administration design of the funding pillar. The simple and equitable way to organize this is to pay Rs X per year per child to parents. The more precise way is to link the rupee value transferred to the incremental knowledge obtained by a child.

- Parents would find it difficult to understand the true contribution made by alternative school providers. This calls for a regulatory strategy. On one hand, regulation may coerce schools to do certain things. In addition, regulation may work through information release which helps parents make decisions about school choice. A public administration strategy is required to design this state capacity in regulation.

- Finally, there may be certain locations where private schools fail to come about. In these locations, the government may choose to provide school services. The key tool for obtaining sound functioning of government schools is to ensure that the flow of resourcing into public schools only runs through parents: funding would flow to parents only, and through them, to the schools chosen by parents. A public administration strategy is required for running government schools, or contracting out the running of government schools, in under-served locations.

There are natural tensions between these three pillars. The people who do production of government schools would like to monopolize the funding, ask for weak regulation and raise entry barriers against nongovernment schools. This calls for strong separation between the three pillars.   ••

Example 52: Skills

Increased skills induce positive externalities, and each individual could possibly under-invest in skilling. This motivates funding by the state. There could be market failure in the form of asymmetric information between the buyer and seller of skilling services. This motivates regulation. Finally, it is possible to have public sector production of skilling services. These three elements constitute clear verticals—regulating, financing, producing.

In India, state production is about running the Industrial Training Institutes (ITIs). Funding is about the flows of public money to private persons who add skills. Regulating is about ensuring high quality training by all providers, public or private. This three-pillar thinking helps us organize the work in our minds, and encourages us to see the tensions within the three areas of work.   ••

Example 53: Infrastructure

In the field of infrastructure, the simple scheme of producing–regulating–financing does not carry through. A more useful classification is Planning, Contracting, Regulating and Producing. Planning pertains to the overall design required in both transportation and energy infrastructure. As an example, it is an act of planning to envision a container terminal at Nhava Sheva, and then the array of connections of roads and railways that have to be made to it. There is a greater role for the union government in planning infrastructure assets that span many states.

Contracting is about establishing the PPP contracts through which private firms are given contracts to build this infrastructure. Regulating is about addressing the market failure of infrastructure monopolies in operation, which involves using state power to uphold quality of service and combat monopolistic pricing. Finally, the state does produce by virtue of owning some infrastructure assets, and an organizational framework is required for the governance and operations of those assets.

At the outset, we had pure state systems. The government would plan a road, the Public Works Department (PWD) would build the road, and roads were neglected after they were inaugurated. The first level increase in skill lay in establishing the contracting capabilities for a private firm to build the road. This required a one-off transactional perspective. The complexity goes up greatly for a PPP contract, where the relationship between the government and the PPP vendor has to work out for many decades. This requires a higher level of capability and good behaviour by the government.[2]   ••

Example 54: Health Care

In the field of health care, it is useful to think in terms of the pillars of Funding, Regulating and Producing. Funding pertains to channels through which public money goes to individuals who require health care. This may include expenditures on public hospitals, or on the new age insurance schemes. Regulating pertains to establishing fair play by all health care providers, public or private. Finally, producing pertains to the ownership, governance and management of government hospitals.

Once again, we see the tension where the persons involved in producing would like to monopolize the funding and have weak regulation upon themselves. All too often, health policy in India reflects the desire of the public sector health care producers; it fails to efficiently harness or regulate private sector production of health care, and it tends to deprioritize public health.   ••

Example 55: Digital Identity

On the problem of digital identity,[3] the pillars are Regulating and Producing. It is possible to envision multiple private persons who produce identity services. It is also possible to think of a public sector enterprise (possibly even a monopoly) that engages in production.[4] Regardless of how production is organized, there are regulatory problems associated with regulation of monopolistic pricing, fair play to users, privacy, etc. In the case of identity infrastructure, monopolistic production creates a single point of failure, which is an unwise design strategy.

In the Unique Identity Authority of India (UIDAI), we have merged a monopoly public sector producer with a regulatory function. This leads to concerns about the extent to which the regulatory function will be performed properly. Monopolistic, taxpayer financed public sector production also closes out the possibilities for technological change and competition.   ••

Example 56: Bond Market

RBI owns and operates the bond depository, the SGL. RBI owns and operates the bond exchange, the NDS. RBI is the regulator of the bond market.

RBI is a player on the bond market.

The conflicts introduced by these functions has induced poor performance. For a contrast, SEBI regulates the equity exchange infrastructure, NSE and BSE are the exchanges, and NSDL/CDSL are the depositories. SEBI does not trade on the exchanges. This has laid a better foundation and helps explain the difference between the Indian story of the equity market versus the bond market.   ●●

An Organizing Framework for Public Administration

These three pillars are a useful organizing framework as each of them involves different kinds of management mechanisms. We can think of the management frameworks in government, and expertise in government, as being organized around these three pillars.

It takes one kind of skill, and organization design, to organize the state to produce services. Regulation is a distinct skill and calls for a different organization design. Finally, financing mechanisms require a third kind of skill and a third kind of organization design. It would be useful to have a book on how to do regulation, another book on how to do financing, and another book on how to do production.

Experience and expertise are transferable between diverse sectors within these three pillars. As an example, a person who knows how to run an education voucher system may be able to readily carry that knowledge into an immunization voucher system. There are many analogies in organization design that carry over from a telecom regulator to a securities regulator. An individual in the world of public policy needs to develop mastery of one of these pillars at a time.

Summing Up

States are generally able to intervene in society in three ways. Coercive power can be used to modify the behaviour of private persons, which constitutes *regulation*. States can *produce* certain services. Finally, states can *finance* the purchase of certain services by private persons from private producers.

Market power, asymmetric information and negative externalities can justify regulation. Positive externalities can justify financing. Public goods can justify production or financing.

The organization design required for each of these three pillars is quite different. A funding organization is very different from a regulating organization, which is in turn very different from a producing organization. There is a need to develop expertise in India, and organization designs, that address each of these three pillars. The knowledge of individuals, and role models of process manuals and IT systems, are portable across sectors within each pillar.

State *production* creates incentives for light regulation of public sector production, an attempt at monopolizing public resourcing for only public production and attempts at utilizing the regulatory power to create entry barriers that impede private production. Where possible, it is better to operate regulatory and financing pillars and not a production pillar.

32

Building the Foundational Processes

The Apollo 11 'lunar module', that landed on the moon, weighed 7333 kg.[1] The Saturn V rocket that got it out of the earth weighed 2.8 million tonnes.

A government agency has a goal, located within a certain specialized sector knowledge. This is about understanding market failure in that domain, and choosing the intervention which addresses the market failure at the lowest cost to society. This is the payload. For this to have a chance of reaching the destination, it requires rockets and a navigation system. In this chapter, we discuss components of every government organization, which are the navigation system, and which are analogous to the rockets.

The Rockets

At the North Block in Delhi, which houses the Ministry of Finance, there are grand discussions about the principal-agent problems faced when the Parliament gives coercive power to agencies like RBI, SEBI or ED. But alongside this, there is a crisis in North Block, on the principal-agent problems faced with the contractor who cleans the toilets, and the monkeys that wander the corridors.[2] It is hard to engage in lofty thoughts about inflation targeting and the Public Debt Management Agency, when the elementary facilities management is not in place.

Every government organization in India has failures in three foundational processes—human resources, finance and contracting. These are cross-cutting problems which influence every government agency. Successful public management requires these 'rockets' to be in place, and then the payload of the sector knowledge stands a chance of getting to the destination. When these basics do not work, doing elementary things is difficult, and doing subtle things is impossible.

Most policy thinkers in India are organized along disciplinary lines, with specialization in one sector or the other. The expert on vaccination thinks about what went wrong in the Ministry of Health on Covid-19 vaccines through the lens of the specialized body of knowledge of health. But problems outside the domain—the difficulties of government contracting and public finance—created the conditions for these failures.

Human Resource Process

The HR process of government was inherited from the British. Their approach to India involved a mixture of arbitrary power, and rule by law, led by about 10,000 white people. It was not an HR process design for state organizations for a liberal democracy.

By and large, their systems have carried over into the present, with incremental modifications that were often in the wrong direction. There is the well-known problem of 'compression' of compensation, of an inadequate wage gap between the top and the bottom. Across the heterogeneity of India, wages are often highly out of line with the local labour market. There is little incentive for civil servants to try harder, and managers in public systems are unable to recruit adequate expertise. There was a time when the UPSC examination papers and interviews made more sense, and the best people in India tried to take this exam, but this is no longer the case.

The HR process in government is broken at a fundamental level. Silver bullet solutions, e.g., the disbanding of the civil service that was done in Pakistan, do not work. The hiring of '500 laterals' does not work; it will merely dilute the steel frame of the civil service and reduce it to a bunch of political appointments. The old-style British civil service demands fundamental reform, e.g., as was done in the UK itself.

The HR process is an extremely complex problem and we have to think through subtle problems of checks and balances. The correct answers will not be monolithic. What works well for defence will be different from what works well for the Ministry of Finance, or for RBI, or for elements of the Indian state at city or state governments.

Finance Process

The finance process comprises budgets, expenditure, accounting and audit. This has broken down over the years to a substantial degree.

The legislature no longer has a meaningful role in budget-making; it is now the exclusive preserve of the cabinet and the executive branch. Budget documents have been released where the numerical values presented do not reconcile across elementary addition. The public release of budget documents in some state governments is now somewhat tenuous.

Budget-making can express political priorities, respond to events, and create accountability mechanisms for spending units. The Indian budget process is largely paralysed; the expenditure plan changes negligibly from one year to the next. This is a lost opportunity for more rational resource allocation.

In some advanced economies, the political leadership writes a document that expresses its political priorities. Departments then compete to propose expenditure plans, in writing, that achieve those priorities. Budget-making is the large-scale debate, between many people, that analyses these documents, and identifies the projects which have the highest bang for the buck while fitting within the envelope of feasible expenditure. And then, after that, careers are on the line in delivering on the promises that were made in the budget process. These mechanisms are absent in India.

On the spending side, in India, the ability of departments to work through the year, and spend a stated budget, has declined over the years. This is partly about the overall decline in state capacity, but it is also about difficulties in the finance process.

Budgets have come to lack sanctity. For the leadership of a spending ministry, the resources budgeted at the start of the year are only tentative: phone calls can appear within the year forcing them to pull back. These phone calls sometimes represent unconstitutional changes in the budget that are not authorized by the legislature.

In the best of times, the expenditure side works poorly, and the contracting work that starts after the budget takes many months to translate into expenditures. As the year unfolds, there is a high risk of budgetary allocations being yanked. This uncertainty reduces the vigour with which an expenditure unit pursues its stated work plan.

Inter-governmental fiscal relations have become more fraught, and states are on weaker ground. Resource flows to states, that are supposed to take place *de jure*, have been interrupted, introducing *ex ante* risk about the future.

Public debt management should play a role in overcoming revenue or liquidity constraints by borrowing. The failures of public debt management and the financial repression pathways to borrowing have many adverse implications, one of which is the translation of shortfalls in revenue or inter-governmental transfers into disruption of bugetary planning.

The finance process is broken at a fundamental level. The silver bullet that is often proposed—more software systems—does not solve these problems. Complex design work is required to envision the appropriate finance process. The correct answers will not be monolithic; many different elements of the Indian state will need different solutions.

Contracting Process

Every government agency buys goods and services from the private sector. In this, it needs to engage in government contracting. Government contracting is the full pipeline from bid preparation to procurement to contract renegotiation to dispute resolution to payments. At present, all elements of this pipeline work poorly.

The best firms in India view the government as a bad customer. At the procurement stage, unethical firms have corrupt relationships with decision makers and are likely to have an inside track on procurement. After a contract is awarded, civil servants and politicians do not respect contracts, and are comfortable making oral or written demands for tasks and conduct that was not contracted. Private firms have low bargaining power, and contract enforcement through the judiciary against the government does not work. As a consequence, many of the best firms have ceded this space, and there is a small set of specialized firms that sell to the government. This, in turn, hampers the ability of the government to buy at efficient prices.

The state is the agent of the people of India, and it should aspire to achieve maximal spending efficiency, i.e., obtain the maximal bang for the buck in spending hard-won tax revenues. However, too many people slip into being comfortable with imposing constraints upon the state such as blocking purchases from overseas producers, or blocking purchases from large firms, etc. Such constraints only worsen the expenditure inefficiency. An accountable government would try to deliver the highest bang for the buck; government purchasing should have only one objective, to obtain the lowest prices for the required quality.

As in every organization, state organizations face 'make' versus 'buy' decisions. A given problem can be solved by contracting out to an external vendor, or an internal team can be set up to do the same work. The failures of the Indian state in contracting have created a bias in favour of 'make'. In the terminology of 'pillars of intervention' of the previous chapter, it creates a bias in favour of production for problems where mere purchase would suffice. This is often inefficient in translating money into outcomes. We also run into conflicts of interest when a state agency, which is a producer, is in competition against the private persons that it regulates.

As an example, NASA in the US primarily works by contracting out. This delivers a higher bang for the buck. In addition, public expenditures on space exploration that are delivered by NASA into private firms (within the US and outside it) have the side effect of generating knowledge spillovers. In contrast, ISRO in India largely works by hiring engineers. This hampers the effectiveness of expenditure, and also induces reduced gains for India from knowledge spillovers.[3] ISRO also regulates private firms that are sending rockets into space, and has flawed incentives in this regulatory task.

Failures on government contracting thus generate an expenditure inefficiency. A widget that costs Re 1 for a competent and well-incentivized private person ends up costing something more than Re 1 when it is *purchased* by the state. Production *by* the state is also well known to be inefficient: a widget that can be purchased for Re 1 by a competent and well-incentivized private person will cost more than Re 1 when it is produced by the state.

The contracting process in government is broken at a fundamental level. Silver bullets, e.g., a computer system for bid submission or a procurement law,[4] do not work. Complex design work is required to envision the appropriate contracting process for government. The correct answers will not be monolithic: the way to buy a fighter plane will be different from the way to buy vaccines.[5]

This perspective gives us a fresh insight into vouchers. In a voucher program, the individual gets a voucher from the government, chooses a service provider, submits the voucher, and the service provider gets reimbursed by the government. This can be done in many situation, e.g., education or vaccines or medical testing. Voucher programs do involve administrative overhead, in getting the voucher to each eligible citizen and in making payments to the service providers chosen by the people. The key insight lies in the fact that the problem of choosing a good service provider is shifted from the government to a well-incentivized person, the individual. Parents will always do well in choosing a good school for their children. Even when state capacity in contracting is low, voucher programs can be effective, as the key decision is made by a self-interested individual and not by the state.

The Navigation System

The rockets get an agency off the ground. We desire that the payload, of sector knowledge on addressing market failure in the least intrusive manner, will reach the destination. What are the checks and balances that will keep the craft pointed in the right direction? There are three elements in this: the problems of wielding coercive power, the governance at the board, and the transparency process.

Government agencies which wield *coercive power* have a severe problem in the corrosive influence of this power. There are grave dangers in the abuse of the power to make law, to investigate a private person, to punish a private person, or to stand in judgement of a private person.

The individuals who man the state are mere mortals. There is a grave danger, when coercive power is present, of the ship going astray. A strong array of checks and balances is required, to keep the organization on track, when these powers are present. At the early stages of learning how to be a republic, these checks and balances are being learned, and it is best if the magnitude of coercive power is kept to the minimum. Many other chapters in this book discuss these mechanisms, of the checks and balances surrounding coercive power.

The next element of the navigation system is *the governance* of an organization. An agency built of officials and controlled by officials is 'the administrative state'; it will not work for the people. The 'long arm of accountability' of elections is too diffused, and failure of this agency will not percolate into meaningful modifications of its behaviour. The everyday function, of keeping the agency on track, is that of the board. For this, the board must be dominated by private persons, and a private person must be the chairman with a separation between the role of the chairman and the role of the MD. Such a board will obtain feedback from the world, about the failures of the agency, and feed these impulses back into course corrections, through which the rocket will head in the correct direction.

The third element of the navigation system is the *transparency process*. Public choice theory guides us in expecting that persons inside the state value secrecy: greater secrecy in the working of the state increases their arbitrary power. Increasing transparency creates greater checks and balances and thereby fosters improvements in the working of the state. The steady rhythm of transparency processes is required in each government agency.

This includes reporting requirements, release of detailed datasets, requirements to publish full documentation packets as part of regulation-making, the need to publish reasoned orders and calculations of ill-gotten gains that lead up to penalties, information flows from executive organizations to the legislature, and the ability of the citizenry to demand information.

Slogans like 'sunlight is the best disinfectant' do not, however guide us to optimal outcomes. Every institution needs an inner life, a space for candid conversations, where ideas are discussed and negotiations take place.[6]

The essence of deliberative democratic politics is a healthy give and take, a world of negotiations and deal making between politicians of diverse parties. This necessarily diverges from the polarization of the modern political discourse. If everything is live streamed, there is a greater emphasis on grandstanding and performance for the benefit of the base. The essence of technical work is forming a judgement when faced with imperfect information and imperfect knowledge. This diverges from the public's notion of all-knowing experts. The glare of cameras is not always conducive to obtaining the best outcomes.

Starting from a tradition of colonial opacity, India made a move towards greater transparency with the Right to Information Act.[7] With the benefit of hindsight, we see many infirmities in this strategy. The RTI has simplistic extremes: in some respects there is too much access to the decision process, thus exerting a chilling effect upon the quality of files and hampering sound decisions. In some respects, such as the broad label 'national security' or the RBI, the old regime of opacity continues. As an example, it is not possible to obtain information about the steps that led up to demonetization, using the RTI.

Advanced economies have well developed and more complex mechanisms for information release. As an example, in the UK, the transparency framework does not exempt the military. But at the same time, there is a graded system of release with greater delays for more sensitive matters. Even today, some facts about the Second World War have not been released, but at pre-scripted future dates, every fact about the Second World War will come out into the public domain.[8]

The three elements of the navigation system—checks and balances over coercive power, governance by the board, and the transparency process—resist simplistic solutions. Sophisticated thinking is required, where we envision how the behaviour of self-interested state agents will change when placed under a given set of rules. Different classes of government agencies, in different settings, will require different rules.

Establishing the Process of Change

In this chapter, we have touched upon six foundational processes—finance, HR, contracting, checks and balances over coercive power, governance by the board, and transparency. Each of these requires an expert community and a body of literature.

A flow of research output and debate should take place, each year, in any living field of Indian policy reform. The early stages of the policy pipeline—data, research, creative policy proposals and public debate—need to be established in each of the six areas, as was done in the field of finance from the early 1990s onwards, which led up to FSLRC (2011–2015).

The problem faced in FSLRC was, however, simpler: it only aspired to setup a few union government agencies correctly, who would perform the tasks of financial economic policy, all of which are on the union list of the Constitution.

The foundational processes are present in all sectors, and more importantly, at each of the three levels of government.

The process of change, then, needs to take place in each government organization. The governance arrangement of each organization needs to establish a process of change where high knowledge is applied to improve these processes in the organization. A good place to initiate this is in state agencies, rather than the departments of government.[9]

The board of an agency should have a majority of independent members, and a separation between the chairman and the MD. The board should feel pressures of accountability, to improve the performance of the organization, and not merely engage in the pleasures of exercising coercive power. Once such accountability mechanisms are in place, the board has an incentive to improve the foundational processes. Under the oversight of such a board, the management of an agency can embark on the autonomous search for sound process designs. By this reasoning, SEBI's search for a sound HR process should be distinct from TRAI's search for a sound HR process.

There will legitimately be a process of experimentation and discovery. A variety of modifications of the foundational processes can and should be attempted. Researchers and practitioners would then develop a body of knowledge on what works well, and an incremental path to progress can be established.

Categories of Expertise

In the Indian policy process today, a person is an expert in a sector like defence or health. In this book, we see new views of expertise.

If we think along the path of pillars of intervention, there is expertise in government financing, in government regulation or in government production. If we think along the six aspects discussed in this chapter, there is expertise in human resources, finance, contracting, coercive power, transparency and board governance. There will be a need for further combinations, e.g., HR for a government regulatory organization (where coercive power is present) will need to be different from HR for a government production organization (where coercive power is absent). A major reason for state failure in India today is the lack of such specialization.

Example 57: Foundational Processes in Defence

There are state capability problems in the Indian military, as there are in every part of the Indian state.[10] Military affairs is seen as a highly distinct field in India from the mainstream of Indian public policy. Experts on defence think about problems like fighting a two-front war or of the costs and benefits of putting multiple carrier groups into the Indian ocean.[11]

The foundational processes have a major significance in defence, as they do in every other field:

HR State capability lies in the doctrine and tactics that the military personnel is able to develop and operate. This requires a commensurate HR process which lays the foundations for autonomous thinking and decision-making all the way to front line soldiers.[12]

As with the civil service more broadly, the pools of talent that choose to enter the Indian military need to be enhanced.

The frameworks for evaluation and promotion need to cater to the construction of a professional military force.

HR for defence is an important element of the overall defence problem. Experts in this can benefit from knowledge of the broader field of HR in government across other elements of government. As an example, experts on HR in defence would have benefited from talking with experts on HR in government more broadly on the problems of pension reforms, in the years that led up to 'one rank one pension'.[13]

Finance Defence thinking requires strategic thinking on *finance* on 25-year horizons. These are the time scales over which fundamental adjustment of the HR process, and acquisition of important weapons systems, takes place. Year-to-year budgeting, and late-year scrambles to spend less, are inimical to building defence capability.

Contracting Limitations of contracting are hobbling Indian defence. It is hard to buy (say) fighter planes, and there is an excessive degree of in-sourcing of production and research.[14]

Transparency The high level of secrecy limits the feedback loops that induce greater performance. As an example, the Indian debate on one-rank-one-pension would have fared better if there was better data on wages and pensions for the military. More generally, we have seen how, in countries such as the US, vigorous debates take place about military operations, and decisions to wage war do not elicit unanimous support within the citizenry. These democratic debates, and control by the civilian authorities, requires the release of facts and the construction of an expert community.[15]

Coercive power The Indian defence forces should not have the right to coerce Indian persons, therefore the problems of checks and balances governing these should not be an issue.

Board governance The concepts of a board which limits the power of senior managers, and holds them accountable, accountable need to be adapted to fit this domain.

The foundational processes and the navigation systems are thus central for enhancing Indian military capacity.[16] They create the possibility of the payload (of sector questions like a two-front war or carrier groups in the Indian ocean) getting through. These issues tend to get under-emphasised by the conventional disciplinary classification of expertise in a domain. In each of these areas, there is value to be obtained from the larger ecosystem of ideas, where there is an expertise in a field such as HR, that is applied all across the Indian state, which is also applied into the military.   ●●

Summing Up

A government agency is like a rocket ship. The tiny payload at the top is the objectives of addressing market failure in a specific sector. The foundations of the agency—HR, finance, contracting—are the propulsion system, that give the actual work a chance of succeeding. The checks and balances surrounding the agency—the processes that constrain the use of coercive power, the transparency process, and the governance arrangement—are the navigation system that determine whether the agency will go astray.

Financial economists are important for thinking about (say) SEBI, and health economists are important for thinking about (say) ICMR. But the possibility of success at organizations like SEBI or ICMR is predicated on high capabilities on the issues described in this chapter, issues that are cross-cutting across sectors.

Each of these fields six fields require experts and expertise, in the context of the full policy pipeline (data to research to creative policy proposals to public debate). Quick proposals, like the Right to Information Act, or 'Bring in 500 laterals', are a statement of angst and not a solution. FSLRC-scale work is required in each of these areas, to build a literature, to build experts, and to build concrete documents where design work is fully thought through.

In the field of public policy today, specialization takes place along the lines of sectors, such as health or defence. There is a need for specialization along the dimensions of the three pillars of intervention (financing, regulation or production) and along the dimensions of the six fields of this chapter (HR, finance, contracting, transparency, coercive power, board governance). An expert community of thinkers and practitioners is required in each of these.

33

The Decision to Spend Public Money

In 1985, Rajiv Gandhi famously said that in redistribution programs, for each Re 1 of expenditure, about Re 0.15 reached the intended beneficiaries. This is a 6.67× inefficiency through flaws of the expenditure process. P. Chidambaram has argued against putting public money down ineffective subsidy programs which he termed as 'leaky pipes'.

All public spending will contain inefficiencies. When should the state spend? In this chapter, we look at the four building blocks of analysis that shape this decision.

Inefficiency at the Entry Gate, the Marginal Cost of Public Funds

At the outset, all public resources are expensive. The mechanisms of state resource mobilization impose harm upon the economy, which results in a large value for the Marginal Cost of Public Funds (MCPF). Roughly speaking, the cost to society of Re 1 of government expenditure is about Rs 3. The decision to spend public money faces a high hurdle rate right at the entry gate. We have to be really confident that the state is adding value through an expenditure program, that it is worth using state coercion to forcibly take money away from private persons and spend it through the political process.

Expenditure Efficiency in Redistribution

A plan for spending public money on redistribution has to reckon with the two layers of inefficiency. First, resource mobilization incurs the MCPF, which is about 3, and then there is the expenditure efficiency in the redistributive program. As an example, with the modern NREGS, suppose we believe that for each Re 1 of expenditure, about Re 0.4 reaches the intended beneficiaries. In this case, the overall cost for society for delivering Re 1 to the intended beneficiary is about Rs 7.5.

To say this differently, in order to deliver Re 1 to the intended beneficiaries, we have to put Rs 2.5 into the NREGS, given the 2.5× inefficiency of the spending program. And, in order to obtain Rs 2.5, we have to impose a cost upon society of Rs 7.5, given the 3× inefficiency in resource mobilization. We must do the NREGS when we are convinced that getting this Re 1 to the intended beneficiaries is so important that it justifies taking away Rs 7.5 from the people.

Expenditure Efficiency in State Production

Suppose we have a public good, such as street cleaning, that can be produced at the cost of Re 1, at the frontier of expenditure efficiency by a private person. When the state hires civil servants and runs a government organiation to do this same work, an inefficiency is introduced. We call this the 'Markup in State Production' (MSP).

Example 58: The Markup in State Production in Elementary Education

Muralidharan and Sundararaman, 2015,[1] find that private schools in Andhra Pradesh spent less than a third of public schools, while delivering slightly better learning outcomes. This suggests a value for the Markup in State Production (MSP) of over three times.

When the state runs schools in Andhra Pradesh, then, there is a 3× inefficiency introduced owing to resource mobilization and another 3× inefficiency introduced by the infirmities of expenditure programs. In order to achieve schooling worth Re 1, the overall cost to society is about Rs 9.   ••

Expenditure Inefficiency in State Contracting

Every expenditure strategy faces the make versus buy decision. Instead of make, we can turn to buy, where the government contracts this task out to a private producer. Here, a different inefficiency is introduced, on account of the deficiencies of state contracting. What can be done for Re 1 by a self-interested private person will end up costing something higher when purchased by the state. We call this the 'Markup in State Contracting' (MSC).

Policymakers thus face three alternative choices when faced with a non-subsidy expense. The first choice is to do nothing, to spend no public money. The second choice is to raise money through taxes and make within the state. This incurs an expenditure inefficiency of 3× MSP times. The third choice is to raise money through taxes and buy from a private person. This incurs an expenditure inefficiency of 3× MSC times.

Wisdom in Expenditure Decisions

Public money is extremely precious, and should be used with care, owing to the marginal cost of public funds (MCPF). Every rupee spent by the state imposes a cost of at least Rs 3 upon society and suffers from an additional layer of inefficiency owing to the infirmities of expenditure programs.

Addressing market failure is, however, enormously valuable for society. Even if there is a 6× inefficiency in achieving high levels of safety with respect to internal or external threats, it is worth spending public money for these, as the gains are very large. Roughly speaking, we can think of about 4 per cent of GDP being spent on external affairs, defence, and the criminal justice system, and this would be a good use of money, even after recognizing the layers of inefficiency in government resource mobilization and government expenditure.

Redistributive programs involve moral choices. Most of us would agree that disaster relief, or sending money to the poorest 10 per cent of society, is worth doing even when the hurdle rate is 5× to 10×, as long as the magnitude of expenditure is small, e.g., 1 per cent of GDP.

In advanced economies, both elements of inefficiency are lower. A better tax system and a better mechanism for public debt management implies that the MCPF is lower. Greater state capability in expenditure means that expenditure inefficiency is lower. It is rational for advanced economies to have a bigger state when compared with poor countries. It is irrational to build a big state in a poor country.

The analysis of this chapter gives us a useful way to think about one spending decision at a time. A large number of expenditure elements in India, at present, are unjustified when viewed in this fashion. A distinct thread of reasoning which needs to take place in the budget process is that of *allocation* between rival pathways to spending. This involves equalizing the gains to society from the last rupee of spending. These skills need to reside in the finance 'foundational process'.

Summing Up

A private person is able to buy a widget for Re 1. When a government buys that widget for Rs 2, there is an overall inefficiency of about 6×, reflecting the twin problems of the marginal cost of public funds (MCPF) of about 3× and the expenditure inefficiency of about 2×.

The 'Markup in State Production' (MSP) is the inefficiency of the government when spending public money to organize production activities within a government organization. The 'Markup in State Contracting' (MSC) is the inefficiency of the government when spending public money to buy goods or services from the private sector. The magnitude of the MSP versus the MSC, on a given problem, shape the decision of make versus buy.

The overall decision about whether to spend public money should be based on the inefficiency at the entry gate (the MCPF) multiplied by the inefficiency at the expenditure step (either MSP or MSC depending on whether make or buy is used). In the example of schools run by the Andhra Pradesh government, there is a 3× inefficiency in resource mobilization and a 3× inefficiency in spending, so there is a 9× inefficiency in all. The decision to spend public money should be shaped by a sense of these numbers.

34

Walk Before You Can Run

In each field of reform (e.g., land market) there are many things that need to be done. In what order should they be done? This is the sequencing question.

Sequencing discussions in India often degenerate into choosing low hanging fruit to begin the work, and proclaiming that an important reform has begun. Sophisticated thinking on sequencing involves five elements:

1. Capacity building in the policy process: We have shown seven elements of the policy pipeline. There is a natural sequencing, going from left to right, of the order in which actions should be undertaken.
2. Prerequisites: When X is a prerequisite for Y, we have to get X in place before Y.
3. Learning-by-doing: Start with simple problems, learn public management, and gradually escalate complexity.
4. Political economy considerations: Weighing the gains and the costs imposed by various alternative components and taking the ones with high economic gain but low political

cost first. Early moves should create a constituency for the late moves. Early moves should not walk into a political economy trap.

5.   Stinginess: Start out small on coercive power and spending, only escalate when capabilities are proven.

Element 1: Capacity Building

Consider the problems of Indian pension reforms in 1995. There was no data, there was no research, there was no policy community incubating ideas for reforms.

Under these conditions, the right thing to have done was to build these early stages of capability in the country. To enact the Employee Pension Scheme (1995), under these low conditions of capability in the early stages of the pipeline, was a mistake. It is no surprise that, with the benefit of hindsight, we now see that the EPS was a bad element of Indian pension policy.

There is a terrible air quality crisis in India today. The right policy response, as of 2022, consists of setting up measurement systems that will gather data, and setting up research centres. To try to rush ahead with solutions, such as odd-even in Delhi, is a mistake. We do not have enough knowledge for the most well-meaning policy process to emerge with the right answers.

Element 2: Prerequisites

The simplest inputs into the sequencing decision come from the question of prerequisites. What systems i, j, k are required for system x to work?

Example 59: Electricity Reforms

Fuel is required by thermal generation plants, and electricity generators need to be able to sell electricity to distribution companies. The natural sequencing for the reforms is then to first reform electricity distribution. At this point, we would have financially sound distribution companies. The next step should have been to reform the energy sector, so that a market for fuel was in place and generation plants would be able to buy fuel. The last step should have been to reform electricity generation.

In the Indian experience, we set about creating a new private industry of electricity generation, without having solved the problems of distribution or of fuel. Very large amounts of capital are blocked in new age generation plants, who are stranded with the lack of fuel and/or the lack of financially sound buyers for their electricity.

With the benefit of hindsight, we see a simple failure of sequencing in the reforms of this sector. Problems in distribution and the energy sector should have been addressed before or at least in conjunction with generation reforms.[1]   ••

Example 60: Sequencing for Infrastructure Reform

Each infrastructure project starts out as a greenfield idea. It overcomes significant political and regulatory risk and gets to the stage of an operating asset. It builds up a certain time-series of toll revenues. At this point, it is a utility in the traditional sense of the term: with low risk and highly stable cash flows.

The nature of ownership, management and financing needs to change greatly as we go down this journey. At the early stage, projects are highly risky and require all-equity private financing. At the end, the return on equity can be juiced up using leverage, and the lowest cost financing for equity and debt from the public market can be harnessed.

When we start out from a state-dominated infrastructure sector, in what order should these arise? If the early stages are opened up, there is a problem as the early investors do not have a viable path to exit. This inhibits interest in investment.

Hence, the optimal sequencing lies in establishing the policy frameworks in reverse order. The first port of call is to have listed infrastructure utility companies, which also raise money from the public bond market, where the cost of capital is low, the assets reliably obtain toll revenue, and valuation benchmarks are established. All policy effort should be devoted to getting the world of listed infrastructure utilities working well. The public equity market should have dozens of very large infrastructure utilities, which operate and toll stable assets, which are sleepy low-risk companies.

Once this is done, these valuation benchmarks, and the certainty of exiting an infrastructure project by selling to an existing listed utility, will invite investments in the risky early-stage projects. Thus, the second stage in infrastructure reforms should be the establishment of mechanisms for private persons developing greenfield infrastructure assets.   ●●

Example 61: Float the Exchange Rate before Trade Reforms

Exchange rate reforms should come prior to trade reforms. This involves removing administrative barriers to the exchange rate and getting up to a floating exchange rate. This gives a continuously self-adjusting price which counteracts changes in competitiveness.

Once this is done, and the local economy is opened up, there will be continuous adjustment of imports and exports in response to changes in the exchange rate. If the country falters in exporting, the market adjustment is an exchange rate depreciation, which improves export competitiveness. The exchange rate is a shock absorber which will move in response to the short term and long-term consequences of trade reforms. ••

Example 62: Finance Comes First

As the economist Josh Felman says, if a great earthquake destroyed Mumbai, the first thing that we would need to restore are the financial firms, as they will provide the capital for the rebuilding of the rest of the city. A capable financial system is the primordial requirement of the market economy.

The infrastructure financing debacle in India is a reminder of finance as a prerequisite. The Bond–Currency–Derivatives Nexus was not in place, and therefore infrastructure financing could not be done in a market-based way. Policymakers were in a hurry, in the early 2000s, to get to infrastructure investment, and felt that financial reforms were a luxury which could be postponed. Infrastructure investment was done, for the short run, by forcing banks to hold infrastructure assets. This led to the worst outcome, visible after 2010, of stalled infrastructure investment and a large stock of stressed banks. It would have been much better to build the Bond–Currency–Derivatives Nexus, before embarking on infrastructure investment.

In similar fashion, we must place financial reforms before macro reforms. This is because macro policy requires the machinery of a sound financial system. Inflation targeting requires a monetary policy transmission, which requires the underlying financial reforms in the form of competition in banking, the Bond-Currency–Derivatives Nexus and capital account liberalization. Fiscal reform requires debt management and the bond market.

These preconditions generate a natural sequencing: First we must build a capable financial system, and then we must undertake monetary and fiscal reforms. In India, we seem to be coming at this in the reverse order.   ••

Example 63: Statistical System Prerequisites

Building a factual foundation is the first step of the policy pipeline. Improved measurement will feed into all areas of decision-making in the private sector and in the policy process. Hence, improvements in measurement should be prioritized for the early stages of building the republic.

If the CPI had not been well measured, it would not have been possible to do inflation targeting.[2]

Some people are excited about the value of nominal GDP targeting as a superior framework for monetary policy. We cannot consider this possibility in India, given the state of GDP measurement.

For most people in the country, GDP measurement has little practical importance. There is one place where numerical estimates of GDP play a direct role: fiscal planning. In January, when the budget is made, numerical targets for tax collection and the borrowing of the government are calculated based on estimated GDP. When the statistical system overstates GDP, this leads to tax targets that are excessively high and a borrowing program that is excessively large.[3]

This suggests a natural sequencing: a country should build trusted GDP estimates before it uses GDP values in fiscal planning. ••

Example 64: Banking Reforms before Bankruptcy Reforms

The essence of the bankruptcy code is transferring the control of a company, from the shareholders to the 'committee of creditors'. This requires rational persons who can become members of this committee and make commercially sound decisions.

Banks are an important element of the committee of creditors. In the Indian case, banking regulation resulted in distortions of the behaviour of bankers on the committee of creditors. Banking regulation had established the comfortable conditions where banks overstate the value of a bad asset, and bad news is kept safely hidden. To fix intuition, consider an asset with the face value of Rs 100, which is truly worth Rs 40, but is carried on the books at Rs 80 (owing to the infirmities of banking regulation). Under these conditions, energetically prosecuting a bankruptcy case results in a loss of Rs 40 for the bank. As a consequence, banks have an incentive in favour of dilatory tactics in the bankruptcy process.[4] As banks are an important source of credit, this interferes with the working of the bankruptcy process.

Before a bankruptcy reform is done, banking regulation needs to be put into order. ••

Element 3: Building Capability Gradually

Our first objective should be to establish *easy* objectives for state capacity, and fully succeed in building this state capacity.

Only after this is done should we try for a more complex problem. 'Easy' here is in the sense described in our treatment of what is easy and what is hard. Simple problems are those that involve low numbers of transactions, low discretion, low stakes and low secrecy.

In the case of taxation, high tax rates kick off vigorous countermeasures by private persons, ranging from tax avoidance to tax evasion. It is much harder to build a tax system with high tax rates. Hence, it makes sense to first learn how to do tax administration at low tax rates. Only after a high-compliance environment is achieved at low tax rates can we examine the possibility of higher tax rates. If, on the other hand, we try to jump to high tax rates, this induces an 'organizational rout', a collapse of the tax administration into high rates of corruption and evasion.

Similarly, a simple single rate GST is easier to implement, as opposed to a complex GST system with multiple rates. It would make sense to first build a single rate GST, achieve a high compliance environment, and then examine the possibility of having multiple rates.

On a related note, at the early stages of learning how to build a tax administration, the officials should have low powers of investigation and punishment. If high powers are given to officials, alongside the poor checks and balances of an early-stage organization, this will yield a collapse into intimidation and corruption. Only after a tax administration is working at high levels of probity with low tax rates, low powers of investigation, and low penalties, can we consider gently raising these powers.

These are natural sequencing opportunities: to build the easy pieces first, to learn state capacity on simple problems, and then come to the more difficult ones.

Example 65: A Success Story: The Indian Pension Reforms

Sequencing issues were central to the Indian pension reforms. There were three elements to the Indian pension reforms problem: mandatory pensions for private firms (that was done by EPFO), mandatory pensions for civil servants and the vast uncovered unorganized sector.

Policymakers chose to build the New Pension System starting with the civil servants. This was motivated by many elements of reasoning. New institutional infrastructure needed to be built and proven, and civil servants was a compact problem where this could commence. The credibility of the reform would be heightened with the 'eat your own dog food' character of the reform starting with civil servants.

Once the NPS worked, the employees of private firms would clamour to exit EPFO. Finally, word of mouth through civil servants (who are credible parties in their engagement with the larger populace) would gradually draw in voluntary unorganized sector participation into the NPS, without requiring the reduced returns for pensioners that are associated with expensive sales campaigns.   ••

Example 66: The Indian Bankruptcy Reform

When a country embarks on setting up a bankruptcy process for the first time, as India did in 2016, at first, the state capacity will be poor. A well-functioning bankruptcy process requires numerous actors to play their role correctly, and at first this ecosystem will not be in place.

Hence, in the early stages of the bankruptcy reform, it is better to carry small bankruptcies through the system. These constitute a smaller load. With larger cases, there will be expensive legal teams in the fray, trying to find any loophole. The collision between high stakes and low state capacity will give poor answers. For this reason, the decision to put 12 large cases into the fledgling Indian bankruptcy process was a problematic one.

Placing a high load, of high-stakes cases, upon a fledgling bankruptcy process can lead to an organizational rout. The economist Josh Felman has a good insight on one channel of influence, which runs as follows.[5] The essence of the bankruptcy process is the sanctity of process. The process creates the right incentives, so even if in one case there can be a higher value realization by sacrificing the process, we should still uphold the process.

Early in the life of the bankruptcy reform, judges are themselves relatively unsure about how this works. If a Rs 10 million case appears, it is more likely that a judge will favour the sanctity of process. But if a Rs 1 trillion case appears, and the prevailing jurisprudence is weak, the judge is more likely to say that the process can be over-ruled as the sums of money to be gained are so large. A few rulings like this can create jurisprudence that permanently hobbles the bankruptcy reform. ••

Example 67: A Success Story: China's Journey in Negotiating Free Trade Agreements

Consider the questions of trade policy faced in China.[6] Coming from a suspicious and protectionist background, much like India's, how was the country to graduate to a bigger engagement with international trade?

The logical place for China to start was New Zealand. New Zealand is a small country, so even if there are large mistakes in the development of a free trade agreement, this would not have important consequences for China. New Zealand is a country where the intellectual and political climate is one with high support for free trade, so removing cross-border restrictions would be easy. This was a good place to develop experience in trade negotiations, and to establish good precedents which could be quoted in future negotiations, either when faced with a recalcitrant government or when faced with difficulties in the domestic political economy.

China started on this negotiation in 2005, and the agreement was signed in April 2008. It was the first free trade agreement by China with a developed economy. It envisaged removing all tariffs by 2016.   ●●

Element 4: Manage Political Economy

Successful reform is about dealing with the allocation of gains and losses, and creating and sustaining winning coalitions. We should think about the most vulnerable, and push costs to them into the future. A good sequencing is one that gives gains to the economy early, and thus boosts GDP growth.

Anne Krueger, Jagdish Bhagwati and T. N. Srinivasan have emphasized the connections between internationalization and the local elite. In the initial condition, we are trapped in a domestic political economy, where large domestic distortions go with a narrow elite that defends those distortions. Policy actions that open up the economy in all possible dimensions are a good first step because they reshape the incentives of the local elite in favour of taking on the domestic barriers to high productivity.

A powerful theme in this political economy thinking lies in early actions that reshape the map of interests. Initial actions should build a new coalition of beneficiaries, who will support the completion of the reform.

Example 68: The Problems of Managing the Exchange Rate

Suppose the government manages the exchange rate. Private persons will see the power of the government in changing their profit rates and organize themselves to lobby for a favourable exchange rate policy. As an example, in China, a large export sector sprang up under a distorted exchange rate and lobbied to preserve the distortion.

These problems are avoided if the first stage in the reform is to achieve a floating exchange rate, i.e., to get the nascent pockets of internationalization to think that lobbying for exchange rate depreciation is not a choice.

A related trap in sequencing is the order in which exchange rate reform versus foreign currency borrowing reform takes place. If domestic agents build up large foreign borrowings early, then they tend to lobby in favour of restrictive exchange rate policy. The correct sequence is to first get to a floating exchange rate, and only then open up to foreign currency debt by local firms. ••

Example 69: A Success Story: India's Petroleum Sector Liberalization

The liberalization of petroleum pricing in India shows an interesting success story in sequencing. First came the decision to do this in stages and not induce any sudden shock. The actions began by giving ONGC the international price for crude oil, so as to establish parity with global price-based incentives for exploration and extraction. This was an easy first move which did not impinge upon the population.

Petroleum products are universal intermediates, and the short-term elasticity of demand is very small. There is a large low-income population for whom, low price inelasticity implies that fuel price hikes are tantamount to an income shock. Hence, price liberalization for consumer products, kerosene and LPG, should be back-ended. Hence, the sequencing for price decontrol that was adopted was industrial products (naphtha, fuel oil) followed by transportation fuels followed by cooking fuel.   ••

Example 70: A Success Story: India's Trade Policy Reform

The story of trade policy reform in India is also similarly interesting. When our policymakers worked on trade policy reforms in 1991, they shrewdly designed the sequencing to counteract the opposition of the 'Bombay Club'. The sequencing of tariff cuts was designed so as to first improve competitiveness of incumbents, through trade liberalization of industrial inputs such as capital goods and intermediates.

The first stage was the liberalization of capital goods imports, where the only losers were incumbent public sector companies such as HMT. This was welcomed by private manufacturers as they got better and cheaper equipment. The second stage was to liberalize intermediate goods. This was also welcomed by private manufacturers. Alongside this, capital controls were eased for portfolio flows in all areas (so that Indian firms got capital at a lower cost of capital) but not for FDI in all areas (so that Indian firms got less competition in the hinterland).

These moves helped many Indian firms gain confidence about dealing with import competition. Indeed, there was a great surge of Indian firms who began *exporting*, when given cheaper inputs, cheaper capital goods and cheaper capital. At the time, we coined the slogan *'Each time we cut tariffs, exports will go up'*.

This strategy helped dilute the organized opposition of Indian industry against tariff cuts. The private sector was now armed with global quality capital goods, buying global quality raw materials and sourcing debt and equity capital at world prices. The stage was then set for liberalization of imports of consumer goods.

A related element was the announcement by Yashwant Sinha that every year, the peak customs tariff rate would go down by five percentage points. This was an extremely wise move. Each decline, of five percentage points, was not big enough to kick off a furore. But the remorseless application of this rule, year after year, created certainty in the minds of the private sector that they had to gear up for a world of free trade. At the same time, they were given time to gear up with globally competitive technology.   ••

Element 5: Restraints against Abuse of Coercive Power

Some of the hardest sequencing problems involve creating organizations that wield the coercive power of the state. At early stages of development, individuals in organizations such as enforcement institutions, will likely have poor checks and balances. This will create the possibility of arbitrary use of the coercive power of the state.

> *I look upon an increase in the power of the state with greatest fear, because although while apparently doing good by minimizing exploitation, it does the greatest harm to mankind by destroying individuality which is at the root of progress. State represents violence in a concentrated and organized form.*

—Mahatma Gandhi

When large punishments can be inflicted upon the people, the power of individuals in enforcement institutions becomes extreme. There is a danger that enforcement organizations become roving bandits, engaging in extortion. There is then the risk of being trapped in the wrong equilibrium, as these incumbents would resist the creation of checks and balances.

A fledgling tax administration agency with a high tax rate and the power to raid will yield an 'organizational rout'.[7] The agency will collapse into corruption and abuse of power.

In the field of customs duties, the 'collected rate' is customs revenue divided by the value of imports. In a perfect state, this should be exactly equal to the official tariff rate. In Pakistan, for goods where the customs rate is below 40 per cent, this broadly works out: the collected rate is near the official ad valorem rate. By the time we get to an official rate of 80 per cent, there is a gap of about 30 percentage points between the official rate and the collected rate. At a customs duty of 120 per cent, the gap rises to 70 percentage points. High tax rates induce a bigger failure in weak organizations.[8]

Once this organizational rout has taken place, there will be grave opposition against well-meaning reforms, by the insiders who are profiting from the abuse of state power.

High powers to obtain information, raid, arrest, imprison, and award draconian penalties are found all across the Indian policy landscape and constitute a serious problem.[9] A government agency should be given such powers only when it has achieved high levels of institutional capability. Swedish-style powers of electronic surveillance by an income tax agency can only be given to an income tax agency that has achieved Swedish levels of the rule of law.

For these reasons, it makes sense to only legislate modest coercion at the early stages of state capacity. In the early stages of development, the focus should be on building a competent organization featuring checks and balances and the absence of extortion. Only after this public policy knowledge has been mastered can powers become larger.

On a similar note, when a new coercive bureaucracy is created, it is wise to limit its footprint upon the economy. As an example, we may envision a narrow SEBI that has coercive power upon stock exchanges and stockbrokers. Until high capabilities have developed, it is better to envision a SEBI that has no powers to summon information, investigate or impose punishments upon any other persons in the economy. After a few decades of a highly successful SEBI, there can be an evaluation about whether the footprint of SEBI should creep up.

This mechanism of containing damage—limiting the footprint—is used worldwide when it comes to regulators, that violate the separation of powers doctrine by fusing the legislative and executive branches. It should be particularly applicable in India, where the invisible infrastructure of checks and balances is weak, and where regulators fuse all the three branches of government.

By this reasoning, the early design work for the proposed Data Protection Authority raises concerns; this will be a brand-new agency that will have criminal powers over every consumer-facing firm in India.[10]

How State Capacity Declines

We seem to go through a cycle in India, which runs roughly as follows: An agency is established with low capabilities and excessive aspirations. Things do not work out, and there is a visible crisis.

We have excessive bureaucratic capture in India: the incumbents in an agency generally have a disproportionate say in the course corrections required after a crisis. It is in the interests of this bureaucracy to amass more personal power. Hence, crises lead to greater powers to do surveillance, greater powers to raid and greater powers to punish.

Each crisis thus leaves the agency with greater discretionary power, which in turn fuels a decline in the capabilities of the agency. This perspective yields interesting insights into the decline of capability at many organizations in the last decade.

As an example of this phenomenon, RBI was the regulator of NBFCs, and there was a large crisis of NBFCs in 2018. In response, RBI's powers were increased. Similarly, when politicians ask for greater tax revenues, the tax bureaucracy asks for more coercive power.

Summing Up

The policymaker has to do many things. In what order should they be done? Too often, in India, policymakers pick one of two easy things, 'the low hanging fruit', and after that the reform peters out. Doing the easiest thing first is generally not the optimal sequencing.

The policy pipeline shapes sequencing. If the data is lacking, it will not be possible to make progress on policy design. Therefore, when the data is lacking, the first thing in the sequencing should be improvements in the data.

In the working of real-world systems, there are prerequisites. An inflation-targeting central bank will require a capable bond market, in order to do the monetary policy transmission. Reforms of electricity generation will not work if the electricity distribution does not work. We have to identify these choke points and solve them first.

State capacity does not come about easily. It is better to solve easy problems first, that put us on the path to higher state capacity in the future. Capability emerges out of the process of learning-by-doing. This calls for low transaction-intensity, low discretion, low stakes and low secrecy, at the early stages.

It is important to think through the political economy. This is not just about buying out the persons who lose from a reform. The early steps should create gainers who will then support and sustain the reform.

In the early stages of building the republic, low coercive power should be given to government organizations, particularly the powers to raid, investigate, and punish. Through this, we reduce the stakes. Only after high success is achieved, in wielding low coercive power, can there be a discussion about whether higher coercive power is desirable.

In India, we are often seeing a negative spiral. An agency has excessive coercive power, and so it fails in its work, but the political response to failure generates greater coercive power for the agency, which further reduces capability. The right response to failure by an agency should be a reduction in its coercive power.

35

Building the Knowledge Foundations

Policymaking, when it is done right, is fundamentally a research problem. It involves hypothesizing about market failure, and the lowest-cost intervention that can address the market failure, and watching the evidence about one intervention at a time based on which pragmatic decisions can be made to retreat or to change course. As a consequence, a state is only as good as the knowledge foundations in society, that it is able to tap into. The knowledge foundations of society comprise facts ('how many teenagers in Kerala are married?') and theory ('what is the impact of early marriage upon the life of a family in Kerala?').

Earlier in this book, we showed the lack of information about the economy as a root cause of why public policy fails. What is a policymaker to do when faced with these constraints?

Skepticism on Public Data

Limitations of state capability are present across the board in India. All aspects of the Indian state perform poorly.

It is not a surprise that the state-run statistical system also performs poorly.

At the simplest, state agencies that produce statistics face the usual constraints of public administration, of achieving the operational competence of making and releasing data. Layered on top of this are the political dimensions of data.[1] Facts about the country are sometimes directly politically salient, e.g., when they shape redistricting, or when they interfere with official propaganda. More generally, Goodhart's law is in operation: once facts have real world implications, a political economy process is set in motion where rival groups aim to distort facts in desired ways.

The uncritical use of data is a major flaw that is hampering numerous research papers that study Indian economics, and policymakers have been often misled when they have relied on public statistics.[2] We cannot assume that when data is released by a government agency, it is sound. There is a need for greater critical thinking about data quality.

A diverse array of non-government data sources has now opened up, which make possible the observation of the economy, on a sustained basis, without requiring state capacity in the official statistical system. As an example, night lights radiance yields an estimate of prosperity, at a monthly frequency, for pixels of India which are 0.5 km × 0.5 km.[3]

The Importance of Private Information Sets

In an ideal world, we would like to have statistics and analytical models. In our reality in India, our ability to undertake formal economic analysis on many problems is limited. This creates the need for informal information channels.

When quantitative analysis is infeasible, we should do more qualitative research. Every policy thinker in India must thus have a strong emphasis on a human network in the real world, on going out on field trips, on looking at our world, listening to people, and trying to assimilate what they are saying. We do not have the luxury of reading papers and looking at data; we have to look directly at the world. Similarly, the knowledge and effectiveness of a policymaker is directly proportional to the intensity of engagement with private persons.

The Bank of England has repeatedly recruited people from outside the UK into leadership roles. It is relatively easy for an expert on monetary policy in any advanced economy to show up in the UK and be useful in the Bank of England. Where does this portability of knowledge come from? Partly, it is based on the fact that the institutional landscape of all advanced democracies is relatively homogeneous.[4] Partly, it is based on the fact that the data and the research literature on the UK is strong, so a new person can rapidly orient herself into that setting.

These features are absent in India, where the data and research literature are weak. The information set is significantly composed of soft information that is picked up over the years from a human network where the truth is revealed only in an environment of trust. For this reason, successful work in public policy in a given field in India requires long years of engagement and trust-building in a deep human network.

Policymakers must rely more on market-based sources of information that help the policy process correct itself. In most sectors of the economy, market participants are producing information that they mostly keep to themselves because it is proprietary. Policymakers can help discover relevant parts of that information by creating incentives for market participants.

For instance, when there is not enough information to price a public service based on a ground-up costing, they can use reverse auctions to discover a reasonable price. Similarly, policymakers may also rely more on competitive market structures to reduce the need for information and analysis. For instance, for tariff-setting in infrastructure sectors, instead of relying on ground-up costing, regulators could set the tariffs based on benchmarks of the industry, so that those performing worse than the average get a disincentive.

Kicking Off Improvements in Measurement

I must study politics and war that my sons may have liberty to study mathematics and philosophy.

—John Adams

We must also prioritize time and resources for improvements of the statistics. Every policymaker should kick off long-range initiatives to improve statistics in her area. Economic statistics is not just the work of the CSO—it is the work of myriad persons all across the economy. We must prioritize the capture of information and the release of information.

When sound new statistical measures come about, at first they will have inadequate and short time series for a long time. Often, we will not be the beneficiaries of the statistical system improvements that we initiate. Just as *a country becomes great when men plant trees that they will not live to enjoy the shade of*, a country becomes great when people initiate data gathering efforts that they will not live to enjoy the fruits of.

Example 71: A Success Story: Outcomes Measurement in Education

The most famous episode in India of outcomes measurement was the work by Pratham, to measure what school children know, through their 'ASER' survey. ASER measurement has two great strengths. First, ASER measures outcomes (what children know) as opposed to the traditional measurement of inputs (school buildings built, teachers hired, etc.) or outputs (kids enrolled). Further, ASER is not part of the government, and it is hence more immune to pressures to distort the data or block the release of data when the data is painting an unflattering picture.

ASER surveys began in 2005 and have been extremely influential in showing the lack of learning achievements by school children in India. When you compare this date against the launch of *Sarva Shiksha Abhiyaan* (2000/2001) and further back to the launch of the District Primary Education Program (1993), there is a sense that we would have fared much better if an ASER-style measurement had begun much earlier. This would have created feedback loops and helped rapidly improve the design decisions from 1993 to 2003, which have proved much harder to reverse when the bad news started coming in from ASER surveys in 2005 onward.   ••

Example 72: Outcomes Measurement in the Criminal JusticeSystem

In each area, it would be wise to start the process of state building with outcomes measurement. The entire enterprise of the criminal justice system should lead to one outcome: young women feeling safe when walking alone in public places at night. This can be directly measured using surveys, where we ask parents the time in the evening when they feel teenage daughters should be back at home. The establishment of crime victimization surveys should be the first milestone in reforms of the criminal justice system.[5]   ••

Episodic versus Long-Term Measurement

Many academic economists initiate a project, gather custom data for that project, and stop measuring when the project is finished. This data is kept confidential by the researcher. While all knowledge is useful, this approach to measurement is less effective from the viewpoint of society.

What is more valuable are methods for measurements which run all the time and and where the resulting data is widely available. When measurement is done all the time, it becomes possible to assess the consequences of an event.

As an example, Andhra Pradesh banned micro-finance in 2010. This called for research on understanding the impact of the ban. CMIE had been surveying 11,000 households in Andhra Pradesh, three times a year, all the time. Households in regions of other states were also observed, where there was no ban on micro-finance. This made possible a comparison of regions within Andhra Pradesh which were hit by the ban against matched regions elsewhere in India which were not hit by the ban.[6]

Similarly, the presence of the CMIE panel data for households made possible estimates of excess death in the pandemic.

It Takes Time to Develop Sound Measurement Systems

Tiger conservation leaped into prominence with the establishment of Project Tiger in 1972. It took about 30 years to lay the foundations of measurement.

Important new development took place in this field from 2002 to 2006. Every four years since 2006, the Indian government conducts a national census of tigers and other wildlife. The All India Tiger Estimation Report 2018 was prepared by the National Tiger Conservation Authority in collaboration with the Wildlife Institute of India, World Wide Fund India (WWF), state forest departments, and many volunteers and non-profits.

The most recent survey deployed 44,000 field staff who conducted habitat surveys across 20 tiger-occupied states of India, checking some 381,400 km for tigers and their prey. The team placed paired camera traps at 26,838 locations across 139 study sites and these collected 34.8 million photos. The WII and NCTA developed the methodology for conducting the tiger survey after extensive consultations with experts and through a rigorous peer review process. The methodology combines field combing to record carnivore tracks, remote sensing data, hidden cameras, four indigenously developed software systems including one that tracks tiger flank stripe patterns, and DNA profiling.

None of this is cast in stone. An active debate continues to take place, in the intellectual community, about the strengths and weaknesses of the measurement program.

Iterative refinement is taking place, every day, based on these debates. The only trusted measurement system is one that is continuously scrutinized, criticized and refined.

This work is an example of the long and slow process required, in laying foundations of measurement, of deep collaboration between the state and civil society, and of the use of old knowledge and new research methods.

For every economic policy researcher or practitioner, who feels exhausted at the thought of measurement in the problem before her—whether it is crime, courts, capital controls or air quality—the scale of work on measurement of tigers is an inspiring story.[7]

Principles for Data Release by the Government

In previous years, the statistical system run by the government involved organizations which utilized a great deal of microeconomic data, that was kept secret, and released useful aggregate data. In the modern world, this can be re-imagined. The most important role that the government can now play is to obtain and release micro data. The private sector will find diverse ways to utilize this well.

Example 73: What Is the Role of the State in Maps?

In the old world, the Survey of India produced a consumer product, maps. In order to build maps, the Survey of India walked around in India and built the underlying maps databases.

The maps database is indeed a public good. Once it is built, and released for download over the Internet, it is non-rival and non-excludable. Even if there are internal inefficiencies in the production of this data by the Survey of India, it is worth spending public money in order to make and release this database.

Once this is done, it would make sense for the Survey of India to retreat from the consumer business of making physical maps.[8] A physical map is a private good (your use of a physical map interferes with my use of the same map). The private sector is quite able to use the data released by the Survey of India, through which a competitive industry will arise around physical maps, electronic maps, etc. The open source 'Open street maps' ('OSM') will be one player that will utilize the databases released by the Survey of India and release it into APIs and consumer products which are free.

If we think in terms of the four dimensions of what is hard, interacting with end-consumers involves a lot of transactions. It is difficult for Survey of India to meaningfully serve individual users. By removing the consumer-facing role for Survey of India, we reduce the difficulty of building a sound Survey of India.   ••

Similarly, the government can release GDP data. It would be better to release all the underlying micro data that is used to compute GDP. After that, different users will process this data in different ways, and form their own picture about what is going on in the economy by modifying the assumptions made in the GDP calculation. Similarly, the only role for the state in the decadal Census is to make a dataset and release it on a website as a free download, as a public good; end-users are quite able to download this data and utilize it themselves.

Two useful principles to think about data release are:

1. If something can be obtained using the Right to Information Act, it should be released pre-emptively. We should progressively expand the scope of items under 'duty to publish' of the RTI Act.

2. If a data set was created using public funding, then it should
    be released into the public domain in machine readable
    form, while taking care to mask identifying information
    that would harm the privacy of private persons.

From Data to Knowledge

The policy process involves identifying market failure in the
landscape, choosing a subset of important difficulties that are
worth working on, and using a process of cost-benefit analysis
to discover the least intrusive intervention through which
each market failure can be addressed. The safe strategy in
public policy is to incrementally evolve, making small moves,
obtaining feedback from the empirical evidence, and refine
policy work in response to evidence.

This process requires intellectual frameworks accompanied
by trusted data sets. It is generally difficult to recruit these
analytical capabilities into the Indian state. The two worlds—
main line civil servant versus intellectual capabilities—are far
apart in terms of organizational culture and recruitment profile.
In the long run, this should change. The ultimate aim of a
knowledge society is an arrangement where all government
intervention is grounded in a research process.

But for many years, we may expect that the organizational
DNA in the state is not conducive to recruiting researchers or
to creating the conditions in which they can be productive.
Under these conditions, it is particularly important for Indian
government organizations to develop deep partnerships with
knowledge institutions.

Policymakers in government tend to be in the din and
noise of the day-to-day policy process. The departments

of government suffer from a high pace of staffing changes. Government organizations tend to defend the prevailing policy positions, which is not conducive to the intellectual process.

Knowledge institutions have the luxury of not getting hijacked by the newspaper headlines of the day. This gives an opportunity for sustained focus, over long years, that is required to think properly on a given question. Knowledge institutions are not bound by the prevailing policy positions of the government, and are thus able to exercise pure rational thinking on the questions of the age.

Knowledge Partnerships That Play in the Market for Ideas

Policy institutions need to establish long-run relationships with multiple research institutions. A knowledge partnership contract has the basic rhythm of building knowledge in the public domain, passing the market test in the market for ideas, criticizing the status quo and participating in the public debate, and then being available to render policy advice to a government institution.

This is not easily done. Just as government suffers from capacity constraints in India, there is limited capacity in academic institutions in India also. However, capacity at research institutions evolves in response to greater engagement with policy institutions.

In a knowledge partnership, the role of government institutions is to foster the supply side of research (by resourcing it with an environment of long-term stability) and the demand side (by asking questions of researchers).

The first priority of research institutions must be to build new knowledge and participate in the public discourse. This involves understanding what is going wrong in the country and criticizing it. Research capabilities must first be proven in the public domain landscape of the research community. The privilege of giving policy advice, and being part of the policy process, should be limited to the persons who achieve the status of public intellectuals, through writing and speaking in the public domain, and earning respect for honesty and knowledge.

Knowledge institutions have a comparative advantage in understanding and measuring market failure, and the costs imposed upon society by state intervention. There is a natural role for knowledge institutions in assessing the extent to which market failure is, indeed present, in inventing new solutions, in cost-benefit analysis, and in concurrent evaluation through which measurement is done about the extent to which the problem is solved.

The healthy functioning of knowledge partnership contracts requires effort and capability on both sides. Government organizations need to be patient, knowing that capacity creation takes time. Government organizations need to avoid falling into the three stereotypes of the contracts with consulting firms, manpower firms and PR firms.

On their side, knowledge institutions also need to change gears in order to be useful partners. The ultimate purpose of a research institution in India is to acquire *metis*, to create authentic knowledge about India, to diffuse knowledge into India, and to be part of the process of changing India. Research institutions need to shift gears away from a focus on publishing in international journals, which goes with catering to the interests and priorities of editors and referees who are far away and have no skin in the game.[9]

What Knowledge Partnerships Are Not

In conventional government contracting, there are three kinds of relationships which are confused as being knowledge partnership contracts.

Governments regularly give out specific assignments to consulting firms or law firms, to deliver a tangible work product. These tangible work products are important, but they come late in the policy pipeline. They do not substitute for intellectual capabilities at a much earlier stage, where more basic questions are being asked. Knowledge institutions are valuable at a more basic level: *What is the problem that we see? Is market failure present? What is the lowest cost intervention? Do the benefits outweigh the costs? How do we build state capacity for achieving this intervention?* Knowledge institutions should invent the New Pension System; a law firm would draft the contract with a pension fund manager much later in the process of policy implementation.

Governments also regularly contract with manpower firms, who supply junior staff who take instructions and perform tasks. Such staffing contracts are also not knowledge partnership contracts.

Governments also have communications specialists who take care of public relations. Crafting and sending out a message, sending out messages into the social media, supporting the government in public debates, this is not the work of knowledge partners. Government organizations need to understand that the freedom of mind in academic institutions is the key to obtaining high quality advice. When you ask a researcher to be a spokesman, you get neither spokesman nor researcher.

Increasing Analytical Capability in Government

Level I: At its best, an Indian government organization should be imbued with analytical capabilities. It should be able to utilize evidence to conduct research and utilize this for the policy process. This would then be comparable to the best policy organizations seen in mature market economies, where the internal staff have research capabilities. Once research capabilities inside the government organization are adequate, the knowledge institutions of society contribute to the policy process through research products that they release into the public domain, which are utilized by government employees, through criticism of the status quo, and through participation in the public debate about policy.

Level II: The second-best path is one where the Indian government organization lacks these capabilities, but is able to forge deep partnerships with research institutions. Through this, evidence and research would be brought into the innermost discussions about policymaking.

Level III: The weakest path is that of a conventional Indian policy institution, which lacks a research culture, and lacks deep partnerships with research institutions. The lack of knowledge partnerships comes about either owing to the lack of interest in ideas, or from the insistence that academic institutions must be subservient to government officials. Such policy institutions are unmoored to knowledge, and produce the lowest-quality work.

The Long-Term Foundations for Policy Research

In the short term, the Indian policy community has to make do with the academic institutions and researchers which are available. We must, however, recognize that these individuals and institutions are part of the fuller research ecosystem, where the key element is the universities.

Research and capability in the humanities and social sciences, all across the country, is what lays the foundations for policy-oriented research. The universities build the foundational papers and the universities build the people. The policy community reaps the fruits of the labours of the universities. A great deal of the difficulties that we have seen in India in recent decades are related to the atrophying of capability in the universities in the humanities and social sciences.

India has invested in building science and technology at universities. In these fields, research done overseas is directly applicable in India, and India can actually free ride on knowledge production overseas. Yet, India has chosen to invest in building human capital for science and technology by having universities in India.

We have cut corners on building humanities and social sciences at universities, and these are fields where knowledge on India can only be produced in India. Through this, we have hampered knowledge on India, and also the human capital in the country. Building the republic will require strong capabilities in the humanities and social sciences in Indian universities.

The Shifting Institutional Architecture of Knowledge Institutions

In the India of old, government funded and government controlled knowledge organizations dominated the landscape. Over the years, however, the difficulties of state capacity have adversely impacted upon their functioning.

The contours of a new map, of the institutional landscape in the humanities, social sciences and policy research, is now visible. The highest growth rates of capability, and in many cases the highest levels of capability, are increasingly found in private organizations. The end notes of this book draw on a powerful literature, and the bulk of these capabilities are now in private organizations. Recognizing these developments has important implications for funders and users of research.

These new organizations are innovating on their internal organization design and processes, when compared with the traditional government-controlled organizations. The best of these innovations will add up to the new foundations of the Indian intellectual system.

Is This a Good Use of Public Money?

Data and knowledge can be public goods: once released into the public domain they can be non-rival and non-excludable. This market failure generates underinvestment by private persons and justifies state expenditures.

The state should do the things that private persons will not do. The private sector has yet to organize itself to systematically fund the creation of statistics and knowledge. This justifies state expenditures. There are, of course, questions of bang for the buck. For example, the simple expenditures into public universities are not working well. The mechanisms for expenditure need to be redesigned.

While the hurdle rate for all public expenditure is high with the MCPF of about 3, the magnitudes of expenditure involved here are small and the gains to society are very high.

Summing Up

A great deal of data in India is of low quality. This includes data that is produced by government agencies and the official statistical system. All official data cannot be trusted. We have to take great interest in the methods and administrative difficulties, of each data source, before deciding to use it.

There are many coping mechanisms. Policy design can plan to discover prices through auctions, rather than assume that adequate information is available up front. There is a greater role for qualitative research, given the weaknesses of quantitative research.

Every policymaker must kick off long-range improvements in measurement. The most valuable thing, for the Indian policy process, is sustained measurement, and not one-off measurement. When a phenomenon is measured, again and again, we develop the long time-series, and the observation of many units and many geographical locations. These are the most useful data sets of the country.

Government needs to release much more information in the public domain, particularly record-level anonymized micro data. What can be obtained through the RTI should be published. Data that is made using public money should always be released to the public. The private sector and the research community will do good things with data files; the only thing required of the government is to release micro data.

Knowledge institutions reshape the intellectual discourse. Complex reforms, such as the GST or inflation targeting, cannot be achieved as a palace coup; they require a shift in the entire discourse. Sustained work by large numbers of intellectuals in knowledge institutions is essential to achieving the new level of thinking.

Every policymaker will benefit by setting up a few knowledge partnership contracts and take effort to make them work. In the short term, they are low-cost initiatives. In the long run, these will yield a qualitatively superior trajectory of the policy process.

This approach needs to be applied in all parts of government. Whether it is in Karnataka or in a city in Karnataka such as Shimoga, policymakers require capable knowledge institutions, which are steeped in the local context, which develop metis.

The intelligentsia in public policy is derived from the broad foundations of the humanities and social science knowledge that is made in the universities. In India, public investments in the universities have emphasized science and engineering and neglected the humanities and social sciences. Building the republic requires capabilities in the universities, in the humanities and the social sciences.

36

Low State Capacity Changes Policy Design

The grand story of infrastructure in India is instructive. By the late 1990s, there was universal mistrust of public production of infrastructure services, and the policy community moved towards private production. It was felt that a private person will run infrastructure assets better, as we lack the state capacity to run these assets.

With the benefit of hindsight, we know that contracting and regulation of private infrastructure providers *also* requires considerable state capacity. The simplistic notion—of shifting infrastructure provision away from a low capability state to private providers—was wrong.

How then should we think more carefully about the optimal pathways when we have low state capacity?

How does our thinking about public policy change when we possess low state capacity?

Just a Down-Sized Sweden?

Consider the contrast between Sweden and India. The expenditure/GDP ratio in Sweden is about twice that of India.

The management capability in public policy in Sweden is much superior to that seen in India. If the Swedish leadership decides to establish universal HPV immunization for children, it is easy to translate this intent into action. But in India, it is quite a challenge for the leadership to implement such a decision. Sweden has more state capacity.

How would we think about public policy differently, when placed in Sweden as opposed to how we would think in India?

The simplest idea is to think of an Indian state that does everything that Sweden does, with inferior resourcing. The Swedish central bank has 360 employees, so we should aim for a central bank with 180 employees.[1]

We would look at the unemployment insurance system in Sweden, and come up with a design in India which requires roughly half the expenditure.

We think this is the wrong way to think about the consequences of low state capacity. The consequences of low state capacity run deep and require fundamentally different answers in a place like India, when compared to a high state capacity country like Sweden.

A Higher Price and a Lower Budget Constraint

One way to think about state capacity is as a layer of inefficiency in all state activities. Low state capacity is like a modified price of engaging in a certain activity.

Sweden gets a central bank done in 360 employees, but we may require 720 people in a central bank, as low state capacity induces greater inefficiency. Here, the cost pertains to financial resourcing but even more to the scarce time of the policy leadership.

It is also useful to think of state capacity is a finite *resource*, as a low budget constraint. The financial resources available in a low-capacity state are more limited. The scarcest resource of all is the time and attention of the senior political and bureaucratic leadership, and of the experts.

The short-term question lies in utilizing these scarce resources wisely. Doing policy under conditions of low state capacity is about making decisions where prices are higher and budget constraints are smaller.

The deeper question lies in how to increase state capacity. How can a country put itself on the journey to increasing state capacity, so that over time, the cost of undertaking a certain activity goes down, and the aggregate resources available to the state go up?

Market Failure That Should Not Be Addressed

In theory, the world contains a lot of market failure and we use state intervention to address them. In practice, we have an imperfect state. In the real world, the outcomes with state intervention are always worse than originally imagined. The policy decisions that flow from the real-world political process are sub-optimal. State capacity is limited, so the implementation of a policy objective is flawed. It is useful to think of three cases:

Market failure solved, but at a high cost:

- Under conditions of low state capacity, there is a greater risk of extremist policy actions.

  For example, consider the market failure (externality) associated with acid rain. It is possible for a government to ban coal-fired thermal plants. This action does put an end to the market failure. But this is an inefficient solution, as the cost imposed upon society is too high.

- Banning an activity is done too often in India. Public choice theory predicts that bureaucracies will favour the peace of mind and laziness. Given the lack of accountability associated with present laws, there is a bias in favour of bans.

Regulatory response, but high cost and low effectiveness:

- Sometimes, the Indian state pursues a situation with market failure by trying to write regulations which reshape the behaviour of private persons. In this, owing to capacity constraints, the regulations that are written fare poorly on the cost-benefit analysis. They impose high costs and achieve low results.

- The market failure is not solved, and the costs imposed upon society are excessive.

Redistribution, but High Cost and Low Effectiveness:

- Government interventions through running government schemes or paying out subsidies are particularly daunting, under conditions of low state capacity, because of the high marginal cost of public funds. The cost to society of public expenditures is very high, so even a well-run program is less attractive under these conditions.

- Further, low state capacity hobbles the working of the scheme or subsidy program, and that further hampers the net gain to society.

- Put together, schemes of the Indian state fare poorly on cost-benefit analysis owing to high cost to society and poor results.

Through these pathways, the cost–benefit analysis associated with government intervention works out differently when there is low state capacity. There is a loss of welfare associated with a certain market failure. Under conditions of low state capacity, the costs associated with the intervention will be large and the market failure itself will be inadequately addressed. We are often better off living with the market failure, rather than trying to address it in an imperfect way.

Under conditions like Sweden, where state capacity is high, we would be more optimistic and set out to address many situations with market failure. But under conditions of low state capacity, it would be efficient to choose a smaller class of problems worth solving.

By this reasoning, we would not do half the effort on addressing all the market failure that Sweden is fighting. The Indian state should not just be a mini-Swedish state. There would be many zero values (i.e., no state intervention required) in the optimal path for India. We would try to go after a smaller set of situations with market failure, where the welfare cost of the free market outcome is particularly large, and where the state capacity required in addressing the market failure is relatively small. Given our capacity constraints today, to quote Kaushik Basu, we have to engage in 'libertarianism of necessity'.

More Intrusive Interventions Are More Dangerous

When state capacity is low, there is a greater chance of making mistakes. In this case, the damage that can be done by a more intrusive action by the state is greater.

When we live in a low state capacity environment, there is a greater chance that the government is wrong. In this case, we should favour small moves, small powers for the government, small punishments, small sums of money. The bigger and more dramatic the action, the greater is the harm inflicted upon society when government is wrong.

Public choice theory drives a wedge between the aspirations of the state, for more control of the people, versus the views of the people. The state will be hungry for more power, more control, more coercion, running beyond what is best for the people. When the political system works well, state coercion has greater legitimacy: even when fairly intrusive things are done by the state, there is a deep democratic foundation to those decisions. Democracy is a system where the people consent to state coercion.

When the political system works less well, we should be more skeptical about the coercive projects of the state. When democracy works poorly, the legitimacy of state coercion is reduced. Policy thinkers would do well to favour a light touch when faced with such circumstances.

For my friends, everything, for my enemies, the law.

—Oscar Benavides, Peruvian politician

The phrase 'the government is wrong' seems like a sterile one. Our mental model may be one in which at random, there is a certain probability of making a mistake. However, the probability of being wrong is itself driven by the incentives of politicians and officials. Under conditions of low state capacity, an official has the power to raid any person, with weak checks and balances. Public choice theory teaches us that the government is not just wrong through random errors; there is malign intent in the errors. Weak checks and balances operating upon the official who controls raids will *induce* a higher probability of malign raids.

Under conditions of low state capacity, a big disruption such as demonetization should be subjected to greater skepticism than it would face in a high state capacity environment. This is because the probability of our being wrong, under Indian conditions of state capacity, is higher.

Do Fewer Things

We in India are late industrialisers. We built a democracy at an early stage of development. Democracy has brought a large number of demands upon the state. It is difficult for elected leaders to ignore these demands. Too often, we have succumbed to mission creep. We tend to go after too many policy problems and end up with inadequate resourcing on each of them. In area after area, there is an organizational rout born of premature load bearing. We are weak in public policy and public administration—across all areas—so the opportunity cost of undertaking any one of those activities is high.

This can be viewed in a more benign way: an organizational rout whereby public expenditures are not translated to good outcomes. There is a more sinister dimension to premature load bearing, however, when coercive power is given to officials with inadequate checks and balances. This leads to a reduction of freedom and a rise in expropriation risk.

There is a lot to gain by paring down to a smaller set of priorities, focusing upon them, and making genuine progress.

If the scarce resources—of money and manhours of key persons—could *focus* on a small set of important problems, we would get a lot more done. Along the way, we would learn how to own and operate a state.

This can be seen as one more message in sequencing. The correct sequence is to first focus on a few problems, learn how to do politics and public management, and then scale out into a larger number of problems.

The economist Joseph Stiglitz has argued that in developing countries, there is rampant market failure, and this calls for a larger scale of state intervention. While we agree on the presence of much market failure, our proposal would run in the opposite direction. We would argue in favour of the largest possible state that is feasible while achieving competence, and this is likely to be a very small state.

The Virtue of Simplicity

When state capacity is high, a government can embark on more complex plans. When state capacity is low, the only things that will work correctly are simple plans.

This was a major theme in the evolution of tax policy in India in recent decades. Reduce the number of rates, reduce exemptions, reduce complexity: these were the themes around which major progress was made.[2]

As an example, consider the prospect of a subsidy, implemented through the tax system, for things that involve positive externalities. In theory, this can be a good thing. There *is* market failure when there are positive externalities, and there *is* a case for a subsidy, and sometimes that subsidy can be delivered through the tax system.

Suppose highway construction is to be financed by tax-exempt bonds. The policy analysis of tax-exempt bonds is, however, a very complicated affair. When we confront a positive externality, and think of a public subsidy, we must have numerical estimates of how large the externality is, which guides the design of the subsidy. Giving an entity or a class of entities the ability to issue tax exempt bonds constitutes a certain magnitude of subsidy, which may or may not be commensurate with the magnitude of the positive externality. A subsidy through the interest cost of bonds straight away favours more leveraged firms, which is unconnected to the magnitude of the positive externality.

Once the precedent is set, that highway developers are able to issue tax-exempt bonds, then there will be a clamour for other kinds of tax-exempt bonds. Should this be given to airports also? What about irrigation? Is the positive externality associated with all kinds of infrastructure the same? Why stop at infrastructure? What about a firm that gives loans to poor people? Why not have tax exempt bonds for hospitals?

Under conditions of low state capacity, the only safe place to be is to have no tax-exempt bonds. If a subsidy has to be paid, it is best to do this through the expenditure programs of government, where there will be better scrutiny of the relative magnitudes of expenditures.

Example 74: Information Utilities

There is an emerging field in India, of 'information utilities' that perform commercial functions. There are two ways in which this industry can come about. One pathway is to have multiple competing private firms, with a layer of consumer protection and checks on market power such as inter-operability regulation. This is the approach taken in the construction of NSDL, CDSL, etc. There is an alternative approach: to build a government monopoly. RBI is in the process of building such a monopoly, which is called the 'Public Credit Registry' (PCR).

This is an inferior path for three reasons. First, concentrating information about private persons in the hands of government is harmful for society. We are generally better off with a government that knows less about us, and this is even more important at the early stages of building the republic, where there are few checks on abuse of information. Second, monopolies generally fare worse than competitive industries at fostering innovation and cost reduction. Third, RBI has quite a challenge on its hands, of learning how to achieve state capacity on its core functions of inflation targeting and regulating banks. The pathway for RBI lies in focusing on its main tasks, and learning to do them well, rather than building a sprawling empire.[3] ●●

Example 75: Competition between Exchanges

Financial exchanges can compete, offering diverse kinds of products for trading, methods of trading, etc. There is a normal market process of listening to what users want, investing in innovations, learning from mistakes, changing course, etc., all playing out at exchanges with rapid feedback from successful adoption (or not) by financial market participants.

The government is involved in the working of financial markets in the form of addressing market failure. While exchanges innovate, the role of the government is to ensure that there is no collapse of the system of financial trading, and to enforce against market abuse. Apart from this, there is no role for the government.

In India, however, we have evolved a central planning system where every detail about the design of the exchange is controlled by SEBI. Every exchange in India looks the same to the user, and the features and capabilities of the exchange are controlled by SEBI.

This has generated a remarkable phenomenon of shadow-boxing, where the process of competition between exchanges is played out as rival influences upon SEBI. Each exchange lobbies in favour of changes in the SEBI-specified product design that will increase its own market share. The only competition between exchanges is for influence at SEBI.

Under Indian conditions of state capacity, SEBI fares poorly when the competitive energy between exchanges is played out at the arena of SEBI. Under Indian conditions of state capacity, the power of central planning placed at SEBI—unmoored of market feedback—yields a poor design of the trading system.

In recent years, this has given a stream of actions by SEBI that have a negative impact upon market quality. At first blush, we may think that the answer lies in improved state capacity at SEBI. However, the real issue is that comprehensive central planning systems work particularly badly when there is low state capacity. The deeper solution is to remove SEBI from the crossfire of competition between exchanges.   ••

Example 76: Industrial Policy

We frequently hear demands for a government to 'pick winners' such as an industry (e.g., making wall clocks) and/or a location (e.g., Morbi, Gujarat), and push the private sector in this direction either through tax incentives or subsidies or coercion.

The experience of mature economies such as Japan or the US shows us that industrial policy works badly, even under those conditions of state capacity. Under Indian conditions of state capacity, industrial policy is best avoided. There is a large chance of mistakes by the state, and there is a large opportunity cost of the human and financial resources that are put into these battles.

We should get uncomfortable when any Indian government agency encourages or discourages any industry or location. As an example, RBI has capital control restrictions that favour nine industries, including nanotechnology and poultry. No economist knows enough about the structure of the Indian economy to make such a decision.[4]

In the 1970s, the Santacruz Electronic Export Processing Zone (SEEPZ) was built by policymakers based on the idea that the electronics industry needed encouragement, and this encouragement was given in the form of zero customs duties. The elimination of customs duties is always a good policy, and this gave gains. The industries that came out of SEEPZ, however, were not what policymakers visualized. India did not start exporting electronics owing to the SEEPZ experiment. SEEPZ instead gave birth to the Indian software and diamond industries. The elixir that worked was not the ability of a policymaker to pick winners; it was the removal of trade barriers.   ••

Learning the Meta Technology of How to Run the State

In the early history of many successful states, the leadership focused primarily on two problems: raising taxes and waging wars. Learning-by-doing took place through the pursuit of these two activities. State capacity in the early UK and the early Sweden was learned by building large, complex organizations which raised taxes and waged wars.

The learning-by-doing that took place was not just about the narrow problems of raising taxes and waging wars. The learning-by-doing that took place was about larger ideas about how to organize the state. The general capability of public policy and public administration was learned in these two areas, which was then transplanted into other areas.

This ladder of capability is useful when thinking about the problem of state capacity in India. The strategy for public policy in India should be to pare down the number of objectives to a few core public goods such as the criminal justice system. Our task for a few decades is to learn how to build state capacity in those areas. The problem is not just the narrow question of learning how to run the criminal justice system, but the larger lessons of how to achieve state capacity.

Once we have these capabilities in the country, there would be the possibility of broadening out to a more expansive set of market failure. That would be a political choice for future generations.

Summing Up

If we were in Sweden, we would do normal public economics: We would identify market failure and address it. If we live in a country with low state capacity, how does this change our thinking?

In the international experience, waging war was an important pathway to developing state capacity. That pathway is not open to India, given the nuclear deterrent.

When there is low state capacity, there is a bigger chance of state power being used in wrong ways. Therefore, it is wise to use coercion mildly. When state capacity is low, tax rates should be low, expenditures on public programs should be low, the investigative powers of the agencies should be low and the punishments that are encoded into laws should be low.

When state capacity is low, we should design simple interventions that are easy to implement. A single rate GST makes lower demands of state capacity, in the annual process of making the budget and in the everyday process of tax administration.

The weak state has highly limited resources of money, of the time of capable staff, and the management time of the leadership. Rather than spread this widely, it makes more sense, under conditions of low state capacity, to attempt doing fewer things.

How to choose these fewer things? One useful test is whether there is a market failure. Many things should not be done, as they do not address market failure. The core of any state is four elements: the criminal justice system, the judiciary, tax collection and financial regulation. Without these, there can be no economy. Hence, these four areas should be the limited areas of focus. We should learn how to run a state by building capability in these four areas.

37

Rolling up Your Sleeves to Build State Capacity

Don't fix the pipes; fix the institutions that fix the pipes.

—Old saying in the field of drinking water

The defining challenge in India is the construction of state capacity. At present, we are limited in our management capabilities in public policy. This imposes important restrictions upon what the state may attempt. We must focus, we must go after important situations with substantial market failure and avoid diffusing effort across a large number of areas. The primal functions of the state are issues like safety, which calls for building armed forces and a criminal justice system. The primal functions of the state are pure public goods like clean air. We should focus on these areas and learn how to do public administration.

There are two temptations that need to be avoided. The first is the pleasure of solving one small problem. A senior policymaker may discern a problem in an action by (say)

FSSAI and may expend a great deal of time and trouble in solving it. This may be satisfying, but this is a poor use of top management time. Top management must delve deeper: Why is it that intelligent and well-meaning personnel at FSSAI came up with a poor outcome? This takes us to deeper questions about incentives and processes at FSSAI.

The second temptation that should be avoided is the great man theory of history. It is all too easy to personalize the poor outcomes at an agency and look for a staffing change. But great men are the *crests of foam that the tides of history carry on their strong backs*.[1]

Conversely, we tend to look for heroes when undertaking recruitment decisions, lionize the hero, and expect all problems to be solved once a great man has been appointed. This line of thought is doomed to failure. The primary determinant of policy outcomes is the organization design and not the personnel. Great men also respond to incentives, and pursue their own self-interest: hence, we have repeatedly been disappointed when great men exited a position and we looked back at their report card.

Dispersion of Power

Public choice theory and political science emphasize the dangers of concentration of power. Concentrated power will generally be abused for personal gains by the persons wielding the power. This encourages us to disperse power. Mature democracies work by limiting the power of every player in public life.

When some in India advocate a more dictatorial form of government, and use the phrase 'presidential system' for it, there is a lack of appreciation of the extent to which the powers of the president in the United States are rather limited. The United States President has a narrow ('enumerated') list of powers under the US Constitution. Unlike the Indian arrangement, the US President does not even control the annual budget, nor does he control the draft legislation that is tabled for discussion by legislators.

> *The accumulation of all powers, legislative, executive, and judiciary, in the same hands, whether of one, a few, or many, and whether hereditary, self-appointed, or elective, may justly be pronounced the very definition of tyranny.*

—James Madison, 1788.

From the 16th century onwards, political philosophers have understood that it is better to have power dispersed between the three wings of government—the legislative, executive and judicial branches. In this, public choice theory takes us to the same argument as the traditional wisdom of liberal democracy on the value of separation of powers. It is better to organize the state around three branches: the legislature (which enacts the Indian Penal Code), the executive (which investigates crimes and prosecutes some) and the judiciary (which conducts hearings and awards punishments and is immune to the displeasure of the executive).

It is better to have a bicameral legislature, and different clocks for the selection of representatives in the Lok Sabha and the Rajya Sabha, in order to avoid the possibility of a momentary infatuation of voters inducing concentration of power. In the design of the Constitution of India, voters have to be infatuated on a sustained basis for many years for one party to gain control of the Lok Sabha and the Rajya Sabha.[2]

It is better to have power dispersed vertically between the union government, state governments and local governments. In this, public choice theory takes us to the same argument as traditional wisdom of liberal democracy on the value of decentralization.

It is better for any one industry to be answerable to many masters ranging from income tax law to competition law to sectoral regulation. If an industry is excessively dominated by one regulatory agency, this generally yields poor outcomes owing to the concentration of power.

It is better for power to be dispersed between the ruling party and the opposition. The standing committees of Parliament are an example of establishing institutions that foster negotiation, and the dispersion of power.

Bills are processed by standing committees, and in every case that we have been personally involved, we have seen that standing committees have improved bills. Standing committees, which are Shivraj Patil's contribution to the Indian institutional infrastructure, have become a forum for negotiation between gentlemen in private, as opposed to the grandstanding and hostility that tends to be on display. This gives us greater power sharing. By clawing back a role for the legislature in the drafting of laws, they reduce the problems of the lack of separation of powers, of the administrative state, where the joint secretary writes bills.

Politicians should go out of office but not out of power.[3]

All lawmakers should have a continuous engagement with the legislative process, and perform the oversight role of the legislature, whether in or out of power. This helps create a repeated game and an environment of reciprocity. This takes the system closer to a cooperative equilibrium.

What Goes into the Law

We normally think that Parliamentary authorization is required, through law, for all coercion of free persons by the state. Hence, our traditional concept has been that the text of the law must authorize the coercion of private persons, and that no coercion should take place unless approved by lawmakers.

Public choice theory gives us a new insight into the drafting of a law. It calls for a second element in every law: the checks and balances that are required to make the state behave. We in India have traditionally been over-optimistic about a benevolent state, and have skimped on the checks and balances that create accountability and performance. We need to take public choice theory to heart, and thereby bring sound procedures into law where agencies and personnel are mistrusted with power, so as to produce better performance by the state apparatus.

As an example, consider the law that creates UIDAI. It has to contain two parts. The first part involves coercing private persons, to say that if they wish to be part of a government welfare program, they have no choice but to submit to intrusive biometric requirements. The second part involves coercing the officials in UIDAI, and all public and private persons who utilize the UIDAI data, to engage in fair play towards the people. The need for this second part flows from public choice theory, the skepticism about the benevolence of the state.[4]

Looking Deeper into Organization Design

The policy community should focus on the medium-term agenda of building state capacity rather than the short-term agenda of fixing one small policy problem at a time. Our prime focus should thus be the subject of organization design. Good policy outcomes come from a sound organization design, and vice versa.

Organization design comprises the specification of objectives, the design of the organogram (the organization diagram), and the process manuals.

Clarity of Purpose of the Agent

A central feature of the road ahead is the concept of 'agencification': the establishment of focused agencies that perform clearly specified public policy objectives. High performance agencies are those with clear objectives, sound design of the organogram and sound processes.

Departments of governments are political creatures, and are led by a minister who is a career politician. They are part of the turbulent world of politics. Agencies are technical organizations, outside departments, that perform a well specified task. Some agencies in India like to see themselves as political players, rivalling the importance of departments of government. However, agencies should be set up with narrow, technical and non-political functions. The political problems should be concentrated in the departments where decisions are ultimately controlled by a politician.

These agencies can be public or private. In a PPP contract, a private agent may build a road. This requires drafting a complex contract, and then engaging in contract management around this complex contract. In a canteen contract, a private agent may run a canteen in a government organization. This also requires drafting a complex contract, and then engaging in contract management around this complex contract.

Alternatively, a parliamentary law may create a regulator like FSSAI or a financial agency such as RBI. This requires drafting a complex contract—the law—and then engaging in contract management around this complex contract. This is the day-to-day functioning of the government department that deals with FSSAI or RBI.

The department can engage in agencification by creating a public agency, or by setting up a PPP contract with a private person. In both cases, there is the principal-agent problem. Neither of these pathways is a fire-and-forget. In both cases, capacity is required in the department for drafting complex contracts and for doing contract management over the years.

Delegate Whatever You Can

Managers of a government department must identify as many clear sub-problems as possible, and kick off a set of agencies (either private or public) that address these sub-problems. If the agent is a government agency, then the relationship is defined in a law or an executive order. If the agent is a private person, then the relationship is defined in a contract. The principal should contract-out everything that can be contracted out, in this fashion.

After this is done, the work of the department splits into two tracks:

1. Contract management for each of these relationships; and
2. Performing, within the department, all the difficult functions which are not easy to specify, where there

are political complexities, which are not mere technical problems.

The maximal delegation of technical problems into a group of agencies is valuable as it frees up capacity in the department for the political problems that cannot be delegated.

We should not think that once something has been delegated, the principal can drop down to zero engagement. The principal–agent relationship will only work correctly when the principal stays engaged in the work of the agent and engages in contract management as specified in the relevant legal instrument. This will require capacity and resourcing at the principal.

Example 77: A Ministry of Finance for the 21st Century

As an example, in 2004, we worked on a Ministry of Finance committee report, Ministry of Finance for the 21st Century.[5] This was an attempt at rethinking the organization design of the Ministry of Finance. Organization design comprises organization structure and processes. A key part of this work was carving out sub-problems from the overall tasks of the Ministry of Finance, and assigning these to a constellation of agencies.

This involves clarifying the role of RBI, setting up the Public Debt Management Agency (PDMA), etc. The separation between policy formulation and policy implementation yields clean thinking in policy formulation. This requires moving towards a unified Internal Revenue Service, which fuses the CBDT and CBEC, and delivers a professional tax administration with political independence, while the formulation of tax policy (leading up to the drafting of the Finance Act) takes place in the Ministry of Finance.   ••

Hygiene in Constructing Agencies

The rule of law is the most important infrastructure of all.

Three elements of wisdom are useful in designing sound agency arrangements. The separation of powers doctrine argues that it is better to separate legislative, executive and judicial powers across three distinct organizations. To the extent that more than one of these is brought into a single organization, there is concentration of power, which inevitably leads to the abuse of power.

We in India are at the early stages of learning how to construct state capacity. We should systematically use separation of powers as a tool for inducing greater performance. Conversely, where separation of powers is absent (e.g., at a regulator like SEBI), we should recognize that it will now be *more difficult* to achieve state capacity, and greater effort will need to be undertaken on other accountability mechanisms, in order to obtain performance.

The second element of wisdom is about the rule of law. Fair play by the state and its agents is a moral and political objective. However, the rule of law is also a valuable tool for achieving state capacity. When there are failures on the rule of law, this places arbitrary power in the hands of officials and politicians. This leads to abuse of power and low state capacity.

The third element of wisdom is about the powers of an agency. At the outset, it is important to give low powers to an agency. Government agencies should have low levels of direct and indirect coercive power. This includes the power to raid a person, the power to tap phone conversations, the power to spend money, the power to punish a person, etc. Power corrupts, and the greater the power of the personnel of an agency, the harder it will be for that agency to achieve state capacity.

Swedish or UK levels of coercive power should only be given to an agency when it has Swedish or UK levels of capability. Conversely, Swedish or UK levels of investigative powers or punishments are always inappropriate in India. The daily expansion of criminal offences increases the likelihood of state failure.

Six Components of the Law That Create an Agency

The law that establishes an agency requires six elements:

1. *Clarity of objective.* Accountability can only come about when there is clarity of purpose. Vague, multiple or conflicting objectives cater to corruption and incompetence.
2. *Formal processes for legislative functions.* The law must write the due process through which the agency wields the power to write law.
3. *Formal processes for executive functions.* The law must write the due process through which the agency performs executive functions like licensing and investigation. This is analogous to the role of the Criminal Procedure Code in binding the police in how they function.
4. *Formal processes for judicial functions.* The law must write the due process through which the judicial functions are performed. There must be a hearing, the person

conducting the proceedings must be unconflicted, orders and penalties must be reasoned, and an efficacious appeal must be possible.

5. *Reporting and accountability.* The agency must release enough information about its own functioning so as to be held accountable for its use of public resources and wielding the coercive power of the state.

6. *Board.* The law must write the role and structure of the board. The board must have a majority of nongovernment members, who must hold the management accountable, and the board must control the design of the organization. A majority of outside directors is essential in switching the board conversations from loyalty to voice.[6]

These six elements are well understood in mature democracies and are the foundation of high-performance government organizations, worldwide, but these are missing in Indian laws that create agencies. These six elements are worked out thoroughly in the draft Indian Financial Code (IFC), that was drafted by the Financial Sector Legislative Reforms Commission (FSLRC).

It is commonly argued that in India, we have fine laws which are badly implemented. We would argue the reverse: the bad outcomes that we see in India flow from badly drafted laws. When laws encode these six elements, we will obtain superior performance from agencies.

If these six elements are not encoded in the law that governs an agency, there is an intermediate stage where the board of an agency adopts these rules with the legal status of board resolutions. As an example, the IBBI has adopted a board regulation that establishes a legislative process in the absence of these elements in the IBC. This can get an agency on the path to high performance while a sound law has not yet been drafted.

Establish a Leadership

There are many elements of the Indian state where the leadership has atrophied. Examples of these include most government hospitals, police stations, colleges, etc. At organizations without a leadership, we have a large number of functionaries operating in fixed process manuals, living each day exactly like they had lived previous days.

The role of the leadership is to have a situational awareness of *the organization*. What is the role of the organization? How are we faring today? What new information has come in? How should we respond to this information? The leadership knows the mandate of the organization, looks at the daily flow of information, and continually takes management decisions that reshape the organization so as to better respond to events in a way that ultimately delivers better on the mandate.

We have low state capacity when there is no leadership that thinks in this fashion, when the organization has a fixed budget year after year, and the organization is impervious to information. All too often, in India, there are no feedback loops, and a state organization has stopped thinking.

The law that establishes an agency should clearly establish its leadership and governance. There must be strong MIS systems, which feed information to the board, which must have a majority of independent directors, and also control the organization design. This will help prevent the organization from collapsing into slumber.

Containing Discretion

In India, we have swung between extremes of executive discretion and executive paralysis. On one hand, in many parts of the Indian state, there is remarkable and excessive executive discretion. At the same time, in many parts of the Indian state, there is now a fear of making decisions which has slowed down routine work. Government museums are unable to acquire works of art as they fear the use of discretion in their purchases.

These two phenomena are closely interconnected. In any liberal democracy, there is a fundamental lack of legitimacy of an executive that possesses extreme discretion. When the basic rules of the game support extreme executive discretion, in time, a backlash develops and then we get snarled in CAG/CBI/CVC/CIC. It is ironic to see that some of the difficulties now visible in the working of (say) CBI are also grounded in the same problem of extreme executive discretion.

When we think about 'what is hard' in state building, it is clear that high quality discretionary decisions are difficult. To the extent that processes can eliminate discretion, that makes things easier. But there is no avoiding discretion in the working of any state. Some of the most important things that states do involve seeing the world, forming a judgement and making a discretionary decision. This is a recurring theme across the criminal justice system, the judiciary, the tax system and financial regulation. State building requires achieving good discretionary decisions. A state that cannot exercise discretion is an ineffectual one.

In the Indian debate, incumbent officials who are used to high discretion are vocal in criticizing reforms proposals which establish due process, and simultaneously complain about the death of discretion. We must see that the old ways are untenable: India has reached a point in its trajectory where the executive discretion that was normal and acceptable from the 1970s to the 1990s is now seen as illegitimate and will run into trouble.

The TRAI 'calls dropped' regulation was struck down by the Supreme Court in 2016 on the grounds that TRAI's process for regulation-making was not adequately transparent.[7] Similarly, the RBI ban on cryptocurrency was struck down by the Supreme Court in 2020 as disproportionate. These decisions show a shifting jurisprudence on regulatory organizations.

The way forward is to find the middle road, of well-defined processes that govern the legislative, executive and judicial functions in all elements of the state. It is only when these processes are sound that officials will be able to have a certain kind of controlled discretion, which is simultaneously surrounded by checks and balances so as to achieve legitimacy and auditability. Formal processes, embedded in the law, are the prerequisite for wielding discretion, which is the prerequisite for state capacity.

Time and Money in Building State Capacity

The conventional Indian way of starting a new agency, e.g., a regulator, consists of enacting a law, hiring a few people, getting some temporary office space, and declaring the agency open for business. This is certain to yield operational rout. The agency drowns under the load that is placed upon it in the early days. It gets consumed in fire-fighting and never recovers.

We do differently, in India, on hard infrastructure. We know that a highway costs Rs 100 million per kilometre. We know that in order to build a highway, we must do systematic project management, enumerate all the sub-tasks that are required, and coordinate them in an overall project plan. Only after all elements are completed do we inaugurate the highway. This same approach is required for building state capacity!

When a new government agency has to be built, or an old government agency has to be fixed, this will require time and money. For instance, building a regulator of doctors and hospitals is an expensive project. We should be willing to commit adequate resourcing to it. We should build this organization in much the systematic way that private equity funds build private organizations: writing process manuals, building IT systems, setting up office facilities, recruiting and training staff, and only then doing the ribbon-cutting.

In the development of capability of the criminal justice system, it makes sense to start with a narrow set of crimes (e.g., riot, or murder) and focus only on these. This will involve writing a manual for investigation, a manual for prosecution, working out the required resourcing, training the staff in working within the manuals, establishing feedback loops for continuous improvement, and a dashboard of performance metrics. We have to establish capabilities in the executive, get judges used to how this will work, and establish a jurisprudence, for one offence at a time. Once this is done, the next crime can be taken up. This constitutes a sequential process of building state capacity.

In similar fashion, for SEBI to learn how to enforce against market abuse, the logical place to start is with exactly one specific offence, e.g., 'price manipulation through a short squeeze'. For this one offence, the correct regulation has to be drafted replacing the vagueness and low evidentiary standards of the present market abuse regulation,[8] the manual for investigation has to be drafted, the manual for prosecution has to be drafted, white papers have to be released into the public domain, the internal staff have to be trained in living by these manuals, and MIS systems have to be built to watch over the enforcement process. The market and the judges have to understand the law, and jurisprudence has to build up illuminating the borderline cases. In about two years, it should be possible to get SEBI up to the ability to detect and enforce against one tangible element of market abuse. Only after this is mastered, the management can then start on a second element of market abuse.

The armed forces have the luxury of not fighting wars on most days, and have developed a sound culture of enormous training schedules that run all through the year. In other parts of government, training tends to be short-changed in an environment of crisis management. This is a vicious cycle: weak institutions are engulfed in crisis management, and cut corners in training, which engenders institutional weakness.

Once a policymaker decides that a highway must be built, everyone is comfortable that it will take *n* years before the highway is inaugurated. In similar fashion, once it has been decided that a new organization like the Insolvency and Bankruptcy Board of India (IBBI) will be built, everyone should be comfortable that this will take two years before it can be inaugurated.[9]

Administrative Law to the Fore

In Indian public policy, it is exciting to work on inflation targeting or net neutrality or Nifty futures trading in Singapore.

A great fraction of conference time is devoted to political economy, to painting the map of interests and envisaging grand bargains.

Administrative law is considered the dull backwater, that should concern junior bureaucrats only. However, we think that the cutting edge of building state capacity lies in the dry detail of formal processes, rules and checks and balances, in the subject of administrative law.

Clean Slate versus Reforming an Existing Organization

The material of this chapter readily fits into the challenge of building a brand-new organization. But most of the machinery of the Indian state is already in place. A great deal of bad decisions and the wrong political economy are now in play.

Public choice theory helps us see the difficulties that we are up against. Incumbents value arbitrary power and do not share the goals of the organization. There will be resistance against the reforms effort. It should not be surprising when (say) CCI employees are hostile to CCI reforms.

Example 78: Reducing Arbitrary Power in Tax Administration

Tax officials obtained draconian powers under the excuse that these were essential for increasing the tax/GDP ratio. Tax officials draft their own procedural law, and thus have excessive control of the steady process through which greater powers are appropriated. Alongside this, tax rates have generally crept up; they are seldom reduced.

Greater coercive power and higher tax rates give us higher stakes: this makes it harder to achieve state capacity. The importance of tax officials has gone up, but the tax/GDP ratio has not.

If there is a proposal to reform the tax system, where reduced powers and greater checks-and-balances are a central issue, the incumbent tax officials will promise the decision makers that this will result in reduced tax revenues.   ••

Summing Up

When there is one practical error that has taken place in one government organization, we should generally resist the impulse of solving it. We should go deeper. Why did intelligent and well-meaning people make such a mistake? What was the structure of incentives that led them to this mistake? This leads us to the question of organization design.

Recruiting famous people or skilled people will not change the organization design. Building state capacity will not come out of hiring IAS or non-IAS or private people.

Government works better when there is dispersion of power. A great deal of failure comes from a few individuals controlling excessive power. Checks and balances are key.

The drafting of law involves two key elements. First, law authorizes the coercion of private people. Second, the law must address the principal–agent problem between the citizen and the state. An array of checks and balances must be built in, when drafting the law, in order to address public choice concerns, to create accountability mechanisms.

Government departments in India are overloaded with many tasks and it is hard to reform this. Agencification will help. Establish an organization outside the department, give it a clear objective, and hold it accountable. Departments must contract out, to such agencies, all technical functions which can be contracted out through well specified laws. Once this process is complete, the work inside the department will consist of (a) Participating in the governance of the external agencies, and solving the principal-agent problem between department and agency, and (b) All the unexpected things and political problems, which could not be contracted out.

Agencification will work better when there is a great focus upon rule of law, separation of powers and low coercion. Agencies must have low powers of investigation, punishment, spending, etc. Only after an agency is proven as having high levels of state capacity can a slow process of giving more power be evaluated. We should only get up to UK-style or Swedish-style powers and punishments when we get up to UK-style or Swedish-style state capacity.

The law that sets up an agency must have clarity of purpose, formal processes for legislative executive judicial functions, reporting and accountability and correct design of the composition and functions of the board. About 140 sections of law, which sets up this machinery, are found in the draft Indian Financial Code, version 1.1.

Agencies can sometimes collapse into every day practical activities, and a loss of strategic thinking. Functionaries would show up to work every day and do the same work that they did yesterday. The board and the top management of the agency have to provide leadership. This involves a feedback loop of taking in information, developing a situational awareness, and undertaking actions that deliver the mandate of the agency. This is related to the teeth-to-tail ratio problem: if an agency is only paying salaries of frontline field operatives, it is all teeth and no tail, it has lost the ability to think.

Discretionary power is routinely abused in the Indian state. The answer is not to remove all discretion. If there is no ability to see the world, and choose the right response, there can be no state capacity. The answer lies in establishing formal procedures with the rule of law, so that discretion is contained in checks and balances.

Administrative law is thus at the heart of the Indian journey.

Building a bridge requires money and time. From the decision to build the bridge, to the inauguration, it takes a long time. In similar fashion, building an agency requires money and time. Merely hiring a few people and renting an office does not give a working agency. When a fledgling agency is asked to do work, this is premature load-bearing and it generates an organizational collapse.

When reforms have to be brought to existing agencies, the incumbent officials resent reductions in their arbitrary power. They argue that if a policeman has to go to a judge and get a warrant before entering a home, we will fail to catch criminals. But *it is only in a police state that a policeman's job is easy*.

38

Do No Harm

Set a High Bar for Coercion

*Dullness in matters of government is a good sign and not a bad
one. In particular, dullness in parliamentary government is a test of
its excellence, an indication of its success.*

—Walter Bagehot

We do not understand the world enough, and every
intervention will work out poorly compared with what was
originally envisaged. Hence, we should be very cautious
before we set out to coerce private persons.

There is now an increasing recognition in India of the
need to be cautious about spending public money. It is now
well understood that the public expenditure process results in
the wastage of most the resources that go in.

It makes more sense to first demand that an expenditure
program successfully addresses market failure, before
committing large sums of money into it. In similar fashion,
we should become stingy in the use of coercion. Before a

government official or agency is given powers to investigate or punish, there must be a high assurance that there are checks and balances, rule of law, and state capacity. More intrusive powers of investigations, and larger punishments, should be written into laws only after ascertaining that less intrusive powers and smaller punishments are being wielded well.

In India, too many people are ready to propose that the state mandate something. One part of the excessive willingness to coerce comes from the public policy establishment. For example, we are not able to get business into GIFT city, so the proposed solution is to force overseas Nifty derivatives activity to go into GIFT city.

Demands for state coercion come from the private sector also. The private sector is comfortable with a government that interferes. The standard procedure for gaining competitive advantage is to try to obtain government coercion against rivals. This perhaps reflects the long history of Indian socialism. Firms have developed capabilities in competing through manipulation of the policy process, instead of developing superior products.

The trigger-happy approach to coercing private persons needs to change, for India to develop a healthy state. The bar, of evidence and argument, that is required before the state coerces a private person, should be set very high. This reflects a Hippocratic oath of public policy: we should have strong foundations of evidence and analysis before we harm certain persons.

A key element of doing better, when compared with gratuitous state intervention, is to require demonstration of harm. In our policy discourse, we should demand proof of harm before state intervention is contemplated. When a government intervenes in the absence of demonstrated harm, this is likely to reflect mere political lobbying by one special interest group or another.

Our weary belief is that the outcome of every policy intervention will surprise us. We should be mindful of our limitations in re-engineering society and crossing the river by feeling the stones.[1] 'Make Haste Slowly' is thus a good rule when thinking about structural change in the economy.

Respecting individuals, and avoiding social engineering, has value in and of itself. No one person should impose a value system upon other persons. In addition, social engineering is fraught with difficulty. We do not know enough to be successful social engineers. If we bumble about, interfering in a machinery that we only dimly understand, we will often make things worse. The Hippocratic oath, when applied into the world of public policy, translates into eschewing social engineering.

We should move fairly briskly on modifications *of the state apparatus*, engaged in the routine management process of understanding areas of failure and undertaking reorganization. But we should be wary of policy plans that aim to remake society.

The Optimist in Her Labyrinth

Policy analysts and engineers generally mean well and are able to see things that a government is doing wrong. It is important to look deeper and understand *why* the government is making mistakes. Every policy intervention will evolve through real world political economy and will not remain in the control of the analysts or engineers who played a role in the ideation or early implementation.[2]

Politicians and officials sometimes lack a technical understanding, but most of the time, the mistakes are emerging out of faulty *incentives*. It does not suffice to (say) have sector knowledge on drug safety and criticize what the Indian state does wrong on drug safety. We have to learn to step into the shoes of the establishment and understand why it fails. The change that matters is the deeper change, of the incentives of politicians and officials.

The optimist proposing a new regulator often slips into the illusion that she, or people like her, will man the new regulator and will make decisions for the good of the people. But in reality, each new regulator will have processes, incentives and staffing much like the existing regulators. Unless deeper changes are made, to the incentives of the politicians and officials, we should expect that a new regulator will be a disappointment just like the others that came before it.

The only grounds for optimism when establishing a new regulator is when there is a deeper change in the working of the regulator, with about 140 sections of law that set it going on a better foundation. If these 140 sections of law are not done correctly, each new regulator will become one more element of the apparatus of central planning, raids and investigations.

Heed the Law of Unintended Consequences

> *I beseech you, in the bowels of Christ, think it possible that you may be mistaken.*

—Oliver Cromwell, 5 August 1650

Our understanding of the world is highly limited. Intervening in social systems is a messy business, and very often, things go wrong. The Indian landscape is littered with outcomes that were the opposite of what was intended. APMCs were not intended to create entrenched power in the hands of traders. Land ceiling acts were not intended to create shortages of real estate and high prices for real estate. Bank nationalization was not intended to hamper growth, stability and inclusion.

Under these circumstances, epistemological modesty is a wise position. The 'law of unintended consequences' has been repeatedly alluded to in this book. At this point, we are ready to sketch the sources of such consistent failure.

Error. Our facts and our analytical models are incomplete; there is a 'knowledge constraint'. The world is a complicated place; we know less than we think. Hence, we make errors.

Wishful thinking. We suffer from 'confirmation bias'; we tend to look for the facts that support our positions. Once a tentative position is taken, we lose objectivity. This has become a bigger issue in the world of electronic and social media, where it has become harder for a policymaker to change positions.

Political economy dominates. The ideal technocratic plan is never implemented in the real world. What will be put to field will always be tugged at by various political considerations, it will always be a sub-optimal version of the starting point of the discussion. The best laid plans of well-meaning intellectuals turn into a mess on the way to execution.

Limitations of execution. There is an administrative constraint holding up the translation of idea into execution. The frail management systems through which policy initiatives are implemented result in an intervention which diverges substantially from what was originally intended. Innovators in policy thinking often find themselves saying, some years later: *I did not mis-lead, you mis-followed.* To the extent that we take implementation constraints seriously in policy design, we will fare better.

The plan gets derailed. As the boxer Mike Tyson said, *Everybody has a plan until they get punched in the mouth.* We start doing something, but unexpected events show up, and we are forced to respond.

Time horizons. A policy strategy may work as intended in the long term, but it can yield unpleasant side effects in the short term.

People respond to incentives. Individuals, officials and politicians, all respond to incentives. The Lucas critique is at work; behaviour changes once a new policy is introduced. This often changes the world when compared with what was understood at the time the policy analysis was undertaken. This is completely unlike physical systems. The behaviour of air molecules does not change when we use them to put planes aloft. But in social science settings, the empirical regularities which were present in the data are modified when policymakers change incentives and thus behaviour.

Nonlinearities. Unintended consequences flow from nonlinear science. Nonlinearities, and the interactions of a large number of moving parts, are notorious for potentially inducing chaos in physical systems. Social systems suffer from the even greater problem that the moving parts are not fixed creatures but optimizing persons. It would be hard enough to analyse non-linear interactions between 1.3 billion people; it is even harder to do this as each one is a sentient being in the quest for life, liberty and happiness.

Consider It Possible You May Be Mistaken

By default, the public policy process is loath to admit failure and change course. Bureaucracies prefer to stay in their comfort zone, they tend to favour intensification of existing programs as opposed to deeper reform. Politicians and officials are loath to admit there was a mistake.

The outcomes will be improved if there are formal processes that encourage questioning. Every intervention into society should be subject to ex-post review, to ask the question: Did this deliver on its objectives? Does the ex-post cost-benefit analysis line up with the ex-ante cost-benefit analysis? Did the benefits, as revealed in operation, actually outweigh the costs as revealed in operation?

Public policy is a process of hypothesis testing, of forming a theory about the world, and experimenting with interventions that are thought to help. This process takes place under conditions of poor knowledge and hostile political economy. Formal rules that shift the process towards greater cogitation and rational analysis will produce better outcomes.

Pathways to Less Government Intervention

> *I asked them to look into the Abyss and both dutifully and gladly they have looked into the Abyss and the Abyss has greeted them with the grave courtesy of all objects of serious study, saying, 'Interesting am I not?'.*
>
> —Lionel Trilling about his students

The field of public policy has a tension at its core. We are exhilarated in understanding market failure, and setting up state machinery that makes everyone better off by addressing it. But we understand how badly the state works, under real world conditions. We roll out state interventions with a heavy heart.

The state is an engine which is supposed to convert coercive power into human welfare. At its best, this results in the blossoming of poetry and science. But coercive power is all too easily abused, and the state is then an engine through which coercive power is used by a few to inflict harm.

A young soldier glorifies warfare, while a wise general knows that war is hell. We feel similarly about public policy. A young person who is not excited about doing good by addressing market failure has no heart. A grown up who is not afraid of state intervention going horribly wrong has no brain. We should know how to setup the machinery of bureaucratic intervention into the economy, but we should always dread rolling this out.

The Single Window Chimera

Every now and then, we hear proposals in India to hold state coercion intact and make life easier for private persons by setting up 'single window approval'. There are two problems with this approach.

First, we do not make the Gestapo nicer by setting up a pleasant front desk. Single window systems do not solve the problem of state coercion, and the threat of raids and punishments including possibly criminal sanctions. Second, absent deeper reform, it is hard to build single window systems that overcome a maze of restrictions. Many or most enthusiastic announcements of single window systems fail to work out in practice.

We must go deeper. We reform by whittling down and correcting state intervention, not putting a user interface on it. The reform required in the early 1990s was not a single-window system governing IPO approvals, it was the abolition of the Controller of Capital Issues. The reform required in trade liberalization was not a single-window system for import approvals, it was the removal of trade barriers. Our problem in India is inappropriate state coercion that limits cross-border activities, and this is not solved by a single-window system governing approvals for cross-border activities.

Elements of Reduced Scope for State Intervention

There are many elements through which the scope of state intervention can be reduced.

Is there market failure? Market failure is the technical core of public policy. There is great value in systematically using the toolkit of public goods, externalities, asymmetric information and market power.

Is a Coasean solution feasible? Many times, the correct way forward lies in establishing property rights and judicial infrastructure. Once this is done, Coasean negotiation will find the optimum answer without requiring the bureaucratic machinery.

Do traditional community solutions work well? Elinor Ostrom has reminded us of the remarkable outcomes through some traditional community arrangements. Those wielding state power should respect the possibilities for purely decentralized solutions to spring up, that allocate common goods without requiring a bureaucratic apparatus.

Can we free ride on state capacity outside India? There is a class of problems where India can free ride on the policy institutions of advanced economies. These should be utilized to the extent possible, while having a full understanding of the limitations of international experience.

Can some of the work of regulation be pushed down to private firms? Sometimes, private firms, privately owned utilities, or other forms of private organization can be established which perform regulatory functions, which use powers achieved through contract law to enforce against market failure. As participants *choose* to submit to this regulation, as opposed to the forced imposition of state power, these solutions are always superior to state-led solutions.

Does modern technology make it possible to remove the market failure? Sometimes, there are clever solutions through which market failure can be eliminated. Consider the electromagnetic spectrum. At first blush, we think that the use of spectrum is rival: one person communicating at a certain frequency precludes others from using it. The state is then needed in establishing property rights to spectrum. This requires creating a bureaucratic machinery which auctions spectrum, and polices for violations.

However, there is an alternative methodology, which is used in cordless phones or WiFi, where intelligent devices establish a self-organizing system through which spectrum is shared. Intelligence at each device coupled with healthy protocols makes sharing of spectrum possible. Such technologies convert spectrum from rival to non-rival.

Once this is feasible, the need for government control of spectrum allocation is removed. This is an attractive path, particularly under conditions of low state capacity. All that the state needs to do is to say that certain frequencies are available for unlicensed use, and back this up with rules for fair play by devices as has been done by the US FCC.

In recent years, there has been a debate in India about the V band and the E band, where the Department of Telecommunications has a choice between making it unlicensed spectrum or auctioning it off to private persons.[3] We would favour the former: a non-state solution is generally superior, particularly under conditions of low state capacity.

Do we have the state capacity? There are many elements of market failure which are legitimate areas for state intervention, and such state intervention is being done in mature market economies. But in India, we have much less state capacity, so certain areas of work are outside our budget constraint and should be dropped.

Intellectual Capacity and Its Limitations

Social systems are complex creatures, and it requires a great deal of intellectual capacity to devise the right interventions. In this book, we repeatedly argue in favour of crossing the river by feeling the stones, an empirical process of introducing small interventions and watching the empirical evidence. We should know that most of the time we are wrong, so we should always be willing to backtrack based on the empirical evidence.

The design of interventions, and the slow careful process of rolling out (and back-tracking) is a research process. We should measure the economy well. We start with a theory about the world, introduce an intervention, find out whether it worked, and then make the next move. The development of this kind of intellectual capability is integral to developing state capacity, and it is hard to obtain this.

Summing Up

There is a bias for action in public policy in India, as muscular intervention into society is rewarded by headlines and a perception of strength. But a great deal of caution is advisable when rolling out a state intervention, as the chances of success are low.

The people devising policy proposals tend to suffer from the illusion that their pet idea will be exempt to the broad based state failure that we see in India. This is overly optimistic.

Social systems are complex, and interventions generally lead to unintended consequences, and induce a lot of harm.

Part VI

Applying These Ideas: Some Examples

39

The Path to Decarbonization

Climate change is a giant threat faced by the human race. The
present distribution of human populations reflects the climate
of the last 10,000 years. When the climate changes, large-scale
movements of people will become essential, which is hard to
organize in a harmonious way. Hence, we must look for the
policy pathways through which CO2 emissions can be reduced
while imposing the lowest economic cost upon society.[1]

The Market Failure

At the heart of the climate crisis is the fact that CO2 is a
pollutant. There is market failure in the form of a negative
externality. Each person that emits CO2 is imposing a small
cost upon every other resident of the planet.

The Carbon Tax Addresses This Market Failure
at the Root Cause

There are many ways in which the adverse consequences of
this market failure can be addressed. But the least intrusive

solution, the lowest cost solution, is found by going to the root cause, and introducing a carbon tax. The person who is polluting needs to suffer that higher cost, of the carbon tax, and thereby change behaviour in favour of polluting less.

This is not a static problem: the world cannot possibly stop emissions suddenly. Near-infinite levels of taxation would be required, today, in order to stop emissions today. In a more dynamic approach, the path for state policy lies in establishing a trajectory of rising carbon taxes for the coming 25 years. This would create incentives for research and investment by consumers, producers and traders of energy. This is analogous to the Indian experience with customs duties, where Yashwant Sinha announced that the peak customs duty would drop by 5 percentage points every year: this reshaped the investment and organization-building strategies of all private firms.

Climate scientists know the trajectory of emissions that is required to avoid a climate catastrophe, which is a high probability. Nobody knows the trajectory of carbon tax rates which will deliver this emissions trajectory.

The right approach, then, involves a starting estimate of the tax rate trajectory, and incrementally refining it every five years based on the best knowledge available at future dates.

For the behavioural responses that are desired from the private sector, the announcement by the state has to be a credible commitment. This falls in the larger problem of state credibility. Is the policy process strategic? Is it capable of making promises over long time horizons? The Indian policy process is weak on these dimensions. To the extent that the private sector does not believe the government when the first announcements are made, there will be an inadequate adjustment ahead of time, and the economy will experience greater shocks when the tax rates actually kick in.[2]

The Price System versus Central Planning Solutions

The carbon tax is the least intrusive state intervention. The state would be silent on all questions of detail, of the technologies and business models that would be used by energy producers and consumers at each location in the country. When fossil fuels are more expensive, the price system will do its work: sending out signals all across society in favour of modifications to consumption, production, research and investment. Millions of decision makers will change their behaviour, guided by a credible commitment to a rising trajectory of carbon taxes.

There is an alternative pathway, which does not involve a carbon tax. This is a central planning system, where the state gets involved in the details of how energy is produced and used, designs the technological architecture of production in the future, and writes hundreds of regulatory rules that force diverse players to behave differently. This will impose greater costs of adjustment upon society, when compared with the carbon tax approach.[3]

By 'central planning' here, we mean a resource allocation that is controlled by the state; we do not mean a resource allocation that is controlled by the *union* government. Electricity is mostly in List 2 of the Constitution, so the bulk of this work would actually take place at state governments. Nevertheless, we refer to this as 'central planning', i.e., directed by the government, as opposed to the organic evolution of the self-organizing system, of information processing and decision-making in the price system.

The Climate Policy Transmission Lies in the Electricity Sector

When the carbon tax is introduced, and steadily increases, there will be a strong incentive for users of fossil fuels to shift to other energy sources and adjust their consumption patterns. The electricity sector is at the heart of the adjustment. Users of LPG or petrol will shift to induction heaters and electric vehicles, thus increasing demand for electricity, and within the electricity sector there needs to be a shift in favour of non-fossil-fuel generation. Renewables are intermittent generators and there will be new complexity in achieving reliable delivery of electricity, through a combination of demand-side behaviour changes, prices that fluctuate, and storage.

The required transformation of the electricity sector, once again, requires the price system. The rising schedule of carbon taxes would set the backdrop, and intra-day electricity price fluctuations would be visible in the foreground, and these would shape the behaviour of consumers and producers. The precise mix of technologies that would be in play at every location in India would be determined locally by economic motivations of buyers and sellers. A process of discovery by the private sector would be set in motion by the price system, involving innovation, risk taking, and investment. At every location, there would be some bankruptcies and some fabulous profits.

Here also, there can be a centrally planned solution, where officials and politicians determine the technology and business models used everywhere in the country. The problem is that bureaucratic decisions do not adequately peer into the future and do not engage in risk-taking. The centrally planned adjustment would induce a higher cost of the climate transition when compared with the adjustment that is achieved through the price system. Under conditions of low state capacity, the superiority of the price system as a path to resource reallocation will be greater, when compared with the possibilities for central planning in an advanced economy.

At present, the Indian electricity sector is largely in a world of central planning. The bulk of decisions about prices and technology are made by officials and not by self-interested market actors. It lacks the ceaseless process of discovery, of innovation, risk-taking and investment. The first step towards India's decarbonization, hence, lies in decontrolling the electricity sector, in placing electricity fully into the price system. Alongside this, regulatory capacity will need to be built, to address market failure in the field of electricity. The main themes of this book—market failure and state capacity—have many useful implications for this task of establishing objectives and processes in electricity regulation.

The bulk of the work on electricity in India takes place at the level of state governments. Hence, the frontier of carbon mitigation lies in the process of electricity reform, one state at a time. This is also consistent with the fact that more internationalized states will be more concerned about the impact of carbon border taxes in advanced economies, and the new world of ESG investing, upon investment and jobs in their states.

The State Capacity Perspective

When central planning is used, in the electricity sector or in the economy more broadly, in order to control the carbon transition, this calls for immense capabilities in the state. The state needs to be omniscient and benevolent. Anywhere in the world, decarbonization that is led by the carbon tax, rather than detailed rules, will work better. In a low state capacity country, like India, the gap between the two approaches will be even greater.

A market-oriented electricity sector will require substantial regulatory capacity in the Indian electricity sector. State- and union-level electricity regulators will need to be established, which have the correct objectives (of addressing market failure) and high capabilities. Cutting-edge knowledge in Indian regulatory theory will need to be brought into establishing these electricity regulators.

Summing Up

CO2 is a pollutant; there is a market failure in the form of a negative externality, which justifies state intervention. India will need to reduce CO2 emissions.

The carbon tax addresses this market failure at its root cause and is thus the least cost intervention. The government would announce a credible 25-year timetable of rising carbon taxes, which would reshape the behaviour of the entire economy. Every five years, the 25-year plan would be modified based on the adequacy of the response by the economy in terms of reduced emissions.

If a centrally planned approach is taken—where the state chooses the technical changes that have to take place by suppliers and buyers of electricity—the cost of carbon mitigation for society will be higher. This is true everywhere, but it is more true in a low state capacity environment.

There are long-standing infirmities in the electricity sector, whereby price signals do not work correctly and there are numerous non-market distortions. The path to decarbonization, then, lies in first reforming the electricity sector and then using the carbon tax to reshape the structure of the economy.

There is market failure in the field of electricity, and a sound foundation needs to be laid in terms of the objectives and procedures of electricity regulators.

40

Building the Perfect GST in a Low-Capacity State

Many of the themes of this book come together in the GST reform. What is the best path to the GST?

From the viewpoint of state capacity, it makes sense to start with a low single rate. This is the easiest GST to implement, as it is administratively simple and the incentives for evasion are lowest. To make this concrete, consider a 10 per cent GST with a comprehensive base. This draws on the global wisdom that the right way to do a GST is to have a single rate. A single 10 per cent rate applied on 70 per cent of the economy yields 7 per cent of GDP as tax revenue, and even if this is only partly achieved, we are broadly okay. At this low rate, it is possible to avoid all exclusions. Petroleum products and real estate would go in.

To many of us in India, a single rate-GST appears sharply different from the present arrangement of indirect tax. However, it is always possible to layer non-VATable taxes on top of the basic GST, which would serve as Pigouvian taxes. Individual state governments can choose how they wish to think about alcohol taxation. A carbon tax can potentially be layered on top of the GST. A state like Sikkim, which prizes environmental protection, may impose a sin tax on plastic consumption. We should decouple our thinking between two distinct problems: a single rate GST and a collection of non-VATables in taxes.

The distortion associated with a tax rate goes up in proportion to the rate squared. Hence, the low value (10 per cent) goes with a reduced distortion, and thus enables a higher level of GDP. The marginal cost of public funds comes down. Government (at all levels) is an important buyer of goods and services, and the low 10 per cent rate has a beneficial impact upon the expenditure side also, thus reducing the net impact on the budget. This is related to the mistaken focus on short-term revenue neutrality, when the right objective is long-term budget neutrality and not short-term revenue neutrality.

The human energy that was spent on negotiations about thousands of products could instead have been devoted to getting a simple administrative process done. The very simplicity of the 'Perfect GST' makes it easier to build the IT system, get payments done on time, and integrate with imports and exports. Simplicity of tax policy makes tax administration feasible, even at low levels of state capacity.

The leadership could have clearly said: This is an experiment. We are going to learn how to make this work, and we are here to discover how much this self-enforcing tax is going to yield in terms of tax revenues for the first two years. The leadership could have made an emotional appeal to taxpayers: Comply with this 10 per cent rate and the rate will not go up, and all of us will be the beneficiaries.

The 10 per cent rate would have induced optimism on the part of the domestic and global private sector. India would have earned respect worldwide for having capabilities in policymaking. This would have fostered investment and thus GDP growth.

In the first two years, significant resource reallocation would have started taking place, with firms discovering more efficient ways of working. This would have fed back into higher GDP growth and thus tax revenues.

If these first two years had worked out well, that would be a triumph. If tax revenues were stubbornly low, the rate could have been raised from 10 per cent to 12 per cent. The right sequencing is to take on a harder problem (a higher tax rate) later in the game, as this requires greater state capacity.

There is an interesting and self-stabilizing phenomenon associated with a large tax shortfall at the 10 per cent rate. Suppose it became clear that 10 per cent was not going to work, that the rate was going to go up to (say) 12 per cent next year. Households would see this and increase their consumption, knowing that prices would go up in the future. This would give buoyant business cycle conditions, and enlarged consumption, which would partly offset the difficulties.[1]

Policy thinkers at the union government and at the state governments need to bring this intuition into rethinking GST at its foundations.

Summing Up

The principles of this book suggest that the right way to design the GST is a single rate, a low rate, a comprehensive base, with an elegantly simple administrative system.

41

Health Policy

Health policy is one of the most difficult fields in public policy. Even in advanced democracies, getting health policy right is a struggle. In the Indian situation, many basic things are as yet not in place.

The standard recipe of public economics is to start from conditions with no state and identify the market failure. What goes wrong when we have pure *laissez faire*, when the government does nothing about health? There is a neat split between 'public health' and 'health care'.

Market Failure in Public Health

Consider the eradication of smallpox in India in 1975.[1]

Once smallpox was eliminated, everyone gained welfare: this joy is non-rival and non-excludable. Controlling communicable diseases, and controlling sources of ill-health such as road safety or natural disasters: these are public goods.

The second class of market failure in the field of health concerns externalities. Pollution of water or air, and the impact of one infected person upon another, involves negative externalities. Here also, there is market failure and thus a case for state intervention.

'Public health' is defined as the population-scale initiatives that address externalities and provide public goods. By definition, it involves activities at the level of the *population* and not the needs of one person. Public health mostly involves prevention and not cure: it obtains a healthier population through reduction in sickness. In contrast, most health care involves private goods and not public goods, and health care transactions are generally about cure and not prevention.

The advanced economies have been engaged in public health for a very long time. As an example, John Snow investigated cholera epidemics in London in 1854, the UK government began work on clean water in in 1858 and on clean air in 1952.[2] In many aspects, the public policy initiatives that address externalities and public goods in health, in advanced economies, are in place.[3]

As a consequence, there is limited interest in public health in the contemporary policy debates of advanced economies.

But in countries such as India, public health is not a solved problem. With a growing focus in the last 50 years on government delivery and financing of hospitals and primary care, there has been a certain loss of focus upon public health. *Swaccha Bharat Abhiyaan*, and efforts to ensure clean drinking water, are small steps in the right direction, but an overall strategy for public health is absent.

There is much confusion on terminology in health policy. Three phrases are commonly misused: 'public good', 'public health' and 'health care'. The phrase 'public health' is often misunderstood to mean 'health care'. Many think that 'public health' is the health of the public, e.g., that gifts of health care services represent 'public health'. Conversely, it is often incorrectly assumed that 'health care' is a 'public good'. The phrase 'public health expenditure' is often applied for government expenditures on health care, and it is particularly confusing because it contains the phrase 'public health' which is the antonym of 'health care'. The phrase 'government health care expenditure' is unambiguous and preferred.

In 2018, the World Health Organization began a 'Common Goods in Health' (CGH) initiative.[4] The attempt here is to bring back a focus upon the population-scale policy actions, i.e., addressing externalities and providing public goods, in health policy. The phrase 'Common Goods in Health' is unambiguous, and may help reduce the confusion associated with the phrases 'public health', 'public goods', and 'health care'.

Market Failure in Health Care

Health care is the medical services which can be purchased by an individual: primary care, hospitals, diagnostics, and pharma. In health care, the consumption of services by one individual precludes it from being consumed by another, thus it is rival, and it is not a public good. There is little market failure in the form of externalities here. The health care market suffers from the other two kinds of market failure: asymmetric information and market power.

People respond to incentives
Doctors are people
Doctors respond to incentives

The economic analysis of the behaviour of doctors and hospitals yields great insights. In an ideal world, doctors are altruistic. However, in the real world, the behaviour of doctors is also shaped by their self-interest and the objective of revenue maximization.

There is high asymmetric information between a doctor and a patient. When a doctor says that an MRI is required, the patient is likely to comply. When the MRI laboratory pays a kickback to the doctor, as is common in India, medical malpractice arises. Prices of health care tend to skyrocket when individuals are unable to engage in comparison shopping for health care services with predictability of expenditures.

In a simple for-profit setting, the incentive of the doctor is not to heal the patient, it is to extract maximal revenue. Alongside this, it is efficient to make the patient feel subjectively better. This is done by over-prescribing antibiotics, by prescribing steroids (that briefly make a person feel better), by having an impressive appearance and a good bedside manner, by earning likes on social media, etc. Such strategies do not heal, but they generate more referrals. In a simple for-profit setting, there is no incentive for the doctor to guide the patient towards wellness, i.e., the behavioural pathways that reduce future requirements of health care.

India has drifted into a largely unregulated health care market produced both by the private sector and government. Unhealthy practices by health care personnel are found all across the health care landscape: across the government and private sector, and across primary, secondary and tertiary care. A government doctor may practice in the evening in private practice and may refer patients for tests and medicines to private pharmacies and labs just outside the government hospitals. A broad array of health care providers may provide antibiotics for quick relief, and not prioritize the long term well-being, of their patients. Private hospitals may undertake unnecessary procedures to inflate billings.

Emphasis on Prevention or Cure?

Policymakers always face two rival pathways in health policy: of utilizing incremental expenditure or coercion for the purpose of preventing ill health versus utilizing it for the purpose of health care. Generally, the gains from prioritizing prevention, i.e., public health, are greater.

Consider road safety. When a person suffers from a road accident that is not fatal, there are three consequences: (a) Pain and unhappiness; (b) If the affected person is a worker, there is the loss of output and possibly income on account of reduced days of work; and (c) Expenditures on health care. Given that India has some of the highest rates of road accidents in the world, on the margin, prevention seems better than cure. We are better off with fewer road accidents, rather than having casualties and then supplying the commensurate health care services. When accidents are prevented, not only does society reduce expenditure on health care, we become better off because those same resources are shifted to producing things that people actually want. Health care expenses, for preventable sickness, are a 'dead weight cost' in the jargon of economics.

Health expenditure is fashionable, but the bulk of the spending that is classified as health expenditure is in health care. A government that prioritizes public health will be criticized on the grounds that it is spending less on health. Greater care on vocabulary is required.

The Indian Journey of Health Policy

Under colonial rule, there was an emphasis on the public goods of sanitation and communicable disease. Local bodies were resourced for improving local sanitation. Advances were made on disease surveillance, prevention and cure. A government committee, led by Sir Joseph Bhore from 1943 to 1946, envisaged a shift in focus from public health to health care, and advocated a government run health care system. This was an extremely influential report, and shaped a large reorientation of health policy in the following decades.[5]

By the 1980s, it was clear that these modifications were working poorly. The disease burden was high, owing to weaknesses in public health. The government-dominated health care system was working poorly.[6] Individuals were increasingly resorting to private health care. Politicians became increasingly aware of the unhappiness of individuals.

Ideally, these difficulties should have generated a fresh focus upon public health. However, building capabilities in public health was not done. Building health care facilities is a more visible marker of a government's commitment to health, as compared with the (say) invisible work of thousands of civil servants controlling mosquitoes.

Health policy in recent decades has taken the path of least resistance: Emphasizing government-provided health care and selectively using public money to buy insurance (often from private health insurance companies), whereby low income households obtain health care from private health care providers.[7] This is an inefficient path in three ways: Weak public health gives a high disease burden, there is market failure in the private health care industry, and there is market failure in the health insurance industry.[8]

Policy Pathways in Public Health

The focus of health policy in India must be upon prevention, i.e., upon public health. This includes immunization, disease vectors such as mosquitoes, monitoring of disease outbreaks and fighting epidemics, drug safety, food safety, air quality, water quality, waste management, disaster risk resilience, disaster response, etc.

It is striking to see that there was greater capability in India, in the 1970s, on fighting mosquitoes than is the case today. We have regressed from preventing malaria by fighting mosquitoes in the 1970s, to treating patients who have malaria, dengue or the Zika virus. Problems such as air quality and road safety have become worse in India today, than was the case many decades ago. There is a need to revive public health, and reduce the extent to which persons require health care. Ironically, the weaker the health care system, the greater the gains from prevention.

Most of public health lies outside the administrative boundaries of the Ministry of Health. As an example, air quality is a key public health crisis that afflicts North India. However, the problem of air quality lies in the Ministry of Environment and not the Ministry of Health. Public health considerations need to shape the working of many ministries. As an example, the Indian road safety crisis is a first order challenge for public health. The agencies building and operating roads should carry targets for accident rates and not just targets for kilometres of highways built. Similarly, the PDS system purchases carbohydrates and distorts the relative price of carbohydrates versus proteins and lays the foundation of bad nutrition in the country. Policy mistakes on food have come together whereby a small set of districts in India consume public subsidies, make cheap carbohydrates, and emit solid particulate matter; it will help to see the costs and benefits of the food system policy paradigm in its entirety.

Decentralization holds much promise for improvement in public health. A great deal of the task of reducing the disease burden in Bombay should lie at the Bombay municipality. The city of Jamshedpur is a good demonstration of a well-structured local government that is successfully delivering clean water, sanitation and vector control. At the same time, problems like air quality and the food system lie beyond the possibilities of the state government or municipal government of Delhi.

Public health is attractive because prevention is better than cure, which is the same as saying that the cost of public health is lower than the cost of health care. It is much cheaper, to put an end to the air quality crisis of North India, when compared with the costs of delivering quality health care that can redress the damage. There are important opportunities for innovation in doing public health better. Consider drinking water. The concept of a water utility is appropriate for cities with a population of at least 10,000. Below this, frugal innovation is required in rethinking the strategy. Gravity-fed water filters, at the household level, costing Rs 2500 each can deliver major gains on water quality, and can be rolled out on scale without waiting for institutional capacity at the village level.

Policy Pathways in Health Care

In the public sector, government management fares poorly in translating expenditure into health care services. In the private sector, the payments by customers are often hijacked by for-profit health care providers. A valuable counterweight in the private system could have been health insurance, but as yet, health insurance companies suffer from poor financial regulation (of insurance) and have not achieved the scale required for them to impinge on the behaviour of private health care providers.

Greater government spending on health care is popular. At present, there are two pathways for this increased expenditure. More money can be put into government health care facilities such as PHCs or government hospitals. Alternatively, more money can be put into health insurance companies who intermediate between individuals and private health care providers. Both these pathways work poorly today. As a consequence, the welfare gains from increased government expenditure on health care, under the present paradigm of health care, are likely to be low today.

Example 79: Market Failure in Health Care versus a Socialized Health Care System

As an example, we may think that there is market failure based on asymmetric information and market power when a private doctor deals with a paying customer. We may have a design for a public health care system through which this market failure is addressed.

But public financing, in and of itself, induces a 3× inefficiency. When money flows from the paying customer to the government, in the form of taxes, a 3× inefficiency is wired in, owing to the large marginal cost of public funds.

In addition, expenditure programs of governments are also inefficient. Where a private person will spend Rs 100, a government organization will perhaps spend Rs 200. This introduces an inefficiency of perhaps 2×, at the expenditure stage.

Putting these together, a socialized government-run health care system might introduce a 6× inefficiency. If the magnitude of the market failure in the private arrangement (through asymmetric information and market power) is smaller than 6×, the socialized health system would prove to be worse than the unregulated private solution.   ••

The private health care system is vast, and the simple rollout of regulators as seen in other areas (e.g., electricity or finance) would not work, given the complexities of state intervention into millions of providers. The poor experience with regulation in many other parts of the Indian economy also gives pause to the simple rollout of bureaucratic regulation as the solution. The first line of attack in the field of private health care is to establish a light touch foundation of law, regulation, information release, private certification, and private associations through which the left tail of bad behaviour by private health care organizations is reduced.

An important insight lies in re-imagining the contractual relationships to achieve incentive compatibility. Imagine a contract between a network of health care providers, and the patient, which underwrites all health care for the patient for life, in exchange for fixed monthly payments. When you get sick, you would go to your health care network, and they would render you health care services, at no additional cost. Such networks are called Managed Care Organizations. This is a risk sharing arrangement with focus on outcomes rather than input production.

Once this style of contracting is done, the incentives of the health care producer change. Now, the managed care organization is paid by you every month, and these payments are clean profit for them, *until you get sick*. When you get sick, you impose costs upon them. They have no incentive to over-prescribe procedures, and their incentive is to keep you healthy.

A doctor in the managed care system who sees a surge of an infectious disease in her neighbourhood would have the incentive to talk with public health officials, and initiate public health responses which address the epidemic at the root cause. This is incentive compatible as the managed care organization makes more money when fewer people get sick.

In the UK, the government runs a managed care system, and it is called the National Health Service (NHS). The patients finance the managed care organization (NHS) through payment of taxes. Under NHS, there is one general practitioner (GP) tied to each person.[9] On average, there are 0.58 GPs per 1000 persons. The GP is a private doctor who is paid a salary and incentive for outcomes, and charges patients nothing at the point of care. The GP's incentive is to keep the person healthy, so that the person comes back to her fewer times per year.

This is a logical and simple design that generates the correct incentives for the GP. However, the sound operation of the UK NHS requires UK-style state capacity and financing.

Managed care organizations also exist in private systems as in the case of Accountable Care Organizations in USA, or managed-care systems in Israel and Colombia. These are more evolved forms of private insurance systems, which take on increasing accountability of health outcomes. Such systems also require careful systems design and enablement on the part of policymakers and regulators.

As with policy pathways in public health, an important part of the policy agenda in health care lies in understanding and harnessing technical change. Market failure in health care is not static. With innovations on transparency and newer health technologies, the landscape of market failure and possible state intervention is changing. E-pharmacy players provide price and formulation transparency for consumers, wellness platforms disseminate information on prevention and primary care to citizens, low-cost point-of-care diagnostics help with correct diagnostics in remote places. The public goods of knowledge, that cater to local conditions in India, are required. This calls for public funding through a body analogous to the US NIH.[10]

The Path to State Capacity

The task before health policy research in India is to translate this strategic thinking into wise organization structures at the union, state and city levels. Careful thinking on coercive power, spending taxpayer resources and establishing accountability mechanisms will be required, so as to build an agency landscape which has sound incentives and achieves competence. A set of laws and organization designs will need to be drafted.

Three organizations appear to be required: a union government public health body, a city-level public goods body and a state-level health care body. The union government public health body may have the objectives of coordinating and design programs for mitigating the adverse impact upon health that is emanating from other ministries such as roads or food. It would deal with national public goods like pandemic preparedness and the financing of research. It would interact with financial regulation of health insurance, and bring health domain knowledge into that task. The city level public goods body would coordinate inter-sectoral public goods of water, sanitation, vector control, blocking fires and other sources of pollution. The state-level health care organization would work on law and regulation governing private health care, and nudge the system towards managed care.

Summing Up

Health policy is one of the hardest parts of public policy. The toolkit of market failure and state capacity gives us important insights into the field. There is a neat and vertical split between two classes of market failure (public goods and externalities) that shape the field of 'public health' or 'common goods for health' and the other two classes of market failure (asymmetric information and market power) that shape health care.

We in India need to change course. Under the present trajectory, GDP growth is inducing greater ill health through problems such as pollution and road safety. In the government, public health capabilities have atrophied: we do worse on critical problems like vector control when compared with many decades ago. Voters are unhappy, and the government is trying to subsidize their purchase of private health care services from a private health care system that suffers from extensive market failure. First principles thinking about market failure and state capacity is required in public health and in health care.

As in many other fields, there is a lot of interest in technological fixes for health policy. There is undoubtedly great opportunity in using better technology, ranging from mundane process automation using better data handling, all the way to AI systems that will replace doctors. However, the foundation of beneficial technology adoption lies in incentives. Our first priority has to be to address the foundations: to reorganize health policy around the problems of market failure and state capacity.

Under each of the two wings—public health and health care—a research community is required and the full policy pipeline is required. We need to establish data sets, develop a research literature, incubate diverse policy proposals, debate them, develop a mature point of view on how the problems will be solved, present these choices to legislators, enact new laws, and then build the state capacity to enforce these laws. Health policy is a less mature field in India, in the development of the policy pipeline, when compared with two other examples shown in companion chapters: GST and financial economic policy.

42

Vaccines for Covid-19

Vaccines in response to the pandemic was a high-decibel policy debate. At two points in time—the deaths in the second wave and the early weeks of Omicron—there was much regret in India about the inadequate number of people that had been vaccinated. Our toolkit yields valuable insights into the role of the state, and the difficulties of state coercion, in the field of vaccination.

The State-Capacity Perspective

There are advanced economies, where the state mobilized itself to vaccinate the entire population, and did this well. As an example, in Israel, 11 doses per 100 persons were in place by the end of 2020, when vaccination in India had not yet begun. On 31 March 2021, right before the Indian second wave, 52 per cent of Israel was double-vaccinated, while India was at 0.7 per cent.[1]

Complete state control of vaccination does not, however, transplant well from a country like Israel into a low state capacity environment. Population-scale vaccination is difficult as it is a transaction-intensive service. When we look back into vaccination programs of the Indian state of the past, there has never been a high success in covering a large population in a short time. We have to learn to walk before we can run: if complete coverage of the population in a few months has never been done before, it is unlikely to come about at short notice.

India is a highly heterogenous country. The pathways to effectively reaching heterogeneous subgroups of the population heterogeneous. It is better to have many lines of attack, in trying to get more vaccination done, rather than have one fixed process design that would be applied all over the country.

The Market Failure Perspective

A mosquito net is a private good with an externality. When person X buys a mosquito net, she benefits from reduced malaria. In addition, she imposes some small gains upon other people, as she is less likely to pass on malaria to others. There is a market failure here: a positive externality. Each person will tend to under-invest in expenditure, and inconvenience, on the purchase and use of mosquito nets.

There may be a case for state intervention here, of using taxpayer resources to part-pay for the purchase of mosquito nets. As an example, the financing pillar can be put into motion, where households are given a voucher that pays Rs 250 to the producer when the household buys a mosquito net. We might choose to use public resources to do this, or we might choose to step back and do nothing.

Vaccines are exactly like mosquito nets: they are a private good with an externality. The vaccination service is a health care transaction. When person X buys a Covid vaccine, she benefits from reduced disease. In addition, she imposes some small gains upon other people, as she is less likely to pass on Covid to others. There is a market failure here: a positive externality. Each person will tend to under-invest in expenditure, and inconvenience, on the purchase of Covid-19 vaccines. There may be a case for state intervention in order to tip more people over into the decision to buy the vaccine.

The standard example of a positive externality is higher education.   The individual tends to under-invest in higher education as the individual does not care about the gains to others that arise out of achieving more knowledge. This analysis involves two real numbers—the rupee value of expenditure on higher education that the person ought to ideally choose, and the rupee value that the person actually chooses, which is always smaller. Market failure is present in the decision of each person, absent state intervention.

A peculiar feature of vaccines is that there are only two possibilities: 0 or 1. If a person chooses to get the vaccine, there is no market failure. Market failure in only present, absent state intervention, for the people who choose to not get a vaccine. Once a person chooses to get a vaccine, market failure is absent in the outcome.

There is one aspect in which the social objective diverges from the individual objective. The objective of public health is not to give everyone the vaccine. The objective of public health is to change the disease dynamics so that the disease dies away. This requires enough immune people in the population, so that one infected person is likely to induce infection of no other person. This state of 'herd immunity' requires about 70 per cent of the population to be immune, through disease experience or vaccination. As the system comes closer to herd immunity, the magnitude of the positive externality (and thus market failure) goes to zero, but some risk-averse individuals have the incentive to continue to buy vaccines.

The Power of the Price System

How would vaccination unfold if there were no government? In some respects, it would be much like the market for mosquito nets.

Multiple private vendors would source bulk supplies of vaccines from all over the world. Multiple health care organizations, all the way to streetside individual doctors, would offer vaccination services. The bulk of Indian health care is in private hands, therefore, the point of contact for most citizens in getting vaccinated would be a private health care facility.

The market for vaccines also differs from the market for mosquito nets in two ways. As knowledge and economies of scale build up, there is a crash in the cost of production. And, as the threat of disease recedes, owing to vaccination or disease experience, the willingness to pay for a vaccine goes down. Hence, the market for vaccines is a short, hot market with a rapid collapse in prices.[2]

The median Indian household income is about Rs 13,000 a month. All families were highly affected by the pandemic and the willingness to pay might have been about Rs 500 per person. Market-based vaccination would, under this environment, have got a vast uptake. Alongside this, the progression to herd immunity was taking place through disease experience. These two large decentralized mechanisms—the market that was getting vaccines across, and the virus that was getting disease across—could have generated strong progress to herd immunity.

No two people are alike. Some people would be willing to pay more for a vaccine (frontline work, elderly persons, elderly parents at home, co-morbidities, low savings and hence high need of wage income, access to health care, risk tolerance, etc.). Each person would have their own judgment about when it was right to get a vaccine and get back to work. No simple rules can express the complexity of these individual choices.

There was a lot of focus on vaccine shortages in late 2020 and early 2021. The mantra of economics is: *Supply curves slope upwards*. Higher prices would create incentives for more vaccine production. The price system sends out incentives to manufacturers by offering higher prices.

There is immense power in the price system; it will move mountains to do vaccination, it will use resources efficiently, it will reach into many use cases and heterogeneous pockets of the economy through customer segmentation, it will innovate and it will take risks.[3]

The basic precept of public policy is: *go with the grain of the price system*.

Policy Concerns and Solutions

Policymakers might think that market-based mechanism works poorly for the people who are below median income. As with other private goods with positive externalities, there is a case for public financing. This is likely to be most efficiently done through vaccine vouchers, which avoids the Markup in State Contracting (MSC). Perhaps the state could have issued vouchers for Rs 500 per person to the bottom 25 per cent of the population. This would also have helped speed up the movement of the system towards herd immunity.

The state could have contracted with private health care firms to go into poor neighbourhoods and carry out door-to-door vaccination. Or, the state could have chosen 'make' instead of 'buy', and run vaccination services, at street corners and going door-to-door, by itself.

Reviewing the Actual Experience

The union government chose a four-part policy strategy:

Centralization There was only one vaccination program for every resident of India.

Constraints on Supply Import of vaccines was banned. State coercion was used to force every health care provider to do no vaccination other than under the control of the government.

Constraints on demand Vaccination at the initiative of the individual was banned. Each individual had to wait for vaccination to be authorized by the government.

Constraints on price Vaccine prices were unilaterally determined by the union government, for three cases: purchase of vaccines by the union government, purchase of vaccines by state governments and purchase of vaccines by private health care facilities. Quantities were also controlled: e.g., half of the vaccines produced in India were forced to be sold to the union government.

This system of control was operationalized through an IT system named 'Cowin'.

India has a primarily private-sector dominated health care system. Doctors and patients engage in conversations and choose medicines, vaccines, surgery, etc. It was a new moment in India's history, where the private conversation between a health care provider and a patient was subject to complete control of the union government. Vaccination for each individual could only happen under the control of the union government, and this was done through simple rules that did not capture the complexity of the lives of the people. Doctors lost the freedom to deliver a vaccination to a patient. We need to wonder how this new level of state power will be utilized in the future. There were many gaps in implementation, and the rules were often made in ways that reflected the interests of the state rather than the interests of the citizenry.

Many alternative paths appear superior to this one. Vaccine vouchers have been mentioned above, where the self-organizing system figures out production, while the state does financing for poor people. Or, state/city governments could have run free vaccination camps at every street corner, or campaigns in poor neighbourhoods going door-to-door, as was done with polio vaccination. This would address concerns about poor people accessing vaccines. It would *augment* vaccination through the price system, without *supplanting* it.

Each vaccination that an unshackled private sector did would only have helped matters in reducing deaths directly (vaccinated people are less likely to die) and indirectly (vaccinated people are less likely to transmit the disease to others; this is the positive externality). For the individuals that step forward to buy a vaccine, there is no market failure and no case for state intervention. The energy of the private sector would have augmented vaccine supply (through imports and domestic production) and delivery (by utilizing the deeply decentralized Indian private health care system to deliver vaccines all over India).

As an example, at the time when Omicron was ramping up and there was great interest in booster shots, Serum Institute halved its production as the union government was not buying vaccines and private persons were prohibited from buying vaccines.[4]

By using state coercion to close down all private initiative and the natural working of the market economy, the overall pace of vaccination was retarded.

The price system is often criticized on the grounds that poor people are left out. We need to bring three insights into this reasoning. (1) Each rich person who gets a vaccine is inducing a positive externality upon everyone else (including the poor) through reduced transmission. (2) A vaccine voucher system should have been setup, to get purchasing power into the hands of the poor. (3) The poor are likely to have faced greater constraints in navigating the complexities of the Cowin/UIDAI based system for getting vaccination: by introducing state control, we do not necessarily help the poor.

Summing Up

Rapid vaccination of the population against Covid-19, led and controlled by the government, worked in some advanced economies. Given low state capacity in India, this would not work comparably in India.

What is the market failure in vaccination? When one person buys the vaccine, she imposes a positive externality upon others as she transmits disease less. The market failure lies in the fact that the willingness to pay by each person only reflects the gains to self, not the full gains to society. This can be addressed through the standard pathways for state intervention when faced with this market failure (a positive externality): a vaccine voucher through which some state financing augments purchase by the individual.

The price system is extremely effective at responding to higher prices with higher vaccine production and with devising myriad business models through which vaccines go out to buyers all over the country. Supply curves slope upwards: high prices at the outset would have induced investments in production, and then prices would have crashed.

In India, the union government chose a policy framework with centralization, constraints on supply, constraints on demand, and constraints on price. This was a suboptimal path. Supplanting private energy, and the working of the price system, is likely to have impeded the quantity of vaccination that got done, at each point in time.

43

Financial Economic Policy

Indian finance works poorly. Whether we think about the efficiency of the resource allocation, vulnerability to systemic crises, or financial inclusion, the present financial system fares poorly. The root-cause analysis takes us to failures of financial economic policy.

Financial economic policy is about the things that the government does in financial markets, financial intermediaries, the creation of money, and the mechanics of government borrowing. While it stands alongside fiscal policy, there is a clear distinction between the two. Fiscal policy decides how much to borrow, and financial economic policy decides how to borrow.

The Market Failure

As with all other questions in public policy, the point of departure is the working of a pure free market. If the government did nothing in this field, what would go wrong? We can identify four main issues:

- There is market failure in the form of *externalities* when there is a crisis in the financial markets. When private persons maximize their own interests, they sometimes do things which impose harm upon others by destabilizing the financial system. Government intervention helps increase the probability of consistent working of the financial system.

   Government intervention helps a lay participant feel certain that when securities are bought on the exchange, there will be no glitch in the payment of money and receipt of securities. Similarly, when a financial firm has made promises to lay persons, and comes to bankruptcy, the government helps clean up the mess and reduce the negative externalities imposed upon others.

- There is a problem of *asymmetric information* with both financial markets and financial intermediaries.

   Government intervention on financial markets, to improve disclosure and combat market abuse, improves the confidence with which individuals participate in financial markets.

   Similarly, an individual will find it difficult to know when the promises of a bank or an insurance company can be trusted. This is analogous to the problem of drug safety: an individual buying medicines is not able to put in the effort required to test the purity of the drug. The government helps by running a regulatory system through which the promises of financial firms are upheld with a high probability.

- The creation of money, which can be done by a state, facilitates transactions in the local economy. The creation of money has features of a public good that facilitates transactions, and a public good of reduced macroeconomic volatility through the working of monetary policy.[1]

- An institutional arrangement is required to perform the investment banking function for the government. This would represent the government in the financial markets and represent the financial markets in the budget process. This is a utility that is required for the fiscal system to borrow.

Financial economic policy is about addressing these four objectives: combat negative externalities, combat asymmetric information, invent money, and establish an investment banker for the government.

> *It is essential to place the function of consumer protection at the heart of financial regulation.*

—FSLRC, Volume 1, page 45[2]

When a household deals with a financial firm such as a bank, the household does not have a reasonable ability to understand the soundness of a bank. Financial firms are often unfair in their dealings with households.[3]

When a bank does fail, the household does not have a reasonable ability to participate in the conventional bankruptcy process. If we insist upon *caveat emptor*, i.e., 'buyer beware', in the relationship between unsophisticated households and financial firms, this would greatly narrow household participation in finance. Government intervention is required from the viewpoint of consumer protection to address these three problems. This is done through three paths:

1. A financial regulator looks at the relationship between financial firms and consumers and coerces financial firms to engage in greater fair play. This includes truthful disclosure, fair contract terms, etc.

2. A financial regulator engages in 'micro prudential regulation', where financial firms that make promises (such as banks and insurance companies) are coerced into low levels of risk. This caps their probability of failure and ensures that the promises that they have made are upheld with a high probability. This is analogous to drug safety regulation, which ensures that with a high probability, the drug purchased by a consumer in a shop is efficacious.

3. Sometimes, financial firms have made intense promises to households and they go bankrupt. At this time, a 'resolution corporation' is required, which is a specialized bankruptcy process. This pays out some money to households in the form of deposit insurance and runs a swift resolution process which minimizes the negative externalities upon the economy as a consequence of firm failure.

Financial markets are the vast impersonal systems for organized trading in securities. Government intervention combats externalities, asymmetric information and market power in the working of financial markets through three pathways.

1. A buyer of securities requires a high level of assurance that after the transaction, money will be paid and securities will be received. This requires micro-prudential regulation of exchange infrastructure.

2. Ample disclosures need to be made available by all issuers of securities, so that financial market speculators are well

informed. This requires regulation of disclosures by issuers
of securities.

3. Participants in the securities markets require a high level
of assurance that market abuse is absent. This requires
that the regulator must enforce against market abuse.
Market abuse comes in two kinds: market-based abuse,
which is about exploiting market power on financial
markets, and information-based abuse, which is about
falsifying the information seen by speculators about
firms.

How to Address the Market Failure

Addressing the market failure in finance requires establishing
a group of government agencies. The problem of 'financial
regulatory architecture' is determining this map of agencies
and the precise functions of each of these organizations.
The design of this map is based on the problems of state
capacity—the need to have a clear objective for each
organization—and the need to avoid imposing inefficiencies
upon the economy.

Within each agency, the law that creates the agency
needs to be drafted, which expresses precise objectives, gives
the minimal coercive power to the agency, and establishes
feedback loops of accountability including the board.

Finance is an unusual field, in that this work lies almost
entirely at the union government. In a field like health, the
bulk of the work happens at the city or the state levels, and
policy work takes place primarily at the sub-national level.
This is not the case here.

The Agency Map, the 'Financial Regulatory Architecture'

To perform these functions, we require a group of four government agencies:

1. A *central bank*, which creates the Indian rupee.
2. A *financial regulator*, which does consumer protection in the sense described above.
3. A *resolution corporation*, a specialized bankruptcy process for the class of financial firms which make intense promises to households, such as banks and insurance companies. All other financial firms—i.e., those which make no promises to unsophisticated households—should utilize the ordinary bankruptcy process of the Insolvency and Bankruptcy Code (IBC).
4. A *public debt management agency*, the investment banker for the government.

Public choice theory comes in the way of the sound working of each of these four organizations. The officials that man these organizations are likely to favour arbitrary power and low accountability. Officials may be over-eager to ban certain kinds of business activity, so as to obtain peace of mind from not having to take responsibility for regulatory functions. Officials may cross the line from regulation into central planning, and micro-manage private persons in their quest for personal power. Regulators can deploy their powers to investigate, prosecute and punish in a selective way.

In each of these four organizations, we must worry about the puzzle of creating the checks and balances which are conducive to good outcomes.

Achieving State Capacity for the Central Bank

When a central bank creates money, there is the possibility of excessive money creation. The creation of money needs to be anchored into the real economy. In addition, the entire work process of creating money—i.e., monetary policy—requires an accountability mechanism. These problems are solved by requiring that the central bank deliver on an inflation target. The 4 per cent CPI inflation target achieves two things. First, it holds RBI accountable.

Second, it establishes a self-adjusting system for the production of money, which creates the public good of macroeconomic stabilization. When the engine of creating money is placed under the control of an inflation target, this becomes a tool for macroeconomic stabilization. When times are tough, inflation will tend to be low, and the central bank will cut rates, and vice versa.

There is a long lag between changes in monetary policy and their impact upon the economy. There is a danger that monetary policy can be used to influence elections: In the year prior to elections, interest rates will be cut by a supportive central bank to help the incumbent government win elections, and the resulting inflation surge will take place after elections are complete. In order to address this, there is a need for central bank independence.

This is achieved by shifting the power of monetary policy away from one person (the RBI governor, who can be pressurized by the ruling party) to a committee that is dominated by non-RBI employees.[4] For an analogy, if there is one judge, there is a greater risk of political pressure upon the judge, but if there is a bench of judges and power is dispersed, it is harder to bring pressure upon all of them.

In the class of public policy problems, monetary policy is a relatively easy problem. It involves a small number of transactions: about four to six meetings of the Monetary Policy Committee every year. It involves low stakes: these are not decisions which induce a very large impact upon any private person. It involves relatively low discretion: The actions of the MPC are anchored to forecasted CPI, and it is easy to look at the headline CPI and know how well the decisions of the MPC have worked out. Finally, it requires low secrecy. There are no state secrets of note, and the entire process can be swathed in transparency. To make a central bank work, we only require a small number of people who understand macroeconomics in the country, and we require that they are appointed upon the MPC.

Achieving State Capacity for the Regulator

In contrast with monetary policy, financial regulation is hard. There are a large number of transactions: roughly speaking there are 1,000 supervisors at financial regulators interacting continuously with about 2,000 significant financial firms. The stakes are very high: huge profit and loss flows from the decisions of financial regulators; the powers to license, raid, investigate and punish can destroy careers and firms. There is extreme discretion in how a certain situation is treated. There is a need for secrecy in the enforcement function. For these reasons, while monetary policy is easy, financial regulation is hard.[5]

In the international experience, regulators fuse legislative and executive functions. The Parliamentary law that establishes a regulator carefully defines the spots where the regulator has the authority to write law in the form of 'regulations'. In addition, regulators have executive functions of licensing, investigation and prosecution.

In the concept of liberal democracy, regulators are an unusual situation in that *law* is written by officials. There is a lack of democratic legitimacy when unelected officials are given the power to write law. Similarly, regulators exercise state power, in licensing and enforcement, without the oversight of elected representatives. Many elements of institutional design are required in order to address the dangers associated with this 'democratic deficit'.

The first element of this is governance of the organization by a board which has a majority of independent directors. The officials who run the organization must be accountable to this board, where a majority of persons are external experts and stakeholders. The board must control the internal processes, organization diagram and budget of the regulator. With a majority of independent members, the board should police the management of the regulator, watching for violations of the rule of law.

For the purpose of writing law (i.e., regulations), a formal process must be followed. Regulation-making projects must emanate from a decision of the board, taken under conditions of transparency (release of board agenda papers and minutes).

Once a regulation-making project is initiated, the staff must be required to build a documentation packet, articulating the problem that is sought to be solved, demonstrating that there is market failure, and demonstrating that the proposed intervention is the least intrusive alternative available. This documentation packet must be put into public consultation, in order to solicit the views of affected persons and intellectuals. This packet, and the responses from the public, should lead up to a discussion, refinement, and decision at the board of the agency. Only the board should be able to release a new regulation.

Public choice theory predicts that the staff of a regulator will favour arbitrary power in the legislative and executive functions. Hence, the Parliamentary law which defines the regulator must write down the processes of regulation-making, licensing, investigation and prosecution in considerable detail. At an early stage of state capacity, the regulator must be given low powers of investigation and punishment, so as to protect the feedback loops of the push-back against regulatory actions from the economy.[6]

Difficulties of the Indian Experience

The Indian experience with financial economic policy features many important deviations from this normative depiction.

Prior to 2015, RBI had no objective, and as public choice theory would predict, many infirmities were observed. The prime function of the central bank is to deliver low and stable inflation. However, India has a long history of high and unstable inflation. From 2015 onward, a formal objective—an inflation target—was placed upon the RBI. This has helped anchor the Indian rupee and has created an accountability mechanism for RBI.[7]

RBI independence has, however, not been achieved, as the RBI governor effectively controls the Monetary Policy Committee. There is thus the possibility of pressure upon this one person (the governor) to cut interest rates, by the ruling party, in the year leading up to the elections. In addition, the Ministry of Finance has the power to give directions to RBI on any subject, without any transparency.

The work of financial regulation is spread across RBI, SEBI, IRDA, and PFRDA. All these agencies feature important deviations from good governance principles for regulators.[8] There is arbitrary power in regulation-making, licensing, investigation, and prosecution. At an early stage of development of state capacity, substantial powers of investigation and punishment have been placed at regulators, which has hampered the emergence of state capacity.

The regulation-making and licensing powers have been used, in India, to create a comprehensive central planning system, where every product and process of the private sector is controlled by the financial agencies. These interventions often have no foundation in terms of market failure. As an example, SEBI controls the time of day at which exchanges start and stop their operations. Similarly, SEBI now has *de facto* control of the names of the board of directors and the management team of exchange institutions. This is a level of central planning that was not found with industrial firms in India in 1991.

An unusual feature of regulators in India, which is not seen elsewhere in the world, is that the judicial function has also been placed at regulators. When this is done, regulators fuse the legislative, executive and judicial branches of the state. There is no separation of powers. This arrangement is inconsistent with sound thinking in regulatory theory and violates the separation of powers that is part of the basic structure of the Constitution of India.

As a consequence of these infirmities in the foundations of public administration of financial regulators, the state capacity in financial regulation which has come about is limited. We have a crisis-ridden financial system that does a poor job of raising financial resources and allocating them into the real economy.

While RBI does monetary policy, it also does many other things. As an example, it does financial regulation and runs exchange infrastructure for the bond market and the currency market. This sprawling agenda has hindered focus and accountability, and engendered low performance.

There are four clear tasks in financial economic policy: monetary policy, financial regulation, resolution, and public debt management. Many other things are done in Indian financial economic policy, going beyond these four tasks, which are deficient in rationale. These include capital controls, government-owned financial institutions to address perceived failures of the financial system (e.g., NABARD or Mudra Bank), government owned banks, directed lending, the system of 'financial repression' through which financial firms are forced to lend to the government, etc.

The Process of Financial Reform

At the outset, equity market trading took place by open outcry at the Bombay Stock Exchange (BSE), which was controlled by its members. Settlement took place through physical share certificates, and there was a chronic problem with counterfeit share certificates. The BSE closed down a few times every year, out of its inability to manage payments efficiently.

The first phase of financial reform in India was triggered by the requirement for foreign capital inflows after 1991 and the Harshad Mehta scandal in 1992. This led to a remarkable phase of change, led by a remarkable community of public minded people. SEBI was established as a new regulator. Modern exchange infrastructure was established in the form of the National Stock Exchange (NSE), the National Securities Clearing Corporation (NSCC) and the National Stock Depository Limited (NSDL). Electronic trading and derivatives trading were introduced. These were transformative reforms. One of the pioneers of this work, Ravi Narain, said that when satellite trading through NSE reached a remote town in India, it was transformative on the scale of a first railway line reaching the town. The improvements of the equity market of that period were an important part of the enabling environment for the high growth of the 1991–2011 period.[9]

This was followed by a series of government committee reports, which mapped out the journey of financial economic policy. These included a report on capital controls led by U. K. Sinha, on consumer protection led by Dhirendra Swarup, on public debt management led by Jahangir Aziz, on international finance led by Percy Mistry, and a report on domestic finance led by Raghuram Rajan.[10] These five reports worked out a broadly coherent vision for the next stage of the reforms.

The changes that were called for required large-scale changes in the laws that created agencies and controlled government intervention in finance.

These ideas were brought together by the Financial Sector Legislative Reforms Commission (FSLRC), which worked in

2011–2015. FSLRC drafted a single law, the Indian Financial Code, which replaces 61 existing laws.[11]

A few elements of this work have been translated into implementation, such as inflation targeting, but most have not. The Indian Financial Code, version 1.1, is the pending agenda for financial reforms.

In this period, the policy pipeline was fully working, from data to research to creative policy proposals, to government committee reports to the drafting of law and the construction of state capacity to enforce new laws. These successes were grounded in a financial reforms community. A coherent set of persons played various roles through this period and brought a consistent intellectual framework into all this work. The reforms process was led by the Ministry of Finance, SEBI and NSE. A large number of individuals across government, academics and financial firms participated in the work. As an example, 146 individuals were involved in FSLRC in various capacities.[12]

After this, this community was largely dispersed, and progress in financial economic policy subsided. For the next phase of the financial reforms, a comparable community will need to be recreated.

Summing Up

Financial economic policy is about the working of financial intermediaries, financial markets, money creation and government borrowing. From a market failure perspective, finance requires regulation to do 'consumer protection' (to improve the fair play as seen by unsophisticated households), 'prudential regulation' (to increase the probability that promises made by financial firms are upheld), 'resolution' (specialized bankruptcy regulation mechanisms for financial firms that have unsophisticated households as customers) and 'systemic risk regulation' (interventions that reduce the probability that the working of the overall financial system is impaired). Alongside this, financial economic policy covers the problems of creating fiat money (through a central bank) and public debt management (e.g., through a public debt management agency).

Financial regulators are like other regulators, in that careful design work is required on the law and on organization design, so that the coercive power is channelled into addressing market failure while operating in the rule of law. For the central bank, there is a clear objective in the form of inflation targeting; for the remaining organizations in the agency landscape, it is harder to establish clear objectives and hold the agency accountable.

Achieving state capacity in financial regulation is extremely difficult. It involves a high number of transactions, high discretion, high stakes and high secrecy.

In the Indian experience, there was a great outburst of financial economic policy starting from the early 1990s, which led to the achievements of establishing NSE (1992), NSDL, SEBI, the transformation of the equity market, merging FMC into SEBI and enshrining inflation targeting as the objective at RBI (2016). The committee process, and a strong community, gave the drafting of the Indian Financial Code, version 1.1, in 2015. All this was made possible through a remarkable combination of knowledge and community. By 2017, this community was dispersed, and the process will now need to restart at the early stages of the policy pipeline.

Part VII

Reimagining the Indian Development Project

44

Institution Building,
Not Just GDP Growth

The dominant imperative for India is to increase GDP, so as to bring prosperity to over a billion people. There are few things more important than our challenge of becoming rich before we become old. We know, from historical experience, that the only way out of mass poverty is to obtain modest rates of growth of per capita GDP that are sustained for many decades. As an example, if per capita GDP grows at 4 per cent per year, then there is one doubling every 18 years. Per capita GDP would go up by 7 times in 50 years, and then we would be a rich country.

The problem with focusing on GDP growth as the immediate determinant of policy decisions is that there are many pathways to obtaining short spurts of GDP growth.

GDP growth can be obtained through a great surge of debt, through a boom in government investment, by destroying the environment, by distorting the exchange rate, by establishing central planning structures that use coercion to mobilize and deploy resources, etc. Each of these pathways gives a short spurt of growth but does not last into the long run.

The experiences of the USSR and Japan are salutary reminders of the ability of states to achieve short and unsustainable bursts of high growth. And, for each USSR or Japan that actually managed to obtain state-led growth for a few decades, the historical experience contains many countries that failed to do even this much when opting for a state-led model of growth.

In a simplistic notion of development, we have to combine capital and modern technology in order to achieve high productivity. This can readily lead to notions of high modernism. In the extreme, we may think of placing modern technology into government-owned monopolies and using state coercion to force everyone to work with these monopolies. In the short run, this does give capital deepening and technical change. But this works out poorly in the medium term. We cannot be assured of benevolent and competent leaders in the public sector. We lose out on the energy of private innovation and competition. The economy loses flexibility and continuous adaptation when it is trapped by dominant state-controlled monopolies. And when we go down this route, we tend to revere and prioritize the big prestige projects over the subtlety of institutions.

A complex modern economy only works when it is a self-organizing system. It has to have the creative efforts of a large number of individuals, all working in their own self-interest. Central planning, and a leadership role for the state, does not work for a modern complex economy.

Building the republic, then, is about the policy institutions which shape the incentives of each person and help intermediate the interactions between individuals. Building these institutions is a slow and complex problem. In the short run, it is always possible to obtain GDP growth without solving these deeper problems. We would all do well to shift focus from the numbers for GDP growth, to the state of health of state institutions.

In the short run, central planning and state-led development can yield GDP growth. But as the economy becomes more complex, the need for state institutions that reshape incentives becomes even greater. Spurts in growth that are state-led tend to peter out. The only way to run the 50-year marathon is through building institutions. We should pursue institution building rather than GDP growth. Sustained improvement in institutional quality is hard, but it is the only way to obtain sustained GDP growth.

Many technologists slip into a different strain of high modernism, with an enthusiasm for designing state-run or state-imposed monopolies upon the economy. Deep knowledge of the humanities and social sciences is an antidote for this optimism. We are generally better off with multiple competing efforts, organic evolution of standards and technologies, and the minimal involvement of the state.

Success Is Not Assured

The early rhetoric about economic development viewed an underdeveloped country as a child. Growth was inevitable, it was only a matter of putting in a few auxiliary actions that helped and enabled that process. In this worldview, we run the risk of thinking that progress is inevitable, that progress involves (say) steel mills, and we can save everyone the time and trouble by having state-run steel mills.

We now know that there is no inevitability about the rise of a country into the ranks of a prosperous democracy. There are only four countries which were poor in 1945, that are now prosperous democracies: South Korea, Taiwan, Chile and Israel.

A Bigger GDP Is Not Synonymous with Higher State Capacity

Many assume because aggregate GDP or per capita GDP has gone up, the state must be in better shape. However, the simple addition of capital, labour and more productive firms yields higher GDP growth, regardless of how the state is faring. When Infosys and TCS are better firms, Indian GDP goes up, and this need not go along with improvements in the Indian state.

We can readily identify some elements of the Indian state which appear to be inferior when compared with a past date. It is likely that the Metropolitan Magistrate's Court in Fort in South Bombay did a better job at adjudicating contract disputes, 100 years ago. In the early decades after Independence, India was at the global frontier with high quality statistics such as NSS, weather data, soil quality surveys, etc.: in many of these respects, the statistical system today appears to have declined in quality. It is likely that the parliamentary debate around the union budget in the 1950s was significantly superior to that seen today. The Survey of India likely created a better maps database, 100 years ago, when compared with its present operations.

State capacity can improve only over long periods of time, with a slow accumulation of human capital and organization designs. But a policy community can be disrupted in a short period and leave behind a substantial decline in state capacity.[1]

Can we go from such anecdotes to data? A prominent measure of state capability in a globally comparable data set is available, for the 1996–2012 period.[2] By this measure, state capability has risen in only a few countries over this period, and state capability in India *declined* in this period. Our institutional capacity got worse in a period of strong GDP growth. We do wrong in equating GDP growth with improvement in the foundations for GDP growth.[3]

Turning to the Indian experience, we can conjecture a mechanism through which higher GDP growth *caused* reduced state capacity. When bigger rupee values are at stake, private persons have more to gain by undermining state institutions. The resources that are brought to bear, to attack the working of state institutions, are larger when GDP is higher.

We vividly saw this in India, in the period after 2005, when India was starting to reap remarkable success by private firms. The prospective gains from subverting state institutions were suddenly larger, and we got bigger investments into attacks on institutions. State apparatus that used to work when million-rupee bribes were offered broke down when the offers went to billions of rupees.

Another pathway runs from success to complacence. In a period of high GDP growth, such as 1991–2011, the incumbents who argue *if it ain't broke, don't fix it* tend to gain the upper hand, as the GDP growth is offered as the proof of success of the status quo.[4]

Perhaps India's growth of 1979–2011 was not adequately grounded in the required institutional capacity to be a prosperous liberal democracy, and perhaps this has something to do with the difficulties that have been seen from 2011 onward.

Keeping Score

The advantage of a well-measured GDP is that it can become a report card for the government. However, as argued above, it is possible to get GDP growth for a short time through all sorts of bad policies. The path to becoming an advanced country lies in many generations of sustained improvement in institutions. If we are not to keep score using GDP growth, what measures could be useful?

There is no one measure of institutional quality, but we can think of a few measures that are useful in thinking about how we are faring in building a republic.

Safety. The number of young women walking alone on a street, at night, shows the extent of perceived safety and the functioning of the criminal justice system. This is a good measure of Indian institutional quality.

Flight of millionaires. The number of millionaires who emigrate out of India, per year, is an important measure. Millionaires in India are not ordinary people. They have acquired deep locale-specific knowledge, have achieved economic success and have roots in India. They do not leave the country looking for better economic opportunities. They are buying homes and citizenship in a mature liberal democracy owing to the fear of expropriation at home. Their departure suggests there are concerns about safety and the rule of law in India. Similar problems are being seen in China as well. Our progress towards the rule of law is measured by the extent to which millionaires do not seek to leave the country.

Flight of India-centric firms. The phenomenon of India-centric firms that do not organize themselves as an Indian company is quite revealing. These firms go through considerable expense to set up a Singapore-based or a London-based entity, so as to avoid the legal and political risk associated with being an Indian company. This is a telling sign of institutional failure in India.

Flight of India-centric trading. Trading activity in the Indian rupee and the Nifty should, by rights, be located in India. However, from 2007 onward, over half of this activity has shifted to overseas locations. This reflects the failure of Indian institutions. Every year, we get new repressive measures in financial regulation, tax policy and capital controls, which pushes a greater proportion of activity overseas. This market share is a revealing indicator of Indian institutional quality.

Flight of India-centric contract enforcement. The extent to which private contracts in India rely on arbitration outside India is a comment on the quality of the Indian legal system. If India's courts, judges, lawyers and laws worked better, it would be much cheaper to settle disputes in India. The fact that vastly greater legal costs are incurred outside India is a demonstration of Indian institutional weakness.

Mocking the powerful. The extent to which comedy shows torment the present leadership is a measure of the *de facto* freedom of speech present in the country. Under the rule of law, a Donald Trump is unable to inflict harm upon all persons who build these shows. The extent to which comedy shows take on the most powerful figures is a measure of institutional quality in India.

45

Looking Forward

Mark 1: The Nehruvian Development State

At Independence, the conceptual framework of policy was developed by Jawaharlal Nehru, B. R. Ambedkar, P. C. Mahalanobis, Pitambar Pant, Sukhamoy Chakravarty and others. This involved a developmental state, and a lead role for the state in the evolution of the country. At the time, it was felt that there was a shortage of capital in India. They also felt that a sophisticated financial system could not be achieved in India and envisioned a significant role for the state in *supplanting* the private financial system in order to address the problem of missing markets.[1]

We call this the 'Mark 1 strategy'. It induced an early growth acceleration compared with the pre-war data, and then ran into many difficulties. By the 1970s, it was clear that the license-permit raj was not working well. Central planning induces stagnation.

Mark 2: Improved Economic Freedom

The conceptual framework of the next phase was developed by Jagdish Bhagwati, T. N. Srinivasan, Manmohan Singh,

D. T. Lakdawala, Ashok Desai, Arun Shourie, Montek Ahluwalia, M. Narasimham, Padma Desai, Anne Krueger, I. G. Patel, Raja Chelliah, and others.[2] The change in course began with the Janata Party in 1977, and rapidly yielded results in the form of higher growth from 1979 onward. Through the 1980s, there was a gradual process of domestic liberalization, while preserving autarky when it came to the international engagement. The reforms of 1991–2004 gave a big step forward in domestic liberalization of the real economy, in financial reforms and in scaling down autarky.[3]

By this time, a sophisticated financial system started emerging, and the appropriate role of the state shifted from *producing* financial services to *regulating* private financial service providers. In addition, opening up to the global financial system eased resource constraints. The gap between investment and savings is financed by capital inflows. This changed the notion in the minds of Indian policymakers that capital is in short supply. The bottlenecks now lay not in capital, but in economic freedom and in institutional quality.

This 'Mark 2 strategy' unfolded from 1977 onwards and yielded a great outburst of growth from 1991–2011.

These two decades stand out as the best growth experience in India's history. For the first time, the growth pessimists were proven wrong, and India got strong growth. This impacted upon all quartiles of the income distribution. For the rich, there was wealth creation of a kind that had never been seen before. The middle class graduated to being able to afford appliances, devices and plane tickets. The poor got poverty reduction on a massive scale. For the first time in India's history, the headcount of the poor shrank.

There was an optimism in this period of a kind that was perhaps last seen immediately after independence. Finally, to many of us, India was getting on its feet.[4]

The Loss of High Growth

The growth of 1991–2011 has not carried forward into the following years.[5] A phenomenon of this size cannot just come about owing to some events. There is a need for a conceptual framework, in understanding what happened, and then in changing it.

The key idea is that a lot of government intervention, and the licence–permit–inspector raj, remains in place. The early dawn of economic freedom, that was promised in 1991, has not evolved into a mature market economy. Private persons are beset with government intervention. As an example, while many think that India achieved convertibility on the current account in 1994, it is hard to describe the maze of rules as 'convertibility on the current account'.[6]

On the policy side, there was a rough idea that there should be less state intervention, and that light touch economic regulation should be done by a new breed of economic regulators. This has worked out unsatisfactorily. The executive powers of regulators, in licensing and enforcement, constitute a new level of intrusive control, of a kind which was not present before 1991. The new regulators are often the new central planners. As was seen prior to 1991, central planning has induced stagnation.

The instincts of central planning are alive and well among policymakers. There is a great deal of arbitrary power in the hands of government. Extensive interference in the economy by the government, the policy risk associated with future interventions, and the fear of how arbitrary power in the hands of the government will be used, has led to a loss of confidence in the private sector. A broad range of government agencies have achieved high power without commensurate checks and balances.[7]

When India was a small economy, the GDP was small, and the gains from violating rules were relatively small. The 10× growth in the size of the economy created new opportunities to obtain wealth. The gains from violating rules went up sharply. Large resources were brought to bear upon subverting state institutions. The foundations of state institutions, in terms of the rule of law and checks and balances were always weak. This combination, of an amplified effort by private persons to subvert institutions, coupled with low state capacity, has resulted in a decline of institutional quality.

In many other countries, the phenomenon of a 'middle income trap' has been observed. At the early stages of development, the simple mobilization of labour and capital suffices to escape from abject poverty. But once the minimal market economy is in place, a different level of institutional quality is required. The maturation of firms and the government creates the need for complex contracts, contract enforcement, economic regulation, and institutions that intermediate and channel the conflicts between social groups. When a middle-income country seeks to rise to a mature market economy, and institutional capacity is weak, growth stalls.

The number of persons working has stagnated at about 410 million in the 2015–2022 period. When the aggregate number of workers stagnates, for each person that gets a job and a livelihood, someone else is losing it. A great deal of our traditional notions of altruism or philanthropy fail to work, in the large, in such an environment. The highest priority in this world must be on the ideas and the action that will restore sustained macroeconomic dynamism.

What Is to Be Done?

Long years ago, we made a tryst with destiny, and we must find our way out of these dark woods. The most important question in Indian economics and policymaking today is that of diagnosing and addressing the sources of under-performance that have arisen from 2011 and building the ideas and actions through which India can emerge into the ranks of advanced countries. This requires building knowledge and building community for the Mark 3 paradigm, the paradigm that will set the stage for India to break out into a prosperous liberal democracy over the next 50 years.

This book distills the insights of the research literature that has emerged in the last 20 years, which has a new level of sophistication in thinking about India, which has moved on from the Mark 1 or Mark 2 paradigms. We have built on the literature and researchers seen in the end notes, and on the ideas of Abhijit Banerjee, Avinash Dixit, Bibek Debroy, Devesh Kapur, Esther Duflo, Jeff Hammer, Kaushik Basu, Lant Pritchett, Nandan Nilekani, Pratap Bhanu Mehta and others.

Addressing these problems requires going to the foundations. Why do we require state intervention? Why is state capacity low? How should state organizations be constructed, so as to cater to a gradual improvement of state capacity? What is the right approach to public policy, when state capacity is low? These are the most important questions of Indian economics today.

Knowledge of macroeconomics, globalization, finance and firms generated the great growth episode of 1991–2011. The fundamentals of economics—the importance of freedom and the role of the state in addressing market failure—lie at the heart of the required Mark 3 paradigm. The puzzle in Mark 3 is that of achieving state capability. This will require building experts and expertise at the intersection of economics, law and public administration.

The policy landscape in India today is a sprawling scene where a large number of state interventions are in place, and most of them work poorly. The path to progress lies in narrowing the scope of the state, picking fewer battles, and first learning how to run the government at high levels of state capacity. The four primal requirements of a state are the criminal justice system, the judiciary, the tax system and financial regulation. Our prime objective should be to learn how to be a capable state in these four areas.

We share the objectives of people working in numerous fields—total factor productivity, infrastructure, better design of poverty programs, urbanization, sustainability, etc. There is intricate sectoral knowledge in each field such as agriculture. Each of these is a compelling area, where there are great possibilities, and where the impact will be enormous. The public economics and public administration of this book is a general toolkit, that can be applied in diverse settings. A virtuous cycles of progress needs to be set off, where the general toolkit helps obtain progress in specific domains, and each domain feeds knowledge and experience to the general toolkit.

Many things work well without government intervention. We need to shift away from notions of a developmental state, where big initiatives originate from the government, towards respect for the self-organizing system that is a free society. We need to rely far more on private negotiations, private contracts, and civil society solutions, rather than turning to the government to solve problems. The state should be the last resort in resolving market failure, not the first resort.

Economic thinkers of the previous decades tended to focus on economics more narrowly, on issues such as the green revolution or heavy industry or trade liberalization. In finding the Mark 3 framework, we need to more explicitly locate ourselves in the intersection of politics and the economy. To make sustained economic growth possible, we require the republic. The founding energy of liberal democracy is the pursuit of freedom, of people being masters of their own fate.

The toolkit of four kinds of market failure, drawn from public economics, helps identify the areas where there is a case for state intervention. Public choice theory steers us away from optimism about the state and shows us the root cause of low state capacity. The state is not a benevolent actor, it is formed of self-interested persons. Individuals and state agencies crave arbitrary power. The path to state capacity lies in checks and balances, and dispersed power.

The laws that define government intervention need to be written with a focus on removing arbitrary power, controlling the ways in which officials engage with private persons, and establishing the rule of law. This new approach to writing law is of essence in building the republic.

Our traditional notion of political economy is about competing coalition of *voters*, where special interests mobilize to block reforms. A remarkable feature of India is the role of established bureaucratic formations as the constituency in favour of arbitrary power, of the administrative state, and as the opponents of reform. The officials like the rule of officials. The central planners and the agencies are arrayed against rule of law and a market economy.

There is a capability trap when coercive power is given to weak organizations. Once an organization has the power to coerce, and the checks and balances are weak, there will be a steady slide into abuse of coercive power. The private sector is fearful of the arbitrary power wielded by officials and does not speak up. There is no voice, but there is an exit in the form of reduced investment. There is a lack of a feedback loop where difficulties kick off improvements. Too often, in fact, we are seeing the opposite kind of feedback loop, where agencies fail in their work, but the political system responds by giving them greater powers to investigate and punish, which induces a further reduction in their capabilities.

The path to state capacity lies in being stingy with public expenditure and with coercive power. Government organizations should have to prove themselves, before significant money or coercive power is placed in their hands. UK levels of coercive power in a tax administration can only be justified when the tax administration rises to UK levels of rule of law. The first step in the Indian journey to state capacity is that of revoking the wide array of coercive powers which have been bestowed upon a large number of government organizations, so that private persons can breathe more freely and so as to get on the journey to sound public administration and thus state capacity.

The challenge of this generation is that of building knowledge and building community for the Mark 3 paradigm. In many traditional fields (e.g., agriculture) and in many non-traditional fields (e.g., government contracting), we need to develop a community that achieves expertise and tells war stories to each other. This needs to happen at the level of the union government, in each state, and at each city. The quest needs to start at public economics, but ultimately it is about becoming a republic.

Acknowledgments

One owes an intellectual debt to so many people. Some of them are no more. With every formal and informal interaction with our fellow economists and thinkers, we chip away at understanding the art and science of economic policy. I particularly wish to thank Abhay Pethe, Arbind Modi, Arjun Sengupta, Arun Shourie, Arvind Panagariya, Arvind Subramaniam, Arvind Virmani, Ashok Desai, Avinash Dixit, Bhanoji Rao, Bimal Jalan, C. Rangarajan, D.K. Shrivastava, Daniel McFadden, Daniel Yergin, Devesh Kapur, George Kopits, Harsh Vardhan Singh, Horst Kohler, I.G. Patel, Indira Rajaraman, Jagdish Bhagwati, Jayanta Roy, M. Govinda Rao, Michael Mussa, Montek Ahluwalia, Morris Adelman, Murillo Portugal, Narendra Jadhav, Nitin Desai, Partho Shome, Patricia Annez-Clarke, Pratap Bhanu Mehta, Raja Chelliah, Rajiv Kumar, Rakesh Mohan, Rathin Roy, Roberto Zagha, Satya Poddar, Shankar Acharya, Sharad Desai, Shubhashis Gangopadhyay, Stan Fischer, Sukhamoy Chakravarty, Surjit Bhalla, Thomas Marschak, Urjit Patel and Yoginder Alagh.

To achieve successful policy outcomes in India, we need the deft hands of accomplished mandarins, and I was fortunate to observe some truly outstanding ones at close quarters. They are a major inspiration for this book. Towards this, I am greatly indebted to Abid Hussain, Amarnath Verma, B. K. Zutshi, B. L. Das, C. R. K. Rao Sahib, Gopi Arora, G. V. Ramakrishna, Lavraj Kumar, Nandan Nilekani, Naresh Chandra, N. K. Singh, P. N. Haksar, R. Vasudevan, S. P. Shukla, S. Venkitaraman and Y. Venugopal Reddy.

In the difficult challenges of the coming years, we require the combination of economic knowledge and the gift for statecraft that they have.

The political leadership, at its best, is able to see opportunities for progress in a difficult situation and seize opportunities for game-changing reforms. This requires strength of character, an entrepreneurial sense of timing and a commitment to progress in the long run. Arun Jaitley, Atal Bihari Vajpayee, Capt. Satish Sharma, D. P. Dhar, George Fernandes, Jaswant Singh, J. Vengal Rao, Dr. Manmohan Singh, Mohan Dharia, P. Chidambaram, Pranab Mukherjee and Yashwant Sinha were the political leaders who gave me the opportunity to experience the highs and lows in some the great 'policy yagnas' of the past 40 years. For this, I am deeply grateful to them. Lessons from these experiences form the core of many sections of this book.

I want to express deep gratitude to my life partner Lata Kelkar, without whose selfless support this exciting journey of policymaking would not even have been possible. Finally, continuous inspiration for this project came from our daughter Sujata, her husband Nitesh, and our grandchildren Akash and Aarav, who have been a boundless source of love and joy.

—Vijay Kelkar

All of us are a linear combination of our influences. At an early stage, at IIT Bombay, I was inspired by Gopal Shevare, K. Sudhakar, D. B. Phatak and Ira Bidkar. At graduate school at the University of Southern California, I was privileged to get an insight into the worldviews and analytical frameworks of Lee Lillard, Andy Weiss, Yoram Weiss, Jeff Nugent, Cheng Hsiao and Richard Easterlin.

I am grateful to all my colleagues from CMIE, IGIDR and the Ministry of Finance and NIPFP, who disagreed with me, criticized me and made me see things in new ways. I thank Yashwant Sinha, Rakesh Mohan and Jaimini Bhagwati for my induction into the UTI crisis at the Ministry of Finance. I was blessed to have observed the work of three great finance ministers leading up to 2005, and to have worked closely with Arbind Modi, Ashok Lahiri, S. Narayan, U. K. Sinha and Vijay Kelkar.

My thinking on public economics and public administration draws from the worldview and wisdom of Reuben Abraham, Junaid Ahmad, Ashok Desai, Jeff Hammer, K. P. Krishnan, Percy Mistry, Rajiv Mehrishi, Kirit Parikh, Lant Pritchett and Shekhar Shah.

My work in macroeconomics and finance was a partnership with K. P. Krishnan, Ila Patnaik, Josh Felman and Susan Thomas. The founders of the modern Indian equity market—R. H. Patil, C. B. Bhave and Ravi Narain—were a source of inspiration for what economic reforms can be.

I learnt enormously from the community that carried out the financial reforms of the 1990s and the first decade of the new millennium: Ashish Chauhan, Chitra Ramakrishna, C. M. Vasudev, Jaimini Bhagwati, Jayanth Varma, L. C. Gupta, Percy Mistry, P. J. Nayak, Raghavan Putran, Rajesh Doshi, Raju Chitale, Rakesh Mohan, Shashank Saksena, S. Narayan, Surendra Dave, U. K. Sinha and Usha Thorat.

Ashish Chauhan, V. Balasubramaniam, Ratna Madeka, Lakshmi Patel, G. M. Shenoy and Shuvam Misra were co-creators, with Susan Thomas and me, in Nifty, PRISM and many other innovations of the early years of the equity market.

My work on pensions was a collaboration with Anand Bordia, A. P. Singh, Dhirendra Swarup, Gautam Bhardwaj, John Piggott, Renuka Sane, Robert Palacios and Surendra Dave.

My work in public finance draws on Vijay Kelkar, Arbind Modi, Ashok Lahiri, M. Govinda Rao, Amaresh Bagchi and Rathin Roy.

My thinking on the statistical system is formed of many decades of watching CMIE build organizational capability in the field, and the perfectionism of Mahesh Vyas.

Discussions with Y. Venugopal Reddy, M. Govinda Rao and Junaid Ahmad shaped my thinking on decentralization.

I learnt about firms and the pathways to transforming firm productivity from Mahesh Vyas, Vishal Nevatia, Pramod Kabra, Harsh Vardhan, T. Koshy, Sanjiv Shah and Deep Narayan.

The cast of 146 persons in FSLRC, particularly B. N. Srikrishna, Dhirendra Swarup, C. K. Gopal Nair, M. Sahoo, Somasekhar Sundaresan, A. P. Singh and Harsh Vardhan, influenced my thinking on financial economic policy, writing laws and building state capacity.

Susan Thomas, Rajeswari Sengupta, Anjali Sharma, Bhargavi Zaveri, T. K. Viswanathan, M. Sahoo and K. P. Krishnan shaped my thinking in bankruptcy, after the handoff from FSLRC to BLRC.

Watching Montek Ahluwalia, D. Subbarao, C. B. Bhave, Ashok Chawla, U. K. Sinha, K. P. Krishnan and Jahangir

Aziz, and the sprawling cast of the Indian crisis response in 2008, shaped my understanding of macroeconomic and financial crises.

Jeff Hammer, Nachiket Mor, Sandhya Venkateswaran, Amrita Agarwal and Shubho Roy have shaped my thinking on public health and health care.

Technology policy now cuts across a broad array of issues in public policy, and my thinking on this was shaped by Sunil Abraham, Rishab Bailey, C. B. Bhave, Sanjay Jain, Vijay Madan, Rahul Matthan, Ameya Naik, Nandan Nilekani, Smriti Parsheera, Gautham Ravichander, Viral Shah, R. S. Sharma, A. P. Singh and Manish Srivastava.

Over the 2007–2020 period, Ila Patnaik and I had the exhilarating experience of building a small research group at NIPFP. We thank C. Rangarajan, Vijay Kelkar, M. Govinda Rao and Rathin Roy for making this research group possible. We were blessed by a procession of young geniuses who came into this work, challenged our assumptions and improved our thinking. In particular, we thank Anirudh Burman, Apoorva Gupta, Bhargavi Zaveri, Bhavyaa Sharma, Chirag Anand, Pramod Sinha, Pratik Datta, Radhika Pandey, Shekhar Hari Kumar, Shubho Roy, Smriti Parsheera, Suyash Rai and Vimal Balasubramaniam for these experiences.

—Ajay Shah

Gurcharan Das, Pratap Bhanu Mehta, Ram Guha and Jerry Rao encouraged us at the early stages of this project and helped us to follow in their footsteps of writing important books.

Bhuvana Anand, Suyash Rai, Shruti Rajagopalan, Renuka Sane and Amit Varma helped us in strategizing the book concept and designing the table of contents.

Given enough eyeballs, all bugs are shallow. This book has benefited from many discerning eyes who came at the arguments and the detail from diverse points of view. Amrita Agarwal, Vikram Aggarwal, Sanjeev Ahluwalia, Bhuvana Anand, Surbhi Bhatia Sumit Bose, Anirudh Burman, Shubhashis Gangopadhyay, Akshay Jaitly, Rajeev Kapoor, Pranay Kotasthane, Kaushik Krishnan Satya Poddar, Arjun Rajagopal, Shubho Roy, Renuka Sane, and Rajeswari Sengupta read drafts and induced numerous improvements. Ayush Patnaik forced us to up our game on numerous weak arguments. Rahul Ahluwalia helped us pin down facts on education. Kusan Biswas and Ashim Kapoor helped us stay organized by setting up elegant Latex solutions for the writing process.

The team at Penguin was a delight to work with. They warmed to the concept of the book early, and steadfastly helped in carrying it through into the form in your hands. We thank Tarini Uppal, Binita Roy and Shantanu Ray Chaudhuri for their skill, enthusiasm and support.

—Vijay Kelkar and Ajay Shah

Notes

Chapter 1.

1. Jon Porter, 'EU proposes mandatory USB-C on all devices, including iPhones', *The Verge*, September 2021, https://www.theverge.com/2021/9/23/22626723/eu-commission-universal-charger-usb-c-micro-lightning-connector-smartphones.

2. Mishaal Rahman, 'Google requires new Android devices with Type-C ports to not break USB-PD compatibility', *XDA Developers*, October 2019, https://www.xda-developers.com/google-new-android-devices-type-c-support-usb-pd/.

3. David Owen, 'How the refrigerator became an agent of climate catastrophe', *The New Yorker*, January 2022, https://www.newyorker.com/news/annals-of-a-warming-planet/how-the-refrigerator-became-an-agent-of-climate-catastrophe.

4. On noise pollution in India, see Chris Berdik, 'The Fight to Curb a Health Scourge in India: Noise Pollution', *Undark*, March 2020, https://undark.org/2020/03/23/india-noise-pollution/.

5. On light pollution in India, see Pavan Kumar et al., 'Analyzing trend in artificial light pollution pattern in India using NTL sensor's data', *Urban climate* 27 (March 2019): 272–283, https://www.sciencedirect.com/science/article/abs/pii/

S2212095518303717; Sahana Ghosh, 'Light pollution on the rise in India', *Mongabay*, January 2019, https://india.mongabay. com/2019/01/light-pollution-on-the-rise-in-india-study/.

6. Ana Swanson, 'Meet the four-eyed, eight-tentacled monopoly.
7. that is making your glasses so expensive', *Forbes*, September 2014, https://www.forbes.com/sites/anaswanson/2014/09/10/ meet-the-four-eyed-eight-tentacled-monopoly-that-is- making-your-glasses-so-expensive/?sh=6d5f7e586b66.
8. Executive Order 12866 is at https://www.archives.gov/files/ federal-register/executive-orders/pdf/12866.pdf and the OMB guidance document is at https://obamawhitehouse.archives. gov/omb/inforeg_riaguide/.
9. Confusion around the word 'infrastructure' is not unique to India; e.g., see Bryce Covert, 'The debate over what "infrastructure" is ridiculous', *New York Times*, April 2021, https://www. nytimes.com/2021/04/26/opinion/biden-infrastructure-child- care.html.

Chapter 2.

1. As an example, *National Food Processing Policy*, 24 December2019, from the Ministry of Food Processing Industries, Government of India.
2. In the jargon of public economics, taxation in order to deter negative externalities is termed a 'Pigouvian tax'.

Chapter 3.

1. This evidence is from the IDFC Institute's 'SATARC' Crime Victimisation Surveys: IDFC Institute, *Safety trends and reporting of crime (SATARC)*, technical report (IDFC Institute, 2017), https://www.idfcinstitute.org/knowledge/publications/ reports/safety-trends-and-reporting-of-crime-satarc/.
2. Wikipedia, 'List of countries by traffic-related death rate', *Wikipedia*, 2019, https://en.wikipedia.org/wiki/List_of_ countries_by_traffic-related_death_rate.

3. The quote is from Dipak Kumar Dash, 'Interview with Nitin Gadkari', *The Times of India*, March 2020, https://timesofindia. indiatimes.com/blogs/the-interviews-blog/the-main-reasons-for-accidents-are-faulty-road-engineering-bad-junction-design-inadequate-signage-and-road-markings/.

4. One organization working on this problem is Save Life Foundation, https://savelifefoundation.org/the-problem/.

5. Karthik Muralidharan et al., *The fiscal cost of weak governance: Evidence from teacher absence in India*, technical report (The World Bank, 2016).

6. Angela N. Kisakye et al., 'Regulatory mechanisms for absenteeism in the health sector: A systematic review of strategies and their implementation', *Journal of Healthcare Leadership*, 2016, https://www.dovepress.com/regulatory-mechanisms-for-absenteeism-in-the-health-sector-a-systemati-peer-reviewed-fulltext-article-JHL.

7. Shalini Rudra, 'Immunization coverage: India far away from meeting targets', *Observer Research Foundation*, 2017, https://www.orfonline.org/expert-speak/immunisation-coverage-india-far-away-from-meeting-targets/.

8. The citizenry walking away from state-run alternatives that are free is found in many settings. As an example, 7.9 per cent of undertrials in prisons utilized the legal aid services they were entitled to. Anup Surendranath and Gale Andrew, 'State legal aid and undertrials: are there no takers?', *Indian Law Review*, 2022, https://www.tandfonline.com/doi/full/10.1080/247305 80.2022.2029018.

9. These facts are drawn from: Avani Kapur, Mridusmita Bordoloi and Ritwik Shukla, 'Sarva Shiksha Abhiyan', *Accountability Initiative*, 2018, https://accountabilityindia.in/publication/sarva-shiksha-abhiyan-ssa/; ASER Centre, 'Annual School Education Report 2016', 2017, Geeta Gandhi King-don, 'The private schooling phenomenon in India: A review', 2017, Azeem Panjwani et al., *Systemic drivers of foundational learning outcomes*, technical report (Central Square Foundation, September 2021), https://www.centralsquarefoundation.org/Systemic%20 Drivers%20of%20FLN_Highlights%20Report.pdf.

10. This material is derived from Ananya Goyal, Renuka Sane, and Ajay Shah, 'What year in the history of an advanced economy is like India today?', *The Leap Blog*, August 2021, https://blog.theleapjournal.org/2021/08/what-year-in-history-of-advanced.html.

11. Exports here is measured in USD and is measured as goods + services exports excluding POL and excluding gold, gems and jewellery.

12. The 2021 results are at https://freedomhouse.org/country/india/freedom-world/2021, and show a score of 67/100. The oldest available data is for 2017 and has a value of 77/100.

13. The 2021 results are at https://rsf.org/en/country/india. The oldest avail-able data is for 2013 where India stood at rank 140.

14. Robert K. Merton, 'The unanticipated consequences of purposive social action', *American Sociological Review* 1, no. 6 (1936): 894–904, https://www.jstor.org/stable/2084615.

15. Populist political movements contain a suspicious streak about the supposed conspiracies of the high-flying elite. The law of unintended consequences has an interesting implication, for understanding conspiracy theories. It is hard enough for a policymaker, working in the open, to achieve a desired outcome, when the problem statement and the instruments adopted are reasonably straightforward. It would be practically impossible for a group of *conspirators* to work in secrecy, to undertake a complex set of steps, and hit a desired target. Conspiracy theories are likely to be often false because social systems are too complex, because complex interventions will generally result in an outcome that is different from what was intended by the initiator. This idea is originally from Karl Popper. Karl Popper, *Conjectures and refutations*, (London: Routledge Kegan Paul, 1972).

Chapter 4.

1. Editorial, 'Liberalise, do not bureaucratise', *Business Standard*, February 2022, https://www.business-standard.com/article/opinion/liberalise-do-not-bureaucratise-122022701190_1.html.

Chapter 5.

1. We are grateful to Suyash Rai for discussions on this classification scheme.

2. Robert E. Lucas, 'Econometric Policy Evaluation: A Critique', in *The Phillips Curve and Labour Markets*, ed. Karl Brunner and Allan H. Meltzer, vol. 1, Carnegie-Rochester Conference Series on Public Policy (Amsterdam: North-Holland Publishing Company, 1976), 19–46.

3. This broad result recurs in various parts of the economics literature, e.g., see Martin Feldstein, 'Tax avoidance and the deadweight loss of the income tax', *The Review of Economics and Statistics* 81, no. 4 (November 1999): 674–680, https://www.nber.org/system/files/working_papers/w5055/w5055.pdf; John Creedy, *The excess burden of taxation and why it (approximately) quadruples when the tax rate doubles*, technical report (New Zealand Treasury, December 2003), https://www.treasury.govt.nz/sites/default/files/2007-10/twp03-29.pdf.

4. C. Rajagopalachari, *Why Swatantra?*, technical report, Swatantra Party, April 1973, https://www.livemint.com/Sundayapp/XlvTGlfJcdJu9mQGZcksTI/C-Rajagopalachari--Why-Swatantra.html.

5. James M. Buchanan and Gordon Tullock, *The calculus of consent: logical foundations of constitutional democracy* (Liberty Fund, 1962).

6. Concerns about the Speaker are articulated in Arvind P. Datar, 'How can we guarantee the Speaker's impartiality?', *Indian Express*, August 2021, https://indianexpress.com/article/opinion/columns/how-can-we-guarantee-the-speakers-impartiality-7460392/.

7. These two examples are from Tom Nichols, 'How America lost faith in expertise, and why that's a giant problem', *Foreign Affairs*, March 2017, https://www.foreignaffairs.com/articles/united-states/2017-02-13/how-america-lost-faith-expertise

8. On the difficulties of cross-border intercourse, see Riya Sinha, *Linking land borders: India's integrated check posts*, technical report (Centre for Social and Economic Progress, June 2021), https://

csep.org/wp-content/uploads/2021/06/WP_Linking-land-borders-ICP-1.pdf.

9. Debates around universal suffrage continue into the modern age, e.g., Jason Brennan, 'The right to vote should be restricted to those with knowledge', *Aeon*, September 2016, https://aeon.co/amp/ideas/the-right-to-vote-should-be-restricted-to-those-with-knowledge.

10. Kenneth J. Arrow, 'A difficulty in the concept of social welfare', *Journal of Political Economy* 58, no. 4 (1950): 328–346, https://www.jstor.org/stable/1828886.

11. On these issues, see Dipankar Gupta, *Revolution from above* (India: Rupa Publications, 2013), Sanjaya Baru, *India's power elite: Caste, class and cultural revolution* (Penguin, April 2021).

Chapter 6.

1. Alexander Hamer, 'The curious case of the great Hanoi rat hunt', *Real History*, October 2018, https://realhistory.co/2018/10/11/great-hanoi-rat-hunt/.

2. Xue Yujie, 'The gadget that boosts your step count while you nap', *Sixth Tone*, June 2018, https://www.sixthtone.com/news/1002530/the-gadget-that-boosts-your-step-count-while-you-nap-.

3. Matthew Wright, 'Amsterdam's taxing narrow houses', *Matthew Wright: Science, writing, reason and stuff*, October 2012, https://mjwrightnz.wordpress.com/2012/10/28/amsterdams-taxing-narrow-houses/.

4. This was done through: Vijay Kelkar, *Report of the Committee on Category-II drugs*, technical report (Ministry of Industry, August 1987).

5. Isaac Frazier and Zachary Frazier, 'Rewarding Bad Behavior', *UN.A.BRIDGED*, February 2017, https://web.archive.org/web/20171102041149/http://www.un-a-bridged.com/rewarding-bad-behavior/.

6. This argument is from Shubho Roy, 'Skepticism about measurement: Hospital beds edition', *The Leap Blog*, June 2020,

https://blog.theleapjournal.org/2020/06/skepticism-about-measurement-hospital.html.

7. Nicholas Bloom et al., 'Are ideas getting harder to find?', *American Economic Review* 110, no. 4 (2020): 1104–1144, https://web.stanford.edu/~chadj/IdeaPF.pdf.

8. Andrew Gelman, 'No, I don't believe etc etc., even though they did a bunch of robustness checks', *Statistical Modeling, Causal Inference, and Social Science*, November 2020, https://statmodeling.stat.columbia.edu/2020/11/13/no-i-dont-believe-etc-etc-even-though-they-did-a-bunch-of-robustness-checks/.

9. Daniel Kahneman, *Thinking, fast and slow* (Farrar, Straus/Giroux, 2011).

Chapter 7.

1. As an example of this phenomenon, see Ajit Kanitkar, 'Case of tur dal farmers shows that hiking minimum support price won't help if implementation is poor', *Scroll.in*, February 2018, https://scroll.in/article/869545/case-of-tur-dal-f%20armers-shows-that-hiking-minimum-support-price-wont-help-if-implementation-is-poor.

2. There are myriad examples of state failure when applying price controls, in the Indian experience. A recent story, on price controls on movie tickets is in Episode 154 of *Anticipating the unintended*, https://publicpolicy.substack.com/p/154-weve-seen-this-movie-before#details.

3. Susan Thomas, 'Agricultural commodity markets in India: Policy issues for growth', in *Derivatives markets in India*, ed. Susan Thomas (Tata Mcgraw Hill, 2003), https://www.semanticscholar.org/paper/Agricultural-commodity-markets-in-India-%3A-Policy-Thomas/41230bf080e599041db428f0c4fb30faa0e38cda.

4. Anirudh Burman et al., *Diagnosing and overcoming sustained food price volatility: Enabling a National Market for Food*, technical report 236 (NIPFP, July 2018), https://www.nipfp.org.in/media/medialibrary/2018/07/WP_236.pdf.

5. Ashok Gulati and Anil Sharma, 'Freeing trade in agriculture: Implications for resource use efficiency and cropping pattern changes', *Economic and Political Weekly*, 1997, https://www.jstor.org/stable/4406230; Kirit S. Parikh et al., *Towards Free Trade in agriculture* (Springer, 2013); Kirit S. Parikh et al., 'Agricultural trade liberalisation: growth, welfare and large country effects', *Agricultural Economics*, 1997, https://www.sciencedirect.com/science/article/abs/pii/S0169515097000170; Ajay Shah, 'India: An agricultural trade powerhouse', *Business Standard*, May 2019, https://www.business-standard.com/article/opinion/india-agricultural-trade-powerhouse-119050500774_1.html.

6. Ajay Shah, 'The tragedy of our farm bills', in *The seen and the unseen* (Amit Varma, February 2021), https://seenunseen.in/episodes/2021/2/7/episode-211-the-tragedy-of-our-farm-bills/; Garry Pursell and Ashok Gulati, *Liberalising Indian agriculture: an agenda for reform* (World Bank Publications, 1993); Anirudh Burman et al., *Diagnosing and overcoming sustained food price volatility: Enabling a national market for Food*, technical report 236 (NIPFP, July 2018), https://www.nipfp.org.in/media/medialibrary/2018/07/WP_236.pdf.

7. The fundamental article on this is F. A. Hayek, 'The use of knowledge in society', *American Economic Review*, 1945, https://www.econlib.org/library/Essays/hykKnw.html.

8. This argument is from Akshay Jaitly and Ajay Shah, *The lowest hanging fruit on the coconut tree: India's climate transition through the price system in the power sector*, technical report 9 (Bombay: XKDR Forum, October 2021), https://xkdr.org/paper/the-lowest-hanging-fruit-on-the-coconut-tree-india-s-climate-transition-through-the-price-system-in-the-power-sector.

9. This section builds on Ajay Shah, 'Prices, fast and slow', *Business Standard*, July 2018, https://www.mayin.org/ajayshah/MEDIA/2018/prices_fast_and_slow.html.

10. Lawrence Summers, 'Interview with Martin Wolf', *The Financial Times*, April 2021, https://www.ft.com/content/380ea811-e927-4fe1-aa5b-d213816e9073.

Chapter 8.

1. Lina M. Khan, 'Amazon's antitrust paradox', *Yale Law Journal* 126, no. 3 (January 2017): 564–907, https://www.yalelawjournal. org/note/amazons-antitrust-paradox; Smriti Parsheera, Ajay Shah, and Avirup Bose, *Competition issues in India's online economy*, technical report 194 (NIPFP, April 2017), https:// macrofinance.nipfp.org.in/releases/ParsheeraShahBose2017_ onlineBusinesses.html.

2. On the Indian bankruptcy reform, see: T. K. Viswanathan, *Bankruptcy law reforms committee: Rationale and design* (Ministry of Finance, November 2015), https://ifrogs.org/POLICY/blrc. html; Ajay Shah and Susan Thomas, 'The Indian bankruptcy reform: The state of the art, 2018', *The Leap Blog*, December 2018, https://blog.theleapjournal.org/2018/12/the-indian-bankruptcy-reform-state-of.html.

3. Megha Patnaik, *Tax, lies and red tape*, technical report (ISI Delhi, 2019).

4. Ajay Shah, 'Indian capitalism is not doomed', *The Leap Blog*, September 2012, https://blog.theleapjournal.org/2012/09/ indian-capitalism-is-not-doomed.html.

5. For a story about how firm exit took place in India in the absence of the bankruptcy code, Ashish K. Mishra, 'Indiaplaza. com: How an Indian e-commerce firm ran out of cash', *Mint*, July 2015, https://www.livemint.com/Companies/ fuuj34vscVDBRjwrBld7sJ/Indiaplazacom-How-an-Indian-ecommerce-ran-out-of-cash.html.

6. This is part of the larger idea that countries with good institutions have shorter slumps, as argued in Richard Bluhm, Denis de Crombrugghe, and Adam Szirmai, *Do Weak Institutions Prolong Crises? On the identification, characteristics, and duration of de-clines during economic slumps*, technical report (CESifo Working Paper series, February 2014), https://papers.ssrn.com/sol3/papers. cfm?abstract_id=2393931.

7. The macro policy view on business cycle stabilization is presented in Ajay Shah and Ila Patnaik, 'Stabilising the Indian business cycle', chap. 6 in *India on the Growth Turnpike: Essays*

in honour of Vijay L. Kelkar, ed. Sameer Kochhar (Academic Foundation, 2010), https://www.nipfp.org.in/media/medialibrary/2013/04/wp_2010_67.pdf.

8. This example is from Ila Patnaik, 'Creative destruction', *Business Standard*, July 2003, http://openlib.org/home/ila/MEDIA/2003/stdbooths.html.

Chapter 9.

1. On Indian agriculture reforms, Ajay Shah, 'The tragedy of our farm bills', in *The seen and the unseen* (Amit Varma, February 2021), https://seenunseen.in/episodes/2021/2/7/episode-211-the-tragedy-of-our-farm-bills/.

2. As an example, N. S. S. Narayana, Kirit S. Parikh, and T. N. Srinivasan, 'Rural works programs in India: costs and benefits', *Journal of Development Economics*, 1988, analyse a rural works program in general equilibrium. https://www.sciencedirect.com/science/article/abs/pii/0304387888900326.

Chapter 10.

1. Ajay Shah, 'Solving market failures through information interventions', *The Leap Blog*, April 2015, https://blog.theleapjournal.org/2015/04/solving-market-failures-through.html.

2. This section builds on Ajay Shah, 'Occam's razor of public policy', *The Leap Blog*, January 2016, https://blog.theleapjournal.org/2016/01/occams-razor-of-public-policy.html.

3. On the plans to make one more public sector infrastructure financing company, in 2020, K. P. Krishnan, 'Deja vu on DFIs', *Business Standard*, September 2020, https://www.business-standard.com/article/opinion/deja-vu-on-dfis-120091502159_1.html.

4. J. N. Bhagwati and V. K. Ramaswami, 'Domestic distortions, tariffs and the theory of optimum subsidy', *Journal of Political Economy* 71, no. 1 (1963): 44–50.

5. On the difficulties of 'KYC' in India, Rishab Bailey et al., *Analysing India's KYC framework: Can we do things better?*, technical report (SSRN, January 2021), https://papers.ssrn. com/sol3/papers.cfm?abstract_id=3776008.

6. As an example, see Peter R. Neumann, 'Don't follow the money', *Foreign Affairs*, July 2017, https://www.foreignaffairs. com/articles/united-states/2017-06-13/dont-follow-money.

7. PRS Legislative Research, *The Companies (Amendment) Bill, 2019*, technical report (PRS, 2019), https://prsindia.org/ billtrack/the-companies-amendment-bill-2019.

8. A populist regime in force for about 10 years knocks off 10 per cent of GDP. Manuel Funke, Moritz Schularick, and Christoph Trebesch, *Populist Leaders and the Economy*, technical report 15405 (CEPR, October 2020), https://www.econstor.eu/ bitstream/10419/226836/1/ECONtribute-036-2020.pdf.

Chapter 11.

1. This fact is from Lant Pritchett, 'Has the randomista revolution gone too far?', in *Vox talks* (Tim Phillips, December 2019), https://voxeu.org/vox-talks/has-randomista-revolution-gone-too-far.

2. S. Mahendra Dev and Ajit K. Ranade, 'Employment Guarantee Scheme and Employment Security', in *Social and Economic Security in India*, ed. S. Mahendra Dev et al. (Institute for Human Development, New Delhi, 2001).

Chapter 12.

1. Ronald H. Coase, 'The problem of social cost', *Journal of Law and Economics III* (October 1960).

2. Partha Sarathi Biswas, 'Pollination opportunity: Money beyond honey', *Indian Express*, March 2017, https://indianexpress. com/article/india/pollination-opportunity-money-beyond-honey-4560991/.

3. G. Hardin, 'The tragedy of the commons', *Science* 162, no. 3859 (December 1968), https://www.science.org/doi/10.1126/science.162.3859.1243.

4. An Indian view of these ideas is: Parth J. Shah and Vidisha Maitra, eds., *Terracotta Reader: A Market Approach to the Environment* (Academic Foundation in association with Centre for Civil Society, 2005).

5. Jayana Bedi et al., chap. Disruption on Demand in *Doing Business in Delhi: A Study of Initiated and Uninitiated Regulatory Reforms*, ed. Bhuvana Anand, Alston D'Souza, and Ritika Shah (Centre for Civil Society, 2018), https://ccs.in/doing-business-delhi-study-initiated-and-uninitiated-regulatory-reforms-0

Chapter 13.

1. William D. Nordhaus, *The Economic Consequences of a War in Iraq*, technical report 9361 (NBER, December 2002), https://www.nber.org/papers/w9361.

2. For a less optimistic view of cost-benefit analysis, see John H. Cochrane, 'Challenges for Cost-Benefit Analysis of Financial Regulation', *Journal of Legal Studies* 43 (June 2014), https://www.journals.uchicago.edu/doi/10.1086/678351.

3. The draft Indian Financial code FSLRC, *Indian Financial Code*, 1.1 (Ministry of Finance, July 2015), places such requirements upon the regulation-making process. https://goo.gl/hdAQoW.

Chapter 14.

1. Vijay Kelkar and Ajay Shah, 'Six battlegrounds for the war on corruption', *Mint*, November 2016, https://www.livemint.com/Opinion/d7V9V6xUulbGWr5LLjttDJ/Six-battlefronts-for-the-war-on-corruption.html.

2. On the links between bilateral trade imbalances and protectionism, Samuel Delpeuch, Etienne Fize, and Philippe Martin, 'Trade imbalances and the rise of protectionism', *voxEU*, February 2021, https://voxeu.org/article/trade-imbalances-and-rise-protectionism.

3. The irrelevance of bilateral trade balances is an ancient idea in economics; for a modern take see Margaux MacDonald et al., *Are Bilateral Trade Balances Irrelevant?*, technical report 20/210 (IMF, September 2020), https://www.elibrary.imf.org/view/ journals/001/2020/210/article-A001-en.xml.

4. Vijay Kelkar, Vikash Yadav, and Praveen Chaudhry, 'Reforming the Governance of the International Monetary Fund', *World Economy* 27, no. 5 (May 2004).

Chapter 15.

1. The recent debate around these terms is well analysed by Mukund P. Unny, 'The "Union government" has a unifying effect', *The Hindu*, June 2021, https://www.thehindu.com/ opinion/op-ed/the-union-government-has-a-unifying-effect/ article34938894.ece.

2. The five poorest HRs are: (1) Jaunpur, Sultanpur, Faizabad, Ambedkar Nagar (UP); (2) Balangir, Kandhamal, Rayagada, Koraput, Kalahandi, Nayagarh (Odisha); (3) Kendujhar, Mayurbhanj, Cuttack, Jajapur, Dhenkanal (Odisha); (4) Satna, Rewa, Panna, Anuppur, Chhatarpur, Damoh, Katni (Madhya Pradesh); (5) Purnia, Katihar, Madhepura, Araria, Supaul, Kishanganj (Bihar).

    The five richest HRs are: (1) Thane (Maharashtra); (2) Sonipat, Rohtak, Gurgaon, Palwal, Panipat, Rewari, Mahendragarh, Mewat, Faridabad, Jhajjar (Haryana); (3) Mumbai, Mumbai Sub-urban (Maharashtra); (4) Chandigarh; (5) Delhi.

3. The five HRs with the lowest female mobile phone ownership are: (1) Jhansi, Lalitpur, Hamirpur, Mahoba, Jalaun (UP); (2) Samastipur, Darbhanga, Begusarai, Bhagalpur, Khagaria (Bihar); (3) Ranchi, Bokaro, Hazaribagh, Dhanbad, Kodarma, Purbi Singhbhum, Khunti, Saraikela-Kharsawan, Ramgarh (Jharkhand); (4) Ganganagar, Hanumangarh, Jhunjhunun, Sikar, Churu (Rajasthan); (5) Giridih, Dumka, Godda, Deogarh, Jamtara (Jharkand).

    The five HRs with the highest female mobile phone ownership are: (1) Kapurthala, Jalandhar, Ludhiana, Patiala, Amritsar, Tarn

Taran, Fatehgarh Sahib (Punjab); (2) Thane (Maharashtra); (3) North Goa, South Goa (Goa); (4) Chandigarh; (5) Bombay (Maharashtra).

4. Ila Patnaik et al., *Distribution of self-reported health in India: The role of income and geography*, technical report 6 (Bombay: XKDR Forum, September 2021), https://xkdr.org/paper/distribution-of-self-reported-health-in-india-the-role-of-income-and-geography.

5. Montek S. Ahluwalia, 'State level performance under economic reforms in India', in *Economic Policy Reforms and the Indian Economy*, ed. Anne O. Krueger (University of Chicago Press, 2002), 91–125; Vivek Dehejia and Praveen Chakravarty, *India's Curious Case of Economic Divergence*, technical report (IDFC Institute, November 2016), https://www.idfcinstitute.org/knowledge/publications/working-and-briefing-papers/indias-curious-case-of-economic-divergence/; Praveen Chakravarty and Vivek Dehejia, *India's income divergence: governance or development model?*, technical report (IDFC Institute, March 2017), https://www.idfcinstitute.org/knowledge/publications/working-and-briefing-papers/indias-income-divergence-governance-or-development-model/.

6. James C. Scott, *Seeing like a state: How certain schemes to improve the human condition have failed* (Yale University Press, 1998).

7. Jairam Ramesh, *Lessons from reorganizing India's states: and why Uttar Pradesh needs to be divided*, technical report (C. D. Deshmukh Memorial Lecture, January 2019), https://scroll.in/article/909436/jairam-ramesh-a-potted-history-of-reorganizing-indias-states-and-why-uttar-pradesh-should-be-next.

8. Vijay Kelkar, 'Towards India's new fiscal federalism', *Journal of Quantitative Economics* 17, no. 1 (March 2019): works out the legal aspects of sharing GST with sub-national governments, which involves the establishment of a consolidated fund at the level of governments of the third tier. https://ideas.repec.org/a/spr/jqecon/v17y2019i1d10.1007_s40953-019-00159-x.html.

Chapter 16.

1. When building government organizations, the Indian state generally does not systematically do organization design. An exception is the bankruptcy regulator (IBBI) where an MCA working group applied its mind to the organization building project: Ravi Narain, *Building the Insolvency and Bankruptcy Board of India*, technical report (Ministry of Company Affairs, 2016), https://www.ibbi.gov.in/Wg-01%20Report.pdf.

2. Similar problems have been seen in Indian agricultural exports, where policy makers flick the switch between ban and unban. As an example for exports of onions, see Subramani Ra Mancombu, 'Fearing export ban, traditional onion buyers abroad switch to other origins', *The Hindu Business Line*, July 2021, https://www.thehindubusinessline.com/economy/agri-business/fearing-export-ban-traditional-onion-buyers-abroad-switch-to-other-origins/article35462982.ece.

Chapter 17.

1. Chandre Dharmawardana, 'A critique of the YouTube broadcast by Dr. Anuruddha Padeniya, entitled: Western doctor gives a thundering slap to Western methodology', *Colombo Telegraph*, May 2021, https://www.colombotelegraph.com/index.php/a-critique-of-the-youtube-broadcast-by-dr-anuruddha-padeniya-entitled-western-doctor-gives-a-thundering-slap-to-western-methodology/.

2. Bent Flyvbjerg, 'What you should know about megaprojects and why: An overview', *Project Management Journal* 45, no. 2 (2014).

3. Nehru's sensitive views on large dams are the subject of Ramchandra Guha, 'Prime Ministers and big dams', *The Hindu*, 2005, http://ramachandraguha.in/archives/prime-ministers-and-big-dams.html.

4. Ajay Shah, 'Bureaucrats are not stakeholders', *The Economic Times*, June 2013, https://www.mayin.org/ajayshah/MEDIA/2013/bureaucrats_stakeholders.html.

Chapter 18.

1. On this experience, K. P. Krishnan, 'The journey of economic reforms', *Business Standard*, August 2020, https://www.business-standard.com/article/opinion/the-journey-of-economic-reforms-120083000944_1.html.

2. A six-part long battle against corruption is sketched in: Vijay Kelkar and Ajay Shah, 'Six battlegrounds for the war on corruption', *Mint*, November 2016, https://www.livemint.com/Opinion/d7V9V6xUulbGWr5LLjttDJ/Six-battlefronts-for-the-war-on-corruption.html.

3. As an example, consider the RBI regulation that prohibits websites from storing card data, an intervention that imposes high costs upon society while giving low gains in terms of reduced fraud. It is estimated that a significant fraction of the Internet-based subscription business in India was lost when the new regulation came in, and Indian residents were blocked from subscribing on many overseas web sites. These mistakes would have been caught in a better structured formal regulation-making process. Renuka Sane, Ajay Shah, and Bhargavi Zaveri, *Should consumers be prohibited from storing card data on the internet?*, technical report 3 (Bombay: XKDR Forum, May 2021), https://xkdr.org/paper/should-consumers-be-prohibited-from-storing-card-data-on-the-internet

4. As an example, in 2018, the US SEC undertook the 'Tick Size Pilot Program', https://www.sec.gov/ticksizepilot.

5. Purva Chitnis, 'Penalty, Jail And More: How Mumbai Will Enforce The Plastic Ban', *Bloomberg Quint*, June 2018, https://www.bqprime.com/business/penalty-jail-and-more-how-mumbai-will-enforce-the-plastic-ban.

6. Samuel R. Gross et al., 'Rate of false conviction of criminal defendants who are sentenced to death', *National Academy of Sciences* 111, no. 20 (March 2014): Kennedy, Edward H. https://www.pnas.org/doi/10.1073/pnas.1306417111.

Chapter 19.

1. Suyash Rai, 'A pragmatic approach to data protection', *The Leap Blog*, February 2018, https://blog.theleapjournal.org/2018/02/a-pragmatic-approach-to-data-protection.html;   Anirudh

Burman, 'Privacy, Aadhaar, data protection: statist liberalism and the danger to liberty', *The Leap Blog*, September 2018, https://blog.theleapjournal.org/2018/09/privacy-aadhaar-data-protection-statist.html.

2. On surveillance by the Indian state, see Rishab Bailey et al., *Use of personal data by intelligence and law enforcement agencies*, technical report (NIPFP, August 2018), https://macrofinance.nipfp.org.in/PDF/BBPR2018-Use-of-personal-data.pdf.

3. On the lack of separation of powers at SEBI, K. P. Krishnan, '"Judicial" regulation at SEBI', *Business Standard*, April 2021, https://www.business-standard.com/article/opinion/judicial-regulation-at-sebi-121042701363_1.html.

4. On the problems of drug safety regulation in India, and the story of Dinesh Thakur and Ranbaxy, Katherine Eban, *Bottle of lies: The inside story of the generic drug boom* (Harper Collins, 2019), Kristin Waterfield Duisberg, 'The whistleblower', *UNH*, Winter 2021, https://magazine.unh.edu/issue/winter-2021/the-whistleblower/.

5. On the complexities of a government that tests devices, see Surajeet Das Gupta, 'Hardware device makers slam govt's mandatory testing and certification plan', *Business Standard*, February 2022, https://www.business-standard.com/article/economy-policy/hardware-device-makers-slam-govt-s-mandatory-testing-and-certification-plan-122022800018_1.html.

6. This is an economists' adaptation of the concepts of Clifford Geertz, *The interpretation of cultures* (Basic Books, 1973), https://books.google.co.in/books?id=pl2NDgAAQBAJ.

Chapter 20.

1. This quote is from the context of vaccine development for Covid-19, in Douglas R. Green, 'SARS-CoV2 vaccines: Slow is fast', *Science Advances*, May 2020, https://www.science.org/doi/full/10.1126/Sciadv.abc7428.

2. Ajay Shah, 'Three page notes considered harmful', *Business Standard*, October 2017, https://www.mayin.org/ajayshah/MEDIA/2017/3pagenotes.html.

3.   Uwe Hoering, 'What it takes to clean a river', *Down To Earth*,
     June   2015,   https://www.downtoearth.org.in/coverage/
     climate-change/what-it-takes-to-clean-a-river-19098;   FE
     Online, 'Germany to help India clean Ganga, says "took
     30 years, 45 bn euros to clean Rhine"', *Financial Express*,
     August 2018, https://www.financialexpress.com/india-news/
     germany-to-help-india-clean-ganga-says-took-30-years-45-
     bn-euros-to-clean-rhine/1297562/; Nikhil Ghanekar, 'Clean
     Ganga Mission: Lessons we can learn from Europe's Rhine river
     cleaning', *DNA India*, April 2016, https://www.dnaindia.com/
     india/report-clean-ganga-mission-lessons-we-can-learn-f%20
     rom-europe-s-rhine-river-cleaning-2203178.
4.   As an example of a project plan to build a new regulator, see
     Ravi Narain, *Building the Insolvency and Bankruptcy Board of India*,
     technical report (Ministry of Company Affairs, 2016), https://
     www.ibbi.gov.in/Wg-01%20Report.pdf.
5.   Mobis Philipose, 'Will the real SEBI please stand up?', *Mint*,
     July 2019, https://www.livemint.com/opinion/columns/will-
     the-real-sebi-please-stand-up-1564594293741.html; Jayanth R.
     Varma, 'A petty money dispute holds market to ransom', *Prof.
     Jayanth R. Varma's Financial Markets Blog*, July 2019, https://
     faculty.iima.ac.in/~jrvarma/blog/index.cgi/Y2019-20/petty-
     money-dispute.html.

Chapter 21.

1.   Lant Pritchett and Michael Woolcock, 'Solutions when
     the solution is the problem: Arraying the disarray in
     development', *World Development* 32, no. 2 (2004): offers a
     two-dimensional scheme based on transaction-intensity and
     discretion-intensity.
2.   This section builds on: Ajay Shah, 'Monetary policy is easy;
     Financial regulation is hard', *Financial Express*, July 2010,
     https://www.mayin.org/ajayshah/MEDIA/2010/finance_vs_
     MP.html.

3. A detailed proposal for a 'Indian Courts and Tribunals Service' (ICTS) is worked out in: Pratik Datta et al., *How to Modernize the working of courts and tribunals in India*, technical report 258 (NIPFP, March 2019), https://macrofinance.nipfp.org.in/releases/icts_concept_note-2019.html.
4. Ajay Shah, 'Sequencing in the construction of State capacity: Walk before you can run', *The Leap Blog*, August 2016, https://blog.theleapjournal.org/2016/08/sequencing-in-construction-of-state.html.

Chapter 22.

1. RBI, *System of ways and means advances : Agreement signed between the Government of India and the Reserve Bank of India*, technical report (RBI Press Release, March 1997), https://www.rbi.org.in/scripts/BS_PressReleaseDisplay.aspx?prid=18542.

Chapter 23.

1. Maria Popova, 'The power paradox: The surprising and sobering science of how we gain and lose influence', *Brain pickings*, September 2016, https://www.themarginalian.org/2016/09/28/power-paradox-dachter-keltner/.
2. C. Rajagopalachari, *Why Swatantra?*, technical report (Swatantra Party, April 1973), https://www.livemint.com/Sundayapp/XlvTGlfJcdJu9mQGZcksTI/C-Rajagopalachari--Why-Swatantra.html.
3. Ajay Shah, 'The undersupply of criticism', *The Leap Blog*, May 2010, https://blog.theleapjournal.org/2010/05/undersupply-of-criticism.html.
4. Chris Buckley, 'A Chinese law professor criticized Xi. Now he's been suspended', *New York Times*, March 2019, https://www.nytimes.com/2019/03/26/world/asia/chinese-law-professor-xi.html.

Chapter 24.

1. See Oset Babur, 'Talking about failure is crucial for growth, here's how to do it right', *New York Times*, August 2018, https://www.nytimes.com/2018/08/17/smarter-living/talking-about-failure-is-crucial-for-growth-heres-how-to-do-it-right.html.

Chapter 25.

1. See Paul Krugman, 'A country is not a company', *Harvard Business Review*, January 1996, Steven Horwitz, 'Countries are not companies', *fee.org*, January 2017, https://fee.org/articles/countries-are-not-companies/.

Chapter 26.

1. The basic structure doctrine laid down by the Supreme Court in the landmark case of Kesavananda Bharati v. State of Kerala, *Supreme Court of India*, 2 Supp. SCR 1, 1973 provides that the Constitution has certain basic features, which cannot be amended by the Parliament. The separation of powers between the Legislature, the Executive and the Judiciary has been held by courts as one of the elements of this basic structure. Also see Mathew, J., in Indira Nehru Gandhi v. Raj Narain, *Supreme Court of India*, SCR 347, 1976.
2. M. S. Sahoo, 'Political economy of neo-governments', *Chartered secretary*, 2012.
3. We are grateful to Akshay Jaitly for useful discussions on this.
4. It is important to distinguish between class action litigation, where members of a class feel they have been harmed, and public interest litigation, which is a vague construct. There are interesting fields of research, on the difficulties of PILs and on what holds back class action litigation in India. Anuj Bhuwania, 'Not always in the public interest', in *Ideas of India* (Shruti Rajagopalan, September 2020), https://www.mercatus.org/bridge/podcasts/09172020/ideas-india-not-always-public-

interest; Karan Gulati and Renuka Sane, 'Why do we not see class-action suits in India? The case of consumer finance', *The Leap Blog*, May 2020, https://blog.theleapjournal.org/2020/05/why-do-we-not-see-class-action-suits-in.html.

5. On these themes, Edward L. Glaeser and Andrei Shleifer, 'The rise of the regulatory state', *Journal of Economic Literature* XLI (June 2003).

6. This removal of power for private persons is done in Section 5A of Ministry of Company Affairs, *Notification under S.227 of IBC*, https://www.ibbi.gov.in/uploads/legalframwork/cb1d53c7fe47f8f22ab36a40f441db2c.pdf

Chapter 27.

1. Lant Pritchett, 'Where has all the education gone?', *World Bank Economic Review*, December 2001, https://lantpritchett.org/schooling-and-growth/.

2. Robert M. Solow, 'We'd better watch out', *New York Times*, July 1987, http://www.standupeconomist.com/pdf/misc/solow-computer-productivity.pdf.

3. For an early analysis of this, Vijay L. Kelkar, Devendra N. Chaturvedi, and Madhav K. Dar, 'India's information economy: role, size and scope', *Economic and Political Weekly* 26, no. 37 (September 1991): 2153–2161, https://www.epw.in/journal/1991/37/special-articles/india-s-information-economy-role-size-and-scope.html.

4. Ajay Shah, 'The industry structure of India's large firms: IT is the biggest industry', *The Leap Blog*, March 2022, https://blog.theleapjournal.org/2022/03/the-industry-structure-of-indias-large.html.

5. As an example of BPR thinking in one field—the working of courts and tribunals—see Pratik Datta et al., *How to modernize the working of courts and tribunals in India*, technical report 258 (NIPFP, March 2019), https://www.nipfp.org.in/media/medialibrary/2019/03/WP_2019_258.pdf.

6. We see these themes in Nayanika Mathur, *Paper tiger: Law, bureaucracy and the developmental state in Himalayan India*, Cambridge Studies in Law and Society (Cambridge University Press, 2015).

7. As an example, the distinction between computer equipment, as opposed to organizational transformation, in the field of defence is made in Ruchin Sodhani, 'What India's military commentators don't get about drones', *The Print*, November 2020, https://theprint.in/opinion/what-indias-military-commentators-dont-get-about-drones-ai/535603/.

8. Surendra Dave, 'India's pension reforms: A case study in complex institutional change', in *Documenting reforms: Case studies from India*, ed. S. Narayan (New Delhi: Macmillan India, 2006), https://www.mayin.org/ajayshah/lfs/Dave2006_saga.pdf; Ajay Shah, 'Indian pension reform: A sustainable and scalable approach', chap. 7 in *Managing globalisation: Lessons from China and India*, ed. David A. Kelly, Ramkishen S. Rajan, and Gillian H. L. Goh (World Scientific, 2006), https://www.mayin.org/ajayshah/PDFDOCS/Shah2005_sustainable_pension_reform.pdf.

9. The best survey of the field is: Nandan Nilekani and Viral Shah, *Rebooting India: Realizing a billion aspirations* (Penguin Allen Lane, 2016).

10. Ajay Shah, 'Improving governance using large IT systems', in *Documenting reforms: Case studies from India*, ed. S. Narayan (New Delhi: Macmillan India, 2006), 122–148, https://www.mayin.org/ajayshah/PDFDOCS/Shah2006_big_it_systems.pdf.

11. We are grateful to Manish Srivastava of eGov Foundation for useful discussions on these questions.

12. The large-scale system building that went into GST, income tax and MCA21 are examples of the limitations of system building in government. Chartered Accountants Association Surat, 'Timely release of Utilities and Stopping of Panic Messaging', *Taxguru.in*, April 2021, https://taxguru.in/income-tax/timely-release-itr-utilities-stop-sending-panic-messages.html; Pranbihanga Borpuzari, 'GST E-way bill: Why business across India came to a virtual stop on February 1', *Economic Times*, February 2018, https://economictimes.indiatimes.com/small-

biz/policy-trends/gst-e-way-bill-why-business-across-india-came-to-a-virtual-stop-on-february-1/articleshow/62752650. cms; Ashish K. Mishra, Varun Sood, and Shreeja Sen, 'Why the MCA21 portal is a pain to use', *Mint*, April 2016, https://www. livemint.com/Companies/RaT3ci2PpOjCKazJSdnakN/Why-the-MCA21-portal-is-a-pain-to-use.html.

Chapter 28.

1. James C. Scott, *Seeing Like a State: How Certain Schemes to Improve the Human Condition Have Failed* (Yale University Press, 1998).
2. Delhi has the highest number of surveillance cameras per unit area among cities of the world, Staff, 'This Indian city has world's most CCTV cameras in public places; beats China', *Mint*, August 2021, https://www.livemint.com/news/india/this-indian-city-has-world-s-most-cctv-cameras-in-public-places-beats-china-11629953170655.html.
3. Singapore is an example of a country where increased legibility came before political system maturation, William Gibson, 'Disneyland with the death penalty', *Wired*, April 1993, https://www.wired.com/1993/04/gibson-2/; Peter Guest, 'Singapore's tech-utopia dream is turning into a surveillance state nightmare', *Restofworld*, November 2021, https://restofworld.org/2021/singapores-tech-utopia-dream-is-turning-into-a-surveillance-state-nightmare/.
4. We are grateful to Anirudh Burman for this idea.
5. Prasanth Regy, 'RBI's proposal for a Public Credit Registry', *The Leap Blog*, August 2017, https://blog.theleapjournal.org/2017/08/rbis-proposal-for-public-credit-registry.html; Vivek Ananth, 'The collateral damage of regulatory roulette', *The Ken*, August 2018, https://the-ken.com/story/regulatory-roulette/?searchTerm=billdesk.
6. Rishab Bailey and Smriti Parsheera, *Data localisation in India: Questioning the means and ends*, technical report (NIPFP, October 2018), https://macrofinance.nipfp.org.in/releases/BP2018_Data-localisation-in-India.html.

7. Rishab Bailey et al., *Analysing India's KYC framework: Can we do things better?*, technical report (SSRN, January 2021), https://papers.ssrn.com/sol3/papers.cfm?abstract_id=3776008.

8. Eric Raymond, *The cathedral and the bazaar*, technical report (Thrysus Enterprises, 2000), http://www.catb.org/~esr/writings/cathedral-bazaar/cathedral-bazaar/.

9. Andrew L. Russell, 'OSI: The Internet that wasn't', *IEEE Spectrum*, July 2013, https://spectrum.ieee.org/tech-history/cyberspace/osi-the-internet-that-wasnt.

10. Ajay Shah, 'Solving market failures through information interventions', *The Leap Blog*, April 2015, https://blog.theleapjournal.org/2015/04/solving-market-failures-through.html.

11. Jayana Bedi et al., 'Disruption on demand', in *Doing business in Delhi: A study of initiated and uninitiated regulatory reforms*, ed. Bhuvana Anand, Alston D'Souza, and Ritika Shah (Centre for Civil Society, 2018), https://ccs.in/doing-business-delhi-study-initiated-and-uninitiated-regulatory-reforms-0.

12. Ajay Shah, 'New thinking on a traditional public good', *Financial Express*, August 2009, https://www.mayin.org/ajayshah/MEDIA/2009/mapsdata.html.

13. Lina M. Khan, 'Amazon's antitrust paradox', *Yale Law Journal* 126, no. 3 (January 2017): https://www.yalelawjournal.org/note/amazons-antitrust-paradox; Smriti Parsheera, Ajay Shah, and Avirup Bose, *Competition issues in India's online economy*, technical report 194 (NIPFP, April 2017), https://macrofinance.nipfp.org.in/releases/ParsheeraShahBose2017_onlineBusinesses.html.

Chapter 29.

1. Peter Brinsden, 'Thirty years of IVF: The legacy of Patrick Steptoe and Robert Edwards', *Human fertility* 12 (January 2009): https://www.researchgate.net/publication/38112869_Thirty_years_of_IVF_The_legacy_of_Patrick_Steptoe_and_Robert_Edwards.

2. The evidence shows that 16 per cent of articles in the 'top' four finance journals study a locale other than the US. Similarly, over

half of important economics journals have over two thirds of their editorial power located in the USA; any one of the states of California, Massachusetts and Illinois has more power than the four continents of Asia, South America, Africa and Australasia combined. G. Andrew Karolyi, 'Home bias, an academic puzzle', *Review of Finance* 20, no. 6 (October 2016): Simon D. Angus et al., *Geographic Diversity in Economic Publishing*, technical report (SSRN, November 2020), https://papers.ssrn.com/sol3/papers.cfm?abstractid=3697906.

3. As an example, Soroush Vosoughi, Deb Roy, and Sinan Aral, 'The spread of true and false news online', *Science* 359, no. 6380 (2018): find that the top 1 per cent of false news cascades on twitter reach 1000 to 100,000 people, while the truth rarely diffused to over 1000 people. https://www.science.org/doi/abs/10.1126/science.aap9559.

4. Jonathan Rauch, *The constitution of knowledge: A defense of truth* (Brookings Institution Press, 2021), https://www.brookings.edu/book/the-constitution-of-knowledge/.

Chapter 30.

1. This sentence is from David Freedlander, 'The Bonnie and Clyde of MAGA World', *Politico*, November 2021, https://www.politico.com/news/magazine/2021/11/19/dustin-stockton-jen-lawrence-trump-profile-522823.

2. Ajay Shah, 'Lessons from the Indian currency defence of 2013', *The Leap Blog*, June 2015, https://blog.theleapjournal.org/2015/06/lessons-from-indian-currency-defence-of.html.

3. Aarushi Kataria, 'Shaping narratives through selective use of numbers: A Covid-19 case study', *Indian Public Policy Review* 2, no. 5 (2021), https://ippr.in/index.php/ippr/article/view/69.

4. Vadilal Dagli, *Report of the Committee on Controls and Subsidies*, technical report (Ministry of Finance, 1979).

5. The full history is at https://www.imf.org/external/np/fin/tad/extarr2.aspx?memberKey1=760&date1key=2020-02-29.

Chapter 31.

1. Prasanth Regy, 'RBI's proposal for a Public Credit Registry', *The Leap Blog*, August 2017, https://blog.theleapjournal. org/2017/08/rbis-proposal-for-public-credit-registry.html.

2. The shift from a transactional approach to a long-term relationship, in PPP, is at the essence of Vijay Kelkar, *Report of the committee on revisiting and revitalising the public private partnership model of infrastructure*, technical report (Department of Economic Affairs, Ministry of Finance, November 2015), https://www. pppinindia.gov.in/infrastructureindia/documents/10184/0/ kelkar+Pdf/0d6ffb64-4501-42ba-a083-ca3ce99cf999.

3. The best exposition of the need for digital identity and the policy possibilities that flow from it are: Nandan Nilekani, *Imagining India: Ideas for the new century* (Penguin Allen Lane, 2010); Nandan Nilekani and Viral Shah, *Rebooting India: Realizing a billion aspirations* (Penguin Allen Lane, 2016).

4. As an example, in Australia, the federal government (the equivalent of the Indian union government) runs an ID system, myGovID. In addition, there are multiple rival identity systems: Australia Post runs a digital ID, OCR Labs is a private firm which offers identity services, and Eftpos is a designated non-government identity exchange. Aimee Chanthadavong, 'Eftpos granted government accreditation as first private ID exchange operator', *ZD-Net*, September 2021, https://www.zdnet.com/article/eftpos-granted-government-accreditation-as-first-private-id-exchange-operator/.

Chapter 32.

1. Richard W. Orloff, *Apollo by the numbers: A statistical reference*, NASA History Series 4029 (NASA, 2005), https://history.nasa. gov/SP-4029/SP-4029.htm.

2. You can't make these things up.

3. These ideas are explored in Ajay Shah, 'Buy, not build, spacecraft', *Business Standard*, September 2019, https://www. mayin.org/ajayshah/MEDIA/2019/isro_spillovers.html.

4. On the question of a public procurement law, see Shubho Roy and Diya Uday, 'Does India need a public procurement law?', *The Leap Blog*, August 2020, https://blog.theleapjournal. org/2020/08/does-india-need-public-procurement-law.html.

5. A research program on government contracting, at XKDR Forum, is https://xkdr.org/publicprocurement.html, and an overview article is Susan Thomas, *What impedes government contracting in India*, technical report 14 (Bombay: XKDR Forum, April 2022).

6. Yuval Levin, 'Behind closed doors', *National Review*, September 2019, https://www.nationalreview.com/corner/behind-closed-doors/amp/.

7. Himanshu Jha, *Capturing institutional change: The case of the Right to Information Act in India* (Oxford University Press, September 2020).

8. As an example, Mark Strauss, 'Eight historical archives that will spill new secrets', *Smithsonian magazine*, August 2010, https://www.smithsonianmag.com/history/nine-historical-archives-that-will-spill-new-secrets-966931/.

9. As an example, see the analysis of the HR process for regulators, K. P. Krishnan, 'Human resources and regulatory autonomy', *Business Standard*, September 2021, https://www.business-standard.com/article/opinion/human-resources-regulatory-autonomy-121092301711_1.html.

10. Some external views of state capacity problems in the Indian military are Abhijnan Rej, 'A Former US Army Officer Examines the World View of the Indian Military', *The Diplomat*, November 2020, https://thediplomat.com/2020/11/a-former-us-army-officer-examines-the-world-view-of-the-indian-military/; Anonymous, 'US officer spent 5 days onboard an Indian navy warship, INS Delhi', *Paluba*, February 2012, http://www.paluba.info/smf/index.php?topic=178970.

11. We are grateful to Shekhar Hari Kumar for discussions on these questions.

12. Leaving aside the problems of state capacity in strategy and operations, the capabilities and management systems for the frontline soldiers are a key constraint. The required tactical

capability, defined by Biddle as 'the modern system', is the *tightly interrelated complex of cover, concealment, dispersion, suppression, small-unit independent maneuver, and combined arms at the tactical level, and depth, reserves, and differential concentration at the operational level of war.* This requirement shapes the knowledge, training and autonomous thinking capacity required of frontline soldiers. Stephen Biddle, *Military power: Explaining victory and defeat in modern battle* (Princeton: Princeton University Press, 2004); Lorris Beverelli, 'The Importance of the tactical level: The Arab-Israeli War of 1973', *The Strategy Bridge*, November 2019, https://thestrategybridge.org/the-bridge/2019/11/19/the-importance-of-the-tactical-level-the-arab-israeli-war-of-1973.

13. The mainstream civil servants graduated from the traditional civil service pension to the New Pension System (NPS) for all recruits from 1/1/2004. For uniformed personnel, things became more problematic through one rank one pension (OROP). Ajay Shah, 'How to think about one rank one pensions', *The Leap Blog*, August 2015, https://blog.theleapjournal.org/2015/08/how-to-think-about-one-rank-one-pensions.html; Prakash Menon and Pranay Kotasthane, 'Is India's rising defence pension bill affecting modernization of military? 5 myths busted', *The Print*, March 2020, https://theprint.in/opinion/indias-defence-pension-bill-affecting-military-5-myths-busted/379289/; Ila Patnaik and Ajay Shah, 'There be dragons: Off-balance-sheet liabilities of the Indian state', *The Leap Blog*, November 2018, https://blog.theleapjournal.org/2018/11/there-be-dragons-off-balance-sheet.html.

14. As an example of defence policy research at the interfaces of defence and government contracting, Venu Gopal, *Revenue procurement practices in the Indian army* (New Delhi: IDSA, January 2013).

15. The story of Abraham Lincoln cycling through numerous generals is in Nigel Jones, 'Firing the generals: Lincoln v McClennan', *The Past*, July 2021, https://the-past.com/feature/firing-the-generals-lincoln-v-mcclellan/.

16. This reasoning draws on, and is consistent with, Prakash Menon and Pranay Kotasthane, 'COVID-19 Warrants Long Overdue

Doctrinal Shifts in Military Planning', *Indian Public Policy Review* 1, no. 1 (2020): https://ippr.in/index.php/ippr/article/view/7/5.

Chapter 33.

1. Karthik Muralidharan and Venkatesh Sundararaman, 'The Aggregate Effect of School Choice: Evidence from a Two-Stage Experiment in India', *The Quarterly Journal of Economics* 130, no. 3 (August 2015): 1011–1066, https://doi.org/10.1093/qje/qjv013.

Chapter 34.

1. Vijay Kelkar and E. A. S. Sarma, 'Development of energy resources', chapter 9 in *India: Development policy imperatives*, ed. Vijay Kelkar and V. V. Bhanoji Rao (Tata McGraw-Hill Publishing, 1996), 336–419.
2. For the onset of inflation targeting in 2015, work was needed ahead of time on assessing the quality of the CPI, Ila Patnaik, Ajay Shah, and Giovanni Veronese, 'How should inflation be measured in India?', *Economic and Political Weekly* XLVI, no. 16 (April 2011): https://www.epw.in/journal/2011/16/special-articles/how-should-inflation-be-measured-india.html.
3. Ajay Shah, 'Consequences of GDP over-estimation', *Business Standard*, May 2018, https://www.mayin.org/ajayshah/MEDIA/2018/gdp_overestimated.html.
4. Ajay Shah, 'Hot spots in the bankruptcy reform', *Business Standard*, August 2018, https://www.mayin.org/ajayshah/MEDIA/2018/prioritise_the_40.html.
5. Ajay Shah, 'Sequencing issues in building jurisprudence: the problems of large bankruptcy cases', *The Leap Blog*, July 2018, https://blog.theleapjournal.org/2018/07/sequencing-issues-in-building.html.
6. We are grateful to Reuben Abraham for this example.

7. This idea, and the phrase 'organizational rout' is from Matt Andrews, Lant Pritchett, and Michael Woolcock, *Building State capacity* (Oxford, 2017).

8. Figure 3.3 from: Matt Andrews, Lant Pritchett, and Michael Woolcock, *Building State capacity* (Oxford, 2017).

9. Vagda Galhotra, 'Why we need to repeal more criminal laws', *The Wire*, September 2018, documents some of this problem, https://thewire.in/law/why-we-need-to-repeal-more-criminal-laws.

10. On arbitrary power of regulators in India, and the proposed DPA, see K. P. Krishnan, 'Protection from Data Protection Authority', *Business Standard*, December 2021, https://www.business-standard.com/article/opinion/protection-from-data-protection-authority-121122701177_1.html; Rishab Bailey et al., 'Comments on the draft Personal Data Protection Bill, 2019', *The Leap Blog*, April 2020, https://blog.theleapjournal.org/2020/04/comments-on-draft-personal-data.html; Trishee Goyal and Renuka Sane, *Towards better enforcement by regulatory agencies in India*, technical report (Data Governance Network, January 2021), https://datagovernance.org/report/towards-better-enforcement-by-regulatory-agencies.

Chapter 35.

1. Ankush Agrawal and Vikas Kumar, *Numbers in India's periphery: The political economy of government statistics* (Cambridge University Press, October 2020).

2. As an example, concerns about GDP data are summarized in: Rajeswari Sengupta, 'The great Indian GDP measurement controversy', *The Leap Blog*, September 2016, https://blog.theleapjournal.org/2016/09/the-great-indian-gdp-measurement.html.

3. On statistical methods for using the night lights radiance data, Ayush Patnaik et al., *But clouds got in my way: Bias and bias correction of VIIRS nighttime lights data in the presence of clouds*, technical report 7 (Bombay: XKDR Forum, October 2021),

https://xkdr.org/paper/but-clouds-got-in-my-way-bias-and-bias-correction-of-viirs-nighttime-lights-data-in-the-presence-of-clouds.

4. To paraphrase Tolstoy, perhaps *all advanced economies are alike, but every weak institutional setting is weak in its own distinctive ways.*

5. IDFC Institute, *Safety trends and reporting of crime (SATARC)*, technical report (IDFC Institute, 2017), https://www. idfcinstitute.org/site/assets/files/12318/satarc_april272017.pdf.

6. The ban on micro-finance in Andhra Pradesh is studied in Renuka Sane and Susan Thomas, 'The real cost of credit constraints: evidence from micro-finance', *The B.E. Journal of Economic Analysis & Policy* 16, no. 1 (January 2016): 151–183.

7. We are grateful to Rajiv Bhartari and Yadvendradev Jhala for guidance on these questions.

8. Ajay Shah, 'New thinking on a traditional public good', *Financial Express*, August 2009, https://www.mayin.org/ajayshah/MEDIA/2009/mapsdata.html.

9. This text draws upon the experience of the NIPFP-DEA Research Program over the 2007–2015 period.

Chapter 36.

1. Sveriges Riksbank, *Annual Report for Sveridges Riksbank 2018*, technical report (March 2019), https://www.riksbank.se/en-gb/press-and-published/publications/annual-report/.

2. There were three Kelkar committees in tax policy: on direct taxes, on indirect taxes and on the FRBM implementation (which designed the GST). The key idea animating all the three reports was this agenda, of simplification. Vijay Kelkar, *Reports of the Task Force on Direct Taxes*, technical report (Ministry of Finance, December 2002), https://prsindia.org/files/bills_acts/bills_parliament/1970/kelkar_direct_taxes.pdf; Vijay Kelkar, *Reports of the Task Force on Indirect Taxes*, technical report (Ministry of Finance, December 2002); Vijay Kelkar, *Report of the task force on implementation of the FRBM Act, 2003*, technical report (Ministry of Finance, July 2004), https://dea.gov.in/sites/default/files/FRBM_report.pdf.

3. Prasanth Regy, 'RBI's proposal for a Public Credit Registry',
    The Leap Blog, August 2017, https://blog.theleapjournal.
    org/2017/08/rbis-proposal-for-public-credit-registry.html.
4. There is a vulnerability in the supply chain of Indian drug
    companies through the use of Chinese 'active pharmaceutical
    ingredients' (APIs). This can motivate simplistic industrial policy
    solutions, or more careful policy design: Gautam Bambawale
    et al., 'India's supply chain vulnerability with Chinese APIs:
    Industrial policy vs. sophisticated policy design', *The Leap Blog*,
    May 2021, https://blog.theleapjournal.org/2021/05/indias-
    supply-chain-vulnerability-with.html.

Chapter 37.

1. Fernand Braudel wrote, '*the history of events*' was merely the
    history of '*surface disturbances, crests of foam that the tides of history
    carry on their strong backs*'.
2. On the role of the Rajya Sabha in legislation, Suyash Rai,
    'Does the role of the Rajya Sabha in the legislative process
    require reform?', *The Leap Blog*, January 2016, https://blog.
    theleapjournal.org/2016/01/does-role-of-rajya-sabha-in-
    legislative.html.
3. Daniel Enemark et al., 'Effect of holding office on the behavior
    of politicians', *Proceedings of NAS*, 2016, shows that persons
    who have formerly held office are more likely to engage in
    reciprocity. https://www.pnas.org/content/113/48/13690.
4. On the checks and balances required in this field, Vrinda
    Bhandari and Renuka Sane, 'A critique of the Aadhaar legal
    framework', *National Law School of India Review* 31, no. 4
    (December 2019), https://www.jstor.org/stable/26918423.
5. This report is Vijay Kelkar, *Ministry of Finance for the 21st Century*
    (Ministry of Finance, 2004).
6. The terminology of exit, voice and loyalty is from Albert O.
    Hirschman, *Exit, voice, loyalty* (Harvard University Press, 1970).
7. Cellular Operators Association of India and Ors.v. Telecom
    Regulatory Authority of India and Ors., AIR 2016 SC 2336, 2016.

8. On low evidentiary standards with SEBI and market abuse, Nidhi Aggarwal and Bhargavi Zaveri, 'Problems with evidentiary standards for proving securities fraud in India', *The Leap Blog*, August 2019, https://blog.theleapjournal.org/2019/08/problems-with-evidentiary-standards-for.html.

9. The MCA Working Group on establishing IBBI had such a philosophy: Ravi Narain, *Building the Insolvency and Bankruptcy Board of India*, technical report (Ministry of Company Affairs, 2016), www.ibbi.gov.in/Wg-01percent20Report.pdf.

Chapter 38.

1. James C. Scott, *Seeing like a state: How certain schemes to improve the human condition have failed* (Yale University Press, 1998), is a remarkably influential book.

2. For a cautionary tale of engineers in the world of public policy, Nathaniel Popper and Ana Vanessa Herrero, 'The coder and the dictator', *The New York Times*, March 2020, https://www.nytimes.com/2020/03/20/technology/venezuela-petro-cryptocurrency.html.

3. Suyash Rai et al., *The economics of releasing the V-band and E-band spectrum in India*, technical report (NIPFP, April 2018), https://macrofinance.nipfp.org.in/releases/DMSS2018-Spectrum.html.

Chapter 39.

1. Akshay Jaitly and Ajay Shah, 'The lowest hanging fruit on the coconut tree: India's climate transition through the price system in the power sector', technical report 9 (Bombay: XKDR Forum, October 2021), https://xkdr.org/paper/the-lowest-hanging-fruit-on-the-coconut-tree-india-s-climate-transition-through-the-price-system-in-the-power-sector; Ajay Shah, 'Climate change for practical people', *Business Standard*, January 2022, https://www.mayin.org/ajayshah/MEDIA/2022/climate_change.html.

2. Yashwant Sinha's announcement on cutting the customs rate was believed. Inflation targeting was believed, and it helped that it was encoded in a law. Credible long-term commitments on the carbon tax are particularly difficult because potentially they can be changed every year in the Finance Bill. Ajay Shah, 'The policy posture as an incomplete contract', *The Leap Blog*, March 2018, https://blog.theleapjournal.org/2018/03/the-policy-posture-as-incomplete.html; Ajay Shah, 'The strategy and the tactics', *Business Standard*, June 2019, https://www.mayin.org/ajayshah/MEDIA/2019/strategy_tactics.html.
3. As an example, see the 'largest public statement of economists in history', https://clcouncil.org/economists-statement/, which summarizes the standard economic logic on this subject.

Chapter 40.

1. The material of this chapter is based on three government reports: Vijay Kelkar, *Report of the task force on implementation of the FRBM Act, 2003*, technical report (Ministry of Finance, July 2004), https://dea.gov.in/sites/default/files/1.pdf; Arbind Modi, *Report of the task force on GST*, technical report (Thirteenth Finance Commission, December 2009), https://prsindia.org/files/bills_acts/bills_parliament/2014/Report_of_Task_Force-_GST.pdf; Vijay Kelkar, *Thirteenth Finance Commission*, technical report (Government of India, December 2009), https://smartnet.niua.org/content/5a0faf4c-0242-4a46-b4ad-0f1be66fff89

Chapter 41.

1. Lawrence K. Altman, 'India declared free of smallpox', *The New York Times*, July 1975, https://www.nytimes.com/1975/07/03/archives/india-declared-free-of-smallpox-2-countries-left.html.
2. The 'Great Stink' was an event in central London in July and August 1858, which led to the beginning of modern sanitation in London. The 'Great Smog of 1952' was a severe air pollution

event in London in December 1952, which set off the policy response that led up to the Clean Air Act in 1956.

3. David D. Parrish et al., 'Air quality progress in North American megacities: A review', *Atmospheric Environment* 45, no. 39 (December 2011): The authors examine air quality in Los Angeles, which was once among the worst in the world. They say, '*It is fair to say that this mega-city has gone from being one of the most polluted in the world 50 years ago to presently one of the least polluted cities of its size.*' http://gahp.net/wp-content/uploads/2017/10/Air-Quality-Progress-in-North-American-Megacities-A-Review-1.pdf.

4. See the special issue of Health Systems & Reform on *Financing Common Goods for Health*, September 2019, https://www.who.int/health_financing/topics/financing-common-goods-for-health/en/.

5. Joseph William Bhore, *Health Survey and Development Committee report*, technical report (Government of India, 1946).

6. Jeffrey Hammer, Yamini Aiyar, and Salimah Samji, 'Understanding government failure in public health services', *Economic and Political Weekly* 42, no. 40 (October 2007): 4049–4057, https://www.jstor.org/stable/40276648.

7. The journey from colonial public health to government-funded health insurance is described in Ila Patnaik, Shubho Roy, and Ajay Shah, *The rise of government-funded health insurance in India*, technical report 231 (NIPFP, May 2018).

8. An analysis of the difficulties in health insurance is in Shefali Malhotra et al., *Fair play in Indian health insurance*, technical report (NIPFP, May 2018), https://macrofinance.nipfp.org.in/releases/MPSS-Fair_play_in_Indian_health_insurance.html.

9. NHS, 'GPs per 1000 patients', *NHS*, 2015, https://www.nhs.uk/Scorecard/Pages/IndicatorFacts.aspx?MetricId=100063.

10. As an example, Section 3.5 of Ajay Shah, 'Indian health policy in the light of Covid-19: The puzzles of state capacity and institutional design', *India Policy Forum*, 2020, that was written early in the pandemic, identifies scientific questions about Covid-19 which were relevant for India, where it did not suffice for India to only free ride on the research done in

advanced economies. https://www.xkdr.org/paper/indian-health-policy-in-the-light-of-covid-19-the-puzzles-of-state-capacity-and-institutional-design.

Chapter 42.

1. As an example, difficulties in government contracting hindered the ability of the Indian state to buy vaccines, as a comparison against advanced economies shows. Staff, *Questions & Answers on vaccine negotiations*, technical report (European Commission, January 2021), https://ec.europa.eu/commission/presscorner/detail/en/qanda_21_48; Charmi Mehta and Susan Thomas, 'Lessons from the COVID-19 vaccine procurement of 2021', *The Leap Blog*, November 2021, https://blog.theleapjournal.org/2021/11/lessons-from-covid-19-vaccine.html.

2. Ajay Shah, 'The market for Covid-19 vaccines and the tipping point to herd immunity', *The Leap Blog*, September 2020, https://blog.theleapjournal.org/2020/09/the-market-for-covid-19-vaccines-and.html.

3. Amrita Agarwal and Ajay Shah, 'An important change of course by policy in Indian Covid-19 vaccination', *The Leap Blog*, April 2021, https://blog.theleapjournal.org/2021/04/an-important-change-of-course-by-policy.html.

4. Staff, 'Serum may cut Covishield's monthly production by half as govt orders dry up', *Business Standard*, December 2021, https://www.business-standard.com/article/companies/serum-may-cut-covishield-s-monthly-production-by-half-as-govt-orders-dry-up-121120800022_1.html.

Chapter 43.

1. Money can be viewed as a public good that facilitates transactions. This function can be equally achieved by US dollars or crypto-currencies; the creation of the Indian rupee is not essential. It is the second dimension of money—reducing business cycle volatility—where the Indian state adds value. There is also a

third element to money creation: seigniorage income. The central bank earns income on the asset side of its balance sheet, which is paid out to the Treasury as a dividend. This income accrues to the Indian government when Indian rupees are used, while this is not the case when the Indian economy transacts through US dollars or crypto-currencies.

2. B. N. Srikrishna, *Report of the financial sector legislative re-forms commission, volume 1* (Ministry of Finance, March 2013), https://dea.gov.in/sites/default/files/fslrc_report_vol1_1.pdf.

3. As an example of the problems of consumer protection in Indian finance, see Monika Halan, Renuka Sane, and Susan Thomas, 'The case of the missing billions: Estimating losses to customers due to mis-sold life insurance policies', *Journal of Economic Policy Reform* 17 (4 2014): 285–302, https://ifrogs.org/releases/HalanSaneThomas2013_missellingLifeInsurance.html.

4. Ajay Shah, 'Designing the monetary policy committee', *The Leap Blog*, January 2014, https://blog.theleapjournal.org/2014/01/designing-monetary-policy-committee.html.

5. See Ajay Shah, 'Monetary policy is easy; Financial regulation is hard', *Financial Express*, July 2010, https://www.mayin.org/ajayshah/MEDIA/2010/finance_vs_MP.html.

6. The demise of 'AT1 bonds' as an asset class was related to weaknesses of the regulation-making process at SEBI, K. P. Krishnan, 'Regulation by circulars?', *Business Standard*, March 2021, https://www.business-standard.com/article/opinion/regulation-by-circulars-121032501460_1.html.

7. The *Monetary Policy Framework Agreement* was signed on 20 February 2015, and established year-on-year CPI inflation of 4 per cent as the objective of the RBI. In 2016, this was placed into the RBI Act.

8. Shubho Roy et al., 'Building State capacity for regulation in India', in *Regulation in India: Design, Capacity, Performance*, ed. Devesh Kapur and Madhav Khosla (Oxford: Hart Publishing, 2019), https://macrofinance.nipfp.org.in/releases/RSSS_building-state-capacity.html.

9. For a treatment of this period, see Ajay Shah and Susan Thomas, 'Securities Markets', chap. 10 in *India Development Report 1997*,

ed. Kirit S. Parikh (Oxford University Press, February 1997), 167–192; Ajay Shah and Susan Thomas, 'David and Goliath: Displacing a primary market', *Journal of Global Financial Markets* 1, no. 1 (2000): 14–21, https://www.mayin.org/ajayshah/PDFDOCS/ShahThomas2000_jgfm.pdf; John Echeverri-Gent, 'Financial globalization and India's equity market reforms', *India Review* 3, no. 4 (2004): 306–332, https://www.tandfonline.com/doi/abs/10.1080/14736480490895598?journalCode=f%20ind20; Susan Thomas, 'How the financial sector in India was reformed', in *Documenting reforms: Case studies from India*, ed. S. Narayan (New Delhi: Macmillan India, 2006), 171–210, bit.ly/3nBaqHx.

10. The five reports are U. K. Sinha, *Working Group on Foreign Investment*, Committee Report (Department of Economic Affairs, Ministry of Finance, 2010), https://www.finmin.nic.in/sites/default/files/WGFI.pdf, Dhirendra Swarup, *Financial Well Being: Report of the Committee on Investor Awarness and Protection*, technical report (Ministry of Finance, Government of India, 2010), http://bit.ly/2K1JLzk, Jahangir Aziz, *Report of the Internal Working Group on Debt Management in India*, technical report (Ministry of Finance, 2008), https://finmin.nic.in/sites/default/files/Report_Internal_Working_Group_on_Debt_Management.pdf, Percy Mistry, *Making Mumbai an International Financial Centre*, Committee Report (Sage Publishing and Ministry of Finance, Government of India, 2007), https://dea.gov.in/sites/default/files/mifcreport.pdf and Raghuram Rajan, *Committee for Financial Sector Reforms*, Committee Report (Planning Commission, Government of India, 2008), https://web.archive.org/web/20190210134845/http://planningcommission.nic.in/reports/genrep/rep_fr/cfsr_all.pdf

11. FSLRC, *Indian Financial Code*, 1.1 (Ministry of Finance, July 2015); Ila Patnaik and Ajay Shah, *Reforming India's financial system*, technical report (Carnegie Endowment for International Peace, January 2014), https://carnegieendowment.org/files/reform_indian_financial_system.pdf.

12. Ajay Shah, 'FSLRC: The cast of 146', *The Leap Blog*, April 2013, https://blog.theleapjournal.org/2013/04/fslrc-cast-of-146.html.

Chapter 44.

1. As an example from an advanced country, Coral Davenport, Lisa Friedman, and Christopher Flavelle, 'Biden's climate plans are stunted after dejected experts fled Trump', *The New York Times*, August 2021, https://www.nytimes.com/2021/08/01/climate/biden-scientists-shortage-climate.html.

2. Matt Andrews, Lant Pritchett, and Michael Woolcock, *Building State capacity* (Oxford, 2017).

3. Daniel Kaufmann and Aart Kraay, 'Growth without Governance', *Economia* 3, no. 1 (2002): is a remarkable result which finds that institutions help growth, but growth harms institutions, https://econpapers.repec.org/article/col000425/008687.htm.

4. An analysis of the decline of state capability in the USSR is Charles King, 'How a great power falls apart', *Foreign Affairs*, June 2020, where Andrei Amalrik is quoted as writing, '*The regime considers itself the acme of perfection and therefore has no wish to change its ways either of its own free will or, still less, by making concessions to anyone or anything*', https://www.foreignaffairs.com/articles/russia-fsu/2020-06-30/how-great-power-falls-apart.

Chapter 45.

1. Latecomers in development have often used this two-part strategy: of a state that first addresses missing markets by supplanting the private market system, and then retreating to a regulatory role as the private sector finds its feet. For the Japanese story of this transition, see Andrea Boltho, *Japan: An economic survey, 1953–1973* (Oxford University Press, 1975).

2. One of the early articles which clearly saw the problems of the Mark 1 strategy is Arun Shourie, 'Controls and the current situation: Why not let the hounds run?', *Economic and Political Weekly* 8, nos 31/33 (August 1973): 1467–1488, https://www.jstor.org/stable/4362927.

3. A big picture of the evolution from Mark 1 to Mark 2 is in Arvind Virmani, *The dynamics of competition: Phasing of domestic*

and external liberalisation in India, technical report 4/2006 (Planning Commission, April 2006), https://niti.gov.in/planningcommission.gov.in/docs/reports/wrkpapers/wp_dc_pdel.doc; Ashok V. Desai, *The economics and politics of transition to an open market economy: India*, technical report 155 (OECD Publishing, October 1999), https://ideas.repec.org/p/oec/devaaa/155-en.html.

4. For a sense of that optimism, see Vijay Kelkar, *India: On the growth turnpike*, Narayanan Oration (Canberra: Australian National University, 2004).

5. Josh Felman and R. Nagaraj were among the first people who saw the difficulties of the 2003–2008 boom, e.g., see R. Nagaraj, 'India's dream run, 2003–08: Understanding the boom and its aftermath', *Economic and Political Weekly* 48, no. 20 (May 2013): 39–51, https://www.jstor.org/stable/23527367.

6. Ajay Shah and Bhargavi Zaveri-Shah, 'Instant cross-border payments vs. current account inconvertibility', *The Leap Blog*, September 2021, https://blog.theleapjournal.org/2021/09/instant-cross-border-payments-vs.html.

7. On the rise of arbitrary power in the agencies, Josy Joseph, *The silent coup: A history of India's deep state* (Chennai: Westland Publications, 2021).

Index

administrative constraint,
54–61, 67
human resource
management, 55–56
from motives of politicians
and officials, 56–57
principal–agent problems, 54
in private firms, 54–55
in public administration, 54
agencification, concept of, 406–
407, 418–419
agency map, 473–474
central bank, 473
financial regulator, 473
public debt management
agency, 473
resolution corporation, 473
Agricultural Produce Market
Committee (APMC),
103
agriculture, 38, 40, 82, 88–89,
103, 109, 111, 497, 500

Ahluwalia, Montek, 97, 241,
316, 493
AirBnB, 137–138, 297
air quality crisis, 40, 45–46,
351, 452
Ambedkar, B. R., 492
amma kitchens, 6
anarchy, 10, 182
antibiotic resistance, 41, 113
antimicrobial resistance (AMR),
113
anti-poverty programs, 122–
123, 126, 128, 155
arbitrage, 86, 89, 94
'ASER' survey, 373
assignment principle, 126,
154–157
Assisted Reproductive
Technology (Regulation)
Bill (ART Bill), 305
asymmetric information, 12, 14,
15, 20, 32, 104, 114, 207,

252, 273, 277, 297, 319, 323, 447–448, 453–454, 457, 469, 471

Banerjee Abhijit, 193, 496
banking, 53, 99, 103–104, 193, 229, 321, 355, 356, 470
banking regulation, 99, 103, 193, 356
Bankruptcy Legislative Reforms Committee, 99
bankruptcy process, 97–98, 101, 102
bankruptcy reform, 213, 219, 356, 358–359
Basu Kaushik, 391, 496
Bhore committee, 450
Bhore Joseph, 450
bilateral trade deficit, 152–153
biometric identity system, 117–118
black money, 49, 150, 189
Board governance, 340, 342–343
Bombay Stock Exchange (BSE), 479
Bombay Tenancy and Agricultural Lands Act (1948), 143
Bond-Currency–Derivatives Nexus, 354, 355
bond market, 320, 326, 353, 355, 367, 479
corporate, 179
financing of, 116
building state capacity, 401–402
delays in, 213

discretion for, 413–414
establishing leadership in, 412
organization design in, 405–406
clarity of purpose of the agent, 406–407
components of the law, 410–412
delegate whatever you can, 407–408
hygiene in constructing agencies, 409–410
ministry of finance for the 21st century, 408–409
power, dispersion of, 402–404
time and money in, 414–416
administrative law, 416–417
clean slate *versus* reforming an existing organization, 417
reducing arbitrary power in tax administration, 417–418
business cycles, macroeconomics of, 101–102
business process engineering (BPR), 282

carbon tax, 443
addresses market failure, 435–437
central bank, 473
achieving state capacity for, 474–475
Central Bureau of Investigation (CBI), 60

central planning, 8, 16, 82–83, 90, 95, 159, 276–277, 289, 294, 298, 397, 424, 437, 439, 440, 473, 478
Central Statistics Office (CSO), 60
China, 166, 490
  authoritarian regime, 9
  Cultural Revolution in, 26
  export sector in, 361
  import of organic fertilizers by Sri Lanka, 184
  murder of sparrows in, 26, 31
  negotiation of Free Trade Agreements, 359–360
  one-child policy, 183
  ShiDian, 193
  urban governance in, 165
  US trade deficit with, 152
climate policy transmission, 438–439
CMIE, 30, 159, 164, 374
coercive power (of State), 14, 20, 33, 34, 47, 54, 55, 342, 499
  for behaviour modification, 21–22
  in constitutional democracy, 22
  to pay taxes, 22
  redistribution as ground for, 17–18
competition, 96
  in banking, 103–105
complexity, four dimensions of, 227–228

judicial reforms, 230–231
monetary policy, 228–230
solutions change from one dimension of complexity to another, 231–232
four hardest problems, 232
confirmation bias, 425
Constitution India, 313, 338
consumer protection, 277, 470, 473, 480–481
corruption, 174
cost-benefit analysis, 139–142, 143, 145–146, 149
  institutionalized application of mind, 147–148
  zone of applicability of, 146
Covid-19, vaccines for
  'Cowin,' 465
  four-part policy strategy, 464–466
  market failure perspective, 460–462
  policy concerns and solutions, 463–464
  power of the price system, 462–463
  state-capacity perspective, 459–460
CPI inflation, 474
credit information systems, 18–19
credit rating, 154
criminal justice system, 14, 44–45, 234, 312
criminal sanctions, 118–119
crypto-currency investment, ban on, 206

Cultural Revolution, China, 26
customs duty, 52, 111, 364, 436
cyber crime, 296

data protection, 210
Data Protection Authority, 198
debt/GDP ratio, 154
decentralization, 165–169
demonetization, 49, 63, 147,
    183, 189
Department of
    Telecommunications (DOT),
    320
derivatives trading, 480
developmental state, 26–27, 31,
    34, 492, 498
digital pathway to state capacity,
    279–281
    computers for the people
        versus computers for the
        state, 281–282
    computer technology in
        the new pension system,
        283–284
    difficulties of digital
        transformation within a
        government organization,
        286–287
    government organization
        versus policy reform,
        282–283
    state capacity in the digital
        age, 284–285
direct democracy, 62–63, 66
dispersion of power, 74, 204,
    254, 266, 270, 402–404, 418
domestic liberalization, 493

domestic market imperfections,
    116–117
Drug Price Control Order
    (DPCO), 207, 208
dual exchange rate regimes, 86
Duflo Esther, 193, 496

economic freedom
    dawn of, 494
    improved, 492–494
education, constraints in, 45–46
education policy, in Kerala, 158
education vouchers, 23–24,
    326
election clock, policymaking
    on, 214–215
    bankruptcy reform, 219
    building a bridge vs building
        institutions, 220–222
    building the republic takes
        time, 222–223
    before the first year, 216–217
    peak customs rate, cutting
        the, 215–216
    playing the long game,
        217–219
    Rhine was not cleaned in a
        day, 220
    slow and gradual approach
        reduces uncertainty,
        223–225
electronic trading, 480
elementary education and
    health, 28–29
Employee Pension Scheme
    (EPS), 351
EPFO, 284, 358

E-pharmacy players, 456
equilibrium
  effects, 108–109
  general, 109–110
  partial *vs* general, 110
  short term *vs* long term, 110
Essential Commodities Act
  (ECA), 291
exchange rate regime, 86, 353,
  361
ex-post evaluation/review,
  143–144
externality, 12, 32
  negative, 12–14, 130, 296
  positive, 13–14, 296

Facebook, 96, 197–198
Federal 'Administrative
  Procedures Act' (APA),
  1946, 191
federalism, 158, 169, 203
feedback loops, 176, 179, 192,
  193
Felman Joshua, 354, 359
FEMA, 119
FERA, 119
fertilizer industry, 123–124,
  126
Finance Act, 22, 24, 25
financial economic policy, 468,
  470
  achieving state capacity for
    central bank, 474–475
    regulator, 475–477
  address the market failure,
    472
  clear tasks in, 479

  financial regulation, 479
  monetary policy, 479
  public debt management,
    479
  resolution, 479
  financial reform, 479–481
  Financial Regulatory
    Architecture, 473–474
  Indian experience, 477–479
  market failure, 468–472
  objectives of, 470
financial market infrastructure
  institutions (FMII), 137
financial reform
  in India
    first phase of, 480
  process of, 479–481
financial regulator, 471, 482
  financial firms and
    consumers, 471
  micro prudential regulation,
    471
  resolution corporation,
    471
financial regulatory architecture,
  472, 473–474
financial repression, 52, 154,
  332, 479
Financial Sector Legislative
  Reforms Commission
  (FSLRC), 98–99, 102, 411,
  480, 481
firms
  productivity gains of, 8
  profits of, 7–8
fiscal policy, 125, 154, 468
fiscal risk, 124–125, 128

Food and Drugs Administration
    (FDA), 202
food and drugs, regulation of,
    207–208
formal processes
    for executive functions, 410
    for judicial functions, 410–411
    for legislative functions, 410
foundational processes, building
    of categories of expertise,
    339–340
        board governance, 342
        coercive power, 342
        contracting, 341
        finance, 341
        foundational processes in
            defence, 340–341
        transparency, 341
    contracting process, 332–335
    finance process, 330–332
    human resource process,
        329–330
    navigation system, 335–338
    process of change, 338–339
    rockets, 328–329
FRBM Act, 241
FRDI Bill, 99
free-market process, 8
free trade, 89, 360, 363
'fruit of the poisonous tree'
    doctrine, 59–60
FSSAI, 271, 402, 407
futures trading, 84, 89, 416

Gandhi, 11, 182, 364
Gandhi, Rajiv, 344

GDP growth, 29, 45, 50, 52,
    100, 102, 105, 109, 110–111,
    122–124, 128, 142, 151, 152,
    153, 167, 186, 485
    great surge of debt, 485
    productive firms, 488
    state-led development, 487
    subsidy programs and,
        128
General Data Protection
    Regulation (GDPR), 197,
    198
government, 3, 6
    agencies are monopolies,
        263–264
    coercive power, 264
    has greater complexity,
        264–265
    has to prize rules over deals,
        265–266
    imposition on technical
        standard, 3–4
    intervention, in consumer
        protection, 470–471
    lacks feedback loops, 262–
        263
    must disperse power, 266–
        267
    operate on longer horizons,
        267
    spending, 115, 453
Government of India Act
    (1935), 270
GST system, 108, 110, 151,
    165, 289, 357, 400, 442
    in low-capacity state, 442–
        444

peak rate of, 52
single rate, 52

Harshad Mehta scandal (1992),
480
health care, 15–16
policy pathways in, 453
market failure, 453–456
health expenditure, 447, 449
health policy
emphasis on prevention, 449
Indian journey of, 450–451
market failure in
health care, 447–449
public health, 445–447
path to state capacity, 456–
457
policy pathways in health
care, 453
socialized health care
system, 453–456
policy pathways in public
health, 451–452
herd immunity, 462–464
high productivity firms, 100,
105
Human Fertilization and
Embryology Act (HFEA),
304

IBBI, 191, 213, 411, 416
IBC, 213, 219, 412, 473
ICICI Bank, 208
ideal democracy, 11
IDFC Institute, 116
IMF, 155–156
incentives, 72–73, 82

around statistical measures,
75–76
deployment of, 74–75
high-powered, 77–78
people's responses to, 78–80
India
financial reform in
first phase of, 480
free riding on state capacity
outside, 206
data protection, 210
regulation of food and
drugs, 207–208
securities listed overseas,
208–209
US FCC design of
spectrum allocation,
209
growth in
1979–2011, 489
1991–2011, 29–30, 493
trade policy reform, 362–363
Indian Bankruptcy Reform,
358–359
Indian Financial Code (IFC),
191, 411, 481
version 1.1, 481, 482
Indian Railways, 54, 264–265,
285
Indian state failure, 37–41,
66–67
four-part thinking, 40–41
government failure, 38–39
policy failure, 39–42
principal–agent problem, 39
Indian-style developmental
state, 26–30

industrial policy, 397–398
Industrial, Scientific and
    Medical ('ISM') bands, 209
information constraint, 44–47,
    66
information utilities, 213,
    395–396
infrastructure, 18–19, 20
financing of, 116
invisible, 201–203, 210, 211, 366
Insolvency and Bankruptcy
    Board of India (IBBI), 191,
    213, 416
Insolvency and Bankruptcy
    Code (IBC), 213, 473
    in 2016, 213, 219
institution building and GDP
    growth, 485–487
    bigger GDP, 488–490
    keeping score, 490–491
    success is not assured,
        487–488
intellectual capacity, 205
    and its limitations, 431–432

judicial functions, formal
    processes for, 410–411
judiciary, 27, 94, 134, 168, 195,
    228, 230, 232, 234, 253,
    272–274, 277, 333, 400, 403,
    413, 497

knowledge constraint, 47–49, 67
knowledge foundations,
    building the, 369
    data release by the
        government, 376

from data to knowledge,
    378–379
develop sound measurement
    systems, 375–376
kicking off improvements,
    372
    episodic versus long-term
        measurement, 374
    outcomes measurement in
        education, 373
    outcomes measurement
        in the criminal justice
        system, 373–374
knowledge partnerships
    in the market for ideas,
        379–381
    increasing analytical
        capability in
        government, 382–383
    what knowledge
        partnerships are not,
        381–382
long-term foundations for
    policy research, 383–384
principles for data release by
    the government, 376
    role of the state in maps,
        376–378
private information sets,
    370–372
public data, skepticism on,
    369–370
public money, good use of,
    384–385
shifting institutional
    architecture of knowledge
    institutions, 384

'know your customer' (KYC) requirements, 117–118, 189

land reform, 143
law of unintended consequences, 32, 34, 39, 425
liberal democracies, 11, 125, 185, 476
licence–permit–inspector raj, 494
Lok Pal, 60
Lucas critique, 49, 426

macro policy, 154, 354
Mahalanobis, P. C., 492
majoritarianism, 63
'Make in India,' 151
Marginal Cost of Public Funds (MCPF), 50, 51, 52, 53, 54, 125, 344
'Mark 1 strategy,' 492
'Mark 2 strategy,' 493
in 1991–2011, 493
Mark 3 paradigm, 497, 498
building knowledge and building community for, 500
market abuse, 472
information-based abuse, 472
market-based abuse, 472
market-based transactions, 14
market failure, 12, 14, 16, 20, 32–33, 40, 96, 112, 114, 115, 121–122, 435
government intervention, 469
in health care, 447–449
how to address the, 472
in the new age, 296
asymmetric information, 296–297
market power, 297
negative externalities, 296
positive externalities, 296
public goods, 297
perspective, 460–462
to the pillars, 318–319
private solutions for, 129–138
in public health, 445–447
second class of, 445
that should not be addressed, 389–390
market power, 14–15, 32
government as a source of, 103–104
Markup in State Contracting (MSC), 346, 464
Markup in State Production (MSP), 346
mass surveillance system on finance, 117–118
Mehta Pratap Bhanu, 496
micro prudential regulation, 53, 471
middle income trap, 495
migration, 166–167
monetary policy, 22, 155, 233
Framework Agreement, 314
Monetary Policy Committee (MPC), 73–74, 475, 478
Moore's law, 8
Muralidharan Karthik, 346

National Company Law
  Tribunal (NCLT), 213
National Map Policy, 21
National Rural Employment
  Guarantee Scheme
  (NREGS), 127–128, 155
National Securities Clearing
  Corporation (NSCC),
  480
National Stock Depository
  Limited (NSDL), 480
National Stock Exchange
  (NSE), 480
  establishment of, 221
National Tiger Conservation
  Authority, 375
Negotiated Dealing System
  (NDS), 263
Nehru Jawaharlal, 492
network effects, 96–97
New Pension System (NPS),
  222, 358
Nilekani Nandan, 496
Nirbhaya rape case (2012),
  312

OASIS Project, 222
organizational capacity and
  capabilities, 176, 177–179
organization design, 174
  board, 176
  coercive power, 175–176
  elements, 174–177
  feedback loops, 176
  formal, 175
  leadership, 175
  objectives, 175

participation, in policymaking,
  190–191
Patel, G. S.
  committee report, 221
Patel Urjit, 240
paternalism, 33
  difficulties with, 121–122
  information constraints and,
    46–47
paternalistic government,
  33–34, 46
path to decarbonization
  carbon tax addresses,
    435–437
  climate policy transmission
    lies in the electricity
    sector, 438–439
  market failure, 435
  price system *versus* central
    planning solutions,
    437–438
  state capacity perspective,
    440
PATRIOT Act, 311
**pension reforms, 222, 341,
351, 358**
PFRDA, 222
pillars of intervention
  mapping from market failure
    to the pillars, 318–319
  public sector production,
    319–320
    banking, 321
    bond market, 326
    digital identity, 325
    education, 321–323

government production of
  financial services, 320
government production of
  telecom services, 320
health care, 324–325
infrastructure, 323–324
skills, 323
Planning Commission, 155,
  167
policymaking, 303
  alternative depiction of the
    policy process, 308
  capacity building for the
    Indian policy process,
    309–310
  policy pipeline, 305–308
  state of maturity of the
    reforms process, 309
  UK policy process on in-
    vitro fertilization, 304–305
policy pathways
  in health care, 453
    market failure in health
      care, 453–456
  in public health, 451–452
policy process, 237
  adverse impact upon, 256–257
policy reversibility, 194–195
pollution, 13, 131
  control, 132–133
poverty, 122–123, 124
PPP contracting, 232
price system, 82, 83, 94–95,
  107, 124
  cobweb model, 88–89
  conditions of economic
    freedom, 92

dual exchange rate regimes,
  86
law of one price, 86
minimum support price
  (MSP), 85, 89
policymakers on price
  control, 86–88
resource allocation, 89–92
responses of supply and
  demand, 92–94
supply and demand, 83–84,
  83–85
price system, power of, 462–463
Pritchett Lant, 122, 199, 200,
  227, 496
private good, 15, 19, 20, 23
private investment, 30, 298
private schools, 28–29
'Production Linked Incentive'
  (PLI) scheme, 117
Project Tiger, establishment of,
  375
property rights, 131, 134
protectionism, 109, 117, 152,
  293, 298
public administration, 31, 54
  organizing framework for,
    326–327
public choice theory, 57, 58,
  59–60, 122, 156, 157, 473,
  477, 498
  limits of, 60–61
Public Credit Registry (PCR),
  320, 396
Public Debt Management
  Agency (PDMA), 408, 473
public goods, 15, 19, 20, 24, 32

public health, 16
    defined, 446
    expenditure', 447
    market failure in, 445–447
    objective of, 461
public money, decision to spend
    expenditure efficiency in
        redistribution, 345
    marginal cost of public funds,
        344–345
    state contracting, expenditure
        inefficiency in, 346–347
    state production, expenditure
        efficiency in, 345–346
    elementary education, 346
    wisdom in expenditure
        decisions, 347–348
public policy, 10, 24, 73, 83,
    121, 134, 181–182, 189
    centralization of, 158–159
    failures, 41–42, 44–66
    health policy, 163–164
    Occam's razor of, 113–115
    pathways, Kerala vs Uttar
        Pradesh, 161–162
    popular ideas, 64–65
    problems, 475
    process, 139–140
    professional capabilities in,
        242–243
    urban transport policy, 163
    work, 212
public-private partnership, 231
Public Works Department
    (PWD), 324

Rajagopalachari C., 57, 248

RBI Act, 155
redistribution, 17–18, 20, 127
    and anti-poverty program,
        122–123
reforms
    of 1991, 316–317
    of 1991–2004, 493
regulation-making projects,
    476–477
representative democracy,
    65–66
Reserve Bank of India (RBI)
    ban on cryptocurrency, 414
    controls the Monetary Policy
        Committee, 478
    monetary policy, 479
Resolution Corporation, 98–99,
    102, 471
resource constraint, 44, 50–54,
    66, 493
road safety, 28, 112, 449
    consequences, 449
RTI Act, 377
rule of officials, 269–270
    colonial state to
        administrative state,
        270–272
    policy possibilities for a
        country, 275–277
    private solutions for market
        failure, 273–274
    people versus the state in
        the bankruptcy process,
        275
    SEBI's monopoly on
        enforcing securities
        law, 274–275

traditional case for strong contract enforcement, 272–273

Sarva Shiksha Abhiyaan, 158, 373
SEBI Act, 189, 201, 274
separation of powers, 201–202, 269–270, 403–404, 409, 419, 478–479
Singh, Manmohan, 492
Sinha, Yashwant, 436
smallpox in India in 1975, eradication of, 445
social engineering, 182–185, 187, 423
Sri Lanka, 184
Srikrishna B. N., 97–98, 240
Srinivasan, T. N., 492
standards wars, 3, 5–6
state
    cities as, 164–165
    as coercive agent, 10–11, 34
    decentralization within, 165–166
    infrastructure development, 19
    intervention, problems with, 30–31
    paternalism, 33
    power of, 6, 23
    role in Coasean solutions, 133–134
    use of force to modify behaviour, 10–11
state capacity, for the regulator, 475–477

state power reshapes society in digital age
    market failure in the new age, 296–297
    pitfalls, 293–295
    premature state control, 292
        state control of Covid-19 vaccination, 292–293
    premature state legibility, 289–291
        restrictions on storage of goods, 291–292
    state-led technology standards versus the internet, 295–296
STD/PCO booth industry, 102–103
subsidiarity principle, 162–163
subsidies, 23, 115–116
subsidy payments, 124–125
successful state, notion of, 11, 179, 398
sunk costs, 142–143, 149
Surrogacy (Regulation) Bill, 305
surveillance, 59, 114, 117, 118, 197–199, 210, 223, 271, 290, 291, 365, 450
Survey of India, 297, 376–377, 488
Swaccha Bharat Abhiyaan, 446

tax administration, reducing arbitrary power in, 417–418
tax information network (TIN), 204, 282
tax policy, 50, 142

reforms of, 53–54
tax system, 22, 24
    bad taxes, 51
    commodity taxation, 50–51
    corporate tax, 51
    cost of tax compliance,
        51–52
    GST, 52, 62, 64, 108,
        151–152
    income tax, 50
    tax/GDP ratio, 151, 157
    transaction taxes, 51
TCS, 54, 267, 488
Telecom Regulatory Authority
    of India (TRAI), 320
**tort(s), 134, 273, 274, 276,
277**
trade liberalization, 110–111,
    236–237, 362, 429, 498
trading
    derivatives, 480
    electronic, 480

Unique Identity Authority of
    India (UIDAI), 190, 325
United Kingdom (UK)
    levels of coercive power, 499
    policy process in-vitro
        fertilization, 304–305
universal basic income (UBI),
    109–110, 111
UPI, 190, 294

vaccines
    for Covid-19
        four-part policy strategy,
            464–466
        market failure perspective,
            460–462
        policy concerns and
            solutions, 463–464
        power of the price system,
            462–463
        state-capacity perspective,
            459–460
    feature of, 461
    production in India, 72
voter rationality constraint,
    61–66, 67
voting system, 253–255
    limits of, 63
    for turning conflict into
        better decisions, 252–254

women's labour force
    participation, 29
workfare programs, 126–127
World Health Organization
    (WHO), 447
writing law, 476, 498

zero customs duties, 398
zombie firms, 99–101, 105